About the Managing Editor

Nicolás Kanellos has been professor at the University of Houston since 1980. He is founding publisher of the noted Hispanic literary journal *The Americas Review* (formerly *Revista Chicano-Riqueña*) and the nation's oldest Hispanic publishing house, Arte Público Press.

Recognized for his scholarly achievements, Dr. Kanellos is the recipient of a 1990 American Book Award, a 1989 award from the Texas Association of Chicanos in Higher Education, the 1988 Hispanic Heritage Award for Literature presented by the White House, as well as various fellowships and other recognitions. His monograph, *A History of Hispanic Theater in the United States: Origins to 1940* (1990), received three book awards, including that of the Southwest Council on Latin American Studies.

Among his other books are the *Biographical Dictionary of Hispanic Literature of the United States* (1989) and *Mexican American Theater Legacy and Reality* (1987).

Dr. Kanellos is the director of a major national research program, Recovering the Hispanic Literary Heritage of the United States, whose objective is to identify, preserve, study, and make accessible tens of thousands of literary documents of those regions that have become the United States from the colonial period to 1960.

Reference Library of

HISPANIC

AMERICA

Advisors

Dr. Edna Acosta-Belén, *Director, Center for Caribbean and Latin American Studies, University of Albany*

Dr. Rodolfo Cortina, *Director, Bibliographic Database, Recovering the U.S. Hispanic Literary Heritage Project, and Professor of Spanish, Florida International University*

Dr. Rodolfo de la Garza, *Professor of Political Science, The University of Texas at Austin*

Dr. Ricardo Fernández, *President, Lehman College, City University of New York*

Dr. Arturo Madrid, *Director, the Tomás Rivera Center, Claremont, California*

Dr. Michael Olivas, *Associate Dean of Law and Director of the Institute for Higher Education Law and Governance, University of Houston*

Contributors

Roberto Alvarez, *Department of Anthropology, Arizona State University*

Gilbert Paul Carrasco, *School of Law, Villanova University*

José Fernández, *Department of Foreign Languages, University of Central Florida*

María González, *English Department, University of Houston*

Gary Keller, *Bilingual Review Press, Arizona State University*

Thomas M. Leonard, *Department of History, Philosophy & Religious Studies, University of North Florida*

John Lipski, *Department of Modern Languages, University of Florida*

Tatcho Mindiola, *Mexican American Studies Program, University of Houston*

Silvia Novo Pena, *Department of English and Foreign Languages, Texas Southern University*

Manuel Peña, *Foreign Languages, California State University, Fresno*

Jacinto Quirarte, *College of Fine and Applied Arts, University of Texas, San Antonio*

Arturo Rosales, *Department of History, Arizona State University*

Guadalupe San Miguel, *History Department, University of Houston*

Federico Subervi, *Department of Radio-Television-Film, University of Texas, Austin*

Dennis Valdez, *Chicano Studies Program, University of Minnesota*

Jude Valdez, *College of Business, University of Texas, San Antonio*

Reference Library of

HISPANIC AMERICA

VOLUME

III

Nicolás Kanellos,
EDITOR

Distributed by Educational Guidance Service

Reference Library of Hispanic America is based upon *The Hispanic-American Almanac,* published by Gale Research Inc. It has been published in this 3-volume set to facilitate wider usage among students.

Nicolás Kanellos, *Editor*

Gale Research Inc. Staff: ————————————————————

Lawrence W. Baker,
Christine B. Hammes,
    Senior Developmental Editors
Rebecca Nelson, *Developmental Editor*
Peg Bessette, Kevin S. Hile,
Neil R. Schlager,
    Contributing Editors

Cynthia Baldwin, *Art Director*
Barbara J. Yarrow,
    Graphic Services Supervisor
Mark C. Howell, *Cover Designer*
Arthur Chartow, *Page Designer*
Willie F. Mathis, *Camera Operator*
Nicholas Jakubiak, *Keyliner*

Mary Beth Trimper, *Production Director*
Evi Seoud, *Assistant Production Manager*
Mary Kelley, *Production Assistant*

Benita L. Spight, *Data Entry Supervisor*
Gwendolyn S. Tucker,
    Data Entry Group Leader
Tara Y. McKissack, Nancy K. Sheridan,
    Data Entry Associates

While every effort has been made to ensure the reliability of the information presented in this publication, Gale Research Inc. does not guarantee the accuracy of the data contained herein. Gale accepts no payment for listing; and inclusion in the publication of any organization, agency, institution, publication, service, or individual does not imply endorsement of the editors or publisher. Errors brought to the attention of the publisher and verified to the satisfaction of the publisher will be corrected in future editions.

♾™ This book is printed on acid-free paper that meets the minimum requirements of American National Standard for Information Sciences Permanent Paper for Printed Library Materials. ANSI Z39.48-1984.

ISBN 0-8103-9621-1

Printed in 1994
Printed in the United States of America
for distribution by
Educational Guidance Service

Contents

VOLUME I

VOLUME II

VOLUME III

Acknowledgments

My most sincere thanks to all the scholars who have contributed to this volume, for indulging me in my obsession and for producing such wonderfully researched and written chapters, despite the pressure I exerted on you for making deadlines and supplying illustrations and other materials. My thanks as well to my editors at Gale Research Inc., especially Christine Nasso, Christine Hammes, and Rebecca Nelson, whose guiding hand was always characterized by a gentle touch, whose advice was always offered with compassion and understanding. I feel very fortunate to have become part of the Gale family.

Thanks also to my scholarly advisors, especially Dr. Michael Olivas, who assisted me greatly in contacting contributors for this volume. My deepest appreciation and thanks to my assistant, Hilda Hinojosa, who helped organize, type, and maintain oral and written communications with the contributing scholars and with my editors. This, the largest project of my career as a scholar, was brought to press, with her able, efficient, and enthusiastic support.

And from my wife Cristelia Pérez and my son Miguel, I beg their forgiveness for the months that I spent communicating more with my computer screen than with them. Without Crissy's love, support, and understanding this project would never have gotten off the ground, much less seen the light of day. Thank you; I love you.

Nicolás Kanellos

Preface

Reference Library of Hispanic America is the research product of a national team of outstanding scholars who unanimously have invested their time, energy, and genius to create the first one-stop source for information about a broad range of important aspects of Hispanic life and culture in the United States. In their labors for *Reference Library of Hispanic America*, as well as in their day-to-day academic work, these scholars have actively engaged in the difficult task of working with original documentary sources, oral interviews, and field work to create a written record of Hispanic life where none existed before. These scholars are among the first in our country's academic history to research, analyze, and preserve much of the information offered here. The scholars, and this work, are dedicated to filling an informational void relating to the history and culture of Hispanics of the United States—a void that has existed for too long in libraries, classrooms, and homes.

Prior to this publication, the scant information that has been available has quite often resulted from prejudice, propaganda, and folklore (quite often created to support the political and economic exploitation of Hispanics) covering a people conquered through war or imported for their labor, but who were never fully incorporated into the national psyche, the national identity, or the national storehouse of educational, economic, and political opportunities.

The vast majority of Hispanics in the United States are working-class citizens. Even those Hispanics in the professional class often share working-class backgrounds. The majority of Hispanics in the United States are *mestizos*—the product of mixed races and cultures, for the American Indian and African heritages have blended in every aspect of everyday life to produce today's Hispanic peoples of the Americas. The Spanish language, which introduced and reinforced a common culture and religion for these peoples for centuries, serves as a unifying factor for Hispanics, regardless of whether or not the individual speaks Spanish in daily life. These central factors—social class, ethnicity, linguistic-cultural background—unify the people and the information presented in *Reference Library of Hispanic America*, while also respecting the tremendous diversity in racial, ethnic, geographic, and historical backgrounds that exists among Hispanics today.

The final result of this endeavor, we hope, is an easy-to-use compendium that presents an up-to-date overview of each subject, summarizing the known data and presenting new, original research. Moreover, *Reference Library of Hispanic America* has been written in a language and style that make it accessible to students and lay people. Illustrations—photographs, drawings, maps, and tables—bring the data to life. For further reading, subject-specific bibliographies (at the end of each chapter) as well as a general bibliography (on pages A-13 and A-14 of each volume) provide ready reference to other important sources. A complete index (on pages A-15 through A-40 of each volume) assists the reader in locating specific information. A glossary of Spanish terms (on pages A-9 through A-11 of each volume) has also been included to facilitate the reading of *Reference Library of Hispanic America*.

As this is the first edition of a very new type of resource, we are aware there may be some gaps in information, resulting from incomplete data or unavailable resources (be they documentary, informational, or human). However, great pains have been taken to ensure the accuracy of the data and the representativeness of the scholarly interpretation and opinion presented in each chapter. Research is ongoing and future editions of *Reference Library of Hispanic America* will update the present volume.

Nicolás Kanellos
University of Houston

Introduction

The Hispanic Population

With a Hispanic population of more than 22 million, the United States is among the largest Spanish-speaking countries in the world. According to the U.S. Census Bureau, the number of Hispanics in this country has grew by 53 percent from 1980 to 1990. It is projected that by the year 2000, there will be almost 33 million Hispanics living in the United States.

Reference Library of Hispanic America, based on *The Hispanic-American Almanac*, is a one-stop source for information on people of the United States whose ancestors—or they themselves—originated in Spain, the Spanish-speaking countries of South and Central America, Mexico, Puerto Rico, or Cuba.

While the Spanish language is a unifying factor among Hispanics, the diversity that exists within the Hispanic community continues to profoundly influence the collective American experience.

Scope and Contents

Reference Library of Hispanic America covers the range of Hispanic civilization and culture in the United States—providing a chronology and Historical Overview, presenting the facts and figures in such chapters as Law and Politics and Population Growth and Distribution, and discussing the arts, including Theater, Music, and Film.

Twenty-five subject chapters were written by scholars in the field of Hispanic studies. These experts have drawn upon the body of their works and new research to compile their chapters, ending each with a list of references that can be used for further research into any of the subjects covered in *Reference Library of Hispanic America*. A bibliography at the back of each volume of *Reference Library of Hispanic America* provides sources for general information on Hispanics.

Concise biographical profiles in many chapters highlight Hispanics who have excelled in their fields of endeavor.

A glossary of Spanish terms, found in each of the three volumes, facilitates the reading of the material.

The keyword index, also found in each volume, provides quick access to the contents of *Reference Library of Hispanic America*.

More than 400 illustrations—including photographs, drawings, tables, and figures—punctuate the discussion in each chapter.

Suggestions Are Welcome

The managing editor and publisher of *Reference Library of Hispanic America* will appreciate suggestions for additions or changes that will make future editions of this book as useful as possible. Please send comments to:

Reference Library of Hispanic America
Gale Research Inc.
835 Penobscot Bldg.
Detroit, MI 48226

Chronology

50,000-10,000 B.C. Asian peoples migrate to North and South America.

ca. 1000 B.C. Celts move into the Iberian Peninsula.

ca. 500 B.C. Carthagenians establish themselves on the south coast of Spain.

200 B.C. The Iberian Peninsula becomes part of the Roman Empire.

350-850 A.D. Teotihuacan civilization flourishes in the central plateau of Mexico.

500 A.D. Vandals and Goths invade and conquer the peoples of the Iberian Peninsula.

700-900 A.D. Nahua peoples gain ascendancy in Mexico's central plateau.

711 A.D. The Moors invade and conquer the Visigothic kingdoms of the Iberian peninsula.

718-1492. The Reconquest of the Iberian peninsula takes place. Queen Isabella and King Ferdinand unify Spain through their marriage in 1469, and culminate the Reconquest by defeating the last Moorish stronghold—Granada.

1000 Mayan civilization flourishes in the Yucatán peninsula and Guatemala.

1492. The native American population of the Western Hemisphere may have reached between thirty-five to forty-five million.

August 3, 1492. Christopher Columbus sails from the Spanish port of Palos de Moguer with three ships: the Pinta, the Niña, and the Santa María, his flagship.

October 12, 1492. The Spaniards land on an island called San Salvador—either present-day Watling Island or Samana Cay in the eastern Bahamas.

October 27, 1492. Columbus and his crews land on the northeastern shore of Cuba. Convinced that it is either Cipango or Cathay (in Asia), Columbus sends representatives to the Great Khan and his gold-domed cities, only to find impoverished Arawak living in *bohíos* (huts).

November 1493. On his second voyage Columbus discovers the Virgin Islands and Puerto Rico.

1494. After establishing Isabela on La Española (Hispaniola), the first permanent European settlement in the New World, Columbus sets sail and encounters Jamaica in the summer of 1494.

1508. Juan Ponce de León sails in a small caravel for Puerto Rico, where he establishes friendly relations with the native chieftain, Agueibana, who presents him with gold.

1509. Ponce de León is appointed governor of Puerto Rico.

1510. Diego Velázquez de Cuéllar departs with more than three hundred men to conquer Cuba, and lands at Puerto Escondido. He is successful in defeating Arawak chieftain Hatuey's guerrilla raids.

1511. Velázquez is commissioned governor of Cuba. That same year the Cuban Indians are subjected to the *encomienda*.

1512. The Jeronymite Fathers in La Española decide to save the decimated Arawak population by gathering them into missions. Soon, missions spread like wildfire throughout the Spanish Empire.

1512. The Laws of Burgos: Promulgated by the Crown, the regulations are in response to the extremely harsh treatment that desperate colonists in the Caribbean imposed on natives through the deplorable *encomienda* system.

1513. Juan Ponce de León lands on the shores of Florida, exploring most of the coastal regions and some of the interior. At the time, there were an estimated 100,000 native Americans living there.

September 27, 1514. Ponce de León is granted a patent, empowering him to colonize the island of Bimini and the "island" of Florida.

1515. Diego Velázquez becomes a virtual feudal lord of Cuba, and establishes what are to become Cuba's two largest cities, Santiago and Havana. He also directs the explorations of the Mexican Gulf Coast by Francisco Hernández de Córdoba and his nephew Juan de Grijalva. These expeditions betray the existence of civilizations in the interior of Mexico.

1518. Hernán Cortés sets out from Cuba to explore the mainland of Mexico in order to confirm reports of the existence of large, native civilizations in the interior.

1519. Alonso Alvarez de Pineda claims Texas for Spain.

1519. Hernán Cortés lands on the coast of Veracruz, Mexico.

1520. Explorer Alvarez de Pineda settles the question of Florida's geography: He proves it is not an island, but part of a vast continent.

1520s. Continuing their maritime adventures, the Spanish explorers cruise along the northern shore of the Gulf of Mexico, seeing Alabama, Mississippi, and Texas, and also sailing up the Atlantic coast to the Carolinas.

July 1, 1520. Under the leadership of Cuitlahuac, Moctezuma's brother, the Aztecs force the Spaniards out of Veracruz, just a year after the Spaniards had come into the city. The Spaniards called this *La noche triste* (The Sad Night). Moctezuma was stoned to death by his own people during this debacle.

1521. Cortés and his fellow Spaniards level the Aztec empire's city of Tenochtitlán, and begin building Mexico City on the same site.

1524. King Charles establishes the Council of the Indies, designed to oversee the administration of the colonies of the New World.

1536. Álvar Núñez Cabeza de Vaca returns to Mexico, indirectly involving Spain in exploring and colonizing what becomes the American Southwest: In Mexico City rumors were that Cabeza de Vaca and his companions had discovered cities laden with gold and silver, reviving the legend of the Seven Cities, which dated from the Moorish invasion of the Iberian Peninsula.

1537. Àlvar Núñez Cabeza de Vaca returns to Spain and spends some three years writing *La relación*, an account of his wanderings in the North American continent. Published in 1542, *La relación* is a document of inestimable value because of the many first descriptions about the flora, fauna, and inhabitants of what was to become part of the United States.

May 18, 1539. From Havana, Cuba, Hernando de Soto sets sail for Florida; he eventually reaches as far north as present-day Georgia and South Carolina. His expedition later crosses the Great Smoky Mountains into Tennessee. From the mountains, the expedition heads southwest through present-day Georgia and Alabama.

1540. There are an estimated sixty-six Pueblo villages in the area of New Mexico, growing such crops as corn, beans, squash, and cotton. On April 23, 1541, Coronado sets out to reach Quivira—thought to be the legendary Cities of Gold—near present-day Great Bend, Kansas.

1542. The New Laws are proclaimed. They are designed to end the feudal *encomienda*.

July 1542. Coronado returns to Mexico City with fewer than one hundred of the three hundred Spaniards that once formed part of his company.

September 28, 1542. Juan Rodríguez de Cabrillo, a Portuguese sailor commissioned by the viceroy to sail north of Mexico's west coast in search of treasures, enters what he describes as an excellent port—present-day San Diego, California.

1563. Saint Augustine, Florida, the earliest settlement in North America, is founded. It remains a possession of Spain until 1819.

1573. The Franciscan order arrives in Florida to establish missions, which a century later would extend along the east coast of North America, from Saint Augustine, Florida, to North Carolina. The Franciscans also establish a string of missions from Saint Augustine westward to present-day Tallahassee.

1580s. Diseases have all but wiped out the Indians of Puerto Rico. The flourishing of sugar production will now have to await the importation of large numbers of African slaves.

1598. Juan de Oñate begins the colonization of New Mexico.

1610. Santa Fe, New Mexico is founded.

1680. A Pueblo Indian named Popé leads a rebellion that forces the Spaniards and Christianized Indians out of northern New Mexico southward toward El Paso, Texas; they found Ysleta just north of El Paso.

1689. In part due to the need to provide foodstuffs and livestock to the rich mining regions in southern Mexico, the first royal *mercedes* (land grants) are granted to Spaniards in the fertile valleys of Monclova, in northern Mexico, just south of the present border.

May 1690. The first permanent Spanish settlement in Texas, San Francisco de los Tejas, near the Neches River, is established.

1691. Father Eusebio Kino, an untiring Jesuit missionary, makes the first inroads into Arizona. By 1700, Kino establishes a mission at San Xavier del Bac, near present-day Tucson; he later establishes other missions in Arizona: Nuestra Señora de los Dolores, Santa Gertrudis de Saric, San José de Imuris, Nuestra Señora de los Remedios, and San Cayetano de Tumacácori.

1693. Despite the fact that Texas is made a separate Spanish province with Don Domingo de Terán as its governor, the Spanish Crown orders its abandonment. Fear of Indian uprisings is the reason given by the Spanish authorities.

1716. Concerns about possible French encroachment prompt the Spaniards to reoccupy Texas in 1716 by establishing a series of missions, serving to both ward off the French and convert the natives to Catholicism. Of these missions, San Antonio, founded in 1718, is the most important and most prosperous.

1718. The San Antonio de Béjar and de Valero churches are built where the city of San Antonio is located today.

1760. After the Seven Years' War, which united France and Spain against Britain, France cedes claims to all lands west of the Mississippi in order not to give them to the victorious British. Overnight, New Spain's territory expands dramatically.

September 17, 1766. The presidio of San Francisco is founded, becoming Spain's northernmost frontier outpost.

1767. King Charles III expels the Jesuits from the Spanish Empire. This event opens the door for the Franciscan conquest of California. This conquest would never have been accomplished without Fray Junípero de Serra.

July 3, 1769. Fray Junípero de Serra establishes the first mission of Alta California in what would become San Diego. Serra eventually founds ten missions, travels more than ten thousand miles, and converts close to sixty-eight hundred natives.

1770-1790. At least 50,000 African slaves are brought to Cuba to work in sugar production.

1774. Pedro de Garcés, a Spanish Franciscan missionary, founds the first overland route to California.

1776. In the American Revolution, because of their alliance with France, the Spaniards are able to obtain lands all the way to Florida.

1776. Anglo-Americans declare their independence from England, and thirty-four years later Hispanics proclaim their independence from Spain. The thirteen former British colonies come to be known as the United States of America in 1781, and the newly independent people of New Spain name their nation the Republic of Mexico.

1783. Spain regains Florida. In July 1821, the sun finally sets on Spanish Florida when the peninsula is purchased by the United States for $5 million.

1790s-1820s. The Apache threat subsides because of successful military tactics and negotiations on the part of local Spanish leaders, and Hispanic settlements begin to thrive in Pimería Alta (California). At one point as many as one thousand Hispanics live in the Santa Cruz Valley.

1798. The Alien Act of 1798 grants the U.S. president the authority to expel any alien deemed dangerous. Opposed by President Thomas Jefferson, the Alien Act expires under its own terms in 1800.

1798. The Naturalization Act of 1798 raises the number of years—from 5 to 14—that an immigrant has to live in the United States before becoming eligible for citizenship.

1800. Large, sprawling haciendas with huge herds of cattle and sheep characterize the economy and society of northeast New Spain.

1803. A powerful France under Napoleon Bonaparte acquires the Louisiana Territory, from Spain which was ceded during the Seven Years' War in the previous century. Napoleon, vying for dominance in Europe and in need of quick revenue, sells the vast territory to the United States, thus expanding the borders of the infant nation to connect directly with New Spain.

1804. To the consternation of Spain, President Thomas Jefferson funds the historical expedition of Lewis and Clark. Spain is obviously worried that the exploration is a prelude to the settlement of the territory by Anglos.

1810. In Mexico, Father Miguel Hidalgo y Castilla leads the revolt against Spain.

September 16, 1810. With the insurrection of Father Miguel Hidalgo y Castilla, the Spaniards withdraw their troops from the frontier presidios.

1819. When Andrew Jackson leads a U.S. military force into Florida, capturing two Spanish forts, Spain sells Florida to the United States for $5 million under the Onís Treaty.

1820. Stephen Long leads a revolt, ostensibly as part of the Texas independence movement against the Spanish, but obviously he is acting as a filibusterer for his countrymen. Spain finally enters into delibera-tions with Moses Austin, a Catholic from Missouri, to settle Anglo-Catholic families in Texas.

1821. Mexico acquires its independence from Spain. By this time permanent colonies exist in coastal California, southern Arizona, south Texas, and in most of New Mexico and southern Colorado. The imprint of evolving Mexican culture is stamped on today's Southwest. Soon after Mexico gains independence, Anglo-American settlers begin to move into the Mexican territories of the present-day U.S. Southwest, especially Texas.

1823. Erasmo Seguín, a delegate to the national congress from Texas, persuades a willing U.S. Congress to pass a colonization act designed to bring even more Anglo settlers to Texas. Between 1824 and 1830, thousands of Anglo families enter east Texas, acquiring hundreds of thousands of free acres and buying land much cheaper than they could have in the United States. By 1830, Texas has eighteen thousand Anglo inhabitants and their African slaves, who number more than two thousand.

1823. Fray Junípero de Serra's death does not stop missionary activity in California. His fellow Franciscans establish another twelve missions. The famous mission trail of California includes the missions San Diego de Alcalá (1769), San Carlos de Monterey (1770), San Antonio de Padua (1771), San Gabriel Arcángel (1771), San Luis Obispo de Tolosa (1772), San Francisco de Asís (1776), San Juan Capistrano (1776), Santa Clara de Asís (1777), San Buenaventura (1782), Santa Bárbara (1786), La Purísima Concepción (1787), Santa Cruz (1791), San José de Guadalupe (1797), San Juan Bautista (1797), San Miguel Arcángel (1797), San Fernando Rey (1797), San Luis Rey (1798), Santa Inés (1804), San Rafael Arcángel (1817), and San Francisco Solano (1823).

1829. Slavery in Mexico is abolished by the new republican government that emerges after independence.

1836. The Anglo settlers declare the Republic of Texas independent of Mexico.

1836. The Texas constitution stipulates that all residents living in Texas at the time of the rebellion will acquire all the rights of citizens of the new republic, but if they had been disloyal, these rights are forfeited. Numerically superior Anglos force Mexicans off their property, and many cross the border to Mexico.

1840. To meet the wage-labor demands, 125,000 Chinese are brought to Cuba between 1840 and 1870 to work as cane cutters, build railroads in rural areas, and serve as domestics in the cities. Also, the influx of European immigrants, primarily from Spain, increases during that period. Newly arrived Spaniards become concentrated in the retail trades and operate small general stores called *bodegas*.

1845. Texas is officially annexed to the United States.

1846. The United States invades Mexico under the banner of Manifest Destiny. The treaty of Guadalupe Hidalgo ends the Mexican War that same year. Under the treaty, half the land area of Mexico, including Texas, California, most of Arizona and New Mexico, and parts of Colorado, Utah, and Nevada, is ceded to the United States. The treaty gives Mexican nationals one year to choose U.S. or Mexican citizenship. Seventy-five thousand Hispanic people choose to remain in the United States and become citizens by conquest.

1848. The gold rush lures a flood of Anglo settlers to California, which becomes a state in 1850. Settlement in Arizona and New Mexico occurs at a slower pace, and they both become states in 1912.

1850. The Foreign Miners Tax, which levies a charge for anyone who is not a U.S. citizen, is enacted.

1851. Congress passes the California Land Act of 1851 to facilitate legalization of land belonging to Californios prior to the U.S. takeover.

1853. General Santa Anna returns to power as president of Mexico and, through the Gadsden Treaty, sells to the United States the region from Yuma (Arizona) along the Gila River to the Mesilla Valley (New Mexico).

1855. Vagrancy laws and so-called "greaser laws" prohibiting bear-baiting, bullfights, and cockfights are passed, clearly aimed at prohibiting the presence and customs of Californios.

1855. The Supreme Court rules that the Treaty of Guadalupe Hidalgo did not apply to Texas.

1857. Anglo businessmen attempt to run off Mexican teamsters in south Texas, violating the guarantees offered by the Treaty of Guadalupe Hidalgo.

1862. Homestead Act is passed in Congress, allowing squatters in the West to settle and claim vacant lands, often those owned by Mexicans.

April 27, 1867. Spanish troops stationed on Puerto Rico mutiny, and are executed by the colonial governor.

1868. Cubans leave for Europe and the United States in sizable numbers during Cuba's first major attempt at independence.

1868. Fourteenth Amendment to the U.S. Constitution is adopted, declaring all people of Hispanic origin born in the United States are U.S. citizens.

September 17, 1868. A decree in Puerto Rico frees all children born of slaves after this date. In 1870, all slaves who are state property are freed, as are various other classes of slaves.

September 23, 1868. El Grito de Lares, the shout for Puerto Rican independence, takes place, with its disorganized insurrectionists easily defeated by the Spanish.

October 1868. Cuban rebels led by Carlos Manuel de Céspedes declare independence at Yara, in the eastern portion of the island.

1872. Puerto Rican representatives in Spain win equal civil rights for the colony.

1873. Slavery is finally abolished in Puerto Rico.

1875. The U.S. Supreme Court in *Henderson v. Mayor of New York* rules that power to regulate immigration is held solely by the federal government.

1878. The Ten Years' War, in which Spanish attempts to evict rebels from the eastern half of Cuba were unsuccessful, comes to an end with the signing of the Pact of El Zajón. The document promises amnesty for the insurgents and home rule, and provides freedom for the slaves that fought on the side of the rebels.

1880s. In Cuba, slavery is abolished by Spain in a gradual program that takes eight years. The influx of new European immigrants has made Cuba more heterogeneous, leading to the social diversity that is still apparent today.

1880s. Mexican immigration to the United States is stimulated by the advent of the railroad.

1892. The Partido Revolucionario Cubano is created to organize the Cuban and Puerto Rican independence movement.

1894. The Alianza Hispano Americana is founded in Tucson, Arizona, and quickly spreads throughout the Southwest.

1895. José Martí and his Cuban Revolutionary Party (PRC) open the final battle for independence.

1896. A Revolutionary Junta is formed in New York to lead the Puerto Rican independence movement.

1897. Spain grants Cuba and Puerto Rico autonomy and home rule.

April 1898. The *USS Maine* mysteriously blows up in Havana Harbor. And on April 28, President William McKinley declares war against Spain.

May 1898. The U.S. military invades San Juan in pursuit of Spaniards, and is welcomed by the cheering crowds, longing for independence.

December 10, 1898. Spain signs the Treaty of Paris, transferring Cuba, Puerto Rico, and the Philippines to the United States.

1900s. Brutality against Mexican Americans in the Southwest territories is commonplace. Lynchings and murders of Mexican Americans become so common in California and Texas that, in 1912, the Mexican ambassador formally protests the mistreatment and cites several brutal incidents that had recently taken place.

1900. The Foraker Act establishes a civilian government in Puerto Rico under U.S. dominance. The law allows for islanders to elect their own House of Representatives, but does not allow Puerto Rico a vote in Washington.

1901. The Federación Libre de los Trabajadores (Workers Labor Federation) becomes affiliated with the American Federation of Labor, which breaks from its policy of excluding non-whites.

1902. The Reclamation Act is passed, dispossessing many Hispanic Americans of their land.

1902. Cuba declares its independence from the United States.

1910. The Mexican Revolution begins, with hundreds of thousands of people fleeing north from Mexico and settling in the Southwest.

1911. In Mexico, the long dictatorship of Porfirio Díaz comes to an end when he is forced to resign in a revolt led by Francisco Madero.

1913. Victoriano Huerta deposes Francisco Madero, becoming provisional president of Mexico.

1914. President Woodrow Wilson orders the invasion of Veracruz in an effort to depose Victoriano Huerta, who soon resigns.

1917. During World War I, "temporary" Mexican farm workers, railroad laborers, and miners are permitted to enter the United States to work.

1917. The Jones Act is passed, extending U.S. citizenship to all Puerto Ricans and creating two Puerto Rican houses of legislature whose representatives are elected by the people. English is decreed the official language of Puerto Rico.

February 1917. Congress passes the Immigration Act, imposing a literacy requirement on all immigrants, aimed at curbing the influx from southern and eastern Europe, but ultimately inhibiting immigration from Mexico.

May 1917. The Selective Service Act becomes law, obligating non-citizen Mexicans in the United States to register with their local draft boards, even though they are not eligible for the draft.

1921. Limits on the number of immigrants allowed to enter the United States during a single year are imposed for the first time in the country's history.

1921. As the first of two national origin quota acts designed to curtail immigration from eastern and southern Europe and Asia is passed, Mexico and Puerto Rico become major sources of workers.

1921. A depression in Mexico causes severe destitution among Mexicans who suddenly find themselves unemployed.

1925. The Border Patrol is created by Congress.

July 1926. Rioting Puerto Ricans in Harlem are attacked by non-Hispanics as the number of Puerto Ricans becomes larger in Manhattan neighborhoods (by 1930 they will reach fifty-three thousand).

1929. With the onset of the Great Depression, Mexican immigration to the United States virtually ceases and return migration increases sharply.

1929. The League of United Latin American Citizens is founded in Texas by frustrated Mexican Americans who find avenues for opportunity in the United States blocked.

1930s-1940s. With the onset of the Great Depression, many Mexican workers are displaced by the dominant southern whites and blacks of the migrant agricultural labor force.

1930. The United States controls 44 percent of the cultivated land in Puerto Rico; U.S. capitalists control 60 percent of the banks and public services, and all of the maritime lines.

1930. Within the next four years, approximately 20 percent of the Puerto Ricans living in the United States will return to the island.

1933. The Roosevelt Administration reverses the policy of English as the official language in Puerto Rico.

1933. Mexican farm workers strike the Central Valley, California, cotton industry, supported by several groups of independent Mexican union organizers and radicals.

1933. Cuban dictator Gerardo Machado is overthrown.

September 1933. Fulgencio Batista leads a barracks revolt to overthrow Cuban provisional President Carlos Manuel de Céspedes y Quesada, becoming the dictator of the Cuban provisional government.

1934. The Platt Amendment is annulled.

1938. Young Mexican and Mexican-American pecan shellers strike in San Antonio.

1940s-1950s. Unionization among Hispanic workers increases rapidly, as Hispanic workers and union sympathizers struggle for reform.

1940. The independent union Confederación de Trabajadores Generales is formed and soon replaces the FLT as the major labor organization in Puerto Rico.

1940. Batista is elected president of Cuba.

1941. The Fair Employment Practices Act is passed, eliminating discrimination in employment.

1941. With the U.S. declaration of war in 1941, Hispanics throughout the country enthusiastically respond to the war effort.

1943. Prompted by the labor shortage of World War II, the U.S. government makes an agreement with the Mexican government to supply temporary workers, known as "braceros," for American agricultural work.

1943. The so-called "Zoot Suit" riots take place in southern California.

1944. Batista retires as president of Cuba.

1944. Operation Bootstrap, a program initiated by the Puerto Rican government to meet U.S. labor demands of World War II and encourage industrialization on the island, stimulates a major wave of migration of workers to the United States.

1946. The first Puerto Rican governor, Jesús T. Piñero, is appointed by President Harry Truman.

1947. More than twenty airlines provide service between San Juan and Miami, and San Juan and New York.

1947. The American G.I. Forum is organized by Mexican-American veterans in response to a Three Rivers, Texas, funeral home's denial to bury a Mexican American killed in the Pacific during World War II.

1950s. Through the early 1960s, segregation is abolished in Texas, Arizona, and other regions, largely through the efforts of the League of United Latin American Citizens (LULAC) and the Alianza Hispano Americana.

1950s. Immigration from Mexico doubles from 5.9 percent to 11.9 percent, and in the 1960s rises to 13.3 percent of the total number of immigrants to the United States.

1950s-1960s. Black workers continue to be the most numerous migrants along the eastern seaboard states, while Mexican and Mexican-American workers soon dominate the migrant paths between Texas and the Great Lakes, the Rocky Mountain region, and the area from California to the Pacific Northwest.

1950s-1960s. As more and more Puerto Ricans commit to remaining on the U.S. mainland, they encounter a great deal of rejection, but at the same time demonstrate a growing concern for social and economic mobility. Their early employment pattern consists of menial jobs in the service sector and in light factory work—in essence low-paying jobs.

1950. In spite of the resurgence of Mexican immigration and the persistence of Mexican cultural modes, Mexican Americans cannot help but become Americanized in the milieu of the 1950s and 1960s, when more and more acquire educations in Anglo systems, live in integrated suburbs, and are subjected to Anglo-American mass media—especially television.

July 3, 1950. The U.S. Congress upgrades Puerto Rico's political status from protectorate to commonwealth.

1951. The Bracero Program is formalized as the Mexican Farm Labor Supply Program and the Mexican Labor Agreement, and will bring an annual average of 350,000 Mexican workers to the United States until its end in 1964.

1952. Congress passes the Immigration and Nationality Act of 1952, also known as the McCarran-Walter Act, reaffirming the basic features of the 1924 quota law by maintaining a restrictive limit on immigration from particular countries. Immigration from the Western Hemisphere remains exempt, except that applicants must clear a long list of barriers devised to exclude homosexuals, Communists, and others.

1952. Batista seizes power of Cuba again, this time as dictator, taking Cuba to new heights of repression and corruption.

1954. In the landmark case of *Hernández v. Texas* the nation's highest court acknowledges that Hispanic Americans are not being treated as "whites." The Supreme Court recognizes Hispanics as a separate class of people suffering profound discrimination, paving the way for Hispanic Americans to use legal means to attack all types of discrimination throughout the United States. It is also the first U.S. Supreme Court case to be argued and briefed by Mexican-American attorneys.

1954-1958. Operation Wetback deports 3.8 million persons of Mexican descent. Only a small fraction of that amount are allowed deportation hearings. Thousands more legitimate U.S. citizens of Mexican descent are also arrested and detained.

1959. The Cuban Revolution succeeds in overthrowing the repressive regime of Batista; Fidel Castro takes power. The vast majority of Cuban Americans immigrate to the United States after this date: between 1959 and 1962, 25,000 Cubans are "paroled" to the United States using a special immigration rule. Large-scale Cuban immigration to the United States occurs much more quickly than that from either Puerto Rico or Mexico, with more than one million Cubans entering the country since 1959.

1959. Most of the two million Puerto Ricans who have trekked to the U.S. mainland in this century are World War II or postwar-era entries. Unlike the immigrant experience of Mexicans, or Cubans before 1959, the vast majority of Puerto Ricans enter with little or no red tape.

1960s. A third phase of labor migration to the United States begins when the established patterns of movement from Mexico and Puerto Rico to the United States are modified, and migration from other countries increases. The Bracero Program ends in 1964, and, after a brief decline in immigration, workers from Mexico increasingly arrive to work under the auspices of the H-2 Program of the Immigration and Nationality Act of 1952, as well as for family unification purposes, or as undocumented workers.

1960s-1970s. The migrant agricultural work force is changing rapidly. With the rise of the black power and Chicano movements, the appearance of modest protective legislation, and the increasingly successful unionization efforts of farm workers, employers seek to recruit and hire foreign workers to replace the citizens.

1961. Aspira (Aspire) is founded to promote the education of Hispanic youth by raising public and private sector funds. Aspira acquires a national following, serving Puerto Ricans wherever they live in large numbers.

April 1961. Anti-Communist Cuban exiles who are trained and armed by the United States, attempt a foray into Cuba that is doomed from the beginning. The failure of the infamous Bay of Pigs invasion embitters thousands of exiled Cubans, while strengthening Castro's position at home. Many observers throughout the world criticize the Kennedy administration for the attempt to overthrow a legitimately based government.

1962. The United Farm Workers Organizing Committee in California, begun as an independent organization, is led by César Chávez. In 1965 it organizes its successful Delano grape strike and first national boycott. It becomes part of the AFL-CIO in 1966. Today the union is known as the United Farmworkers of America.

October 1962. Kennedy redeems himself from the Bay of Pigs disgrace by blocking a Soviet plan to establish missile bases in Cuba. Soviet Premier Khrushchev agrees to withdraw the missiles with the proviso that the United States declare publicly that it will not invade Cuba.

1964. Congress enacts the first comprehensive civil rights law since the Reconstruction period when it passes the Civil Rights Act of 1964. One result of the act is the establishment of affirmative action programs. Title VII of the Act prohibits discrimination on the basis of gender, creed, race, or ethnic background, "to achieve equality of employment opportunities and remove barriers that have operated in the past." Discrimination is prohibited in advertising, recruitment, hiring, job classification, promotion, discharge, wages and salaries, and other terms and conditions of employment. Title VII also establishes the Equal Employment Opportunity Commission (EEOC) as a monitoring device to prevent job discrimination.

1964. The Economic Opportunity Act (EOA) is the centerpiece of President Lyndon B. Johnson's War on Poverty. The EOA also creates the Office of Economic Opportunity (OEO) to administer a number of programs on behalf of the nation's poor. These include the Job Corps, the Community Action Program (CAP), and the Volunteers in Service to America (VISTA).

1965. The experienced *braceros* (manual laborers) inspire other Mexicans to immigrate to the United States. Many of these contract laborers work primarily in agricultural communities and in railroad camps until the program ends in 1965.

1965. A border industrialization program, the *maquiladora* (assembly plant), is initiated. Mexico hopes to raise the standard of living in its northern border region, while the United States hopes to avoid the possible negative political and economic consequences of leaving hundreds of thousands of Mexican workers stranded without employment as the Bracero Program is ended.

1965. Although the single aim of the Voting Rights Act of 1965 is African-American enfranchisement in the South, obstacles to registration and voting are faced by all minorities. The act's potential as a tool for Hispanic Americans, however, is not fully realized for nearly a decade.

1965. For the first time, the United States enacts a law placing a cap on immigration from the Western Hemisphere, becoming effective in 1968.

1965. Fidel Castro announces that Cubans can leave the island nation if they have relatives in the United States. He stipulates, however, that Cubans already in Florida have to come and get their relatives. Nautical crafts of all types systematically leave Miami, returning laden with anxious Cubans eager to rejoin their families on the mainland.

1965. A major revision of immigration law results when Congress amends the Immigration and Nationality Act of 1952. The national origin quota system is abolished.

Late 1960s-early 1970s. Intellectual foment and rebellion reign in the United States. Caught up in the mood, young Mexican Americans throughout the country seek a new identity while struggling for the same civil rights objectives of previous generations. This struggle becomes known as the Chicano movement. The word "Chicano" is elevated from its pejorative usage in the 1920s when it denoted lower-class Mexican immigrants, and from its slang usage of the 1940s and 1950s, to substitute for "Mexicano."

1966. Hundreds of Chicago Puerto Rican youths go on a rampage, breaking windows and burning down many of the businesses in their neighborhoods. Ostensibly, the riots are in response to an incident of police brutality, but the underlying causes are broader, linked to the urban blight that characterizes their life in Chicago.

1966. A program is initiated to airlift Cubans to the United States. More than 250,000 Cubans are airlifted to the United States before the program is halted by Castro in 1973. About 10 percent of the island's population immigrates to the United States between 1966 and 1973.

1968. Chicano student organizations spring up throughout the nation, as do barrio groups such as the Brown Berets. Thousands of young Chicanos pledge their loyalty and time to such groups as the United Farmworkers Organizing Committee, which, under César Chávez, has been a great inspiration for Chicanos throughout the nation. An offshoot of both the farm worker and the student movements, is La Raza Unida party in Texas, an organization formed in

1968 to obtain control of community governments where Chicanos are the majority.

1969. After the establishment of the Central American Common Market in the 1960s led to economic growth and improved conditions in the region, the border war between Honduras and El Salvador leads to the collapse of the common market and the rapid decline of economic conditions in Central America.

1970s. Immigration and Naturalization Service (INS) Commissioner Leonard Chapman seeks to increase funding and expand the power of his organization, claiming that there are as many as 12 million undocumented workers in the country. Other observers most commonly place the number in the range of 3.5 million to 5 million people.

1970s-early 1980s. The rise in politically motivated violence in Central America spurs a massive increase in undocumented immigration to the United States.

1970. Eighty-two percent of the Hispanic population of the nation lives in nine states, with the proportion rising to 86 percent in 1990. The major recipients of Hispanic immigrants are California, Texas, and New York, and to a lesser degree Florida, Illinois, and New Jersey.

1970. A Chicano Moratorium to the Vietnam War is organized in Los Angeles. Journalist Rubén Salazar is accidentally killed by police.

1970. The struggle over affirmative action continues when opponents coin the term "reverse discrimination," suggesting that white males are victims of discrimination as a result of affirmative action on behalf of women, blacks, Hispanics, and other underrepresented groups.

1970. Brutality against Mexican Americans continues. In *López v. Harlow*, a case filed in an attempt to bring the violence under control, a police officer shoots and kills López, a Mexican American, allegedly in self-defense, because he thought López was about to throw a dish at him.

1970. The amendments constituting the landmark Voting Rights Act of 1970 add a provision that is designed to guard against inventive new barriers to political participation. It requires federal approval of all changes in voting procedures in certain jurisdictions, primarily southern states. This act prevents minority votes from being diluted in gerrymandered districts or through at-large elections.

1971. La Raza Unida Party wins the city elections in Crystal City, Texas.

1972. Ramona Acosta Bañuelos becomes the first Hispanic treasurer of the United States.

1973. The right of the Puerto Rican people to decide their own future as a nation is approved by the United Nations. In 1978, the United Nations recognizes Puerto Rico as a colony of the United States.

1973. An employment discrimination case, *Espinoza v. Farah Manufacturing Company*, argues discrimination toward an employee, Espinoza, on the basis of his citizenship status under the Civil Rights Act. However, the Supreme Court holds that there is nothing in Title VII, the equal employment opportunities provisions of the Civil Rights Act of 1964, that makes it illegal to discriminate on the basis of citizenship or alienage.

1973. The Labor Council of Latin American Advancement (LCLAA) forms to promote the interests of Hispanics within organized labor.

1974. Congress passes the Equal Educational Opportunity Act to create equality in public schools by making bilingual education available to Hispanic youth. According to the framers of the act, equal education means more than equal facilities and equal access to teachers. Students who have trouble with the English language must be given programs to help them learn English.

1975. The Voting Rights Act Amendments of 1975 extend the provisions of the original Voting Rights Act and makes permanent the national ban on literacy tests. Critical for Hispanic Americans, the amendments make bilingual ballots a requirement in certain areas.

1977. The INS apprehends more than one million undocumented workers each year.

1977. A group of young Cuban exiles called the Antonio Maceo Brigade travels to Cuba to participate in service work and to achieve a degree of rapprochement with the Cuban government.

1978. The median income of Hispanic families below the poverty level falls from $7,238 in 1978 to $6,557 in 1987, controlling for inflation.

1978-1988. Hispanic female participation in the work force more than doubles, from 1.7 million to 3.6 million. In 1988, 56.6 percent of Hispanic women are in the work force, compared with 66.2 percent of white women and 63.8 percent of blacks.

1978-1988. The proportion of Hispanic children living in poverty rises more than 45 percent, and by 1989, 38 percent of Hispanic children are living in poverty.

1979. Political upheaval and civil wars in Nicaragua, El Salvador, and Guatemala contribute to large migrations of refugees to the United States.

1980s. Japanese industrialists take advantage of the maquiladoras by sending greater amounts of raw materials to Mexico where they are finished and shipped duty-free to the United States.

1980s. The rates of immigration approach the levels of the early 1900s: legal immigration during the first decade of the century reached 8.8 million, while during the 1980s, 6.3 million immigrants are granted permanent residence. The immigrants are overwhelmingly young and in search of employment, and Hispanic immigrants continue to account for more than 40 percent of the total.

1980s. Programs to apprehend undocumented immigrants are implemented, and reports of violations of civil rights are reported.

1980. A flotilla converges at Cuba's Mariel Harbor to pick up refugees. By year end, more than 125,000 "Marielitos" migrate to the United States. Castro charges that the exiles he allowed to return on visits had contaminated Cubans with the glitter of consumerism.

1980. The Refugee Act of 1980 removes the ideological definition of refugee as one who flees from a Communist regime, thus allowing thousands to enter the United States as refugees.

April 1980. A bus carrying a load of discontented Cubans crashes through the gates of the Peruvian embassy in Havana and the passengers receive political asylum from Peru. Castro begins to revise his policy of gradually allowing Cubans to leave.

1980-1988. The Reagan administration maintains that affirmative action programs entail quotas, constituting a form of reverse discrimination.

1980-1988. The number of Hispanics in the work force increases by 48 percent, representing 20 percent of U.S. employment growth.

1986. After more than a decade of debate, Congress enacts The Immigration Reform and Control Act (IRCA), creating an alien legalization program: legal status is given to applicants who held illegal status in the United States from before January 1, 1982, until the time of application. The program brings legal status to a large number of undocumented Hispanics.

1987. 70.1 percent of Hispanic female-headed households with children are living in poverty.

1988. Ronald Reagan appoints the first Hispanic Secretary of Education: Dr. Lauro F. Cavazos.

1989. Median family income for white families is $35,210; for blacks, $20,210; and for Hispanics, $23,450. Per capita income is $14,060 for whites, $8,750 for blacks, and $8,390 for Hispanics.

1989. Immigration from the Americas rises from 44.3 percent in 1964 to 61.4 percent. Of the major countries, Mexico accounts for 37.1 percent of total documented immigration to the United States, the next highest number of immigrants being from El Salvador, 5.3 percent.

1990. George Bush appoints the first woman and first Hispanic surgeon general of the United States: Antonia C. Novello.

1990. The erosion of past civil rights legislation by the Supreme Court during the Reagan and Bush administrations results in efforts by representatives of civil rights, black, and Hispanic organizations to initiate a push for a new Civil Rights Act. A series of compromises produces a watered-down Civil Rights Act in 1991.

1991. The proposed North American Free Trade Agreement between Mexico, the United States, and Canada expands even further the *maquiladora* concept, offering potentially greater tax abatements for U.S. businesses.

March 1991. Unemployment among U.S. Hispanics reaches 10.3 percent, roughly double the rate for whites.

Theater

✺ Hispanic Theater in the United States: Origins to 1940 ✺ Post World War II to the Present
✺ Outstanding Figures in Hispanic Theater

✺HISPANIC THEATER IN THE UNITED STATES: ORIGINS TO 1940

The Southwest

The roots of Hispanic theater in the United States reach back to the dance-drama of the American Indians and to the religious theater and pageants of medieval and Renaissance Spain. During the Spanish colonization of Mexico theater was placed at the service of the Catholic missionaries, who employed it in evangelizing the Indians and in instructing them and their mestizo descendants in the mysteries and dogma of the church. Throughout the seventeenth and eighteenth centuries in Mexico there was developing a hybrid religious theater, one that often employed the music, colors, flowers, masks, even the languages of the Indians of Mexico while dramatizing the stories from the Old and New Testaments. In Mexico and what eventually became the Southwest of the United States there developed a cycle of religious plays that, while dramatizing these stories from the Bible, nevertheless became so secular and entertaining in their performances that church authorities finally banned them from church grounds and from inclusion in the official festivities during feast days. They thus became folk plays, enacted by the faithful on their own and without official sanction or sponsorship by the church.

At the center of this cycle of folk plays that dealt with Adam and Eve, Jesus lost in the desert, and other favorite passages of the Holy Scriptures was the story of the Star of Bethlehem announcing the birth of Jesus Christ to humble shepherds, who then commence a pilgrimage in search of the newborn Christ Child. On the way to Bethlehem Satan and the legions of hell attempt to waylay and distract the shepherds, and a battle between Good, represented by

the Archangel Michael, and Evil takes place. Among the other various dramatic elements in this shepherd's play, or *pastorela* as it is called in Spanish, are the appearance of a virginal shepherdess, a lecherous hermit, and a comic bumbling shepherd named Bato. Pastorelas, presented by the common folk from central Mexico to northern California, are still performed today, especially in rural areas during the Christmas season. Originally the whole cycle of mystery plays was performed from December 12, when the play that dramatized Las Cuatro Apariciones de Nuestra Señora de Guadalupe (the four appearances of Our Lady of Guadalupe) was presented, through the Easter season and its pageants. The famed *Las posadas* is a Christmas pageant dealing with Mary and Joseph looking for shelter, and originally belongs to this cycle as well. In one form or another these folk plays are still with us today and have especially influenced the development of Mexican-American theater in the United States. The most noteworthy parts of the legacy of the pastorelas and other religious drama have been their missionary zeal, their involvement of the community of grass roots people, their use of allegory and masks, their totally mestizo nature, and their sense of comicality and slapstick.

In 1598, Juan de Oñate led his colonizing mission into what is today New Mexico. As stated earlier, the missionaries introduced religious theater, and Juan de Oñate's soldiers and colonists brought along the roots of secular drama. It has been recorded that while camped at night the soldiers would entertain themselves by imrovising plays based on the experiences of their journey. They also enacted the folk play that has been spread wherever Spaniards have colonized, *Moros y cristianos*, which is the heroic tale of how the Christians defeated the Moors in northern Spain during the Crusades and eventually drove them from the Iberian Peninsula. For many scholars these represent the roots of an authentic secular folk theater that developed in what became the Southwest of the United States and that gave rise to such New Mexican plays in the eighteenth and early nineteenth centuries as *Los comanches* and *Los tejanos*, both of which deal with military conflict in an epic manner. But as late as the early twentieth century, reenactments of *Moros y cristianos*, even performed on horseback, have been documented in New Mexico, which seems to be the state, because of its rural culture, that has most preserved its Hispanic folk traditions.

But the most important part of the story of Hispanic theater in the United States is not one of a folk theater, but of the development and flourishing of a full-blown professional theater in the areas most populated by Hispanics: throughout the Southwest, New York, Florida, and even the Midwest. The origins of the Spanish-language professional theater in the United States are to be found in mid-nineteenth-century California, where troupes of itinerant players began touring from Mexico to perform melodramas accompanied by other musical and dramatic entertainments for the residents of the coastal cities that had developed from earlier Franciscan missions—San Francisco, Los Angeles, San Diego. These three cities were more accessible from Mexico than San Antonio, Texas, for instance, because of the regularity of steamship travel up and down the Pacific coast.

There is evidence that plays were being performed as early as 1789; the manuscript copy of a three-act cloak-and-dagger play, *Astucias por heredar un sobrino a su tío* (*The Clever Acts of a Nephew in Order to Inherit His Uncle's Wealth*) bears that date and shows eveidence of having been toured through the California settlements. Records of professional theatrical performances become more numerous some decades later. In the 1840s, various troupes of itinerant players visited the ranches and inns around the San Francisco and Monterey areas of northern California, performing in Spanish for both Spanish- and English-language audiences. During this time at least one semiprofessional theater house existed in Los Angeles. In 1848, don Antonio F. Coronel, later to become mayor of Los Angeles, opened a theater that seated three hundred as an addition to his house; it included a covered stage with a proscenium, a drop curtain, and a good supply of scenery. In the following decades various other theaters opened to accommodate both Spanish- and English-language productions: Don Vicente Guerrero's Union Theater existed from 1852 to 1854, don Abel Stearn's Hall from 1859 to 1875, and don Juan Temple's Theater from 1859 to

1892. In the 1860s and 1870s, the Hispanic community also frequented the Teatro de la Merced, Teatro Alarcón, and Turn Verein Hall. In the 1880s, Spanish-language productions were even held in the Grand Opera House in Los Angeles.

By the 1860s, the professional stage had become so established and important to the Spanish-speaking community that companies that once toured the Mexican republic and abroad began to settle down as resident companies in California. Such was the case of the Compañía Española de la Familia Estrella, directed by the renowned Mexican actor Gerardo López del Castillo, in its choosing of San Francsico for its home. The company was typical of those that toured interior Mexico in that it was composed of Mexican and Spanish players, was organized around a family unit, into which López del Castillo had married, staged mostly Spanish melodrama, and held its performances on Sunday evenings. Each program was a complete evening's entertainment that included a three- or four-act drama; songs, dances, and recitations; and a one-act farce or comic dialog to close the performance. The full-length plays that were the heart of the program were mostly melodramas by peninsular Spanish authors, such as José Zorrilla, Mariano José de Larra, and Manuel Bretón de los Herreros. Productions by this and the other companies that settled in or toured California were seen as wholesome entertainment appropriate for the whole family, and a broad segment of the Hispanic community, not just the elite, subscribed and attended. This departs somewhat from the English-language tradition and Protestant attitudes at that time, especially west of the Mississippi, which considered the theater arts to be improper for women and immoral, even to the extent of using such euphemisms as "opera house" in naming theaters. In the Hispanic community actors were quite often seen as upstanding citizens, at times even as community leaders, as was the case of López del Castillo, who was elected president of one of the most important Mexican organizations in San Francisco: Junta Patriótica Mexicana (The Mexican Patriotic Commission).

Gerardo López del Castillo was considered to be an outstanding leading man, but it was his wife, Amalia Estrella del Castillo, who won the hearts of many a newspaper critic. On January 26, 1866, the *Los Angeles News* issued the following praise: "Mr. and Mrs. Castillo will rank with the best performers in the state. Mrs. Castillo's imposing and attractive form, handsome features and graceful and charming ease with which she moves through all of her representations is alone well worth the price of admission. When fond of looking at a beautiful woman in the theatrical costume, we would advise you to purchase a ticket."

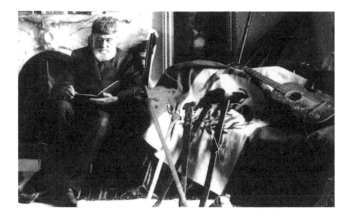

Don Antonio F. Coronel, who had served as mayor of Los Angeles, was an early theater owner and impresario.

Among the twelve or fourteen companies that were resident or actively touring California during the 1870s and 1880s, the Compañía Dramática Española, directed by Pedro C. de Pellón, and the Compañía Española de Angel Mollá were two resident companies in Los Angeles that extended their tours to Baja California and up to Tucson, Arizona; from there they would return to Los Angeles via stagecoach. During this time Tucson boasted two Spanish-language theater houses: Teatro Cervantes and Teatro Americano. In 1878, Pellón established himself permanently in Tucson, where he organized the town's first group of amateur actors, Teatro Recreo. Thus, the 1870s mark Arizona's participation in Hispanic professional theater. It is in this decade as well that troupes began to tour the Laredo and San Antonio axis of Texas, first performing in Laredo and then San Antonio in open-air markets, taverns and later in such German-American settings as Meunch Hall, Krish Hall, and Wolfram's Garden in San Antonio; but it is only at the turn of the century and afterward

Los Angeles's California Theater.

that companies touring from Mexico began making San Antonio and Laredo their home bases.

The last decade of the nineteenth century experienced a tremendous increase in Mexican theatrical activity in the border states. More and more companies that had previously only toured interior Mexico were now establishing regular circuits extending from Laredo to San Antonio and El Paso, through New Mexico and Arizona to Los Angeles, then up to San Francisco or down to San Diego. It was the advent of rail transportation and the automobile that was bringing the touring companies even to smaller population centers after the turn of the century. Between 1900 and 1930, numerous Mexican theaters and halls were established in order to house Spanish-language performances all along this circuit. By 1910, even some smaller cities had their own Mexican theaters with resident stock companies. The more mobile tent theaters, circus theaters and smaller makeshift companies performed in rural areas and throughout the small towns on both sides of the Rio Grande Valley.

Theatrical activities expanded rapidly when thousands of refugees took flight from the Mexican Revolution and settled in the United States from the border all the way up to the Midwest. During the decades of revolution, many of Mexico's greatest artists and their theatrical companies came to tour and/or take up temporary residence; however, some would never return to the homeland.

Mexican and Spanish companies and an occasional Cuban, Argentine, or other Hispanic troupe toured the Southwest, but they found their most lucrative engagements in Los Angeles and San Antonio. They at times even crisscrossed the nation, venturing to perform for the Hispanic communities in New York, Tampa, and the Midwest. By the 1920s, Hispanic theater was becoming big business, and important companies like Spain's Compañía María Guerrero y Fernando Díaz de Mendoza had its coast-to-coast tours into major Anglo-American theaters booked by New York agents, such as Walter O. Lindsay. The company of the famed Mexican leading lady Virginia Fábregas was of particular importance in its frequent tours because it not only performed the latest serious works from Mexico City and Europe, but also because some of the troupe members occasionally defected to form their own resident and touring companies in the Southwest. Virgina Fábregas was also important in encouraging the development of local playwrights in Los Angeles by buying the rights to their works and integrating the plays into her repertoire.

The two cities with the largest Mexican populations, Los Angeles and San Antonio, became theatrical centers, the former also feeding off the important film industry in Hollywood. In fact, Los Angeles became a manpower pool for Hispanic theater. Actors, directors, technicians, and musicians from throughout the Southwest, New York, and the whole Hispanic world were drawn there looking for employment. Both Los Angeles and San Antonio went through a period of intense expansion and building of new theatrical facilities in the late teens and early twenties. Los Angeles was able to support five major Hispanic theater houses with programs that changed daily. The theaters and their peak years were Teatro Hidalgo (1911-34), Teatro México (1927-33), Teatro Capitol (1924-26), Teatro Zendejas (later Novel; 1919-24), and Teatro Principal (1921-29). There were as many as twenty other theaters operating at one time or another during the same time period.

San Antonio's most important house was the Teatro Nacional, built in 1917 and housing live productions up through the Great Depression. Its splendor and elite status was not shared by any of the other fifteen or so theaters that housed Spanish-language productions in San Antonio during this period. While it is true that in the Southwest, as in Mexico, Spanish drama and *zarzuela*, the Spanish national version of operetta, dominated the stage up until the early 1920s, the clamor for plays written by Mexican playwrights had increased to such an extent that by 1923 Los Angeles had developed into a center for Mexican playwriting unparalleled in the history of Hispanic communities in the United States. While continuing to consume plays by Spanish peninsualr authors, such as Jacinto Benavente, José Echegaray, Gregorio Martínez-Sierra, Manuel Linares Rivas, and the Alvarez Quintero brothers, the Los Angeles Mexican community and its theaters encouraged local writing by offering cash prizes in contests, lucrative contracts, and lavish productions. Various impresarios of the Spanish-language theaters maintained this tradition throughout the 1920s, offering at times as much as two hundred dollars in prize money to the winners of the playwriting contests. It was often reported in the newspapers of the time that the Hispanic theaters drew their largest crowds every time they featured plays by local writers.

The period from 1922 to 1933 saw the emergence and box office success of a cadre of playwrights in Los Angeles composed mainly of Mexican theatrical expatriates and newspapermen. At the center of the group were four playwrights whose works not only filled the theaters on Los Angeles's Main Street, but were also contracted throughout the Southwest and in Mexico: Eduardo Carrillo, an actor; Adalberto Elías González, a novelist; Esteban V. Escalante, a

newspaperman and theatrical director; and Gabriel Navarro, poet, novelist, composer, orchestra director, columnist for *La Opinión* newspaper, and editor of the magazine *La Revista de Los Angeles*. There were at least twenty other locally residing writers who saw their works produced on the professional stage, not to mention the scores of authors of vaudeville revues and lighter pieces.

The serious full-length plays created by these authors addressed the situation of Mexicans in California on a broad, epic scale, often in plays based on the history of the Mexican-Anglo struggle in California. Eduardo Carrillo's *El proceso de Aurelio Pompa* (*The Trial of Aurelio Pompa*) dealt with the unjust trial and sentencing of a Mexican immigrant; it was performed repeatedly on the commercial stage and in community-based fund-raising events. Gabriel Navarro's *Los emigrados* (*The Emigrées*) and *El sacrificio* (*The Sacrifice*) dealt, respectively, with Mexican expatriate life in Los Angeles during the revolution and with the history of California around 1846, the date of the outbreak of the Mexican-American War.

By far the most prolific and respected of the Los Angeles playwrights was Adalberto Elías González, some of whose works were not only performed locally, but also throughout the Southwest and Mexico, and made into movies and translated into English. His works that saw the light on the stages of Los Angeles ran the gamut from historical drama to dime-novel sensationalism. The most famous of his plays, *Los amores de Ramona* (*The Loves of Ramona*), was a stage adaptation of Helen Hunt Jackson's novel about early California, *Ramona: A Story*; it broke all box office records when it was seen by more than fifteen thousand people after only eight performances, and soon it became a regular item in many repertoires in the Southwest. Two of González's other plays dealt with the life and culture of Mexicans in California: *Los misioneros* (*The Missionaries*) and *Los expatriados* (*The Expatriates*). Probably his second most successful work was the sensationalist *La asesino del martillo o la mujer tigresa* (*The Assassin with the Hammer or Tiger Woman*), based on a real-life crime story reported in the newspapers in 1922 and 1923. A dozen other plays dealt with love triangles and themes from the Mexican Revolution, including *La muerte de Francisco Villa* (*The Death of Francisco Villa*) and *El fantasma de la revolución* (*The Ghost of the Revolution*).

Adalberto Elías González and these other authors addressed the needs of their audiences for reliving their history on both sides of the border and for reviving the glories of their own language and cultural tradition with the decorum and professionalism befitting the type of family entertainment that the

The Mason Theater, a movie and popular vaudeville house in Los Angeles.

community leaders believed served the purposes of reinforcing Hispanic culture and morality while resisting assimilation to Anglo-American culture. But with the rise of vaudeville and the greater access of working-class people to theatrical entertainment, vaudeville-type revues and variety shows became more and more popular and gradually displaced more serious theater. But Mexican vaudeville and musical comedy did not avoid the themes that were so solemnly treated in three-act dramas. Rather, the Mexican stage had developed its own type of revue: the *revista*. Revistas were musical revues that had developed in Mexico under the influence of the Spanish zarzuela and the French *revue* and vaudeville, but had taken on their own character in Mexico as a format for piquant political commentary and social satire. Also, like the zarzuela, which celebrated Spanish regional customs, music, and folklore, the Mexican revista also created and highlighted the character, music, dialects, and folkore of the various Mexican regions. Under the democratizing influence of the Mexican Revolution, the revista highlighted the life and culture of the working classes. During the revolution, the *revista política* in particular rose to prominence on Mexico City stages, but later all revista forms degenerated into a loose vehicle for musical and comedic performance in which typical regional and underdog characters, such as the *pelado* (literally, skinned or penniless), often improvised a substantial part of the action.

Many critics and historians of Mexican theater see in the revista the birth of a truly Mexican theater. In the words of Miguel Covarrubias, "These rebellious Mexican *commedias dell'art* have produced not only a new national theater, the only one worthy of the name, but a fine corps of actors and comedians whose style and careers have been strongly influenced by the dominant politics of the time" (p. 588).

The Los Angeles stages hosted many of the writers and stars of revistas that had been active during the time of formation of the genre in Mexico, including Leopoldo Beristáin and Guz Aguila. In the theaters of Los Angeles and the Southwest were staged most of the revistas that were popular in Mexico and that were of historical importance for the development of the genre. Such works as *El tenorio maderista* (*The Maderist Tenorio*), *El país de los cartones* (*The Country Made of Boxes*) and *La ciudad de los volcanes* (*The City of Volcanoes*) and numerous others were continuously repeated from Los Angeles to Laredo. Such innovators of the genre as Guz Aguila was for a time a perennial attraction at the Los Angeles theaters. Even important composers of scores for the revistas, such as Lauro D. Uranga, graced the Los Angeles Hispanic stages. With their low humor and popular music scores, the revistas in Los Angeles articulated grievances and poked fun at both the U.S. and Mexican governments. The Mexican Revolution was satirically reconsidered over and over again in Los Angeles from the perspective of the expatriates, and Mexican-American culture was contrasted with the "purer" Mexican version. This social and political commentary was carried out despite the fact that both audiences and performers were mostly immigrants and thus liable to deportation or repatriation. The Los Angeles writers and composers were serving a public that was hungry to see itself reflected on stage, an audience whose interest was piqued by revistas relating to current events, politics, and the conflict of cultures that was produced while living in the Anglo-dominated environment. The revistas kept the social and political criticism leveled at the authorities, be they Mexican or American, within the light context of music and humor in such pieces as Guz Aguila's *México para los Mexicanos* (*Mexico for the Mexicans*) and *Los Angeles vacilador* (*Swinging Los Angeles*), Gabriel Navarro's *La ciudad de irás y no volverás* (*The City of You Go There Never to Return*), and Don Catarino's *Los efectos de la crisis* (*The Effects of the Depression*), *Regreso a mi tierra* (*The Return to My Country*), *Los repatriados* (*The Repatriated*), *Whiskey, morfina y marihuana*, and *El desterrado* (*The Exiled One*).

It is in the revista that we find a great deal of humor based on the culture shock typically derived from following the misadventures of naive, recent immigrants from Mexico who have difficulty in getting accustomed to life in the big Anglo-American metropolis. Later on in the 1920s, and when the depression and repatriation took hold, the theme of culture shock was converted to one of outright cultural conflict. At that point Mexican nationalism became more intensified as anti-Mexican sentiments become more openly expressed in the Anglo-American press as a basis for taking Mexicans off the welfare rolls and deporting them. In the revista, the Americanized, or *agringado* and *renegado*, became even more satirized, and the barbs aimed at American culture become even sharper. It is also in the revista that the raggedly dressed underdog, the *pelado*, comes to the fore with his low-class dialect and acerbic satire. A forerunner of characters like Cantinflas the pelado really originates in the humble tent theaters that evolved in Mexico and existed in the Southwest of the United States until the 1950s. With roots in the circus clown tradition, and a costume and dialect that embody poverty and marginality, the pelado was free to improvise and exchange witticism with his audiences that often embodied working-class distrust of societal institutions and the upper classes. Although the pelado or *peladito*, as he was affectionately called, was often criticized for his low humor and scandalous language, theater critics today consider the character to be a genuine and original Mexican contribution to the history of theater.

One actor who played the pelado to perfection was not even a Mexican but a Spaniard: Romualdo Ti-

Actress Rosalinda Meléndez (left) as a shoe-shine boy during the Depression.

rado. He is without a doubt the most important figure in the history of the Hispanic stage of this period. Tirado was an impresario, director, singer, actor, and the author of numerous revistas. Tirado had immigrated to Mexico around the turn of the century and developed a career on the stage there for fifteen years before resettling in Los Angeles in the late teens. In the City of Angels Tirado became a prime mover in the Hispanic theatrical and cinematic industries as a theater owner and movie producer, and just as important, he was also one of the catlysts that brought about the writing and staging of local plays and revistas.

But the most important author of revistas was Antonio Guzmán Aguilera, who went by the stage name Guz Aguila. Unlike Tirado, who settled in Los Angeles expressly to become a theater impresario and movie producer, Guz Aguila became a journalist for *El Heraldo de México* newspaper, but still managed to tour his theatrical company as far south as Mexico City and as far west as San Antonio. Guz Aguila rose to fame in Mexico City as a newspaperman and prolific revista author, but as a result of a falling out with President Obregón and subsequent imprisonment, Aguila went into exile in Los Angeles in 1924. His production has been estimated as high as five hundred theatrical works, none of which were ever published, but it is certain that many of his revistas were reworked, renamed, and recycled to accommodate different current events, locations, and audiences. In Los Angeles in 1924 Aguila was given a contract that paid one thousand dollars per month to write for the Teatro Hidalgo. In a June 7, 1924, interview for "El heraldo de México," Aguila stated that the Hidalgo had also formed a company of thirty performers for him and commissioned special scenography and costumes. In the same interview, he revealed that his personal motto was *corrigat riendo mores* (customs are corrected through laughter). And an abundance of laughter, color, patriotic symbolism, and naturalism is what Aguila gave his audiences by pulling out and producing his most famous and time-proven revistas: *Alma tricolor* (*Three-Colored Soul*), *La huerta de Don Adolfo* (*Don Adolfo's Garden*; a reference to President Adolfo de la Huerta), and *Exploración presidencial* (*A Presidential Exploration*). After presenting many of his well-known works, Aguila began to produce new revistas based on culture and events in Los Angeles: *Los Angeles vacilador* (*Swinging Los Angeles*), *Evite peligro* (*Avoid Danger*), and *El eco de México* (*The Echo from Mexico*). Aguila returned to the stages of Mexico City in 1927, but he never regained the level of success that he had previously experienced there. He continued to tour the republic and the southwestern United States in the years that followed.

Eusebio Pirrín decided on his stage name, don Catarino, while in Los Angeles after developing his acts from childhood in his family's tent theater. It was on the Los Angeles stage during his teens that Pirrín gained prominence, principally in the role of a tiny old man with a bushy moustache. Pirrín was so small that women from the chorus line would pick him up like a baby. Pirrín directed and starred in his family show, which became a perennial presence on the Los Angeles stages in the late 1920s and early 1930s; he somehow even managed to get bookings during the Great Depression. All of the revistas, songs, and dance routines of the Pirríns were original, most of them creations of the enormously innovative Pirrín. Although don Catarino's role was that of a little old ranchero, much of the humor, settings, and situations for his work truly represented urban culture through picaresque adventures. In his numerous revistas, all built around the character of don Catarino, Pirrín explored the themes of Los Angeles night life, culture conflict, and amorous adventures, but he did not shy away from the real-life dramas of the depression, exile, and repatriation in his generally lighthearted works. Eusebio Pirrín did not appear on the stages of Mexico City until the depression and then he was chagrined to realize that many of his imitators in the Mexican capital had been exploiting the don Catarino character that he had created in Los Angeles.

Unlike Los Angeles, the stages of San Antonio did not attract or support the development of local playwrights, and while they hosted many of the same theatrical companies and performers, such as don Catarino and Los Pirríns, as did the California stages, theater in the Alamo City did not support as many resident companies. To be sure, as stated above, there were many Mexican theater houses and various stock and resident companies, many of which used San Antonio as a base from which to launch tours of Texas and both sides of the Rio Grande Valley. While the story of Los Angeles's Hispanic theater is one of proliferation of Spanish-language houses, companies, and playwrights, the story of San Antonio is one that illustrates the persistence of resident companies, actors, and directors in keeping Hispanic drama alive in community and church halls after being dislodged by vaudeville and the movies from the professional theater houses during the depression. San Antonio's is also the story of the rise of a number of vaudevillians to national and international prominence. Finally, San Antonio also became a center for another type of theater, one that served an exclusively working-class audience: tent theater.

In San Antonio, Los Angeles, and throughout the Southwest, the Great Depression and the forced and voluntary repatriation of Mexicans depopulated not only the communities but also the theaters. Theater owners and impresarios could no longer afford to present full companies, accompanied by orchestras and technicians; the economic advantage of showing movies was devastating to live theater. After receiving the triple blow of depression, repatriation, and cinema, the Hispanic theater industry continued to writhe and agonize from 1930 until the middle of the decade, when only a few hardy troupes acquiesced to entertaining briefly between films or donated their art to charity; some also toured rural areas in tent theaters, struck out to perform for New York's growing Hispanic population, or simply returned to Mexico. Many were the artists from Los Angeles to the Midwest who stubbornly continued to perform, only now their art was staged in church and community halls for little or no pay in the service of community and church charities, which were especially numerous during the depression. And there was no more heroic battle waged anywhere than that of the San Antonio resident directors and their companies to keep their art alive and in service of the communities. Directors Manuel Cotera, Bernardo Fougá, and Carlos Villalongín, along with such stars as Lalo Astol and María Villalongín, continued to present the same theatrical fare in the same professional manner in church and neighborhood halls throughout San Antonio and on tour to Austin, Dallas, Houston, Laredo, and smaller cities and towns during the 1930s. At the same time, in order to fill the vacuum that had been created with the return of many performers to Mexico and the cessation of tours from there, amateur theatrical groups began to spring up and proliferate, often instructed and directed by theater professionals; quite often these groups also used the church halls and auditoriums for their rehearsals and performances. It is worth reemphasizing that most of the professional and community groups did not exist to present religious drama, but church facilities and church sponsorship were often offered because the theater and most of the serious plays presented were seen as wholesome entertainment and instruction in language and culture for the youth of the community, which was even more cut off during the depression from the culture of interior Mexico.

Besides providing the environment for this important community theater movement, San Antonio was also the center for the Hispanic circus and tent-theater industry in the United States. Circus and theater had been associated together since colonial days in Mexico, but during the nineteenth century there developed a humble, poor man's circus that traveled the poor neighborhoods of Mexico City and the provinces. It would set up a small tent, or *carpa*, to house its performances; later these theaters were called carpas by extension of the term. It was in the carpa during the revolution that the Mexican national clown, the pelado developed. In general, besides offering all types of serious and light theatrical fare, the carpa came to be known for satirical revistas that often featured the antics and working-class philosophy and humor of the pelado. The carpas functioned quite often as popular tribunals, repositories of folk wisdom, humor, and music, and were incubators of Mexican comic types and stereotypes. They continued to function in this way in the Southwest, but particularly in San Antonio, which had become, especially after the outbreak of the revolution, a home base and wintering ground for many of the carpas.

Probably because of their small size, bare-bones style, and organization around a family unit, the carpas could manage themselves better than large circuses or theatrical companies. Furthermore, they were able to cultivate smaller audiences in the most remote areas. The carpas became in the Southwest an important Mexican-American popular culture institution. Their comic routines became a sounding board for the culture conflict that Mexican Americans felt in language usage, assimilation to American tastes and life-styles, discrimination in the United States, and *pocho*, or Americanized status, in Mexico. Out of these types of conflicts in popular entertainment arose the stereotype of the pachuco, a typically Mexican-American figure. Finally, the carpas were a refuge for theatrical and circus people of all types during the Great Depression, repatriation, and World War II. More important, their cultural arts were preserved by the carpas for the postwar generation that was to forge a new relationship with the larger American culture.

From the turn of the century through World War II, San Antonio was home to many carpas. Two of the most well known resident tent shows of San Antonio were the Carpa García and the Carpa Cubana, whose descendants still reside in the Alamo City. The Carpa García was founded by Manuel V. García, a native of Saltillo, Mexico. He relocated his family to San Antonio in 1914, after having performed with the Carpa Progresista in Mexico. Featured in his Carpa García was the famed *charro* (Mexican-style cowboy) on the tightrope act. One of the comic actors of the carpa, Pedro González González ("Ramirín"), later had a successful career in Hollywood Westerns. Other members of the family performed magic, ventriloquism, song and dance, and comedy. The highlight of the show was the peladito Don Fito. As played by Manuel's son Rodolfo, Don Fito became a typical

The García girls chorus line from the Carpa García Tent show.

wise guy from the streets of west San Antonio, speaking an urban Mexican-American dialect, or *caló*. He also satirized the language of Mexicans and pachucos and often engaged audiences in repartee. The Carpa García at times also hosted Don Lalo (Lao Astol) and the famous singer Lydia Mendoza and her family of performers. Daughter Esther García, an acrobat, went on to the center ring of the Barnum and Bailey Circus. By 1947, the Carpa García decided to retire after a final run-in with the fire department about making its tents fireproof. In Latin American and U.S. circus history, the Abreu name appears frequently at the end of the nineteenth century and beginning of the twentieth. The Abreu company, directed by Virgilio Abreu, owned and operated the Carpa Cubana—also known as the Cuban Show and the Circo Cubano—that made San Antonio its home base in the 1920s and 1930s. But before that various members of the family had appeared as acrobats, tumblers, and wire walkers with such famous shows as Orrin, Barnum and Bailey, Ringling Brothers, John Robinson, and Sells-Floto. In San Antonio the Cuban circus included trapeze artists, rope walkers, jugglers, clowns, dancers, and its own ten-piece band.

Although based in San Antonio, the company toured as far as California and central Mexico by truck and train, but mostly limited its tours to the Rio Grande Valley in the south and Austin to the north during the 1930s. Virgilio Abreu and his wife, Federica, owned a home on the west side of San Antonio but lived in tents with the rest of the company when on the road. The company would tour for four or five months in the spring until summer heat set in and then not leave San Antonio again until the fall, returning home for the Christmas season. The members of the company would also do variety acts in the local San Antonio cinemas.

New York City

It was during the 1890s in New York that regular amateur and semiprofessional shows began, as the Hispanic community, made up mostly of Spaniards and Cubans, was growing in size, reflecting once again the patterns of internal conflict in the homeland and immigration to the United States that would be repeated time and again during the development of Hispanic communities and culture in the United States. Of course, the diaspora brought on by the

Don Fito, the Carpa García *peladito* from the Carpa García tent show.

Mexican Revolution (1910) more than any other factor characterized the theater in the Southwest during the first half of the twentieth century. In the 1890s New York became an organizing and staging center for Cuban, Puerto Rican, and Dominican expatriates seeking the independence of their homeland from Spain. Later in the century, heavy migration of Puerto Ricans, now U.S. citizens, and the Puerto Rican nationalist movement in pursuit of independence from the United States also manifested itself on the city's Hispanic stages, as did the efforts by exiled Spanish Republicans fighting fascism during the Spanish Civil War in the mid thirties.

Documentary evidence of the Hispanic stage in New York begins in 1892 with *La patria* newspaper reporting on the dramatic activities of actor Luis Baralt and his company. Until 1898, the year of the Spanish-American War, this newspaper which supported the Cuban revolutionary movement, occasionally covered performances by Baralt and his troupe, which included both amateurs and actors with professional experience. The company had an irregular performance schedule in such auditoriums and halls as the Berkeley Lyceum and the Carnegie Lyceum, where it presented standard Spanish melodramas as well as Cuban plays, such as *De lo vivo a lo pintado* (*From Life to the Painted Version*), by Tomás Mendoza, a deceased hero of the revolutionary war, and *La fuga de Evangelina* (*The Escape of Evangelina*), by an unknown author, the dramatization of the escape from prison by a heroine of the independence movement. The last performance reported took place at the Central Opera House on January 16, 1899; funds were raised for the sepulcher of the great Cuban philosopher-poet and revolutionary José Martí. After this last performance there is no further mention in surviving newspapers of theatrical performances in Spanish until the advent of a truly professional stage some seventeen years later in 1916.

Unlike the theatrical experience of Los Angeles, San Antonio and Tampa, in the mid teens of the new century the New York Hispanic community could not claim any theaters of its own. Rather, a number of impresarios rented available theaters around town, but mainly those located in the Broadway area, from midtown Manhattan up to the eighties: Bryant Hall, Park Theater, Amsterdam Opera House, Leslie Theater, Carnegie Hall, and so forth. The first impresario to lead companies on this odyssey through New York theater houses was a Spanish actor-singer of zarzuelas (Spanish operettas) who had made his debut in Mexico City in 1904: Manuel Noriega. Noriega became a figure in New York who in many ways was comparable to Romualdo Tirado in Los Angeles. Like Tirado, he was a tireless and enthusiastic motivator of Hispanic theater, and for a number of years he had practically the sole responsibility for maintaining Spanish-language theatrical seasons. Like Tirado, he became one of the first impresarios to establish a Hispanic motion picture company. Also like Tirado, Noriega's genius as a comic actor could always be relied upon to bring in audiences during difficult financial straits. Noriega found his way to New York in 1916 from the Havana stage to perform with another singer, the famous and charming María Conesa, at the Amsterdam Theater. That very same year he founded the first of his many theatrical companies, Compañía Dramática Española, which performed at the Leslie Theater from June to September and then went on to other theaters in the city. In Noriega's repertoire was the typical fare of Spanish comedies, zarzuelas, and comic afterpieces. During the first two years, Noriega had difficulty in getting the Hispanic community out to the theater, so much so that a community organization, the Unión Benéfica Española had to have a fund-raiser for his poverty-stricken actors. It was in 1918 at the Amsterdam Opera House that Noriega's company began finding some stability, performing each Sunday, with an occasional special performance on Thursdays. By November of that year the company was so successful that it added matinee showings on Sundays, and by December it began advertising in the newspaper for theatrical artists. As Noriega hired on more actors, mostly Cuban, Spanish, and Mexican, the nature of the company began to change, at times highlighting Galician or Catalonian works, at others Cuban blackface comedy. In 1919, Noriega formed a partnership with Hispanic, Greek, and Anglo-American businessmen to lease the Park Theater and make it the premier Hispanic house, rebaptizing it El Teatro Español. After a short performance run all the parties concerned bailed out of the bad business deal; the Noriega company went on to other theaters to perform in its usual manner until 1921, when Noriega slipped from sight.

The 1920s saw a rapid expansion of the Hispanic stage in New York, which was now regularly drawing touring companies from Cuba, Spain, Mexico, and the Southwest and which had also developed many of its own resident companies. Most of the companies followed the pattern of renting theaters for their runs and relocating afterward to different neighborhoods or to Brooklyn, New York, Bayonne, or Jersey City, New Jersey, or even Philadelphia. Beginning in 1922, the Hispanic community was able to lay claim to several houses on a long-term basis, at times even renaming the theaters in honor of the Hispanic community. The first two theaters that began to stabilize Hispanic theater culture in New York were the Dalys

and the Apollo. After 1930, the Apollo no longer offered Hispanic fare; the leadership then passed in 1931 to the San José/Variedades, in 1934 to the Campoamor, and finally in 1937 to the most important and longest-lived house in the history of Hispanic theater in New York: El Teatro Hispano.

As in the Southwest, these houses also experienced the same evolution of Hispanic theater in which melodrama and zarzuela reigned at the beginning of the 1920s to be gradually displaced by musical revues and vaudeville, while in the 1930s artists of serious drama took refuge in clubs and mutualist societies—rarely in church auditoriums as in the Southwest. However, the kind of musical revue that was to rein supreme in New York was not the Mexican revista, but the *obra bufa cubana*, or Cuban blackface farce, which featured the stock character types of the *negrito* (blackface), *mulata*, and *gallego* (Galician) and relied heavily on Afro-Cuban song and dance and improvised slapstick comedy. Like the revistas, the obras bufas cubanas often found inspiration in current events, neighborhood gossip, and even politics. The most famous of all the *bufos*, Arquímides Pous, who played in New York in 1921, was the creator of more than two hundred of these obras, many of which were kept alive by his followers after his death in Puerto Rico in 1926. Pous, who always played the negrito, was famous for his social satire and especially his attacks on racism. The bufo genre itself had been influenced in its development during the second half of the nineteenth century by the *buffes parisiennes* and the Cuban circus. Under the Spanish in Cuba the bufos were particularly repressed for being native Cuban, causing many of them to go into exile in Puerto Rico, Santo Domingo, or Mexico.

Beginning in 1932, the Mt. Morris Theater (inaugurated in 1913) began serving the Hispanic community under a series of various impresarios and names, first as the Teatro Campoamor, then the Teatro Cervantes, and on August 19, 1937, finally metamorphosing into El Teatro Hispano, which lived on into the 1950s. A somewhat mysterious Mexican impresario who never used his first names, Señor del Pozo, surfaced at the head of a group of backers made up of Hispanic and Jewish businessmen. Del Pozo administered the theater and directed the house orchestra. Under Del Pozo, besides movies, the Teatro Hispano offered three daily shows at 2:00, 5:30, and 9:00 P.M., except Sundays, when four shows were given. To maintain the interest of his working-class audiences, Del Pozo instituted a weekly schedule that included bonuses and surprises: on Tuesdays and Fridays banco was played at the theater and prizes were awarded, Wednesday audiences participated in talent shows that were broadcast over radio

WHOM, on Thursdays gifts and favors were distributed to audiences, and on Saturday mornings there was a special children's show. There were also occasional beauty contests, turkey raffles, and such. Weekly programs changed on Friday evenings and were billed as debuts. Del Pozo used the radio, his weekly playbills, and personal appearances to promote the theater as a family institution and himself as a great paternal and kindly protector of the community.

Upon opening in August 1937, Del Pozo immediately began to elaborate the formula of alternating shows relating to the diverse Hispanic nationalities represented in the community. For one week he played to the Puerto Ricans with the revue *En las playas de Borinquen* (*On the Shores of Puerto Rico*); then he followed in September with an Afro-Caribbean revue, *Fantasía en blanco y negro* (*Fantasy in Black and White*) and then *De México vengo* (*I Come from Mexico*); this was followed by the Compañía de Comedias Argentinas, then a week celebrating Puerto Rico's historic proclamation of independence, El Grito de Lares; by the end of September Del Pozo was again announcing Cuban week, featuring a *Cuba Bella* (Beautiful Cuba) revue. Each week a movie was shown to coincide with the country featured in the revue or plays.

In the months and years that ensued, numerous revues and an occasional zarzuela were staged, always balancing out the ethnic nationality represented. The Puerto Rican negrito Antonio Rodríguez and the Cuban negrito Edelmiro Borras became very popular and were ever present. The cast at the Teatro Hispano was constantly being reinforced by refugees from the Spanish Civil War, such as Rosita Rodrigo of the Teatro Cómico de Barcelona, and artists from the failing stages of the Southwest, like La Chata Noloesca and even Romualdo Tirado. By 1940, the Teatro Hispano had fixed its relationship to the predominantly working-class community, which by now was becoming Puerto Rican in majority.

Unlike the theaters in Los Angeles, the Teatro Hispano and the other theaters did not sponsor playwriting contests nor support the development of a local dramatic literature. While the dramatic activity was intense in New York City, the Big Apple did not support a downtown center where five or six major Hispanic houses located side by side competed with each other on a daily basis, as did the theaters in Los Angeles. Unlike the communities in the Southwest, the community of Hispanic immigrants in New York was not cognizant of a resident Hispanic tradition. And, while the relationship between journalism and playwriting had been well established in Mexico and the Southwest, this does not seem to have been the case in Cuba, Puerto Rico, or Spain. Then, too, many playwrights had been drawn to Los Angeles to work in the Hispanic film industry. And finally, the New York Hispanic public was not as large as Los Angeles's during the 1920s and could not support so large a business as the theater represented in the City of Angels.

By far the most productive playwrights and librettists in New York were the Cubans, especially those riding the crest of poularity of the irreverent, bawdy, satirical obras bufas cubanas. Of these, the most prolific and popular were Alberto O'Farrill and Juan C. Rivera. The former was a successful blackface comic and literary personality who edited the weekly "Gráfico" newspaper and produced zarzuelas and obras bufas cubanas based on Afro-Cuban themes. All of them debuted at the Apollo Theater. Juan C. Rivera was a comic actor who often played the role of the gallego and is known to have written both melodramas and revistas. Only a few of the works by these authors are known by name; it is assumed that they produced a considerable body of works to be staged by the companies in which they acted.

While it is true that Cubans and Spaniards made up the majority of theater artists in New York City and that their works dominated the stage in the 1920s and 1930s, it is also true that Puerto Rican drama emerged at this time and, it seems, accounts for a more serious and substantial body of literature. Two of the first Puerto Rican playwrights appear to have been socialists whose dramas supported the Spanish republican cause and working-class movements: José Enamorado Cuesta (1892-1976) and Franca de Armiño (a pseudonym). Of the former, all that is known is that *La prensa* on May 22, 1937, called him a revolutionary writer when it covered his play *El pueblo en marcha* (*The People on the March*). Of Franca de Armiño, all we have is her published drama *Los hipócritas* (*The Hypocrits*), whose notes and introduction reveal that she was the author of various other plays, essays, and poems, and that *Los hipócritas* was staged in 1933 at the Park Palace Theater. The play, which begins with the stock market crash, sets a Romeo and Juliet story to the background of the Spanish Civil War and the foreground of conflict between the workers and management at a shoe factory. While full of propaganda, Marxist theory, and stereotyped characters, *Los hipócritas* is a gripping and entertaining play that reflects the tenor of the times.

While Franca de Armiño and José Enamorado Cuesta were calling for a workers'' revolution, Gonzalo O'Neill was championing Puerto Rican nationalism and independence from the United States. Immediately upon graduation from Puerto Rico's Instituto Civil, O'Neill moved to New York, where he became a very successful businessman and somewhat of a protector and godfather to newly arrived Puerto Rican immigrants. A published poet and literary group organizer as a youth in Puerto Rico, he continued his literary vocation in New York by writing poetry and plays, some of which he published. From his very first published dramatic work, *La indiana borinqueña* (1922, *The Indians of Puerto Rico*), O'Neill revealed himself to be intensely patriotic and interested in Puerto Rican independence. His second published play, *Moncho Reyes* (1923), was a three-act biting satire of the current colonial government in Puerto Rico. Although both of these works enjoyed stage productions, it was his third play, *Bajo una sola bandera* (1928, Under Just One Flag), which debuted at the Park Palace Theater in New York in 1928 and at the Teatro Municipal in San Juan in 1929, that deserves the greatest attention for its artistry and thought, which also made it a popular vehicle for the Puerto Rican nationalist cause. In *Bajo una sola bandera* the political options facing Puerto Rico are personified in down-to-earth flesh-and-blood characters. The plot deals with the daughter of a middle-class Puerto Rican family residing in New York who must choose between a young American second lieutenant—the personification of the United States and military rule—and a young native Puerto Rican, whom she really loves. Both parents oppose each other in their preferences. Of course, the Puerto Rican youth wins the day and the play ends with sonorous, patriotic verses that underline the theme of independence for Puerto Rico. Although O'Neill is sure to have written other plays, the only other title that is known, *Amoríos borincanos* (*Puerto Rican Episodes of Love*), appeared at the Teatro Hispano in 1938; O'Neill was one of the investors in the theater.

Most of the other Puerto Rican and Hispanic playwrights of New York were minor in comparison to these and to the highly productive writers in Los Angeles. The true legacy of the New York Hispanic stage was its cosmopolitan nature and its ability to represent and solidify an ethnically diverse Hispanic community.

Tampa

In the late nineteenth century, the Tampa area witnessed the transplant of an entire industry from abroad and the development of a Hispanic enclave that chose the theater as its favorite form of art and culture. To remove themselves from the hostilities attendant on the Cuban war for independence from Spain, to come closer to their primary markets and avoid import duties, and to try to escape the labor unrest that was endemic to this particular industry,

various cigar manufacturers from Cuba began relocating to Tampa. In the swampy, mosquito-infested lands just east of Tampa, Ybor City was founded in 1886. By the 1890s, the Spanish and Cuban tobacco workers had begun establishing mutual aid societies and including theaters as centerpieces for the buildings they constructed to house these societies. Many of these theaters eventually hosted professional companies on tour from Cuba and Spain, but, more important, they became the forums where both amateurs and resident professionals entertained the Hispanic community for more than forty years without interruption. These theaters were also the training grounds where numerous tobacco workers and other community people developed into professional and semiprofessional artists, some of whom were able to make their way to the Hispanic stages of New York, Havana, and Madrid. Also, Tampa played a key role in one of the most exciting chapters of American theater history: it was the site of the Federal Theater Project's only Hispanic company under the Works Progress Administration.

Unlike Los Angeles, San Antonio, and New York, there was very little truly commercial theatrical activity in the Tampa-Ybor City communities. The six most important mutual aid societies—Centro Español, Centro Español de West Tampa, Centro Asturiano, Círculo Cubano, Centro Obrero, and Unión Martí-Maceo—each maintained a *comisión de espectáculos* (show committee) to govern the use of their theaters, a task that included renting the theater to touring companies and others, scheduling events, hiring professional directors, scenographers and technicians, and even purchasing performance rights to theatrical works. Along with this comisión, which obviously took on the theater management role, most of the societies also supported a *sección de declamación*, or amateur theatrical company, made up mostly of the society's members. For a good part of each year the company rehearsed on weeknights and performed on Sundays. For the most part, the audiences were made up of tobacco workers and their families. The tobacco workers prided themselves on their literary and artistic tastes; they were considered an intellectual or elite labor class that had gained an informal education from the professional *lectores* (readers) they hired to read aloud to them from literary masterpieces, newspapers, and other matter while they rolled cigars. Neither the demanding audiences nor the managing committees were satisfied by strictly amateurish renditions, especially since they could compare performances with those of the professional companies that often visited their theaters. It therefore became the custom to recruit and hire professional actors and directors from Ha-

The cover of a program for the performance of an operetta at the Centro Español in 1919.

vana to train and direct the resident sección de declamación, which was paid for its performances. Over the years numerous professional artists either settled in Tampa or were recruited to become part of the companies. But Tampa's Hispanic societies also prepared such important actors as Manuel Aparicio, Cristino R. Inclán, and Velia Martínez, who later abandoned the cigar factories to dedicate themselves completely to the world of the footlights and marquees. By the 1920s, a good number of the local artists considered themselves professionals and demanded reasonable salaries for their performances.

Of the six societies, the Centro Asturiano was the most important and the longest-lived; in fact, it is still functioning today as a theater, hosting theater and even opera companies. While the Centro Español of Ybor City was the oldest society—founded in 1891 (the Asturiano in 1902)—and for a time the most prestigious, the Asturiano held the distinction of hosting in its twelve-hundred-seat, first-class theater some of the greatest names in Hispanic theater in the world and even opera companies from New York and Italy during the period before World War II; and it was to the Centro Asturiano that Spain's first lady of

the stage, María Guerrero, took her company in 1926. That was a stellar year in which, besides producing the works of its own stock company directed by Manuel Aparicio, the Asturiano also hosted the Manhattan Grand Opera Association. But the socially progressive, even liberal, Centro Asturiano—it extended its membership to all Latins, even Cubans and Italians—held the further distinction of housing the only Spanish-language Federal Theater Project (FTP).

It was during the tenure of the FTP, for eighteen months in 1936 and 1937, that the Centro Asturiano made American theater history by housing the only Hispanic unit of the Works Progress Administration's (WPA's) national project. It is a chapter in which the two theatrical traditions, the Hispanic and the Anglo-American, which had existed side by side for so long, finally intersected to produce at times exciting theater but also examples of cultural misunderstanding. From the start the FTP administration's attitude seems to have been a model of condescension and, ultimately, the Hispanic unit had to disband because of congressional xenophobia.

It is somewhat ironic that Hispanic units were not created in Los Angeles or New York, where there was far greater Hispanic theatrical activity of a professional nature and more in line with the main purposes of the WPA. But in all of the documents of the FTP there is no mention of Hispanic theater outside Tampa and there seems to have been no awareness at all of the remarkable activities documented previously. The project's basic objective of creating work-relief theater of a relevant nature would best have been served where the full-time professionals were suffering unemployment, not in Tampa, where many of the artists still gained a good part of their living rolling cigars. Commercial Hispanic companies were suffering the ravages of the Great Depression in Los Angeles, San Antonio, and to some extent New York; Hispanic actors were hungry in these cities and many of them could not even raise the money to return to their homeland.

The activities sponsored under the FTP were not much different from what was already ongoing in Tampa's Hispanic theater. The project hired Manuel Aparicio to direct the Hispanic unit in the production of what was for the most part a repertoire of well-worn zarzuelas and revistas. The greatest difference was brought about, however, by the infusion of capital for scenery, properties, and costumes, which were all new and first-rate. And, even more significant, the Hispanic actors became integrated for the first time into the shows of the Tampa FTP vaudeville unit and, in general, began to associate more and more with non-Hispanic artists and personnel. It must be stated,

A full house at the Centro Asturiano with director Manuel Aparicio at the center front of the audience in 1937. (Courtesy of the Dorothea Lynch Collection, Special Collections, George Mason University Library.)

however, that when it came time for that integrated vaudeville unit to perform at the Centro Asturiano, the FTP was not able to get Anglos to cross the tracks to see the show. In all, the Hispanic unit of the FTP produced fourteen shows in Spanish in forty-two performances for more than twenty-three thousand spectators. The unit achieved its greatest success with *El mundo en la mano* (*The World in His Hand*), a revista written by Aparicio and the entire company, which was a musical tour through Spain, Cuba, Italy, Mexico, and China. It was so popular that additional performances were scheduled and the revue even toured in the area and down to Miami. The nadir was the production in Spanish of Sinclair Lewis's *It Can't Happen Here,* which was all but forced on the company in an awkwardly literal translation in an equally awkward attempt to synchronize the production opening with the national debut.

The Hispanic community was very proud of its unit and of its leading man and director, Manuel Aparicio, who was selected to attend a conference of FTP directors in Poughkeepsie, New York. But the FTP administrators, who always referred to the Hispanic unit as one of the strongest in the South, took pride in having

successfully "brought" theater to the Hispanics; they also decried the Spanish-speakers backwardness, or fawned at their quaint habits. Ultimately, because of language differences and misunderstandings about citizenship, the Hispanic unit lost twenty five of its members in 1937 when Congress passed the ERA Act (Emergency Relief Administration), which effectively removed foreigners from the WPA. Included among these was director Manuel Aparicio. Other members, such as Chela Martínez, were lost when they were decertified because their family income was too high. The remaining citizens were integrated into the "American" vaudeville company of the federal project. The Hispanic unit had met its end.

A unique theatrical experience was that of the Unión Martí-Maceo, Tampa's Afro-Cuban mutual aid society, whose very existence resulted from the doubly segregationist forces of the Jim Crow South and Cuba's own racism. While the union hosted many of the same theater companies touring to Tampa and also sponsored performances by its own and the other society's secciones de declamación, the union's theatrical and cultural activities were rarely covered in the press, rarely attracted audiences from the His-

A scene from *El niño judío* at the Centro Asturiano. (Courtesy of the Dorothea Lynch Collection, Special Collections, George Mason University Library.)

panic "white" population, and, on the whole, were hardly integrated into the social life of the Hispanic, the Anglo American, or the black communities. In the archives of the union, however, are plays and fragments of plays that provide some interesting glimpses into the nature of the theatrical performances of this society. Two of these works, a one-act play, *Hambre* (*Hunger*), and the obra bufa cubana *Los novios* (*The Betrothed*), are notable for their relevance to the social and economic ambience of the Martí-Maceo. *Hambre* is a gripping and angry social drama that protests the poverty and hunger suffered by the working class while the rich enjoy the life of luxury. *Los novios*, a much lighter and more entertaining play with mistaken identities and ridiculously complex love triangles, also deals with the supposed trespassing of race and class barriers and miscegenation. A buffoon of a Galician servant and a negrito spread mistaken information about the landowner having illicitly fathered a mulata and the landowner's daughter being caught embracing a black. The play also includes asides that elaborate on race relations, and throughout the negrito and the mulata maintain the greatest dignity in the play, with the upper-class whites shown to be the most bungling and prejudiced. In the end, order is restored when everyone finds his rightful place and his rightful partner to marry. But the social satire from a black perspective is unmistakable.

Another society that offered a unique theatricl experience was the Centro Obrero, the headquarters for the Union of Tampa Cigarmakers, which served as a gathering place for workers and as a vehicle to promote their culture. Through its various classes, workshops, publications, and other activities, the Centro Obrero promoted unionism and, quite often, socialism. While the Centro Obrero also hosted touring and local companies and even frivolous shows of obras bufas cubanas, it was within its halls and auspices that plays were developed and shown that promoted workers" interests, using their dialect and ideology. In the Centro's weekly newspapers, *El Internacional* and *La Federación*, various of these plays were published, including *Julia y Carlota* (*Julia and Carlota*), in which Julia exhorts Carlota to break the bonds of family and religion that are meant to keep women in their place, oppressed, and divorced from politics so that they do not help to reform evil laws.

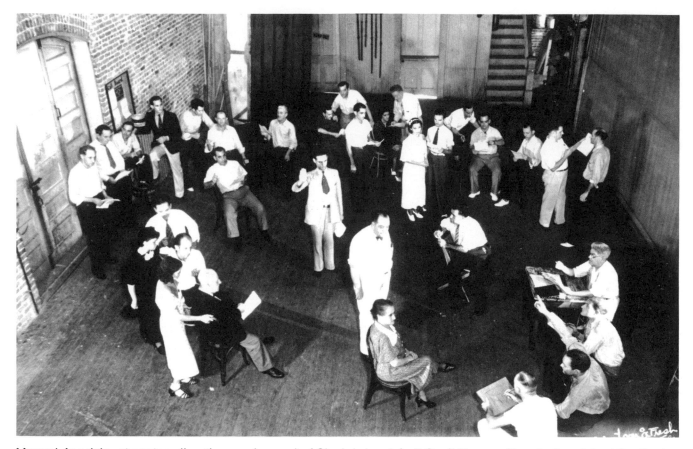

Manuel Aparicio, at center, directing a rehearsal of Sinclair Lewis's *It Can't Happen Here* in Spanish at the Centro Asturiano. (Courtesy of the Dorothea Lynch Collection, Special Collections, George Mason University.)

Other works were clearly agitational and propagandistic, attempting to inspire workers to action. Finally, the Centro Obrero went all out to support the republican cause in the Spanish Civil War. It sponsored numerous fund-raising performances of such plays as *Milicianos al Frente* (*Militia to the Front*), *Abajo Franco* (*Down with Franco*), and *Las luchas de hoy* (*The Struggles of Today*), all of unknown authorship.

There are thus many parallels that can be drawn between the Tampa Hispanic stage and the Hispanic theater as it flourished in the Southwest and New York: the relationship of the theater to politics and to patterns of immigration; the dominance of the Spanish zarzuela and melodrama, eventually ceding to more popular forms, such as the revista and the obra bufa cubana; the effects of the Great Depression; the role theater played in protecting Hispanic cultural values and the Spanish language and in the education of the youth; the isolation of Hispanic culture and theater from the larger society, and so on. But Tampa's Hispanic theatrical experience was unique in that it provided a successful example of deep and lasting community support for theater arts, so deep

and so strong that private enterprise could not compete with the efforts of the mutual aid societies. And because the Hispanic stage had become such a symbol of achievement, that legacy lives on today in the memory of the Tampeños, in the Hispanic theatrical groups that still exist there and in such actresses as Velia Martínez who still are enjoying careers on the stage and in film.

✹POST-WORLD WAR II TO THE PRESENT

The Southwest

The post-World War II period has seen the gradual restoration of the amateur, semiprofessional, and professional stages in the Hispanic communities of the Southwest. From the 1950s on, repertory theaters have appeared throughout the Southwest to produce Latin American, Spanish, and American plays in Spanish translations. In San Antonio, the extraordinary efforts of such actors as Lalo Astol, La Chata Noloesca, and her daughter Velia Camargo were responsible for keeping plays and vaudeville routines alive in the communities, even if they had to be presented for free or at fund-raisers. Actors like Lalo Astol made the transition to radio and television, usually as anouncers, at times as writers and producers. Astol even wrote, directed, and acted in locally produced television drama during the 1950s and 1960s. In Los Angeles, veteran actor-director Rafael Trujillo-Herrera maintained a theater group, almost continuously during the war and through the 1960s, made up of his drama students and professionals, who quite often performed at a small theater house that he bought, El Teatro Intimo.

While there are a few stories of valiant theater artists managing to keep Hispanic theater alive during the war and postwar years, in most cases the tale is of theater houses that once housed live performances becoming cinemas forever, or at least phasing out live performances during the war and through the 1950s by occasionally hosting small troupes of vaudevillians or subscribing to the extravagant "caravanas de estrellas," or parades of recording stars, that were syndicated and promoted by the recording companies. Through these shows prominaded singers and matinee idols, with former peladitos and other

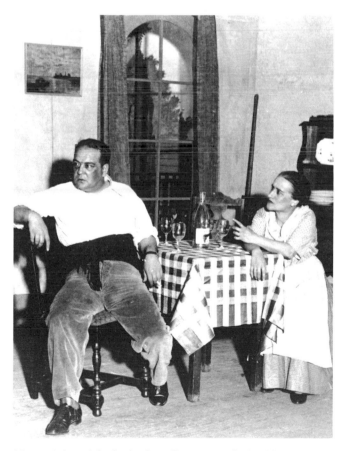

Manuel Aparicio in Jacinto Benavente's *La Malquerida*. (Courtesy of the Dorothea Lynch Collection, Special Collections, George Mason University Library.)

vaudevillians serving as masters of ceremonies and comic relief. Vestiges of this business strategy still survive today in the shows of Mexican recording and movie stars of the moment, which are produced, not at movie houses, but at convention centers and sports and entertainment arenas of large capacity.

The most remarkable story of the stage in the Southwest is the spontaneous appearance in 1965 of a labor theater in the agricultural fields, under the directorship of Luis Valdez, and its creation of a full-blown theatrical movement that conquered the hearts and minds of artists and activists throughout the country. Under the leadership of Luis Valdez's El Teatro Campesino, for almost two decades Chicano theaters dramatized the political and cultural concerns of their communities while crisscrossing the states on tour. The movement, largely student- and worker-based, eventually led to professionalism, Hollywood and Broadway productions, and the creation of the discipline of Chicano theater at universities. In 1965, the modern Chicano theater movement was born when aspiring playwright Luis Valdez left the San Francsico Mime Troupe to join César Chávez in organizing farm workers in Delano, California. Valdez organized the workers into El Teatro Campesino in an effort to popularize and raise funds for the grape boycott and farm-worker strike. From the humble beginning of dramatizing the plight of farm workers, the movement grew to include small, agitation, and propaganda theater groups in communities and on campuses around the country and eventually developed into a total theatrical expression that would find resonance on the commercial stage and screen.

By 1968, Valdez and El Teatro Campesino had left the vineyards and lettuce fields in a conscious effort to create a theater for the Chicano nation, a people which Valdez and other Chicano organizers of the 1960s envisioned as working-class, Spanish-speaking or bilingual, rurally oriented, and with a very strong heritage of pre-Columbian culture. By 1970, El Teatro Campesino had pioneered and developed what would come to be known as *teatro chicano*, a style of agitprop theater that incorporated the spiritual and presentational style of the Italian Renaissance commedia dell'arte with the humor, character types, folklore, and popular culture of the Mexican theater, especially as articulated earlier in the century by the vaudeville companies and tent theaters that had toured the Southwest.

Almost overnight, groups sprang up throughout the United States to continue along Valdez's path. In streets, parks, churches, and schools, Chicanos were spreading a newly found bilingual-bicultural identity through the *actos*, one-act pieces introduced by

Valdez that explored all of the issues confronting Mexican Americans: the farm-worker struggle for unionization, the Vietnam War, the drive for bilingual education, community control of parks and schools, the war against drug addiction and crime, and so forth.

El Teatro Campesino's acto, *Los vendidos* (*The Sell-Outs*), a farcical attack on political manipulation of Chicano stereotypes, became the most popular and imitated of the actos; it could be seen performed by diverse groups from Seattle to Austin. The publication of Actos by Luis Valdez y El Teatro Campesino in 1971, which included *Los vendidos*, placed a ready-made repertoire in the hands of community and student groups and also supplied them with several theatrical and political canons: (1) Chicanos must be seen as a nation with geographic, religious, cultural, and racial roots in Aztlán. Teatros must further the idea of nationalism and create a national theater based on identification with the Amerindian past. (2) The organizational support of the national theater must be from within, for "the corazón de la Raza (the heart of our people) cannot be revolutionized on a grant from Uncle Sam." (3) Most important and valuable of all was the principle that "The teatros must never get away from La Raza . . . . If the Raza will not come to the theater, then the theater must go to the Raza. This, in the long run, will determine the shape, style, content, spirit, and form of el teatro chicano."

El Teatro Campesino's extensive touring, the publicity it gained from the farm-worker struggle, and the publication of *Actos* all effectively contributed to the launching of a national teatro movement. It reached its peak in the summer of 1976 when five teatro festivals were held to commemorate the Anglo bicentennial celebration. The summer's festivals also culminated a period of growth that saw some of Campesino's followers reach sufficient aesthetic and political maturity to break away from Valdez. Los Angeles's Teatro Urbano, in its mordant satire of American heroes, insisted on intensifying the teatro movement's radicalism in the face of the Campesino's increasing religious mysticism. Santa Barbara's El Teatro de la Esperanza was achieving perfection, as no other Chicano theater had, in working as a collective and in assimilating the teachings of Bertolt Brecht in their plays *Guadalupe* and *La víctima* (*The Victim*). San Jose's El Teatro de la Gente had taken the corrido-type acto, a structure that sets a mimic ballet to traditional Mexican ballads sung by a singer-narrator, and perfected it as its innovator, El Teatro Campesino, had never done. El Teatro Desengaño del Pueblo from Gary, Indiana, had succeeded in reviving the techniques of the radical thea-

A scene from El Teatro Urbano's *Anti-Bicentennial Special* in 1976.

ters of the 1930s in their *Silent Partners*, an expose of corruption in a local city's construction projects.

The greatest contribution of Luis Valdez and El Teatro Campesino was their inauguration of a true grass roots theater movement. Following Valdez's direction, the university students and community people creating teatro held fast to the doctrine of never getting away from the raza, the grass roots Mexican. In so doing they created the perfect vehicle for communing artistically within their culture and environment. At times they idealized and romanticized the language and the culture of the *mexicano* in the United States. But they had discovered a way to mine history, folklore, and religion for those elements that could best solidify the heterogeneous community and sensitize it to class, cultural identity, and politics. This indeed was revolutionary. The creation of art from the folk materials of a people, their music, humor, social configurations, and environment, represented the fulfillment of Luis Valdez's vision of a Chicano national theater.

While Campesino, after leaving the farm worker struggle, was able to experiment and rediscover the old cultural forms—the carpas, the corridos, the Virgin of Guadalupe plays, the peladito—it never fully succeeded in combining all the elements it recovered or invented into a completely refined piece of revolutionary art. *La gran carpa de la familia Rascuachi* (*The Tent of the Underdogs*) was a beautiful creation, incorporating the spirit, history, folklore, economy, and music of la raza. However, its proposal for the resolution of material problems through spiritual means (a superimposed construct of Aztec mythology and Catholicism) was too close to the religious beliefs and superstitions that hampered la raza's progress, according to many of the more radical artists and theorists of people's theater.

The reaction of critics and many Chicano theaters playing at the fifth Chicano theater festival, held in Mexico, was so politically and emotionally charged that a rift developed between them and El Teatro Campesino that has never been healed. El Teatro Campesino virtually withdrew from the theater movement, and from that point on the Chicano theaters developed on their own, managing to exist as agitation and propaganda groups and raggle-taggle troupes until the end of the decade. The more successful theaters, such as El Teatro de la Esperanza, administered their own theater house, created playwriting workshops, and took up leadership of TENAZ, the Chicano theater organization, while taking over El Teatro Campesino's former role as a national touring company. Other groups, such as Albuquerque's La Compañía, set down roots and became more of a repertory company. The decade of the 1980s saw many Chicano theater groups disbanding, as some of their members became involved in local community theaters, with their own performance spaces and budgets supplied by state and local arts agencies.

Thus, such companies as Houston's Teatro Bilingüe, San Antonio's Guadalupe Theater, and Denver's Su Teatro began serving their respective communities as stable, repertory companies. Other former Chicano theater artists successfully made the jump to television and movies, such as Luis Valdez himself. In fact, Valdez's play *Zoot Suit* had a successful two-year run in mainstream theaters in Los Angeles and made its way to a Broadway and a film version. He followed up with stage and television productions of his play *Corridos* (*Ballads*) and then the overwhelming box office success of his movie *La Bamba*. Other former Chicano theater directors, like Jorge Huerta, became university professors of theater and directors of productions in such mainstream organizations as San Diego's Globe Theater. Thus, while the 1980s saw a disappearance of the grass roots, guerrilla, and street theater movement among Chicanos, these were the years when greater professionaliza-

tion took place and greater opportunity appeared for Chicano theater people to make a living from their art in community theaters, at universities, and even in the commercial media—the latter facilitated, of course, by the great rise of the Hispanic population and its spending power.

But the decade of the 1980s also saw the emergence of a corps of Chicano and Latino playwrights in communities from coast to coast, as the repertory theaters in the Southwest, New York, and Miami began clamoring for works dealing with Hispanic culture and written in the language of Hispanics in the United States. Numerous playwriting labs, workshops, and contests, such as Joseph Papp's Festival Latino in New York, sprung up from New York to Los Angeles. In the mid 1980s, a major funding organization, the Ford Foundation, took official interest in Hispanic theater and began funding, in a very significant way, not only the theater companies in an effort to stabilize them (including El Teatro de la Esperanza) but also the efforts by mainstream companies and theaters, such as the South Coast Repertory Theater and the San Diego Repertory Theater, to produce Hispanic material and employ Hispanic actors. Furthermore, the Ford Foundation even funded the nation's leading Hispanic press, Arte Publico Press, to publish a line of Hispanic play anthologies and collections of works by the leading Hispanic playwrights. By 1991, Arte Publico Press had produced a new anthology of plays by Luis Valdez, Milcha Sánchez Scott, Severo Pérez, and others (*Necessary Theater: Six Plays of the Chicano Experience*, edited by Jorge Huerta), as well as anthologies of Hispanic women's plays, Cuban-American plays, Puerto Rican plays, and collections by Luis Valdez, Dolores Prida, Edward Gallardo, Iván Acosta, and Carlos Morton. It also reissued its historic (1979) anthology that had been out of print for a decade: *Nuevos Pasos: Chicano and Puerto Rican Theater*, edited by Nicolás Kanellos and Jorge Huerta.

New York

During the war years and following, serious theater in the Hispanic community waned, as first vaudeville drove it from the commercial stage, as it did the Teatro Hispano, and then, as in the Southwest, the movies and the caravans of musical recording stars began to drive even vaudeville from the stage. Under the leadership of such directors as Marita Reid, Luis Mandret, and Alejandro Elliot, full-length melodramas and realistic plays were able to survive in mutualist societies, church halls, and lodges during the 1940s and 1950s, but only for smaller audiences and for weekend performances. With such attractions as La Chata Noloesca's Mexi-

A scene from El Teatro de la Esperanza's production of Rodrigo Duarte Clark's *Brujerías*.

can company and Puerto Rican vaudevillians, including famed recording star Bobby Capó, vaudeville survived into the early 1960s, playing to the burgeoning working-class audiences of Puerto Ricans. One notable and valiant effort was that of Dominican actor-director Rolando Barrera's group Futurismo, which for a while during the 1940s was able to stage four productions a year of European works in Spanish translation at the Master's Auditorium. Beginning in 1950, Edwin Janer's La Farándula Panamericana staged three and four productions a year of classical works, as well as contemporary Spanish, Puerto Rican, and European works at the Master's Auditorium and the Belmont Theater.

In 1953, a play was staged that would have the most direct and lasting impact ever of any theatrical production in New York's Hispanic community. A young director, Roberto Rodríguez, introduced to a working-class audience at the Church of San Sebastian *La carreta* (*The Oxcart*), by an as yet unknown Puerto Rican writer, René Marqués, after its first production in Puerto Rico. The play, which deals with the dislocation of a family of mountain folk from their farm and their resettling in a San Juan slum and then in New York City, effectively dramatized the epic of

Puerto Rican migration to the United States in working-class and mountain dialect. René Marqués went on to celebrity and many more plays and productions in Puerto Rico and the continental United States, but his *La carreta* became a key for building a Puerto Rican and Hispanic theater in New York in that it presented serious dramatic material based on the history, language, and culture of the working-class communities. Roberto Rodríguez joined forces with stage

New York's Teatro Hispano in 1939.

and screen actress Miriam Colón to form El Nuevo Círculo Dramático, which was able to administer a theater space in a loft, Teatro Arena, in Midtown Manhattan. Although there were other minor and short-lived companies, it was El Nuevo Círculo Dramático, along with La Farándula Panamericana, that dominated the New York Hispanic stage into the early 1960s, when two incursions were made into the mainstream: in 1964 Joseph Papp's New York Shakespeare Festival began producing Shakespearean works in Spanish, and in 1965 there was an off-Broadway production of *La carreta*, starring Miriam Colón and Raúl Juliá.

The 1960s also saw the introduction of improvisational street theater similar to Latin American people's theater and Chicano theater, which attempted to raise the level of political consciousness of working-class Hispanics. Among the most well known, although short-lived groups were the following ensembles, which usually developed their material as a collective: El Nuevo Teatro Pobre de las Américas (The New Poor People's Theater of Americas), Teatro Orilla (Marginal Theater), Teatro Guazabara (Whatsamara Theater), and Teatro Jurutungo. But the most interesting of the improvisational troupes, and the only one to survive to the present, has been the Teatro Cuatro, named so for its first location on Fourth Avenue in the lower East Side and made up at first of a diverse group of Puerto Ricans, Dominicans, and other Latin Americans. Under the directorship of an Argentine immigrant, Oscar Ciccone, and his Salvadoran wife, Cecilia Vega, the Teatro Cuatro was one of the most serious troupes, committed to developing a true radical art and to bringing together the popular theater movement of Latin America with that of Hispanics in the United States. As such Teatro Cuatro became involved with TENAZ and the Chicano theater movement and with *teatro popular* in Latin America, and sponsored festivals and workshops in New York with some of the leading guerrilla and politically active theatrical directors and companies in the hemisphere. During the late 1970s Teatro Cuatro became officially associated with Joseph Papp's New York Shakespeare Festival and began to organize the biennial Festival Latino, a festival of Hispanic popular theater. Today, Ciccone and Vega manage the Papp organization's Hispanic productions, including the festival and a playwriting contest, while the Teatro Cuatro has gone its own way, functioning as a repertory company in its own remodeled firehouse theater in east Harlem.

The type of theater that has predominated in New York's cosmopolitan Hispanic culture since the 1960s is that which more or less follows the patterns established by the Nuevo Círculo Dramático and the

Poster from La Farándula Panamericana theater group's 1954 production of *Los árboles mueren de pie*, starring Marita Reid.

Farándula Panamericana mentioned previously, in which a corps of actors and a director of like mind work as a repertory group in producing works of their choosing in their own style. Styles and groups have proliferated, so that at any one time over the last twenty to twenty-five years at least ten groups have existed with different aesthetics and audiences. Among these theaters, many of which have their own houses today, are International Arts Relations (INTAR), Miriam Colón's Puerto Rican Traveling Theater, Teatro Repertorio Español, Nuestro Teatro, Duo, Instituto Arte Teatral (IATE), Latin American Theater Ensemble (LATE), Thalia, Tremont Arte Group, and Pregones. In addition to the reason that New York has over one million Hispanic inhabitants, another reason that so many organizations are able to survive--although many of them do not flourish—is that the state, local, and private institutions that provide financial support for the arts have been generous to the theaters. Compared with that in other cities and states, the financial support for the arts, and theater in particular, in the capital of the U.S. theater world, has been excellent.

Postcard photo of the Bronx's Pregones theater company in 1985.

The three most important theater companies have been the Puerto Rican Traveling Theater (PRTT), Teatro Repertorio Español, and INTAR. The PRTT, founded in 1967 by Miriam Colón, takes its name from its original identity as a mobile theater that performed in the streets of Puerto Rican neighborhoods. At first it performed works by some of the leading Puerto Rican writers, such as René Marqués, José Luis González, and Pedro Juan Soto, alternating Spanish-language performances with English-language ones. The company also produced Latin American and Spanish works and in the early 1970's pioneered productions of works by Nuyorican (New York Rican, discussed later in this chapter) and other U.S. Hispanic authors, such as those of Jesús Colón and Piri Thomas. In addition to its mobile unit, the theater maintained a laboratory theater and children's theater classes. Its most important development came in 1974 when it took over and remodeled an old firehouse in the Broadway area, on Forty-seventh Street, and opened its permanent theater house. To this day, the PRTT provides the stage, audience, and developmental work for New York Hispanic playwrights, such as Jaime Carrero, Ed-

ward Gallardo, Manuel Ramos Otero, Pedro Pietri, and Dolores Prida.

Founded in 1969 as an offshoot of Las Artes by exiled members of Cuba's Sociedad Pro Arte, the Teatro Repertorio Español has grown into the only Hispanic theater in the nation specializing in the production of both classical Spanish works, such as Calderon's *La vida es sueño* and Zorrilla's *Don Juan Tenorio*, and works by contemporary authors from Latin America. It is also one of the few companies in the nation to also stage nineteenth-century zarzuelas. Operating today out of a theater, the Gramercy Arts Theater, which has a tradition of Spanish-language performances that goes back to the 1920s, the Teatro Repertorio Español caters both to educational as well as community-based audiences, with productions in both Spanish and English. It is the only New York Hispanic theater to tour around the country. This is possible because, of the major Hispanic companies in New York, the Teatro Repertorio Español is the only one still working basically as an ensemble, while the others are production companies that hold open auditions for all of their parts.

INTAR was founded in 1967 as ADAL (Latin American Art Group), dedicated to producing works by Latin American authors. By 1977, under the name INTAR the company had achieved equity status as a professional theater. After converting a variety of structures into theater spaces, the company currently occupies a theater on West Forty-second Street near the Broadway theater district. Under the direction of Max Ferra, the company has offered workshops for actors and directors, and staged readings for playwrights and a children's theater. Today INTAR is known for its production of classical works in new settings and innovative directing, such as María Irene Fornés's *La vida es sueño* (*Life Is a Dream*) and Dolores Prida's *Crisp*, based on Jacinto Benavente's *Los intereses creados* (*Vested Interests*). INTAR also presents works in English, including some standard non-Hispanic fare. INTAR has been particularly instrumental in developing Hispanic playwriting through its playwright's laboratory and readings, quite often following up with full productions of plays by local writers.

While the Hispanic theatrical environment in New York has been of necessity cosmopolitan and has lent itself to the creation of companies with personnel from all of the Spanish-speaking countries, there

The elaborate costuming of a Miami production of José Zorrilla's *Don Juan Tenorio*.

have been groups that have set out to promote the work and culture of specific nationalities, such as the Puerto Ricans, Cubans, Dominicans, and Spaniards. Most notable, of course, has been the Puerto Rican Traveling Theater, but also the Centro Cultural Cubano was instrumental in the 1970s in developing Cuban theatrical expression, most significantly in producing the work of Omar Torres and Iván Acosta. Acosta's play *El super* (*The Super*), has been the biggest hit to ever come out of a Hispanic company and even led to a prize-winning film adaptation. And, in general, Cuban-American theater is well represented in almost all the Hispanic companies of New York, with Dolores Prida, Iván Acosta, Manuel Martín, and Omar Torres included among the most successful playwrights.

Puerto Rican playwriting is also well represented at most of the Hispanic companies, but during the 1960s an important new focus developed among New York Puerto Ricans that had long-lasting implications for the creation of theater and art in Hispanic working-class communities; it was called Nuyorican (New York Rican), meaning that it emerged from the artists born or raised among New York's Puerto Rican working classes. Nuyorican theater is not a specific form of theater per se. It has included such diverse theatrical genres as collectively created street theater as well as works by individual playwrights produced in such diverse settings as the Puerto Rican Traveling Theater, the Henry Street Settlement's New Federal Theater, Joseph Papp's New York Shakespeare Festival, and on Broadway itself. Although the term was first applied to literature and theater by playwright-novelist Jaime Carrero in the late 1960s and finds some stylistic and thematic development in his plays *Noo Jall* (a wordplay on the Spanish pronunciation of "New York" and "jail") and *Pipo Subway no sabe reír* (*Pipo Subway Doesn't Know How to Laugh*), it was a group of playwright-poets associated with the Nuyorican Poets" Café and Joseph Papp that first defined and came to exemplify Nuyorican theater. Included in the group were Miguel Algarín, Lucky Cienfuegos, Tato Laviera, and Miguel Piñero, all of whom focused their bilingual works on the life and culture of working-class Puerto Ricans in New York. Two members of the group, Lucky Cienfuegos and Miguel Piñero, were ex-convicts who had begun their writing careers while incarcerated, and they chose to develop their dramatic material from prison, street, and underclass culture. Algarín, a university professor and proprietor of the Nuyorican Poets" Café, created a more avant-garde aura for the collective, while the virtuoso bilingual poet Tato Laviera contributed lyricism and a folk and popular culture base. It was Piñero's work (and life), however, that became most celebrated; his prison drama *Short Eyes* won an Obie and the New York Drama Critics Best American Play Award for the 1973-74 season. His success, coupled with that of fellow Nuyorican writers ex-convict Piri Thomas and street urchin Pedro Pietri, often resulted in Nuyorican literature and theater's being associated with a stark naturalism and the themes of crime, drugs, abnormal sexuality, and generally aberrant behavior. This led to a reaction against the term by many writers and theater companies that were in fact emphasizing Puerto Rican working-class culture in New York. Today there is a new generation of New York Puerto Rican playwrights who were nurtured on the theater of Piñero and the Nuyoricans and who have also experienced greater support and opportunities for developing their work. They quite often repeat and reevaluate many of the concerns and the style and language of the earlier group, but with a sophistication and polish that has come from drama workshops, playwright residencies, and university education. Among these are Juan Shamsul Alam, Edward Gallardo, Federico Fraguada, Richard Irizarry, Yvette Ramírez, and Cándido Tirado, most of whom have had their works included in the historic anthology *Recent Puerto Rican Theater: Five Plays from New York* (1991), edited by John Antush.

Florida

Today Hispanic theater still finds one of its centers in Florida. However, most of the theatrical activity in Tampa has disappeared, with only the Spanish Repertory Theater continuing to perform in the old playhouses (Centro Asturiano) with a fare that varies from the standard zarzuelas to Broadway musicals in Spanish. With the exodus of refugees from the Cuban Revolution of 1959, Hispanic theater in Florida found a new center in Miami, where the Cuban expatriates—many from middle-class or upper-class backgrounds and used to supporting live theater in Cuba—founded and supported theater companies and laid fertile ground for the support of playwrights. During the last thirty years the type of theater that has predominated in Miami has produced standard works from throughout the Spanish-speaking world and from the theater of exile, which is burdened with attacking communism in Cuba and promoting a nostalgia for the pre-Castro past. While the Cuban playwrights of New York, many of whom have been raised and educated in the United States, have forged an avant-garde and openly Cuban-*American* theater, the Miami playwrights have been more traditional in form and content and, of course, more politically conservative. Most frequent in the exile theater is the form and style inherited from the theater of the

absurd, from theatrical realism, and, to some extent, from the comic devices and characters of the teatro bufo cubano; however, the predominant attitude among Cuban exile playwrights is the intellectual one, the creation of a theater of ideas. The exile playwrights whose works are most produced in Miami are Julio Matas, José Cid Pérez, Leopoldo Hernández, José Sánchez Boudy, Celedonio González, Raúl de Cárdenas, and Matías Montes Huidobro. An effort to bring together some of these with some of the newer voices, such as that of Miami's Miguel González Pando, is Rodolfo Cortina's important anthology *Cuban American Theater* (1991), in which the exile theater is considered as part of the total Cuban-American experience and aesthetic.

But over all, the theatrical fare in Miami is eclectic, with audiences able to choose from a variety of styles and genres, from vaudeville to French-style bedroom farce, serious drama, Broadway musicals in Spanish, and Spanish versions of classics, such as Shakespeare's *Taming of the Shrew* and *Othello*. The theater companies offering the most "serious" fare have included the Teatro Bellas Artes, the Teatro La Danza, Grupo Ras, and Pro Arte Gratelli. Among the longest-lasting theaters in Miami are Salvador Ugarte's and Ernesto Cremata's two locations of Teatro Las Máscaras, which for the most part produce light comedy and vaudeville for mostly working-class audiences. Two of impressario Ernesto Capote's three houses, the Martí Theater and the Essex Theater, have a steady lineup of comedies and vaudeville; and his third house, the Miami Theater, provides an eclectic bill, including such hard-hitting dramas as *The Boys in the Band* in Spanish. The Teatro Miami's stage also serves for the taping of soap operas for television. The theater, which plays more to the working classes in Miami, as exemplified by some of the Miami theaters named above and by some that use movie houses after the showing of the last films, produces a type of reincarnation of the teatro bufo cubano that uses working-class language and culture and uses comic style and characters from the bufo tradition to satirize life in Miami and Cuba under Castro. Here, comic characterizations of Fidel and his brother Raúl (Raúl Resbaloso-Slippery Raúl) join some of the traditional character types, such as Trespatines (Three Skates) and Prematura (Premature). This theater is the most commercially successful Cuban theater, while the other, more artistically elite and intellectual theater often begs for audiences and depends on grants and university support for survival.

Romeo and Juliet being performed in Spanish in Miami.

❋OUTSTANDING FIGURES IN HISPANIC THEATER

Miguel Algarín

See Chapter 17

Iván Acosta (1943-)

Iván Mariano Acosta is an outstanding playwright and filmmaker. Born in Santiago de Cuba on November 17, 1943, he immigrated to the United States with his parents as a result of the Cuban Revolution. He is a graduate in Film Direction and Production of New York University (1969), and has worked as a playwright and director at the Centro Cultural Cubano and the Henry Street Settlement Playhouse. His play *El super* (*The Super*), produced at the Centro Cultural Cubano, is probably the most successful Hispanic play to come out of an ethnic theater house; it not only was highly reviewed and won awards but also was adapted to the screen by Acosta in a feature film that has won twelve awards for best script and best director). *El super* was published in book form in 1982, and four other plays were published in his anthology *Un cubiche en la luna y otras obras* in 1989. Among Acosta's other awards are the following: Cintas Fellowship (1980); Ace Award, Best Writer (1980); Thalia Best Writer (1972); Ariel Award, Best Writer (1971).

Manuel Aparicio (?-)

Manuel Aparicio was a Tampa cigar-roller who in the 1920s and 1930s rose to become an outstanding actor and director in Hispanic theater in Tampa and New York. From the humble beginnings of acting in amateur performances at the mutualist societies in Tampa, Aparicio went on to head up his own theatrical companies and take them on tour to Havana and New York. Tampa remained his home base, even during the Great Depression, which was the economic cataclysm that eventually resulted in his name going down in Hispanic theater history, for he became the only director of a Hispanic company under the U.S. Government Works Progress Administration's (WPA's) Federal Theater Project (FTP). In this role he led one of the FTP's most successful theater companies and was even selected for the FTP's conference of directors in Poughkeepsie, New York, in 1937. The Hispanic troupe of the FTP produced some of its own collectively created material, such as the revue *El Mundo en la Mano*, under his directorship and including his acting and singing talents. Like some twenty-five other actors, Aparicio lost his job when Congress passed the ERA Act of 1937, which prohibited the employment of aliens under the WPA.

La Chata Noloesca

See Beatriz Escalona.

Denise Chávez

See Chapter 17

Miriam Colón (1945-)

Miriam Colón is the first lady of Hispanic theater in New York. She is the founder and artistic director of the Puerto Rican Traveling Theater and a genuine pioneer in bringing Hispanic theater to broad audiences. Born in Ponce, Puerto Rico, and raised in Ponce and in New York, Colón attended the University of Puerto Rico and the Erwin Piscator Dramatic Workshop and Technical Institute, as well as the famed Actors Studio, both in New York. Colón developed a long and distinguished career on New York stages and in Hollywood films and television series. Included among her stage credits are *The Innkeepers* (1956), *Me, Cándido!* (1965), *The Oxcart* (1966), *Winterset* (1968), *The Passion of Antígona Pérez* (1972), *Julius Caesar* (1979), *Orinoco* (1985), and *Simpson Street* (1985). In 1989, she was made an honorary doctor of letters by Montclair (New Jersey) State College; she also received the White House Hispanic Heritage Award in 1990.

Beatriz Escalona (1903-1980)

Known by her stage name, La Chata Noloesca (a rearranged spelling of Escalona), Beatriz Escalona became the greatest stage personality to come out of U.S. Hispanic communities. Born on August 20, 1903, in San Antonio, Texas, Escalona was discovered while working as an usherette and box office cashier at the Teatro Nacional. She became associated with the Spanish-Cuban troupe of Hermanos Areu—she married José Areu—and played everything from melodrama to vaudeville with them, beginning in 1920, when she made her stage debut with them in El Paso. Over the course of the 1920s Escalona developed and perfected her comic persona of the streetwise maid, a *peladita* or underdog character who maintained a spicy and satirical banter. By 1930, La Chata Noloesca had split from the Areus and formed her own company, Atracciones Noloesca, and continued to tour the Southwest and northern Mexico. In 1936, she reformed her company in her native San Antonio and set out to weather the depression by performing in Tampa, Chicago, and New York—as well as Puerto Rico and Cuba—as the Compañía Mexicana. La Chata's novel idea was to take to the Cubans, Puerto Ricans, and others Mexican vaudeville, music, folklore, and her own brand of humor. In 1941, the company set down roots in New York for a stretch of nine years, during which time it was a mainstay on the Hispanic vaudeville circuit made up of the Teatro Hispano, the Teatro Puerto Rico, the Teatro Triboro, and the 53rd Street Theater. Back in San Antonio, she periodically performed for special community events until her death.

José Ferrer (1912-)

José Ferrer is one of the most distinguished actors of Hispanic background to have made a career in mainstream films and on stage in the United States. The star of numerous Hollywood films and many stage productions, he was born in Santurce, Puerto Rico, on January 8, 1912. Raised and educated in Puerto Rico, he graduated from Princeton University in 1933. As an actor and/or director, his stage credits include *Let's Face It* (1942), *Strange Fruit* (1945), *Design for Living* (1947), *Twentieth Century* (1950), *Stalag 17* (1951), *Man of La Mancha* (1966), and *Cyrano de Bergerac* (1975), among many others. As an actor, director, or producer, he has been associated with some of the most famous Hollywood films, including *Joan of Arc* (1947), *Moulin Rouge* (1952), *The Caine Mutiny* (1954), *Return to Peyton Place* (1962), *Lawrence of Arabia* (1962), *Ship of Fools* (1966), and others. His awards include the Gold Medal from the American Academy of Arts and Sciences (1949), the Academy Award for Best Actor in *Cyrano de Bergerac* (1950), induction into the Theater Hall of Fame (1981), among many others.

María Irene Fornés (1930-)

María Irene Fornés is the dean of Hispanic playwrights in New York, having enjoyed more productions of her works and more recognition, in the form of six Obie awards, than any other Hispanic. Born on May 14, 1930, in Havana, Cuba, she immigrated o the United States in 1945 and became a naturalized citizen in 1951. This sets her off considerably from most of the other Cuban playwrights who immigrated to the United States as refugees from the Cuban Revolution. Since 1960, she has been a playwright, director, and teacher of theater with Theater for New York City (1973-78) and various other workshops, universities, and schools. In the theater, Fornés has had more than thirty plays produced, including adaptations of plays by Federico García Lorca, Pedro Calderón de la Barca, and Chekhov. Her plays have been produced on Hispanic stages, on mainstream Off-Off-Broadway, Off-Broadway, Broadway, in Milwaukee, Minneapolis, Claremont, California, London, and Zurich. Fornés's works, although at times touching upon political and ethnic themes, generally deal with human relations and the emotional lives of her characters. Her plots tend to be unconventional, and at times her characters are fragmented, in structures that vary from musical comedy to the theater of ideas to very realistic plays. Many of her plays have been published in collections of her work: *Promenade and Other Plays* (1971), *María Irene Fornés: Plays* (1986), and *Lovers and Keepers* (1986).

Leonardo García Astol (1906-)

Leonardo García Astol was born into a theatrical family in Mexico and as a child began touring with his mother, a famous actress divorced from his father, and with the companies of his father and his brother in northern Mexico and later in the Rio Grande Valley of the United States. Prepared as an actor of the grand melodramatic tradition, Astol had to accommodate his considerable acting talents throughout his life in the United States to the needs of the moment, which were usually dictated by economic conditions and working-class audience demands. He began performing in the United States in 1921 and from that time on was associated with many of the most popular theatrical companies and with the famed Teatro Nacional in San Antonio. As the Great Depression hit, he continued to work with one company after another, at times managing the companies. For years he survived doing vaudeville, especially with the role he created of Don Lalo, a comic hobo, for which he is still remembered in communities of the Southwest. In 1938, Astol became a member of the stock vaudeville company for the Teatro Nacional and the Teatro Zaragoza in San Antonio, and during this time he began doing comic dialogues on Spanish-language radio. By 1940, he had become the emcee of an hour-long Mexican variety show on the radio; this later led to his doing soap operas on the radio in the 1950s, as well as other dramatic series. In the late 1950s and early 1960s, Astol broke into television and even wrote, directed and acted in a serial entitled "El Vampiro" ("The Vampire"). While developing the various phases of his career, Astol was always active in maintaining serious theatrical performances for the community, usually staged at church halls and community centers for little or no remuneration. Over the years, Astol's has been a heroic effort to keep Hispanic theater alive in the United States.

Adalberto Elías González (?-?)

Adalberto Elías González was by far the most prolific and successful playwright ever in the Hispanic communities of the United States. A native of Sonora, Mexico, who probably immigrated to Los Angeles in 1920 to further his education after graduating from the Escuela Normal in Hermosillo, he is known to have worked as a newspaperman and professional playwright there at least until 1941. Because of the subject matter of various of his plays, it is assumed that he also had military experience in Mexico before moving to the United States. By 1924, González had steady employment as a movie critic for *El Heraldo de México* newspaper in Los Angeles and had four new plays debut that year. By 1928, his fame as a playwright was so great that in that one year alone his works were staged in Hermosillo, Mexicali, El Paso, Nogales, and, of course, Los Angeles. González's works ran the gamut from historical drama to dime-novel sensationalism. The most famous of his plays was *Los Amores de Ramona* (*The Loves of Ramona*), a stage adaptation of Helen Hunt Jackson's California novel, *Ramona: A Story*, which broke all box office records when it was seen by more than fifteen thousand people after only eight performances in 1927. His second most successful work, *La Asesino del Martillo o La mujer tigresa* (*The Hammer Assassin or The Tiger Woman*), was based on news stories of 1923 and 1924. González also wrote historical drama, based both on Mexican history in California and on the Mexican Revolution, such as his *La Conquista de California* (*The Conquest of California*), *Los Expatriados* (*The Expatriates*), *La Muerte de Francisco Villa* (*The Death of Francisco Villa*), and *El Fantasma de la Revolución* (*The Ghost of the Revolution*). González was the leading winner of playwriting contests in Los Angeles at the height of a playwriting boom never before seen among Hispanics in the United States. In all, González is known to have written some fourteen or fifteen plays that were successfully produced in Los Angeles during the 1920s and 1930s.

Celedonio González

See Chapter 17

Guz Aguila

See Antonio Guzmán Aguilera

Antonio Guzmán Aguilera (1894- ?)

Antonio Guzmán Aguilera, whose pen name was Guz Aguila, was one of Mexico's most prolific and beloved librettists and composed scores of popular theatrical revues. Born in San Miguel del Mesquital on March 21, 1984, Guzmán studied in Mexico City at the Jesuit Instituto Científico de México, and by 1916 had his first play produced at the Teatro Juan Ruiz de

Alarcón. After that he began developing his career as a journalist at various newspapers; while still a journalist he became a famous author of *revistas* (revues) that commented on current events. He became the friend of presidents and politicians and suffered the ups and downs of these associations, so much so that he was arrested when a political rival became president (Obregón); he later went into exile in Los Angeles in 1924. A portion of Guzmán's career was developed in Los Angeles; just how many of his supposed five hundred revues he wrote there is unknown—none of his works were ever published. Besides working as a journalist in Los Angeles, Guzmán Aguilera was contracted by the Teatro Hidalgo for one thousand dollars a month to write revues for its stage. It was at the Teatro Hidalgo that he wrote and debuted one of his only full-length plays, *María del Pilar Moreno, o la Pequeña Vengadora* (*María del Pilar Moreno or the Tiny Avenger*), based on the story of a young girl recently exonerated of murder in Mexico City. While at the Hidalgo he also wrote and staged the following new revues based on culture and events in Los Angeles: *Los Angeles Vacilador* (*Swinging Los Angeles*), *Evite Peligro* (*Avoid Danger*), and *El Eco de México* (*The Echo from Mexico*). In 1927, Guz Aguila returned to the stages of Mexico City, but he never regained the level of success that he had experienced there earlier.

Raúl Juliá (1940-)

See also: Chapter 20

Raúl Juliá is one of the most popular stage and screen actors in the United States. His career was initiated on the Hispanic stages of New York, most notably with important productions of René Marqués's *La Carreta* (*The Oxcart*) in association with Miriam Colón. Born in San Juan, Puerto Rico, on March 9, 1940, Juliá was raised there and attained his bachelor of arts degree from the University of Puerto Rico. As a stage actor he has had important roles in serious theater and on Broadway, including *The Emperor of Late Night Radio* (1974), *The Cherry Orchard* (1976), *Dracula* (1976), *Arms and the Man* (1985), and various Shakespearean plays. His films include *Panic in Needle Park* (1971), *Gumball Rally* (1976), *Eyes of Laura Mars* (1978), *One from the Heart* (1982), *Kiss of the Spider Woman* (1985), *Compromising Positions* (1985), and many others. Raúl Juliá received Tony Award nominations in 1971, 1974, 1976, and 1982.

Tato Laviera

See Chapter 17

Gerardo López del Castillo (?-?)

Gerardo López del Castillo was a leading man and director of the Compañía Española, a Spanish-Mexican theatrical company that first toured and then became a resident company in San Francisco in the mid-nineteenth century. A native of Mexico City, López del Castillo was a professional actor from age 15. Today he is known as the first Mexican actor to take companies on tour outside Mexico. By the time he arrived in California, he was already well known throughout Mexico, the Caribbean and Central and South America. An intensely patriotic individual, López del Castillo often used theatrical performances to raise funds for Zaragoza's and Juárez's liberation armies, and he interrupted his theatrical career on various occasions to serve Mexico as a soldier. He is also known as a great promoter of the creation of a national dramatic art for Mexico. By 1862, López del Castillo and his theatrical company had made San Francisco their home. From there the company occasionally ventured out on tours up and down the coast of California and Baja California, but it mostly performed its melodramas at Tucker's Music Academy, the American Theater, and other San Francisco stages. News of the López del Castillo troupe in California exists until 1867; by 1874, he and his family company had resurfaced in Mexico City, where he was actively promoting the creation of a national dramatic literature. In Mexico City, he was considered a grand old man of the stage, but somewhat old hat, and it is said that he died a pauper.

Julio Matas (1931-)

Julio Matas is a playwright, poet, and fiction writer. Born in Havana, Cuba, on May 12, 1931, Matas was encouraged to follow in the steps of his father, a judge, and he thus obtained his law degree from the University of Havana in 1955. But he never practiced as an attorney. He had enrolled in the University School for Dramatic Arts and by the time of his graduation in 1952, he had already organized a drama group, Arena. In his youth he worked on literary magazines and film projects with some of the figures who would become outstanding in these fields, such as Roberto Fernández Retamar, Néstor Almendros, and Tomás Gutiérrez Alea. In 1957, Matas enrolled at Harvard University to pursue a Ph.D. degree in Spanish literature; however, he remained active as a director, returning to Cuba to work on stage productions. It was during the cultural ferment that accompanied the first years of the Communist regime in Cuba that Matas saw two of his first books published there: the collection of short stories *Catálogo de imprevistos* (1963, *Catalog of the Unforeseen*), and the three-act play *La crónica y el suceso*

(1964, *The Chronicle and the Event*). In 1965, Matas returned to the United States to assume a position in the Department of Hispanic Languages and Literatures at the University of Pittsburgh, a position that he still holds today.

Matas's plays and short stories have been published widely in magazines, anthologies, and textbooks. One of his most popular plays, *Juego de Damas* (*Ladies at Play*), has been performed often and has been published in both Spanish and English.

René Marqués (1919-1979)

René Marqués is considered Puerto Rico's foremost playwright and writer of short fiction. Born in Arecibo, Puerto Rico, on October 4, 1919, to a family of agrarian background, Marqués studied agronomy at the College of Agriculture in Mayagüz and actually worked for two years for the Department of Agriculture. But his interest in literature took him to Spain in 1946 to study the classics. Upon his return, Marqués founded a little-theater group dedicated to producing and furthering Puerto Rican theater. In 1948, he received a Rockefeller Foundation Fellowship to study playwriting in the United States, which allowed him to study at Columbia University and at the Piscator Dramatic Workshop in New York City. After his return to San Juan, he founded the Teatro Experimental del Ateneo (the Ateneum Society Experimental Theater). From that time on, Marqués maintained a heavy involvement not only in playwriting, but also in development of Puerto Rican theater. He also produced a continuous flow of short stories, novels, essays, and anthologies.

While Marqués's best-known work is still the all-important play *La carreta* (debuted in 1953, published in 1961, *The Oxcart*, 1969), he has been writing since 1944, when he published his first collection of poems, *Peregrinación* (*Pilgrimage*). His published plays include *El hombre y sus sueños* (1948, *Man and His Dreams*), *Palm Sunday* (1949), *Otro día nuestro* (1955, *Another of Our Days*), *Juan Bobo y la Dama de Occidente* (1956, *Juan Bobo and the Western Lady*), *El sol y los MacDonald* (1957, *The Sun and the MacDonalds*), and a collection, *Teatro* (1959), which includes three of his most important plays: *Los soles truncos* (*The Fan Lights*), *Un niño azul para esa sombra* (*A Blue Child for that Shadow*), and *La muerte no entrará en palacio* (*Death Will Not Enter the Palace*). Many are the other published plays, novels, collections of short stories, and essays. Marqués is one of the few Puerto Rican writers who has had international audiences and impact; he is truly one of the high points of all Latin American drama. The style, philosophy, and craft of his works, as produced in New York, have had

long-lasting influence on the development of Hispanic theater in the United States.

Matías Montes Huidobro (1931-)

Matías Montes Huidobro is a prolific writer of plays, fiction, and poetry, and he has been a theatrical producer and scriptwriter for television and radio. Born in Sagua la Grande, Cuba, Montes was educated there and in Havana. In 1952, he obtained a Ph.D. degree in pedagogy from the University of Havana, but from 1949 on he had already begun publishing creative literature and literary criticism. He served as a professor of Spanish literature at the National School of Journalism in Havana, at which point he had a falling out with the political powers and immigrated to the United States. In 1963, he became a professor of Spanish at the University of Hawaii, a position he holds to this date.

The dramas of Matías Montes Huidobro vary in style, theme, and format, ranging from expressionism to surrealism, from the absurd to the allegorical and political. His published plays include *Los acosados* (1959, *The Accosted*), *La botija* (1959, *The Jug*), *Gas en los poros* (1961, *Gas in His Pores*), *El tiro por la culata* (1961, *Ass-Backwards*), *La vaca de los ojos largos* (1967, *The Long-Eyed Cow*), *La sal de los muertos* (1971, *Salt of the Dead*), *The Guillotine* (1972), *Hablando en chino* (1977, *Speaking Chinese*), *Ojos para no ver* (1979, *Eyes for Not Seeing*), *Funeral en Teruel* (1982, *Funeral in Teruel*), and *La navaja de Olofé* (1982, *Olofé's Blade*). Montes has also published important novels, including *Desterrados al fuego* (1975, *Exiled into the Fire*) and *Segar a los muertos* (1980, *To Blind the Dead*).

Cherríe Moraga

See Chapter 17

Rita Moreno (1931-)

Rita Moreno is an outstanding actress, dancer, and singer who has acted in important mainstream stage, film, and television productions. Born in Humacao, Puerto Rico, on December 11, 1931, she immigrated to New York at an early age and was one of the first Puerto Ricans to break into the stage there. Among the many musicals and plays in which she performed are *The Sign in Sidney Brustein's Window* (1964-65), *Elmer Gantry* (1969-70), *The Last of the Red Hot Lovers* (1970-71), *The National Health* (1974), *Wally's Café* (1981), and *The Odd Couple* (1985). Her films include *West Side Story*, *Carnal Knowledge*, *The King and I*, *Singing in the Rain*, and *The Four Seasons*. Moreno has won an Oscar for Best Supporting Actress (1962), a Grammy (1973), a Tony, and an Emmy. She is also an activist in her profession and in the community for Hispanic rights.

Carlos Morton (1947-)

Carlos Morton is the most published Hispanic playwright in the United States. Born on October 15, 1947, in Chicago, to Mexican-American parents, Morton received his education in various states, as his father's assignments in the army as a noncommissioned officer changed. Morton obtained a bachelor's degree from the University of Texas, El Paso (1975), an M.F.A. degree in theater from the University of California, San Diego (1979), and a Ph.D. degree in drama from the University of Texas, Austin (1987), after which he embarked on a career as a professor of drama. Today he is an associate professor at the University of California, Riverside. His writing career began much earlier, with the publication of his first chapbook of poems, *White Heroin Winter*, in 1971, followed by the publication of his most famous play, *El Jardín* (*The Garden*) in an anthology in 1974. The majority of his plays have been produced on stages at universities and Hispanic community arts centers, with *Pancho Diablo* being produced by the New York Shakespeare Festival and *The Many Deaths of Danny Rosales* by Los Angeles's Bilingual Foundation for the Arts. Most of his plays are contained in two published collections, *The Many Deaths of Danny Rosales and Other Plays* (1983) and *Johnny Tenorio and Other Plays* (1991).

Juan Nadal de Santa Coloma (?-?)

One of the grandest Puerto Rican theatrical figures in the 1920s and 1930s was Juan Nadal de Santa Coloma, the leading actor, singer, director, and impresario. The overriding theme of his life was the development of a Puerto Rican national theater. Born and raised in Puerto Rico at the end of the nineteenth century, Nadal left his engineering studies at San Juan's Instituto Civil to begin a career on the stage. He worked his way through various touring companies in Puerto Rico and South America, and by 1902 was directing his own company, the Compañía de Zarzuela Puertorriqueña. For the next couple of decades he toured continuously in Latin America and Spain, and he even for a while managed Mexico City's Teatro Principal and Madrid's Teatro Eslava. From 1927 through 1934, he was on and off New York and San Juan stages, with his Compañía Teatral Puertorriqueña, promoting Puerto Rican theater. In 1930, he wrote and staged his musical comedy *Día de Reyes* (*The Day of the Magi*), which had 156 performances in New York City alone. In 1935, he returned to Puerto Rico after what he described as "the cold shower" that was New York, and

on the island he continued to direct several companies during the rest of the decade.

Gabriel Navarro (?-?)

Originally from Guadalajara, Gabriel Navarro moved to Los Angeles as an actor and musician in 1922 in the Compañía México Nuevo. In Los Angeles, he developed into a playwright; he also worked as a journalist and theater critic. During the Great Depression and the demise of the theater industry, he became a movie critic. In 1923, he launched a magazine, *La revista de Los Angeles* (*The Los Angeles Magazine*); it is not known how long it lasted. In 1925, he became associated with a newspaper in San Diego, *El Hispano Americano* (The Hispano American), which that same year published his novel, *La señorita Estela* (*Miss Estela*). As a playwright and composer, Navarro experimented with all of the popular dramatic forms, from drama to musical revue. Navarro's favorite genre was the *revista* (revue); it allowed him to put to use his talents as a composer and writer, in addition to the technical knowledge he had accrued as an actor and director. In the revista, Navarro was the celebrant of Hollywood nightlife and the culture of the Roaring Twenties. His known works include the following revues: *Los Angeles al día* (1922, *Los Angeles to Date*), *La Ciudad de los extras* (1922, *The City of Extras*), *Su majestad la carne* (1924, *Her Majesty the Flesh*), *La ciudad de irás y no volverás* (1928, *The City of To Go and Never Return*), *Las luces de Los Angeles* (1933, *The Lights of Los Angeles*), *El precio de Hollywood* (1933, *The Price of Hollywood*), *Los Angeles en pijamas* (1934, *Los Angeles in Pajamas*), and *La canción de Sonora* (1934, *The Song of Sonora*). His dramas include *La Señorita Estela* (1925), *Los emigrados* (1928, *The Emigrées*), *La sentencia* (1931, *The Jail Sentence*), *El sacrificio* (1931, *The Sacrifice*), *Loco amor* (1932, *Crazy Love*), *Alma Yaqui* (1932, *Yaqui Soul*), and *Cuando entraron los dorados* (1932, *When Villa's Troupes Entered*). Navarro's serious works draw upon his experience growing up in Guadalajara and his twelve years in the Mexican army in Veracruz and Sonora during the Mexican Revolution. *El sacrificio* and *La sentencia* use California as a setting; the latter play examines the expatriate status of Mexicans in Los Angeles and shows the breakdown of family and culture, with an Anglo-Mexican intermarriage ending in divorce and bloody tragedy.

Josephina Niggli

See Chapter 17

Manuel Noriega (?-?)

Manuel Noriega was the first director and impresario to really try to develop Hispanic theater in New York by founding various companies, renting and/or buying theaters, and even establishing a motion picture studio. Noriega was a Spanish singer-actor of zarzuelas (operettas) who made his debut at the Teatro Principal in Mexico City in 1904. Noriega found his way to New York in 1916 via the Havana stage. That same year he founded the Compañía Dramática Española, which began touring theater houses in the city for the next few years. In 1919, he formed a partnership with various businessmen and opened the first Spanish-language theater house in New York, El Teatro Español, but because of poor financial management, it closed its doors almost as soon as it opened. Noriega continued to direct companies until 1922, when he left New York. He resurfaced in Los Angeles in 1927, where he had been developing his career in film.

Alberto O'Farrill (1899-?)

Alberto O'Farrill was born in Santa Clara, Cuba, in 1899 and had begun his career as an actor and playwright in Havana in 1921 before emigrating to the United States. In New York O'Farrill was the ubiquitous negrito (black face) of obras bufas cubanas (Cuban farce) and Cuban zarzuelas who made a career playing all the major Hispanic stages in New York's stock and itinerant companies. O'Farrill was also an intensely literate man who had been the editor of *Proteo*, a magazine in Havana, and had become in 1927 the first editor for New York's *Gráfico* newspaper, which he led in becoming the principal organ for the publication and commentary of literature and theatre. In *Grafico*, O'Farrill also published various stories and essays of his own. Despite his literary interests, as of 1926 none of O'Farrill's dramatic works had been published. O'Farrill debuted two zaruelas (Spanish operetta) at the Teatro Esmeralda in Havana in 1921: *Un negro misterioso* (*A Mysterious Black Man*), and *Las pamplinas de Agapito* (*Agapito's Adventures in Pamplona*). His other known works were all debuted at the Apollo Theatre in 1926: one sainete (comedy), *Un doctor accidental* (*An Accidental Doctor*), and the four zarzuelas *Los misterios de Changó* (*The Mysteries of Changó*), *Un negro en Adalucía* (*A Black Man in Andalusia*), *Una viuda como no hay dos* (*A Widow like None Other*), and *Kid Chocolate*. In most of these, as in his acting, he seems to have been concerned with Afro-Cuban themes.

Gonzalo O'Neill (?-?)

Gonzalo O'Neill was a key figure in the cultural life of the Puerto Rican community in New York during the 1920s and 1930s. While a young man on the island of his birth, Puerto Rico, he began his literary career as a poet and as a founder of the literary magazine *Palenque de la juventud* (*Young People's Forum*), which published the works of many who would become Puerto Rico's leading writers. A graduate of Puerto Rico's Instituto Civil, he moved to New York City and soon became a prosperous businessman, but he also maintained his love of literature, culture, and his drive for Puerto Rican independence from the United States. The latter is seen in all his known published dramatic works: *La indiana boirinqueña* (1922, *The Indians of Puerto Rico*), a dramatic dialogue in verse; *Moncho Reyes* (1923), a biting satire of the colonial government in Puerto Rico, named after the fictional governor; and *Bajo una sola bandera* (1928, *Under Just One Flag*), a full-length drama examining the political options for Puerto Rico as personified by a young girl's choice of betrothed. O'Neill was a type of godfather who offered assistance to writers and Puerto Rican immigrants and who invested in cultural institutions, such as the Teatro Hispano. Various of his plays were staged at this theater, including one that was not published: *Amoríos borincanos* (1938, *Puerto Rican Loves*). It is certain that O'Neill wrote many other works, including other plays, poetry, and possibly essays, but they are as yet lost to us today. The works that we do have of his have been preserved probably because he was wealthy enough to underwrite their publication.

Edward James Olmos (1947-)

Edward James Olmos is an outstanding actor, singer, and producer who has broken into mainstream film and television after having developed his career in theater. Born on February 24, 1947, in East Los Angeles, Olmos received an associate arts degree from East Los Angeles City College and attended California State University, Los Angeles. He was the founder and principal singer of the rock band Eddie James and the Pacific Ocean and had the role of the pachuco narrator in Luis Valdez's hit play *Zoot Suit* in Los Angeles. He has had starring or leading roles in films that have been breakthroughs for Hispanics in the movie industry: *Zoot Suit* (1981), *The Ballad of Gregorio Cortez* (1983), *Stand and Deliver* (1988), for which he also served as a coproducer, and *Macho!* (1992). He is one of the first Hispanic actors to have a principal role in a long-lasting television dramatic series: "Miami Vice," 1984-1988. He has appeared in many other television shows and movies.

His honors include the Los Angeles Drama Critics Circle Award (1978), Theatre World Award for Most Outstanding New Performer, Tony Award Nomination for Best Actor in *Zoot Suit* and an Emmy for Best Supporting Actor in "Miami Vice" (1985).

Pedro Pietri

See Chapter 17

Miguel Piñero (1946-1988)

Miguel Piñero is the most famous dramatist to come out of the Nuyorican school. Born in Gurabo, Puerto Rico, on December 19, 1946, he was raised on the lower East Side of New York, the site of many of his plays and poems. Shortly after moving to New York, his father abandoned the family, which had to live on the streets until his mother could find a source of income. Piñero was a gang leader and involved in petty crime and drugs while an adolescent; he was a junior high school dropout and by the time he was twenty-four he had been sent to Sing Sing Prison for armed robbery. While at Sing Sing, he began writing and acting in a theater workshop there.

By the time of his release, his most famous play, *Short Eyes* (published in 1975), had already been prepared in draft form. The play was produced and soon moved to Broadway after getting favorable reviews. During the successful run of his play and afterward, Piñero became involved with a group of Nuyorican writers in the lower East Side and became one of the principal spokespersons and models for the new school of Nuyorican literature, which was furthered by the publication of *Nuyorican Poets: An Anthology of Puerto Rican Words and Feelings*, compiled and edited by him and Miguel Algarín in 1975. During this time, as well, Piñero began his career as a scriptwriter for such television dramatic series as "Barreta," "Kojac," and "Miami Vice." In all, Piñero wrote some eleven plays that were produced, most of which are included in his two collections, *The Sun Always Shines for the Cool, A Midnight Moon at the Greasy Spoon, Eulogy for a Small-Time Thief* (1983) and *Outrageous One-Act Plays* (1986). Piñero is also author of a book of poems, *La Bodega Sold Dreams* (1986). Included among his awards were a Guggenheim Fellowship (1982) and the New York Drama Critics Circle Award for Best American Play, an Obie, and the Drama Desk Award, all in 1974 for *Short Eyes*. Piñero died of cirrhosis of the liver in 1988, after many years of hard living and recurrent illnesses as a dope addict.

Eusebio Pirrín (Don Catarino, ?-?)

Eusebio Pirrín (Pirrín was a stage name, the real family name possibly being Torres) was born into a circus and vaudeville family that toured principally in the U.S. Southwest and somewhat in South America. Born in Guanajuato, Eusebio developed his famous Don Catarino act on the Los Angeles stage; Catarino was named for a character in a comic strip that ran in Los Angeles's newspaper *El Heraldo de México*. Although Eusebio was only a teenager at the time, Don Catarino was a tiny old many with a bushy moustache. Don Catarino became so famous that he spawned many imitators of his dress, speech, and particular brand of humor throughout the Southwest and in Mexico. The Pirrín family troupe enjoyed great fame and fortune and was able to continue performing in the Southwest from the early 1920s through World War II, even surviving the Great Depression. Although Don Catarino was a rural, ranch type, most of his humor was urban; Eusebio Pirrín created all of the revues and music in which Don Catarino took center stage. Eusebio Pirrín's revues are too numerous to list here, but many of them celebrated urban nightlife in Los Angeles, while others commented on and satirized such important political and social themes as the depression, deportations, exile, and the use of alcohol and drugs.

Dolores Prida (1943-)

Dolores Prida is a playwright and screenwriter whose works have been produced in various states and in Puerto Rico, Venezuela, and the Dominican Republic. Born on September 5, 1943, in Caibairén, Cuba, Prida emigrated with her family to New York in 1963. She graduated from Hunter College in 1969 with a major in Spanish-American literature. Upon graduation she began a career as a journalist and editor, first for Collier-Macmillan and then for other publishers, quite often using her bilingual skills. In 1977 her first play, *Beautiful Señoritas*, was produced at the Duo Theater. Since then she has seen some ten of her plays produced. Prida's plays vary in style and format, from adaptations of international classics, such as *The Three Penny Opera*, to experiments with the Broadway musical formula, as in her *Savings* (1985), to her attempt to create a totally bilingual play, as in *Coser y cantar* (1981, *To Sew and to Sing*). Her themes vary from an examination of the phenomenon of urban gentrification, as in *Savings*, to the generation gap and conflict of culture, as in *Botánica* (1990). Prida's plays, which are written in Spanish or English or bilingually, have been collected in *Beautiful Señoritas and Other Plays* (1991). Prida is also a talented poet who was a leader in the 1960s of New York's Nueva Sangre (New Blood) movement of

A scene from the Los Angeles production of Dolores Prida's *Beautiful Señoritas*. (Archives, Arte Público Press.)

young poets. Her books of poems include *Treinta y un poemas* (1967, *Thirty-One Poems*), *Women of the Hour* (1971), and, with Roger Cabán, *The IRT Prayer Book*. Among her awards are an honorary doctorate from Mount Holyoke College (1989), Manhattan Borough President's Excellence in the Arts Award (1987), and a Cintas Fellowship (1976).

Anthony Quinn (1915-)

Anthony Quinn, the famous actor and two-time Oscar winner, was born on April 21, 1915, in Chihuahua, Mexico, and raised in East Los Angeles. After an impoverished childhood, Quinn broke into the movies in the 1930s playing bit roles as an Indian and other ethnic parts. He has appeared in over 175 films, including some of the most famous to be produced in Hollywood, such as *Guadalcanal Diary* (1943), *Viva Zapata* (1952), *Lust for Life* (1956), *The Hunchback of Notre Dame* (1959), *Beckett* (1961), *Lawrence of Arabia* (1963), *Zorba the Greek* (1964), *The Shoes of the Fisherman* (1968), *The Greek Tycoon* (1978), *Lion of the Desert* (1981), and *Revenge* (1990). His plays include *Clean Beds* (1936), *Gentleman from Athens* (1947), *A Street Car Named Desire* and *Beckett* (1961), and

Zorba the Greek (1983). Quinn is also a painter with numerous exhibitions and has written an autobiography, *The Original Sin* (1972).

Marita Reid (? -)

Marita Reid was one of the most famous actresses in New York's Hispanic theater, and she was a tireless promoter of serious drama in the Hispanic community during the difficult years of the Great Depression and World War II. Born in Gibraltar, Spain, to a Spanish mother and an English father, Marita Reid grew up bilingual and began her life on the stage at age 7. Her early experience was performing on tours in extreme southern Spain. She began performing in New York in the early 1920s in Spanish-language companies. In 1922, she formed her own company, and during the 1930s and 1940s her leadership was crucial as she headed up a number of companies that kept Spanish-language theater alive by performing in the mutualist societies and clubs, as well as in conventional theaters. For nearly three decades she was the leading lady of the Hispanic stage in New York and one of its leading directors. Because of her English background, Reid was able to cross over to American,

English-language mainstream theater. Her career extended to Broadway, cinema, and television, including live television drama in the "Armstrong Circle Theater," "The U.S. Steel Hour," and "Studio One." Reid was also the author of four unpublished plays: *Patio gilbraltareño* (*Gibraltar Patio*), *Luna de mayo* (*May Moon*), *El corazón del hombre es nuestro corazón* (1933, *The Heart of Man Is Our Heart*), and *Sor Piedad* (1938, *Sister Piety*).

Gustavo Solano (? - ?)

Gustavo Solano, whose pen name was El Conde Gris (The Grey Count) was a prolific Salvadoran playwright, poet, and prose writer. In addition to his extensive record as a creative writer, Solano led a very fruitful career as a journalist, beginning in his native El Salvador and later developing in New Orleans, where he was the managing editor of the *Pan American Review* and the founder and editor of the bilingual weekly *La Opinión* (*The Opinion*) from 1911 to 1912. In 1912, he moved to Laredo, Texas, to become the editor of *El Progreso* (*The Progress*), then later to Saltillo, Mexico, as founder and editor of *La Reforma* (*The Reform*). During the late teens he was a soldier in the Mexican Revolution and in 1916 he also served time in the penitentiary in Mexico City for his political activities. In 1920, he began a long relationship with Los Angeles's *El Heraldo de México* (*The Mexican Herald*) as an editorial writer. While in Los Angeles, he was under contract to at least two of the theater houses as a playwright charged with producing original material. He remained in Los Angeles until 1929; during this time he also maintained relationships with various publications in Mexico.

Of all the Los Angeles playwrights, Solano had the greatest number of works published. In his book of poems *Composiciones escogidas* (1923, *Selected Compositions*), Solano lists the following published works: *Verso, Fulguraciones, Trinidad de arte (poesía)* (*Verses, Ponderings, Trinity of Art [poetry]*), *Nadie es profeta en su tierra* (*No One Is a Prophet in His Own Land, a play*), *Apóstoles y judas* (1915, *Apostles and Judases*, an allegorical play of the Mexican Revolution), and *La sangre, Crímenes de Estrada Cabrera* (*The Blood, Crimes of Estrada Cabrera*, a play satirizing the Salvadoran dictator). In *Uno más—Prosa y verso* (1929, *One More—Prose and Verse*) he added the following: *México glorioso y trágico (Revolución Mexicana en escena—Prosa y verso)* (*Glorious and Tragic Mexico [The Mexican Revolution Onstage—Prose and Verse]*) and *Con las alas abiertas (Prosa)* (*With Wings Spread Open [Prosa]*); he also mentioned various other works of drama, poetry, and prose about to be published. In his *Volumen de una vida* (1932, *Volume of a Life*) are

included four of the plays that were staged in Los Angeles: *El homenaje lírico a la raza* (*The Lyric Homage to Our People*), *La casa de Birján* (*Birján's House*), *Las falsas apariencias* (*Mistaken Impressions*), and *Tras Cornudo, Apaleado* (*Beaten on top of Being Cuckolded*).

Piri Thomas

See Chapter 17

Romualdo Tirado (? - ?)

The most important figure in the history of the Los Angeles Hispanic stage was the great impresario, director, singer, and actor Romualdo Tirado, who was also the author of numerous librettos for revues. Tirado was a Spaniard who had immigrated to Mexico and developed a career on the stage there during his fifteen years of residence. From the time of his arrival in Los Angeles in the late teens, Tirado was a prime mover in the Hispanic theater and movie industries, and he was also the catalyst that brought about the writing and staging of local plays. Tirado celebrated the highs of the 1920s and stayed on for the lows of the Los Angeles stage during the Great Depression. During the 1940s, however, he was able to obtain some work in Puerto Rico and in New York at the Teatro Hispano.

Tirado developed many of his own musical revues around his own comic persona in various satirized situations, such as *Clínica moderna* (1921, *The Modern Clinic*), *Tirado dentista* (1921, *Tirado the Dentist*), *Tirado bolshevique* (1924, *A Bolshevik Tirado*), and *Tirado en el Polo Norte* (1925, *Tirado at the North Pole*). In 1930, Tirado and Antonieta Díaz Mercado wrote a full-length play based on Mariano Azuela's novel of the Mexican Revolution, *Los de abajo* (*The Underdogs*), but it was a complete flop. None of Tirado's compositions is available today.

Estela Portillo Trambley

See Chapter 17

Omar Torres (1945-)

Omar Torres is an actor, playwright, poet, and novelist. Born and raised in Las Tunas, Cuba, he immigrated to Miami, Florida, with his family in 1959. There he attended both junior and senior high school. The family moved to New York and there he attended Queens College for a while, only to drop out to study on his own. He later took acting classes at the New York Theater of the Americas and subsequently graduated from the International Television Arts School. He has had an active career in radio, television and movies. In 1972, he cofounded, with

Iván Acosta, the Centro Cultural Cubano, and in 1974 he founded the literary and arts journal *Cubanacán* (a nonsense word meaning "Cuba" here). Torres's produced plays include *Abdala-José Martí* (1972, *Abdala-José Martí*), *Antes del Vuelo y la Palabra* (1976, *Before the Flight and the Word*), *Cumbancha cubiche* (1976, *Cumbancha Low Class Cuban*), *Yo dejo mi palabra en el aire sin llaves y sin velos* (1978, *I Leave My Word in the Air without Keys and without Veils*), *Latinos* (1979), and *Dreamland Melody* (1982). Torres is the author of three novels—*Apenas un bolero* (1981, *Just a Bolero*), *Al partir* (1986, *Upon Leaving*), and *Fallen Angels Sing* (1991)—and five books of poetry: *Conversación primera* (1975, *First Conversation*), *Ecos de un laberinto* (1976, *Echoes from a Labyrinth*), *Tiempo robado* (1978, *Stolen Time*), *De nunca a siempre* (1981, *From Never to Always*), and *Línea en diluvio* (1981, *Line in the Deluge*).

Rafael Trujillo Herrera (1897-)

Rafael Trujillo Herrera is a prolific playwright, drama teacher, and impresario. Born in Durango, Mexico, Trujillo immigrated to Los Angeles and remains there to this date. In the late 1920s and early 1930s, he began writing plays for the stage and for the radio; in 1933 he began directing his own radio show. In 1940, Trujillo became associated with the Works Progress Administration (WPA), for which he wrote a play, *Bandido* (*Bandit*); it was later published under the title of *Revolución* (*Revolution*). During the 1960s, Trujillo published numerous works in various genres in Los Angeles, Mexico, and elsewhere, including some through his own publishing house, Editorial Autores Unidos (United Authors Publishing). All told, Trujillo claims to have written some fifty one-act plays, two in four acts, and twelve in three acts. During these years he also directed at least five theater groups. In 1974, he opened the doors to his own little theater, the teatro Intimo, in Los Angeles. Trujillo's most famous three-act plays are *Revolución*, *Estos son mis hijos* (*These Are My Children*), *La hermana de su mujer* (*His Wife's Sister*), *Cuando la vida florece* (*When Life Flourishes*), and *A la moda vieja* (*Old Style*).

Luis Valdez (1940-)

Luis Valdez is considered the father of Chicano theater. He has distinguished himself as ana actor, director, playwright, and filmmaker; however, it was in his role as the founding director of El Teatro Campesion, a theater of farm workers in California, that his efforts inspired young Chicano activists across the country to use theater as a means of organizing students, communities, and labor unions. Luis Valdez was born into a family of migrant farm

Playwright-director Luis Valdez.

workers in Delano, California. The second of ten children, he began to work the fields at age 6 and to follow the crops. Valdez's education was continuously interrupted; he nevertheless finished high school and went on to San Jose State College, where he majored in English and pursued his interest in theater. While there he won a playwriting contest with his one-act "The Theft" (1961), and in 1963 the drama department produced his play *The Shrunken Head of Pancho Villa*.

After graduating from college in 1964, Valdez joined the San Francisco Mime Troupe and learned the techniques of agitprop (agitation and propaganda) theater and Italian *commedia dell'arte* (comedy of art), both of which influenced Valdez's development of the basic format of Chicano theater: the one-act presentational *acto* (act). In 1965, Valdez enlisted in César Chávez's mission to organize farm workers in Delano into a union. It was there that Valdez brought together farm workers and students into El Teatro Campesino to dramatize the plight of the farm workers. The publicity and success gained by the troupe led to the spontaneous appearance of a national Chicano theater movement. In 1967, Valdez and El Teatro Campesino left the unionizing effort to expand their theater beyond agitprop and farm worker concerns. From then on Valdez and the theater have explored most of the theatrical genres that have been important to Mexicans in the United States, including religious pageants, vaudeville with the down-and-out pelado (underdog) figure, and dramatized corridos (ballads). During the late 1960s and the 1970s, El Teatro Campesino produced many of Valdez's plays, including *Los vendidos* (1967, *The Sell-Outs*), *The Shrunken Head of Pancho Villa* (1968), *Bernabé* (1970), *Dark Root of a Scream* (1971), *La carpa de los Rascuachis* (1974), and *El fin del mundo* (1976). In 1978, Valdez broke into mainstream theater in Los Angeles, with the Mark Taper Forum's production of his *Zoot Suit* and the 1979 Broadway production of the same play. In 1986 he had a successful run of his play *I Don't Have to Show You No Stinking Badges* at the Los Angeles Theater Center.

Valdez's screenwriting career began with early film and television versions of Corky González's poem "I Am Joaquín" (1969) and "Los vendidos," and later with a film version of *Zoot Suit* (1982). But his real incursion into major Hollywood productions and success came with his writing and directing of *La Bamba* (the name of a dance from Veracruz), the screen biography of Chicano rock-and-roll star Ritchie Valens. Valdez's plays, essays, and poems have been widely anthologized. His only collection of work still in print is *Luis Valdez—The Early Works* (1990), which includes the early actos that he developed with El Teatro Campesino, his play *Bernabé*, and his narrative poem "Pensamiento Serpentino." Valdez's awards include an Obie (1968), Los Angeles Drama Critics Awards (1969, 1972, and 1978), a special Emmy Award (1973), award for Best Musical from the San Francisco Bay Critics Circle (1983), and honorary doctorates from San Jose Sate University, Columbia College, and the California Institute of the Arts.

Daniel Venegas

See Chapter 17

Carmen Zapata (1927-)

Carmen Zapata is an actress and producer of Mexican heritage. Born on July 15, 1927, in New York City, she was raised and educated in New York, and later attended the University of California, Los Angeles, and New York University. Zapata has had a very successful career in Hollywood films and on television, including children's television. She is most important, however, as the founder and director of the Bilingual Foundation for the Arts in Los Angeles, which is a showcase for Hispanic playwrights, actors, and directors and has resulted in introducing new talent to the television and movie industries. In-

Actress-director Carmen Zapata portrays Isabel la Católica in the Bilingual Foundation for the Arts's production of *Moments to Be Remembered*.

cluded among her awards are the National Council of La Raza Rubén Salazar Award (1983), the Women in Film Humanitarian Award (1983), Hispanic Women's Council Woman of the Year (1985), best Actress Dramalogue (1986), and an Emmy (1973).

References

Antush, John, ed. *Recent Puerto Rican Theater: Five Plays from New York*. Houston, Tex.: Arte Publico Press, 1991.

Cortina, Rodolfo, ed. *Cuban American Theater*. Houston, Tex.: Arte Publico Pres, 1991.

Covarrubias, Miguel.

Huerta, Jorge. *Chicano Theater. Themes and Forms*. Tempe, Ariz.: Bilingual Press, 1982.

Huerta, Jorge. *Necessary Theater. Six Plays about the Chicano Experience*. Houston, Tex.: Arte Publico Press, 1989.

Kanellos, Nicolás. *Hispanic Theatre in the United States*. Houston, Tex.: Arte Publico Press, 1984.

———. *A History of Hispanic Theatre in the United States: Origins to 1940*. Austin, Tex.: University of Texas Press, 1990.

———. *Mexican American Theatre: Legacy and Reality*. Pittsburgh, Pa.: Latin American Review Press, 1987.

————. *Mexican American Theatre Then and Now*. Houston, Tex.: Arte Publico Press, 1983.

Miller, John C. "Contemporary Hispanic Theatre in New York." In *Hispanic Theatre in the United States,* edited by Nicolás Kanellos. Houston, Tex.: Arte Publico Press, 1984.

Valdez, Luis. "Notes on Chicano Theatre" and "Actos." In *Luis Valdez—The Early Works*. Houston, Tex.: Arte Publico Press, 1991.

Watson-Espener, Maida. "Ethnicity and the Hispanic American Stage: The Cuban Experience." In *Hispanic Theatre in the United States*, edited by Nicolás Kanellos. Houston, Tex.: Arte Publico Press, 1984.

Nicolás Kanellos

Film

This chapter focuses on the depiction of Hispanics by the American film industry from its beginnings around the turn of the century through the contemporary period. The first two sections deal with how the depiction of minority groups, including Hispanics, developed in the earliest U.S. cinema. A host of early trends and personal contributions combined to create the extraordinarily harsh American style of racial and ethnic depiction. These factors were further reinforced in the 1920s and 1930s with the conglomeration of the American film industry in a fashion that emphasized theatrical distribution, the assembly line production of many films, the star system, and production formulas that were later turned into a production code.

The third section reviews the early cinematic depiction of Hispanics. It also describes the prevailing stereotypes: bandidos, buffoons, dark ladies, caballeros, and gangsters. The fourth section describes the changes in the depiction of Hispanics and other minority groups brought about by the Great Depression, World War II, and the advent of the "Hollywood social problem film." Section five reviews Hispanic-focused films as well as the careers of Hispanic actors and filmmakers against the backdrop of important social developments such as the emergence of the civil rights movement and the decline of the production code.

Section six is devoted to films that were produced since 1980, and section seven reviews the emergence of U.S. Hispanic film, including both Chicano produc-

tions and films made in Puerto Rico (often with Mexican or Hollywood control) or by Puerto Ricans both on the island and in the continental United States. Finally, a list of outstanding Hispanic figures in the film industry is provided, as well as a bibliography of further, more specialized readings.

✳ DEPICTION OF MINORITY GROUPS IN EARLY AMERICAN FILM

During a period of a few years, primarily between 1903 and 1915, several technological, aesthetic, economic, and cultural developments in the United States came together that were important in determining how American cinema was to depict race and ethnicity for decades to come. An unfortunate filmic style emerged that was much harsher in its depiction of race and ethnicity than the cinema of other nations. American cinema delighted in the depiction of such stereotypes as "chinkers," "Micks," "darkies," "Hebrews," "greasers," "redskins," and "guineas," and actually used these epithets in the titles and publicity or in the films themselves.

Five governing factors converged and interacted with one another around the turn of the century to produce a definable style of racial stereotyping in American cinema: (1) the developing technological sophistication of filmmaking, particularly in projection and editing, (2) the developing philosophy of illusionism that began to gain ascendancy in film aesthetics, (3) the economic necessity in the U.S. film industry to produce westerns and to produce epic, prestige pictures of middle-class appeal, (4) the attitudes toward race and ethnicity that prevailed in society and that governed the popular novel of the period, and (5) the racial attitudes of the most prominent filmmakers of the period, especially D. W. Griffith.

The early years of cinema witnessed an explosion of technology similar to that of the contemporary computer industry. Advances in film technology were instrumental in determining the art of the possible for the emerging American cinematic filmmakers of the period, such as Edwin S. Porter, D. W. Griffith, Mack Sennett, Thomas H. Ince, William S. Hart, and Charles Chaplin. The development of more powerful projection and editing technologies permitted the production of what audiences of that period perceived to be more realistic films (although the contemporary viewer of these forerunners would find it difficult to understand this). These more "realistic" and longer films, included epics, which lent themselves to the depiction of minority group types, including Mexicans, blacks, Orientals, and native Indians, in a way that was not technologically possible before.

In 1903, Edwin S. Porter produced the landmark film *The Great Train Robbery*. Significantly, the film was a Western and reigned for about ten years, until the emergence of D. W. Griffith's features, as the most important American cinematic production. *The Great Train Robbery* was of epic proportions for its time, an incredible twelve minutes. Yet, by 1915 technological advances and artistic will had stretched the concept of epic to three hours with Griffith's *The Birth of a Nation*. It is in the nature of epics that they deal with race and ethnicity, and it was no coincidence that Griffith's most famous epic was the most ambitious attempt to date, a flawed and racist depiction of ethnic and racial types: tender and sensitive Southern whites, vain white Northern liberals, vicious or brutal blacks, merciless Northern soldiers, heroic Ku Klux Klansmen, and evil mulattoes, the result of deplorable mixing of the races.

Filmmakers quickly came to realize, as the result of the reactions of the viewers of the first "flickers," the potential for manipulating emotions on the basis of heretofore unimagined optical effects. The first movies, only fifty feet long, had the most rudimentary of plots, or were plotless. In any event, the operating element was not plot but effects never before experienced under controlled conditions: a speeding locomotive, a barrel going over a waterfall, a galloping horse. Filmmakers found that they could induce fear, vertigo, suspense, and other intense emotions in the viewers through recourse to special-effect shots. *The Great Train Robbery* is famous for the last shot, a non sequitur close-up of a bandit firing his pistol at the audience. Within a few years, more complex emotions were induced. Griffith's films, through their depiction of kidnappings, attempted rapes, destruction of homesteads or Indian villages, and most of all, war, were able to bring forth feelings of outrage, simultaneous horror, and titillating anticipation, pity, and remorse more intensely than other available media—theater, fiction, poetry, or journalism.

The earliest period of cinema, which had its roots in magic and lantern shows and in vaudeville, emphasized the illusionism of special effects (trains, horses, running water, flights to the moon, and soon). However, as the result of rapid advances in technology that permitted longer and more sophisticated films, together with the increasing staleness of purely optical effects such as waves beating against a pier, cinema began to both borrow from and more closely approximate the stage. The early film directors, Edwin S. Porter, Stuart Blackton, Sidney Olcott, and others, quickly discovered that film had a distinct advantage over the stage in presenting melodrama. The devices available to film could have a reality that was impossible to attain on the stage. For example, the count of Monte Cristo need not escape from his prison through a canvas sea; the film showed a real ocean.

Moreover, the early filmmakers, Griffith the leader among them, soon made changes in style based on the aesthetics of illusionism. Film moved from a style based on special optical effects (where the cameraman was supreme) to a photographic record of legitimate theater, to an emotionally heightened superrealism where the auteur/director reigned supreme. The aesthetics and ideology of this change are well indexed in the motion picture column begun in 1909 in the trade journal *The New York Dramatic Mirror*. Writing under the pseudonym The Spectator, Frank Woods stated the ideal later identified as that of a transparent fiction whose appearance of reality is strong enough to efface an awareness on the part of a viewer of the actual production of the illusion. Woods was convinced that the unique power of the cinema lay in its singular illusion of reality. This illusion gave cinema a "strange" psychological power over its audience:

> . . . the strange power of attraction possessed by motion pictures lies in the semblance of reality which the pictures convey; that by means of this impression of reality the motion picture exerts on the minds of the spectators an influence akin to hypnotism or magnetism by visual suggestion; that this sort of limited hypnotic influence

is capable of more powerful exertion through the medium of motion pictures than is possible in any sort of stage production or in printed fact or fiction, and that it is therefore the part of wisdom to cultivate absolute realism in every department of the motion picture art. Artificial drama and artificial comedy appear to have no attraction for the public mind when displayed in motion pictures, no matter how satisfactory they may be on the stage or in printed literature (*The New York Dramatic Mirror,* May 14, 1910, 18).

The conscious economic policy of attempting to raise the social respectability of films and consequently attract a middle-class audience also had an important ideological and aesthetic consequence, propelling film toward the classical narrative style of illusionism and, in turn, the depiction of ethnic and racial stereotypes in the distinctive American manner. In 1908, the Motion Picture Patents Company (MPPC) was established with the goals of establishing a controlling monopoly of film distribution and achieving acceptance of the "flickers" by the middle class.

The push to make film respectable (that is, acceptable to the middle class) opened on two basic fronts: censorship of film content and improvement of the theaters in which the films were shown. Film censorship had two aims: to "improve" film content and therefore attract a "better class" of audience, and to keep censorship out of the hands of the government and the clergy, which might deal more harshly with the films than the producers wanted. Of course, the goal was to make films that still catered to the working class (many of them recently arrived immigrants from western and, increasingly, eastern Europe), even as they attracted the middle class.

To woo the middle class, filmmakers began to produce films with more complicated narrative plots and characterization, films with "educational" or "instructive" values or a "moral lesson," and films with happy endings. As an editorial in *Nickelodeon* states: "We are living in a happy, beautiful, virile age. . . .We do not want sighs or tears. . . .We are all seeking happiness—whether through money or position or imagination. It is our privilege to resent any attempt to force unhappy thoughts on us." (Gunning, 1981, 15) All of these initiatives lent themselves to the creation of racial antagonists (Mexicans, blacks, Indians), whose interactions with white males and females, however simplistic and formulistic by contemporary standards, were considerably more complex from a narrative and psychological point of view. Moreover, their defeat could be the basis of a moral

lesson for both the character on-screen and the audience, and for happy endings evoking the moral and physical superiority of Anglo values over the degenerate or primitive mores of other cultures.

The central impetus behind the production of vast numbers of Westerns, many using Mexicans or Indians as foils to Anglo heroes and heroines, was a ready international market for such films. The genre became proprietary to the American film industry.

Each of these factors—the increasing sophistication of filmmaking technology, the developing style of illusionism, and the ready market for epics and Westerns—determined that filmmakers would either turn to the prevailing literature of the day and adapt it to film, or hire scriptwriters to produce screenplays closely modeled on that prevailing literature. Before 1908, the primary sources for films were vaudeville and burlesque sketches, fairy tales, comic strips, and popular songs. These forms stressed spectacular effects or physical action, rather than psychological motivation. Although still in an elementary form, film now looked toward more respectable narrative models and the problems they entailed, as outlined below. With respect to Westerns, a vast literature existed, almost all of it formulaic pulp fiction, that could be either adapted or imitated in kind.

Westerns, as Arthur Pettit has observed, are "at least as rigid in their conventions as any medieval morality play" (Pettit, 1980, xv). The genre has a finite number of categories, such as the cattle empire, the ranch, revenge, cowboys and Indians, outlaws, law and order, and conquest. The depiction of Mexicans and Indians in these stories, and their adaptation to the screen by filmmakers seeking to introduce narrative and psychological complexity into their works as well as woo a new audience, was strictly in accordance with the prevailing canon and formula for racial interaction. Pettit, in a review and analysis of hundreds of nineteenth-and twentieth-century popular Western novels, has distilled the following conclusions about the genre, conclusions that are valid in turn for the films that began to emerge around the turn of the century, these having been modeled on the literary productions:

When [the Anglo] set out to bring democracy, progress, and Protestantism to the Hispanic Southwest, he could find a place for the Mexican in what he soon regarded as "his" Southwest only if the Mexican would become, insofar as his limited talents permitted, what the American perceived himself to be: enterprising, steady, and Protestant—in a word, civilized. Yet somehow the Mexican remained something else in the Anglo-American's eye: shiftless, unreliable, and alternately decadent or barbaric. Thus, it seemed to be the American's manifest destiny to conquer and convert this errant race. In the process it was also necessary to destroy a culture the Mexican would not willingly surrender. Operating from such moral absolutes, the Anglo was able to achieve a satisfactory interpretation of his racial and cultural superiority. He could flatter himself that he was not deprecating a race but standing up for civilization. He could persuade himself, in fact, that he was not guilty of racism in any sense that we understand the term. For if the Mexican could be evaluated only in terms of the civilization to which, by the laws of nature, God, and history alike, he had to give way, then how could the conqueror be blamed for what was destined to happen? The Anglo-American thus came to see the indigenous way of life in what became the American Southwest as inherently and irrevocably inferior and hostile to his own institutions (Pettit, 1980, xvii-xviii).

Finally, the work of the early filmmakers, David Wark Griffith supreme among them, has had an enormous impact on American and international filmmaking. Griffith's posthumous autobiography (published in 1972; Griffith died in 1948), without too much exaggeration, is entitled *The Man Who Invented Hollywood*. Griffith's most important contribution to film was his development of the techniques through which the motion picture became an art form, an instrument able to express emotions and ideas. Griffith's instinctive sense of the unique expressive properties of the cinema also extended beyond the technical means into the art of acting. Early on, he recognized the need for a new style of performing for the screen, a style more subtle and restrained than the bombastic, exaggerated delivery then current on the stage. As early as 1909, he gathered a group of young actors and rehearsed them continually until he was able to extract from them performances that could withstand the magnifying eye of the motion picture camera. He thus established a stock company of players that at one time or another included future stars Mary Pickford, Dorothy and Lillian Gish, Blanche Sweet, Mabel Normand, Mae Marsh, Florence LaBadie, Claire McDowell, Henry B. Walthall, Robert (Bobby) Harron, Alfred Paget, Donald Crisp, Arthur Johnson, Jack Pickford, James Kirkwood, Owen Moore, Wallace Reid, and Harry Carey. Griffith had a major role in establishing the star system, with all of its glories and drawbacks, upon

which American films are scripted, produced, and marketed to this very day.

Griffith also made a major contribution to the development of the epic. With the premier of his greatest success, *The Birth of a Nation*, in 1915, the previously little-known Griffith became the best-known motion picture director in the industry. With the help of some publicity hype, he became known as the "Shakespeare of the screen." *The Birth of a Nation* is considered by many historians to be the single most important film in the development of cinema as an art. It was certainly the most influential. Originally running about three hours in length, it was a stunning summary of all that was known about filmmaking at the time, as well as an elaborately constructed, complex production that to this day retains its emotional impact.

Griffith's contributions to film technique and technology, to cinematic acting, and to the development of genres, including the epic, are all well documented. Also carefully reviewed by historians has been the content of his major films, such as *The Birth of a Nation* and *Intolerance*, with respect to their expression of racial and ethnic attitudes. It would be hard to avoid an analysis along these lines inasmuch as *The Birth of a Nation* caused a firestorm of controversy over its anti-Negro bias and its positioning the Ku Klux Klan as heroes who come to the rescue of beleaguered white Southerners.

It appears that Griffith's racial attitudes were readily passed into American cinema style. These attitudes were embedded in Griffith's film technique. They were integral to the way he developed many of his plots and the way he developed several of his epic films. American cinema took not only the technical (relatively content-free) contributions from Griffith and other early filmmakers, but also the content-intensive ones. What emerged, partially as a contribution of these racial attitudes and their narrative and thematic elaboration in film, partially from the convergence of the four factors reviewed earlier (technological, aesthetic, economic, and sociocultural), was a distinctively American style of racial and ethnic depiction, one that was uniquely derogatory unfortunately.

Griffith's racial attitudes can be summarily characterized as somewhat typical for a Southerner of his station during this period, although he carried certain notions to extremes, such as a romantic admiration for the "noble savage" and a profound fear of miscegenation. Both of these notions were quite popular with his viewers. There was a close match between what fed on Griffith and what he fed his public in the privacy of a darkened movie theater. According to Iris Barry's book, *D. W. Griffith: American Film*

Master, Griffith's views on race and culture as they were elaborated cinematically have been separated into six factors. First, Griffith believed in the superiority of the white race. Every other race was evaluated in relationship to the attainments of the white race and with respect to its approximation to the white race, which provided the standard for emulation.

Second, Griffith displayed respect for and admiration of other races and cultures in their "pristine state," for example, peaceful Indians living in their villages far from the white man, Zulus in their jungle habitat, blacks in the antebellum South being cared for like children by white aristocrats, and so on. Griffith directed several movies such as *The Greatest Thing in Life*, in which evil whites come and destroy this pristine beauty of "noble savages" or "natural men."

In addition to his belief in white superiority, the director had an overriding obsession with color, and this feature of Griffith's was directly transferred to the advertisements for his films, which often feature references to "redmen," "yellow chinkers," "smokies," "tawny blacks," "greasers," and so on.

A fourth tenet held by Griffith was a belief in the ability of the less civilized races to overcome their inferiority to the degree that they showed their commitment, obeisance, and fealty to Anglo-Saxon values, and to the degree they had good, positive Anglo-Saxon role models available to them. This theme appears in movies such as *The Redman and the Child* and *Broken Blossoms,* which he directed.

Fifth, he had a profound abhorrence of what he called "mongrolization." For Griffith, half-breeds, such as mulattoes, were among the worst, most deplorable human types. Part and parcel of this attitude, which was so motivating for him that it cannot be overemphasized, was his great fear of miscegenation, which at the same time produced considerable titillation in him. Many of Griffith's films have "fate worse than death" scenes, and Griffith typically used some mongrolized (either racially or culturally) character as the would-be rapist. Interracial rape (attempted but never consummated) was a specialty of his. This sort of primal scene in his psyche profoundly moved him, and it was terrific box office as well. The "fate worse than death" element of American cinema became one of the staples that spurred the careers of many an actress, usually a blonde whose fairness contrasted beautifully on celluloid with the ominous, darker-hued attempted rapists.

A sixth interest of Griffith's revealed in his films was the interaction of sex and race and sex and class. These movies stirred him as well as his viewers. The films were popular with everyone, but they were especially appealing to women, for whom going to the movies represented, apart from the content of the film itself, a certain emancipation from traditional strictures. To go to the movies and then see women in situations profoundly provocative for the historical moment and for the sensibilities of the time genuinely led to a degree of addiction to the experience. Griffith was both a consumer and master purveyor of shared fantasies in the dark pitched at a level that shook the consumer but did not go so far as to induce an emotional or intellectual aftertaste. His audience could enter the darkened movie theater and privately and without remorse experience forbidden thoughts of rape, ravishment, interracial sex, gore and glory, and the like . At the end of the film, the light was turned back on and one could go merrily on one's way without giving the film content a worry. And besides, no one really did get raped or ravished. Griffith's films featured the close call and the close encounter and the salvation of the maiden by the white hero so that in the end everything was right and social decorum and the social order were merely tasted and tested but ultimately maintained.

Thus, in the space of some twelve years shortly after the turn of the century, technological, aesthetic, economic, and sociocultural factors converged in the American film industry and led to the creation of a distinctive and exceptionally derogatory style of depicting racial and ethnic minorities, including Hispanics.

✺ CONGLOMERATION OF THE FILM INDUSTRY AND THE PRODUCTION CODE

The first wave of ethnic stereotyping that so distinguishes American film from the silver screen of other nations was further reinforced by the development of film as big business. Capital investment in the American film industry became centered not in production but in distribution, particularly in the form of movie theaters. By the early 1930s, power rested with a mere eight major, vertically structured corporations that had consolidated production, distribution, and exhibition in monopolistic fashion: MGM, Warner Brothers, Paramount, Twentieth Century Fox, Universal, RKO, Columbia, and United Artists. This fact indicated that the industry gave a steady priority to making a large quantity of pictures rather than to making good ones. A steady turnover of product was needed to ensure revenue at the box office, which was dependent on regular attendance at many theaters on a continual basis, not on high attendance for any one movie during a single run. From an industry point of view, then, making good pictures was secondary to making a lot of pictures.

María Montez, an early Hispanic film star.

The studios operated the newly developed film technology in an assembly line style not dissimilar to the newly established Detroit automobile industry. Writers and directors were assigned projects to be started Monday morning. The various departments—costume, makeup, art construction, musical scores, and so on—concentrated solely on their specific spheres of activity from film to film. The assembly line method was essential to getting a large quantity of product into the theaters, but unlike most assembly lines, the studios were not mass-producing exactly the same product over and over. While each car off the assembly line was no different from all the others, each movie was unique. Means were quickly developed for the mass production of different products. A series of basic conventions—character, narrative, thematic, stylistic—was established as a standard mode of expression. This formula was broad enough to be applied in a wide variety of ways and flexible enough to shift with changing times and tastes, yet fixed enough to serve as a pattern for production and marketing.

This assembly line methodology or homogenization of craft, which governed the "high technology" of the early twentieth century and had a profound influence on the stylistic, thematic, and performance components of U.S. film, is usually known as the Hollywood Formula. With respect to style, film was produced and marketed to the public by genre: Western, musical, screwball comedy, horror, gangster, or woman's film. The easily identifiable genres provided variations on familiar movie experiences and made moviegoing a sort of ritual. Repetition of this sort ensured a basically effortless participation by the audience. There was absolute trust, for example, that the hero would prevail and get the girl. It was just a matter of how and when. With respect to performance, typecasting (the human resource analog to the production of standard fenders or automobile bodies) led to the highly salesworthy star system. After several films, the public came to know a star very well, so much so that it became difficult for actors to stray very far beyond their normal range. Moviegoers all knew clearly what to expect from a Bette Davis or James Cagney vehicle, and the studios protected the stars" screen persona by developing filmscripts that would enhance the performance qualities of each star. The star system was the most important aspect of film marketing. Character, story line, and production qualities were built around the star. The hype derived from advertisements to magazines and press coverage about the glamorous world of Hollywood served the same function.

Given the circumstances of marketing by the star system, it is small wonder that Hispanic film actors and actresses had the option of either retaining their Hispanic identity and being typecast negatively or denying their Hispanic identity by what the industry euphemistically calls "repositioning" themselves. Examples of actors who took the former option include Leo Carrillo, who played his stereotype faithfully as a gambling, murdering, extorting, pimping, border bandido in some thirty films. Lupe Vélez, dead at age 34 in no small measure due to the humiliations of the Hollywood star system, played to perfection the stereotype of the Hispanic "dark lady" with her hip swinging and her amusing difficulties with the English language. Lupe would invariably go down to defeat when confronted with female Anglo-Saxon competition in the struggle to infatuate an Anglo male star. Examples of the repositioned actor include Rita Cansino and Raquel Tejada, who changed their images to Rita Hayworth and Raquel Welch in order not to be typecast as mere Hispanic dark ladies.

The influence of the Hollywood Formula on the development of movies themes or messages did extreme damage to minority groups, including Hispanics. The two fundamental thematic components of the formula were that the movie should communicate Americanism and that it should provide wish fulfillment. Often films combined both notions—nationalism and hedonism—at the deleterious expense of minorities. As Roffman and Purdy observe:

> The dramatic conflict was always structured around two opposing poles definitively representing good and evil, with a readily identifiable hero and villain. But since the hero was also the star, his goodness must conform to the star's personality. Absolute virtue, however, is generally unexciting and inhibits many of the star's qualities of illicit wish fulfillment. Thus the hero often embodied slightly tainted moral traits. As long as there was no doubt as to the hero's ultimate allegiance to the side of good, the audience could indulge in his minor transgressions. By subtly combining moral uprightness with an endearing toughness, the star was made more provocative and the hero a more effective combatant of villainy. He had the air of having been everywhere and seen everything. He was the Indian fighter who was raised by the Indians, the marshal who used to be an outlaw gunfighter, the police agent who once was one of the mob, and the ultimate good bad guy, the private eye who skirts between the world of law and the underworld of crime. This helped rationalize the hero's use of violent, even immoral means to achieve righteous ends. In the same way (though not nearly as often) sympathy could be extended to the criminal without ever upholding criminality (Roffman and Purdy, 1981, 6).

As a result, in American film the ethnic *other* strictly and almost invariably played the outcast or the evildoer. Film, and for that matter, television in its early period, was an instrument of socialization that took as its guiding premise the assimilation of all racial, ethnic, and religious differences into the harmonizing credo of the American melting pot. There was no room whatsoever for divergence from this requirement. Even more painful, those races and ethnicities that could not be readily assimilated because of their difference of color and physiognomy—which would be readily apparent on the black-and-white celluloid—for example, blacks, Hispanics, and Indians, were drummed into the fold of evildoers and outcasts, a priori and without recourse. Blacks, Hispanics, and Indians consequently functioned as the slag in the melting-pot alchemy of American film. Scholars have documented with massive and indisputable evidence how the early cinematic depiction of

the Hispanic (particularly the Mexican), from its turn-of-the-century beginnings with the "greaser" films of D. W. Griffith until World War II, resided at the basest, crassest level of prejudiced racial and ethnic stereotype (see Cárdenas and Schneider, 1981; Cortés, 1983; García, 1988; Keller, 1985, 1988; Lamb, 1975; Mora, 1982; Pettit, 1980; Roeder, 1971; Roffman and Purdy, 1981; Treviño, 1982; Woll, 1974a, 1974b.)

The usual components of wish fulfillment, such as romance and true love, destroying evil (even as we relish evil actions fiendishly depicted on the screen), rewarding good, happy endings, and so on, ensured that Hispanic and other minority characters would perform for the assembly line the roles of vamps, seductresses, greasers, gangsters, and the like, ad nauseam.

The formula became Hollywood law in 1934 with the introduction of the Production Code. The code states in pontifical and hypocritical fashion the moral value system behind the Hollywood formula, decrying criminal violence and intimate sexuality, upholding the sanctity of marriage and the home and other traditions that had already become heartily compromised in the movies. The code stated that entertainment is "either HELPFUL or HARMFUL to the human race." Because of this, "the motion picture . . . has special MORAL OBLIGATIONS" to create only "correct entertainment" that "raises the whole standard of a nation" and "tends to improve the race, or at least to re-create or rebuild human beings exhausted with the realities of life" (Roffman and Purdy, 1981, 6).

In a very broad sense, an ideological vision of the world was acted out in each formula movie. Each individual—of the correct ethnic background, that is—can aspire to success. You are limited only by your own character and energies (if you are of the correct ethnic background, of course). Wealth, status, and power are possible for everyone (Anglo, that is) in America, the land of opportunity where the individual (Anglo) is rewarded for virtue. Such Americana as home, motherhood, community, puritanical love, and the work ethic are all celebrated. All issues are reduced to a good versus evil, black-and-white conflict, an us-against-them identification process where good equals the American (Anglo) values and social system ("us"). "Them," the villains, are defined as those who reject and seek to destroy the proper set of American (Anglo) values. Conflict is always resolved through the use of righteous force, with Anglo values winning out. "Them" not only includes blacks, Hispanics, and Indians—that is, those ethnics whose color and racial features overtly identify them as "others"—but usually any ethnic group when it is depicted ethnically.

✳FIRST DECADES: THE BANDIDO, BUFFOON, DARK LADY, CABALLERO, AND GANGSTER

The early cinematic depiction of the Hispanic was an almost unrelieved exercise in degradation. Summaries exist for some three hundred early "Mexican" films (Roeder, 1971). The word "greaser" was commonly used in these films. For example, D. W. Griffith's *The Thread of Destiny* and *The Greaser's Gauntlet* make commonplace of the epithet. *Guns and Greasers* (1918) was the last film to use the epithet in a film title, but the term continued to be used in advertising. According to Lamb (1975), the crowds loved these films and reacted to them in the movie theater along lines common to theatrical melodrama.

To appreciate fully the brown-white moral dichotomy established in these early movies, one would probably have to be able to view them with a contemporary audience. *Moving Picture World*, the leading trade journal of the first two decades of the century, reported that audiences viewing *Across the Mexican Line* applauded almost every move made by the good Americans, while the actions of Castro, the bandido, met with loud hisses (Lamb, 1975, 8).

During the first two decades of U.S. filmmaking, the Hispanic stereotypes were the bandido, the buffoon, and the dark lady. By the 1920s, two additional roles were added to the repertoire, the caballero and the gangster. Typically, in accordance with the traditional role of minorities in American film, the Hispanic was one to be killed, mocked, punished, seduced, or redeemed by Anglo protagonists.

Some greasers meet their fate because they are greasers. Others violate Saxon moral codes. All of them rob, assault, kidnap, and murder. ...Greed plays a primary role in the early movie greaser's misconduct. Occasionally, as in *The Mexican*, a covetous Mexican landlord demands too much rent from the heroine and gets his "yellow cheeks" slapped by the girl's fiancé. More often, the greaser attempts to steal horses or gold. . ..The greaser of the early films is as lustful as he is greedy. In *The Pony Express* a bandido abducts the Saxon heroine. The hero summons a posse and in one of the first of many cinematic chases, pursues the bandido and his henchmen, shooting them down one by one without sustaining casualties. In the final showdown the greaser leader tries to stab the hero several times but is overcome by a knockout blow (Pettit, 1980, 133).

The earliest Westerns generally followed the conventions of that period's dime novels—popular, cheaply made books that sold in the mass market. There were two differences, however. One is that in some films the greaser was allowed to reform or redeem himself, usually by saving a beautiful Anglo heroine. *The Greaser's Gauntlet* and *Tony, the Greaser* cultivate the theme of Hispanic redemption through obeisance to the physical and moral splendor of an Anglo-Saxon beauty. This theme, to which D. W. Griffith made a significant contribution, was the first example of the Hispanic of low birth but good heart. "His is an unenviable lot, as he is doomed to wander between the longed-for world of the Anglo and the stigmatized world of the Mexican, held forever in a middle position between Saxon heroes and greaser villains. It is the faint beginning of a pattern to be developed more fully in a later generation of books and films" (Pettit, 1980, 135).

The second way films were different from the dime novels reflected the historical reality of the Mexican Revolution (1910-1920), which the American film industry depicted with the customary quality of cinematic exaggeration, but occasionally showing no Americans at all. These films actually depicted the emergence of revolutionaries from the peon class and treated them as heroes. Thus, in *The Mexican Joan of Arc,* where only Mexican characters are featured, a woman whose husband and son are arrested and murdered by the *federales* becomes a rebel leader. In a similar film, *The Mexican Revolutionists*, a rebel named Juan is captured but escapes the *federales* only to help the revolutionaries capture Guadalajara. Films of this type were rare, however. As has been described earlier, American film needed to operate on the basis of stark moral conflicts where whites represented good and nonwhites represented evil. Thus, even the Mexican Revolution provided the backdrop for the famous early actor Tom Mix. In his movies, such as *An Arizona Wooing* and *Along the Border,* the plot features rebels who are really bandidos in masquerade interested in kidnapping a beautiful blonde and providing her with a "fate worse than death." The plot required an Anglo hero to outwit them and give them a suitable punishment.

The Mexican Revolution also served as a vehicle for low comic mockery of the ethnicity and language of Hispanics. In *The Bad Man,* the villain boasts in a greaser action:

I keel ze man sis morning,
Heem call me dirty crook.

I keel some more zis noontime
And steal ess pocketbook (Roeder, 1971, 21).

Reformed in the end, this low-down cartoonlike bandido ultimately returns stolen cattle to their upright Anglo owners.

The Caballero's Way in 1914 marked the first of the Castilian caballero films, promoting personages such as Zorro, Don Arturo Bodega, and later the Cisco Kid. The formula for this cycle of films is very much within the convention of how American film treated ethnicity, since the heroes of these movies, by virtue of their pure Spanish ancestry and Caucasian blood, are able to put down the degraded mestizos who inhabit the Mexican California setting. The caballero cycle owed its inspiration to the North Carolina-born writer O. Henry (pen name of William Sidney Porter). The Cisco Kid was directly modeled on the writer's story "The Caballero's Way" (1907). O. Henry, who spent several years in Austin and Houston and went to jail for embezzlement of an Austin bank, was among the last of the American writers to present Mexicans in a totally prejudicial and stereotypical manner. His usual method when writing about the West, aptly reflected in the caballero film cycle, was

Henry Darrow as Zorro.

to spice up his stories with Spanish characters and motifs and to have pure-blooded Castilians thwart the mestizos and Indians. O. Henry's short stories, extremely popular at the time, were ideal for movies, since they were a type of formula fiction based on contrived plots, shallow characterization, strange turns of events, and surprise endings. Many of his stories were turned into films.

The gay caballero had a few minor variations. The Cisco Kid cycle was the most popular. It began in the silent era with films such as *The Caballero's Way* and *The Border Terror* (1919), and during the sound era large numbers were made. Warner Baxter starred (typically with Hollywood, at first Anglos did the role, Hispanics only later) in three such films from 1929 to 1939. César Romero did six between 1939 and 1941, Duncan Renaldo did eight between 1945 and 1950, and Gilbert Roland did six in 1946-1947 (Zinman, 1973). The Cisco character stressed the amorous side of the gay caballero, a charming brigand who prized a beautiful woman as a gourmet savors a vintage wine (from a contemporary perspective he was a plain and simple cad). Like his Anglo counterparts of similar Western series, his method was to ride in, destroy evil, and ride out, leaving a broken heart or two. If Cisco flirted with Anglo women, his status as a serial hero made marriage inconceivable—it would end the series! The formula worked tremendously well on television as well, since this syndicated serial garnered the largest receipts of its time.

There is one film in which the gay caballero actually gets the girl. The exception actually proves the point that Hispanics within the plot of the film (as well as in the film industry itself) can only succeed if they are willing to deny their own culture and identity in favor of Anglo mores. Cornel Wilde as Don Arturo Bodega, after joining Fremont's Freedom Forces in *California Conquest* and helping defeat the greaser scum of the Pacific province, proposes to his Anglo bride-to-be. The heroine mulls over the proposal by Don Arturo and responds, "You *would* give a lot to be an American, wouldn't you?"

Even before the demise of the gay caballero series, the popularity of this type of film was outstripped by the appearance of the dark lady films, particularly the Mexican spitfire in the person of Lupe Vélez, who elevated the stereotype from a minor role to star billing. Rita Hayworth also got her start this way. Born Margarita Carmen Cansino of a Spanish-born dancer father and his Ziegfield Follies partner Volga Haworth, she was discovered at 13 dancing at Mexican night spots in Tijuana and Agua Caliente. Her early movies, under the name Rita Cansino, included work in the "Three Mesquiteers" series (a takeoff on both the *Three Musketeers* and the mesquite plant), a seemingly unending cycle of movies featuring trios of cowboys. Everyone did them, including John Wayne, Bob Steele, Tom Tyler, Rufe Davis, Raymond Hatton, Duncan Renaldo, Jimmy Dodd, Ralph Byrd, Bob Livingston, Ray (Crash) Corrigan and Max Terhune. Rita played, of course, the dark lady, and she was notable in dancing a barroom "La Cucaracha" in *Hit the Saddle* (1937). It was that year that she married the shrewd businessman Edward Judson, who wised her up that being a Hispanic limited her to work as a cinematic loose woman. Under his guidance she changed her name to Rita Hayworth and was transformed from a raven-haired Hispanic dark lady into an auburn-haired sophisticate. By the early 1940s she attained Anglo recognition as the hottest of Hollywood's love goddesses." Her picture in *Life* magazine was so much in demand that it was reproduced in the millions and adorned the atomic bomb that was dropped on Bimini. Raquel Welch (formerly Raquel Tejada) had a similar career as a non-Hispanic and was therefore more acceptable as a love goddess to the mainstream.

Lupe Vélez went the other way and was dead at age 34. Born Guadalupe Vélez de Villalobos in San Luis Potosí, Mexico, in 1910, she was the daughter of an army colonel and an opera singer. Her arrival in Los Angeles was auspicious. She did eight movies in the "Mexican Spitfire" series, had a tempestuous romance with Gary Cooper, married Johnny Weismuller, with whom she had celebrated rows, and committed suicide, reportedly because she could not face the shame of bearing a child out of wedlock to a man she felt bore her no love (actor Harold Ramond). She was five months pregnant. Ironically, her last film was *Mexican Spitfire's Blessed Event* (1943) (Zinman, 1973).

Blood and caste reign supreme in the dark lady films just as with the gay caballero. If the dark lady, with her hip swinging and her amusing difficulties with the English language, encountered female Anglo competition, she surely went down to defeat. If, however, as in *Border Café*, there were no blondes in sight, she could eventually win her hero, as long as her "Hispanic" heritage was pure Spanish. In *Río Grande,* the dark lady is permitted to be of mixed American-Mexican ancestry—a hotpepper, cold cucumber combination of extremely erratic behavior advertised as "passionate, revengeful, brave, unreasonable and most cussedly lovable" (Pettit, 1980, 141). In a few films featuring only Mexican characters (*Love In Mexico, Papita, When Hearts Are Trumps*) (Pettit, 1980, 141), the dark lady usually rejects a rich but obese and corrupt Mexican suitor in favor of a poor but pure and handsome Indian or mestizo. Pettit (1980, 142) finds that

. . .by far the most popular type of dark lady is only half-Spanish and therefore must undergo a long apprenticeship before gaining the Saxon hero. These tests of loyalty invariably require the dark lady to desert her race, her native country, or both. Dozens of films exploit her precarious position. She may fall in love with a captured American and rescue him from imminent execution at the hands of the Mexican army. Perhaps she must turn against a member of her family—a brother, as in *Chiquita, the Dancer,* or a father, as in *His Mexican Sweetheart*—thus demonstrating both her loyalty to the hero and her allegiance to "the land of the free." Whatever the variations on the theme, the outcome is the same. The dark lady gains the hero only by renouncing her past.

In the early 1930s, Hollywood began to produce a number of gangster films, and as one might have predicted, there quickly appeared a greaser-gangster subgenre. The greaser gangster differed from the dark heroes of Prohibition and the Great Depression (such as James Cagney, George Raft, and the early Humphrey Bogart) in crucial ways. He was a treacherous coward, oily, ugly, crude, overdressed, unromantic, and with no loyalty even to his criminal peers. Leo Carrillo played the stereotype faithfully as a gambling, murdering, extorting, pimping, often border bandido in some twenty-five or thirty films. In *Girl of the Río* (1932), he attempted to steal the hand of the glamorous Dolores del Río, a cantina dancer called The Dove. That particular film earned a formal protest on the part of the Mexican government, especially because it portrayed Mexican "justice" as a reflection of who could pay the most for the verdict of their liking.

Another facet of representation has been animated cartoons with Hispanic figures. The Hanna-Barbera creation of mice Speedy González and Slowpoke Rodríguez can still be viewed on television today. These insensitive cartoon images are animated versions of the greaser buffoon, as earlier depicted in Cisco's sidekick. Slowpoke, for example, is the stereotypical sleepy, lazy Mexican. And while Speedy González is energetic enough, neither his frenetic activity accompanied by shouts of *¡Arriba, arriba, arriba!* nor his triumphs over cats and coyotes ever overcome his greaser image. Children may not be aware of it, depending on their age, but his name evokes countless obscene jokes focusing on Mexican sexuality.

Ironically, one of the most positive things to happen on behalf of Hispanics with respect to animation was the advent of World War II and the need to be sensitive to Hispanics during wartime. During World War II, Nelson D. Rockefeller's Office for Coordination of Inter-American Affairs asked Walt Disney to make a goodwill tour of Latin America in support of the Good Neighbor policy. The result was two films, *Saludos amigos* (1943), oriented toward Brazil, and *The Three Caballeros* (1945), set in Mexico. The latter film featured Panchito, a sombrero-wearing, pistol-packing rooster. A bit of the stereotype remained in Panchito, but he was a likable, fun-loving, and highly assertive type who showed *el pato Pascual* (a Hispanic Donald Duck) and José Carioca (a Brazilian parrot from *Saludos amigos)* the wonders of Mexico, such as piñata parties, Veracruzan jarochos (dances), posadas (Christmas pageant), and other celebrations of Mexican folklore. Mexico had never been given such a benign, positive image by Hollywood, wherein in the persons of Donald, José, and Panchito, the United States, Brazil and Mexico were three pals, none more equal than the others. Latin American audiences were enchanted by both of these films.

✳HISPANICS IN FILM DURING THE 1930s AND THE ERA OF SOCIAL CONSCIOUSNESS

As noted earlier, the Great Depression brought with it the gangster movie genre, which produced a new spate of negative Hispanic stereotypes. The depression also brought with it a new genre as well, the "Hollywood social problem film." For the first time, U.S. Hispanics were portrayed in a somewhat different, and occasionally radically different, light in these Hollywood movies.

The economic breakdown represented by the depression, the rise of fascism and other totalitarianism movements worldwide, the war against these political forms of oppression, and the idealistic vigor of the post-World War II years (up to the advent of McCarthyism) all fostered concern with social conditions, an impulse toward political change. The theater of Clifford Odets, the novels and screenplays of John Steinbeck, and the songs of Woody Guthrie all found a large public response to their criticism of American society, government, and business during the period.

This era of social consciousness also found reflection in Hollywood social problem films, which usually were produced in accordance with the conventions of the Hollywood Formula. The Hollywood conventions were that America is a series of social institutions that from time to time experience "problems" that, like those of an automobile, need to be tinkered with and corrected. For the most part, the films attacked such problems in order to inspire

limited social change or restore the status quo to an "ideal" level of efficiency. While the Hollywood social problem genre places great importance on the surface mechanisms of society, there is only an indirect or covert treatment of broader social values (those of the family, sexuality, religion, and so on) that function behind and govern the mechanisms.

Certainly the depiction of minorities improved markedly in films formulated according to the conventions of the social problem film. For example, anti-Semitism was grappled with, and indeed in 1947 in such films as *Crossfire* and *Gentleman's Agreement* the issue generated large box office returns. Just as anti-Semitism was the theme of 1947, the Negro became the problem of 1949 in films such as the Stanley Kramer production *Home of the Brave* (the central character in the Arthur Laurents book was a Jew; Kramer changed the character to a black), *Lost Boundaries,* and *Pinky* (directed by Elia Kazan), where the "problem" centers around mulattoes who can pass for white. The most unaffected and best realized of the cycle was *Intruder in the Dust (1949)*, adapted from the William Faulkner novel. In 1950, *No Way Out* introduced Sidney Poitier in what was to become his standard role as a noble and loyal black who endures and patiently waits for white society to recognize his rights rather than go out and demand them. To be too insistent would only threaten white society and thereby prolong racial inequality, or so the Hollywood convention went. Subsequent films followed the integrationist solution to the social problem, both reflecting growing integration in some American institutions, such as sports, and emphasizing the need for blacks, with infinite tolerance and patience, to prove themselves worthy: *The Jackie Robinson Story* (1950), *The Joe Louis Story* (1953), *Bright Victory* (1951), *The Well* (1951), and numerous others.

The social problem genre was the occasion for some atonement for the earlier deplorable treatment of the American Indian by the studios. *Massacre* (1931), *Broken Arrow* (1950), *Jim Thorpe—All American* (1951), and many others presented a positive depiction of the American Indian. The Japanese, who during the war had been demonized, were permitted back into the human race and depicted sympathetically by means of social problem films: King Vidor's *Japanese War Bride* (1952), *Go for Broke* (1951), *Bad Day at Black Rock* (1954), and *Three Stripes in the Sun* (1955) all dramatize the Japanese as victims of American bigotry.

In depicting Chicanos, Mexicans, and other Hispanics, the social problem vehicle produced some noteworthy if flawed films, but a review of the overall film production reveals that the positive depiction of

Hispanics was still the exception rather than the rule. *Bordertown* (starring Paul Muni in brownface and Bette Davis in her standard performance as a lunatic, 1935) is the first Hispanic social problem film. The central concern is not the oppression of Chicanos but rather who committed a murder. What social comment there is exists as a sedative against militancy by Hispanics. The filmic creation of Johnny Ramírez was certainly a more complex one than the standard Hollywood border type. Relative psychological complexity aside, the soothing conventions of the Hollywood Formula determine the finale. The film ends with Ramírez, disillusioned over the corruption and meanness of success, returning to his barrio home. He says his confession to the priest, prays with his mother, and all three walk down the church aisle. The padre asks, "Well, Johnny, what are you going to do now?" and Johnny gives the expected reply, "Come back and live among my own people where I belong." *Bordertown* hypothesizes that for a Chicano, success is fruitless and undersirable, that true virtue lies in accepting life as it is. Ramírez has learned the padre's lesson of patience and no longer holds impractical ambitions. *Bordertown* celebrates stoic acquiescence to the status quo and denigrates the aspiration for social change.

Despite the limitations of the social problem film, it is certainly true that psychologically complex and occasionally resolute and strong characters emerged from this genre. Among them are several Chicano protagonists in *Giant* (1956), including the proud and dedicated nurse María Ramírez, who experiences the racism of Texans; the family of Leo Mimosa, who is buried alive in a New Mexico cave in Billy Wilder's notable *The Big Carnival* (1951), which depicts a tragic act of God turned into a public relations event; and the women in *One-Eyed Jacks* (starring Marlon Brando, 1961), Katy Jurado and Pina Pellicer. Occasionally the strong and resolute character is also "evil," as in *Washington Masquerade* (1932), one of the earliest of the "political machine and country crusader" series of films that include *Washington Merry-Go-Round* (1932) and the Frank Capra series: *Mr. Deeds Goes to Town* and *You Can't Take it With You* (1938), *Mr. Smith Goes To Washington* (1939), and *Meet John Doe* (1941). *Washington Masquerade* proclaims that "the running of the U.S. has fallen into bad hands!" and proceeds to clearly identify whose hands they are—Hispanic ones! Unbelievable as this may be, given the lack of political visibility, much less power, of Hispanics in the real world in 1932, the villain is an oily, Latin-like (and hence un-American) lobbyist whose influence extends through all levels of government.

The socially conscious era of the Great Depression and its aftermath brought in a new wave of Anglo good samaritans who acted on behalf of innocent and defenseless Mexicans. There was some of this character development and plot in the silent era as well: *Mexicans on the Río Grande* (1914), *A Mexican's Gratitude* (1909), *Land Baron of San Tee* (1912). In films such as *Border G-Man* (1938), *Durango Valley Raiders* (1938), and *Rose of the Rancho* (1936), or for that matter in the pertinent films of Hopalong Cassidy, Gene Autry, The Lone Ranger, Roy Rogers, and Tex Ritter (*In Old Mexico,* 1938, *Song of Gringo,* 1936, *South of the Border,* 1939, and numerous others), the emphasis changes from the hero as implacable and brutal conqueror of greasers to the hero as implacable and devoted defender of Mexican rights, typically as he tramps touristlike through the exotic local Hispanic community, whether it be north or south of the border. Often the Anglo is fighting bad Mexicans on behalf of good, defenseless, passive Mexicans. The acts of these good samaritans strongly reinforce the stereotype of Mexicans as people who are unable to help themselves.

A variation of the white good samaritan acting on behalf of the Hispanic is developed in *Right Cross* (1950), a Ricardo Montalbán B picture, notable in that it depicts a love relationship between a Chicano male and a white female that is set in the contemporary time frame. Montalbán plays a "neurotic" boxer, bitter with Anglos, who resentfully spurns society, assuming that he is accepted only because he is a boxing champ and will be rejected as soon as he loses his crown. Johnny is cured of these so-called neurotic assumptions—which most Hispanics would view as highly accurate and normal—by his manager's all-American girl-next-door blonde daughter (June Allyson), who convinces him through her love and loyalty (she herself is a female stereotype in deep need of the women's movement) that the "gringos" really like him for himself. Two years later, Montalbán did another B-picture, *My Man and I,* which is vintage social problem formula, promoting the social cliché that if the oppressed are forebearing enough, the good that exists in American society will ultimately come to the rescue and overturn the bad. Here he depicts a fruit picker exploited by a nasty white boss who cheats him out of his wages and then has him arrested. Yet, throughout his ordeal, this upstanding Citizen Chicano (Noriega, 1991b) with the name of Chu Chu maintains his patriotic optimism (he even becomes a naturalized citizen), confident that everything will work out, which is precisely the case. Montalbán in this film is the standard friendly, happy Mexican whose faith in America is upheld when the injustice is rectified.

The most daring and best realized of the Hispanic-focused social problem films are *The Lawless* (1950) and *Salt of the Earth* (1954). The former was a low-budget independent released through Paramount, while the latter was made outside the studio system altogether by blacklisted artists, including writer Michael Wilson, producer Paul Jarrico, and director Herbert Biberman. It is precisely because neither was made within the confines of the studio that a profounder and more artistically elaborated interpretation of racial oppression is realized. In contrast to the usual treatment, which views racial prejudice against minorities as the product of a white sociopath or other such deranged troublemaker who is then blamed for inciting a mostly ingenuous but somewhat blameless populace, the lynch mob violence in *The Lawless* and the vicious labor strife in *Salt of the Earth* are deemed to be typically middle American. In these films, by stereotyping "spics" as lazy and no-good, people find a scapegoat for their hatreds and a rationale for injustice.

Both *The Lawless* and *Salt of the Earth* expose the deplorable working and living conditions of the Chicano community. The only employment opportunities open to Chicanos in *The Lawless,* directed by Joseph Losey and scripted by blacklisted Daniel Mainwarning using a pseudonym, are as fruit pickers earning subsistence wages. Because of their meager, unstable income, the only houses the workers can afford are flimsy shacks lacking indoor plumbing and located "on the other side of the tracks." *Salt* goes further and provides historical background on how the Chicanos" rights were violated by Anglo industrial interests. The community once owned the land, but the zinc company moved in, took over the property, and offered the Chicanos the choice of moving or accepting employment at low wages. They are forced to live in management-owned houses and buy at management-owned stores. The houses are shacks with poor sanitation and plumbing; the stores sell goods at inflated prices and entrap the workers in a state of continual debt. Safety provisions for the Chicano miners are lax, especially when compared to those in neighboring mines worked by whites. Whereas Anglo miners are allowed to work in pairs, the Chicanos must perform dangerous chores individually. When the Chicano workers protest to the company, the manager warns them that he will find others to replace them. "Who? A Scab?" asks a Chicano. "An American," retorts the manager.

In both films racism is clearly linked to social authority. In *The Lawless,* a peaceful dance in the Chicano community is invaded by white hoodlums and a rumble erupts. When the police arrive, eleven Mexicans and only one white are arrested. White business leaders unofficially intervene and the Chi-canos are forced to accept full responsibility for the violence. The newspapers then report that the incident was a battle between two gangs of "fruit tramps." In *Salt*, the police conspire with the mine owners to defeat the strike, disrupting the picket line and arresting one of the spokesmen. Snarling racial epithets, two deputies viciously assault the Chicano and then charge him with resisting arrest. Later, as the strike continues, the police evict the miners from their homes, carelessly damaging their possessions in the process.

The films' portrayal of the Chicano personality does not conform to the conventional Hollywood social problem film stereotype of the noble victim seeking only to gain acceptance from the white man. For example, in *Salt* the strikers are militant and articulate. They debate the issues at union meetings, thoroughly defining their goals and examining the nature of their enemies. Every tactic the company uses against the Chicanos they ultimately are able to thwart, and every cunning argument for a return to work they refute with solid reasoning.

The Lawless is a social problem film that deserves recognition in the history of Hispanic-focused cinema for its artistry, its ability to transcend the social cant of the genre, and the depth of its psychological analysis. *The Lawless* presents us with characters whose attitudes and behavior are as diversified as human experience. The characters range from the idealistic to the confused and fearful, to the destructively embittered, to the resigned and defeated. The Anglos are similarly varied. For example, some police officers are blatant racists but others offer genuine sympathy, even while they follow orders and arrest the Chicanos. The character of Prentiss, a well-meaning, guilt-ridden "liberal" businessman whose actions compromise Chicano youths, is an excellent depiction of the type. The film well evokes the effects of such double-edged benevolence.

Salt of the Earth, of course, has won a place in the international history of film not only as one of the best works on Chicano subjects but also as one of the most significant feminist films. Just as important, *Salt* is notable for the historical circumstances of its production. As Paul Jaricco puts it, it was "the first feature film ever made in this country of labor, by labor and for labor" (Rosenfelt, 1978, 93). The film had only the most limited theatrical distribution because of virulent attacks on it by Howard Hughes, the American Legion and others, but it has become a classic on university campuses and seems to grow yearly in importance. Williams (1980) points out that *Salt* as well as the Chicano film, *Alambrista!* (described later in this chapter) are artistically successful as depictions not of Hollywood "heroes" or stereotypes, but true Chicano types. Rather than individual triumphs of particular heroes, a genuine sense of Chicano reality is evoked through a documentary-style presentation of the social and historical context. Moreover, the vexed history of *Salt* is instructive, for this film serves to define the limits of the Hollywood social problem film and the consequences for filmmakers who would seek to overreach the boundaries of the Hollywood Formula. Film in the United States has not been a medium noted for its respect of artistic freedom.

Closely aligned to the social problem films were the historical "message" pictures such as Warners" Paul Muni biography cycle initiated with *The Life of Emile Zola* (1937), which devoted considerable attention to the Dreyfuss affair (the anti-Semitic element is only fleetingly alluded to, however). Two major films focused on Mexico emerged from this cycle, *Juárez* (1939) and the renowned *Viva Zapata!* (1952). *Juárez* featured Paul Muni in the title role, Bette Davis as Carlota, and John Garfield as a youthful Porfirio Díaz learning Lincolnesque democracy at the master's feet. This was another film marked by renewed efforts on the eve of the war by Franklin Roosevelt's administration to enhance the Good Neighbor policy (Woll, 1974). The film itself is not only a tribute to Juárez, but as Pettit (1980, 147) observes, "also stars Abraham Lincoln. His spirit haunts the film from start to finish. Juárez rarely appears in his office without a portrait of the Great Emancipator peering over his shoulder." The passage of the years has not been good to *Juárez*, but despite its faults, which include the cultural chauvinism of an omnipresent Lincoln, the film rises way above the standard degrading stereotypes of Hollywood. *Juárez* reflects relatively accurate documentation of Mexican history and society, and it impressed not only the American audience for which it was intended, but the Mexican public as well.

The clear masterpiece of the "message" biographies, *Viva Zapata!* (screenplay by John Steinbeck, direction by Elia Kazan, and starring Marlon Brando and Anthony Quinn) is also one of the best Hollywood Hispanic-focused films. The film is not free of problems and stereotypes, many of which relate to turning Zapata into a Hollywood-style "hero" at the expense of historical veracity; nevertheless, it is the most comprehensive and attentive Hollywood film ever produced about the Mexican Revolution—with the possible exception of *Old Gringo* (1988), which is not accurately a "Hollywood" film. One of the reasons for the enduring popularity of the film is precisely the nature and complexity of the message. The film is not only about power and rebellion but also about the ways of corruption and how easy it is for a social

movement to be debased. Zapata resists the corruption of his brother, the power-hungry Fernando, who betrays the revolution and goes to the side of Huerta, and he even resists the tendency of the *campesinos* to look for heroes or leaders to whom they can abdicate their own responsibilities. As Zapata says to his people shortly before he goes to his death in the film, "You've looked for leaders. For strong men without faults. There aren't any. . ..There's no leader but yourselves. . . a strong people is the only lasting strength" (Morsberger, 1973, 104-5).

In addition to *Viva Zapata!,* John Steinbeck did several other treatments of Hispanic material. His other contributions make for a mixed, but on balance, positive record. In 1941, he wrote the screenplay and collaborated with director/producer Herbert Kline to film *The Forgotten Village,* an artistic semidocumentary about science versus superstition in a small Mexican mountain village. This film, which was done outside the studio system, won numerous prizes as a feature documentary but played only in small independent art theaters because it did not benefit from studio distribution. In 1954, Steinbeck helped write the screenplay for *A Medal for Benny,* adapted from one of his paisano (rustic Hispanic) short stories. Starring Arturo de Córdova and Dorothy Lamour, this comedy treats the hypocrisy of town officials who exploit the posthumous awarding of the Congressional Medal of Honor to a brawling paisano. It contains many of the stereotypes of Hispanics that mark the novel *Tortilla Flat* (drunkenness, immaturity, brawling, but also a chivalric sense of honor), which was also adapted into a film (1942, starring Spencer Tracy, John Garfield, Hedy Lamarr, Akim Tamiroff, and Academy Award nominee for supporting actor Frank Morgan), but without Steinbeck's participation. *Benny* was a critical and box office success, and Steinbeck and his cowriter received Academy Award nominations. This film, however, is hardly his best effort at depicting Hispanics, although the Chicano actually wins the hand of an Anglo girl.

The 1948 production *The Pearl* was cowritten by Steinbeck, Emilio "El Indio" Fernández, and Jack Wagner (who also cowrote *Benny*). In addition, "El Indio" Fernández directed it, and it starred Pedro Armendáriz. *The Pearl* was in fact a Mexican movie, the first to be widely distributed (by RKO) in the United States. The film, an adaptation of the novella, is a well-made, sensitive, and genuine treatment of Mexican fishermen, as might be expected of the Mexican director and crew. The plot itself is a parable of a poor Mexican fisherman who learns that wealth brings corruption and death. The critical response and the box office receipts on this film were respectable, but it has not endured.

Even as significant Hispanic films of the social problem and historical message varieties were being produced, in parallel fashion other films of the earlier genres continued unabated. Enormous numbers of Westerns were produced in the period between the Great Depression and the civil rights movement. A small fraction of those containing significant Hispanic elements include the following, in chronological order, concentrating on the more notable Westerns: *Billy the Kid* (1930, King Vidor, director), *The Ox-Bow Incident* (1943, William Wellman, director; Anthony Quinn, Henry Fonda), *The Outlaw* (1943, Howard Hughes, director; Jane Russell), *My Darling Clementine* (1946, John Ford, director; Linda Darnell, Victor Mature), *Treasure of the Sierra Madre* (1947, John Huston, director; Humphrey Bogart, Alfonso Bedoya), *The Fugitive* (1947, John Ford director; Henry Fonda, Pedro Armendáriz, Dolores del Río), *The Furies* (1950, Barbara Stanwyck, Gilbert Roland), *Branded* (1951, Alan Ladd), *High Noon* (1952, Gary Cooper, Katy Jurado), *Rancho Notorious* (1952, Fritz Lang, director; Marlene Dietrich), *Ride Vaquero* (1953, Anthony Quinn), *Veracruz* (1954, Robert Aldrich, director; Gary Cooper, Sarita Montiel), *The Burning Hills* (1956, Tab Hunter, Natalie Wood), *The Sheepman* (1958, Glenn Ford), *The Left-Handed Gun* (1958, Arthur Penn, director; Paul Newman), and *Río Bravo* (1959, Howard Hawks, director; John Wayne, Dean Martin, Ricky Nelson).

Billy the Kid, The Outlaw, The Left-Handed Gun, and much later *Pat Garrett and Billy the Kid* (1973) form part of the cycle on that folk hero; each of these films perpetuates the legend of the Kid as the friend of oppressed Hispanos and the foe of the Anglo cattle barons.

Most of these films perpetuate the three major Hispanic stereotypes of the Western—dark lady, bandido, and buffoon. The more substantial dark lady roles of the Westerns of the 1930s through the 1950s have been assigned to mistresses of white gunmen. This is the case in such films as *My Darling Clementine, Veracruz,* and, above all, the classic *High Noon,* which is undoubtedly the best of these films. Katy Jurado, playing the role of Helen Ramírez, the former mistress of both the murderer and the marshal who sent the villain to prison, is memorable for her sensitive and original treatment of a Chicana. Unlike the shallow stereotyped Hispanic mistress who flits from man to man with no qualms, Helen Ramírez articulates the essential moral posture of the film: the "respectable" townspeople are hypocrites acting in bad faith and self-delusion; Marshal Kane must confront the murderer, even if he does it on his own in order to preserve his integrity.

While some opportunities for Hispanics to work in the film industry remained in the Western genre between the Great Depression and 1960, although even here many of the parts were played by Anglos, in other genres the Hispanic presence in fact was greatly diminished. Some World War II movies contained a bit part from time to time for a Hispanic character, presumably to promote patriotism, a sense of unity, and the brotherhood (not yet sisterhood in these self-satisfied times) of races against the Fascist menace. In *Bataan* (1943), Desi Arnaz is cast as Félix Ramírez, a "jitterbug kid" from California who promptly dies of malaria before anything significantly heroic transpires.

From time to time a Hispanic shows up in a boxing film. In *The Ring* (1952), a sequel to *The Lawless,* the main protagonist, Lalo Ríos, under the guidance of an Anglo manager is renamed Tommy Kansas. As a denatured Hispanic, things go pretty well at first. The manager eventually realizes that Lalo is not champion material, however, and ultimately that judgment is borne out. Lalo is defeated and resolves to leave the ring forever.

The courtroom trial genre can boast of the 1955 anti-Communist potboiler, *The Trial,* starring Glenn Ford as a law professor who successfully defends an innocent teenage Chicano accused of killing a white girl at a beach party. The absurd and highly insulting point of this film is to show how the Communists can score points with gullible people (in this case, the Chicano community) in order to spread their nefarious designs. It takes an Anglo hero to see that the ingenuous Chicanos are being misused and to set things straight.

❋DECLINE OF THE PRODUCTION CODE, EMERGENCE OF THE CIVIL RIGHTS MOVEMENT, AND NEW DEVELOPMENTS IN FILM: 1960s AND 1970s

The 1960s witnessed two important social developments that had significant impact on filmmaking: a liberalizing or loosening of social values, often referred to as the sexual revolution, and the emergence of the civil rights movement. The first phenomenon was a factor in the decline of the production code. Beginning in the 1960s, films became much bolder in their depiction of both sex, including interracial sex, and violence. However, this was a double-edged sword for Hispanics and other minorities because often they were cast in roles where their villainy was far more graphic and horrifying than the snarling but ineffective criminal or would-be rapist of blander times. In this sense, the stereotypes of many Hispanic characters were actually intensified by the relaxation of Hollywood moral codes. The 1960s and 1970s were marked by far more diversity in films but also by a group of films that featured even more serious, racially damaging put-downs of U.S. Hispanics. For example, the bandidos were often engaged in visually explicit and gory violence, and the torrid Hispanas were now engaged in R-rated loose sex with Anglo heroes or an occasional black superstud. The Hispano became the toy of Anglo producers, directors and audiences, all competing in the effort to create for Anglos ever more titillating and vicariously experienced films. As a result, new subgenres of film emerged, such as the fiendish group of plotters (particularly the group Western), featuring casual brutality and other actions that Anglos stereotypically and inaccurately identify under the rubric of "macho." The word "macho" entered the Anglo lexicon in a way that is ungrammatical in Spanish as an abstract quality in adjective form ("mucho macho" could be heard from time to time in bars or seen on T-shirts around the nation).

Moreover, by the 1960s there emerged the "good-bad bandidos" that "close the once unbridgeable gap between the heroic Saxon and the wicked greaser" (Pettit, 1980, 214). An example is Clint Eastwood in *The Good, the Bad, and the Ugly* (1967), where the Anglo hero teams up with the Mexican bandit, Tuco the Terrible (Eli Wallach), to steal gold. In this film, typical of the new, amoral Western, both Anglos and Mexicans are equally evil from the moral perspective and good becomes merely identified with technical skills such as a quick draw or creative thievery.

While in *The Good, the Bad, and the Ugly* the Anglo descends to the level of the stereotypical greaser, the converse is true in the extremely popular group Western, *The Magnificent Seven* (1960) (which spawned sequels: *Return of the Seven*, 1966, and the 1969 *Guns of the Magnificent Seven* in which two Mexican characters on the good samaritan team are uplifted along with the Anglos in their battle against Calavera, the bad bandido. Unfortunately for Hispanic actors in this film about the defense of a Mexican village against a Mexican bandit, the stereotypical greaser role is not even played by a Hispanic, but by Eli Wallach, who was to become the new Leo Carrillo, replaying the greaser-style performance in a number of Italian and Spanish-based spaghetti Westerns.

This trend toward amorality reached its extremes in the 1960s and 1970s films that revolved around the Mexican Revolution of 1910, taking the image of Hispanics and the understanding of those events a giant step backward from the peak that was established by *Viva Zapata!* In the amoral Westerns of director Sergio Leone—*A Fistful of Dollars* (1967), its sequel, *For A Few Dollars More* (1967), and *Duck, You Sucker* (1972)—the viewer is given no moral guidelines to measure or judge the revolution. Both the *federales* and the rebels are repulsive. If the former are sadistic, pretentious, class-conscious, and stupid, the latter are sadistic, filthy, promiscuous, contemptuous, and stupid.

The cycle of Pancho Villa movies displays the same sort of denigration. The first Villa film of the sound era, *Viva Villa!* (1934), presented the revolutionary hero "as a cross between Robin Hood and the Marquis de Sade" (Pettit, 1980, 220). Subsequent films, *Villa!* (1958) and *Villa Rides* (1968), stray little from this general depiction. The latest film to depict Villa, *Old Gringo* (1989), based on a novel by Mexican novelist Carlos Fuentes and produced by Jane Fonda with the avowed intention of injecting realism into the relationship between the United States and Mexico, stands in marked positive contrast to the rest of the cycle.

Set against the simplistic, amoral standard of most of the other Westerns of these years, the work of Sam Peckinpah, particularly *The Wild Bunch* (1969), *Pat Garrett and Billy the Kid* (1973), and *Bring Me the Head of Alfredo García* (1974), developed a more sophisticated view of Hispanics, particularly in the context of the Mexican Revolution in the case of *The Wild Bunch*. In that film the two Mexico's of the revolution are rendered in the contrast between Angel, the morally pure *villista* who represents Mexican village life, and Mapache, the degenerated revolutionary. In a film that is, ironically, one of the most violent on record, Angel occupies a pivotal role in that by his Christlike example he turns the drifting, amoral Anglo mercenaries to good purpose and sacrifice, thus redeeming them. *The Wild Bunch* is one of the most memorable films of the period, combining outsized violence and explicit sex with a certain sense of high moral purpose and interethnic camaraderie. In its own way, it is a distinctively realized combination of the decline of the moral code and the rise of civil rights.

Out of this milieu of loosened production censorship and increased sensitivity to civil rights also emerged the figure of the Hispanic avenger. This figure was modeled on the example of the black avenger. Both of these aggressive, "superstud" types reflected growing Hollywood awareness of the changing population distribution of its market, namely that ever-increasing percentages of blacks and Hispanics were attending the movies. Although this demographic fact provided the underpinning for the "superstud" phenomenon, it does not explain the reason for the sudden, inciting creation of the genre or its content. For an explanation of the mechanisms that triggered the black and Hispanic "superstud" characters, the climate of civil rights legislation and the changes in prevailing cultural attitudes in the 1960s and 1970s must be examined.

Periodically in the late 1950s and early 1960s, *Variety* and other trade journals took note of the "growing Negro audience," which was "now a sizable segment of film patronage as a whole" (*Variety,* May 9, 1956, 5; May 8, 1957, 3). These observations made little difference at the time. In 1963, however, in the midst of the civil rights movement and after the National Association for the Advancement of Colored People (NAACP) abandoned mere persuasion and threatened to take legal and economic action against the industry, blacks began to play policemen, civil servants, students, and workers both in features and in movies and shows filmed and taped for television. Chicano scholar Carlos Cortés (1983, 1984) has documented a similar practice of giving bit parts to Hispanos.

Goaded by the civil rights movement and sensing that the mood of black militancy could be used to its advantage in the creation of a new film type, Hollywood responded with the "superspade" formula (Leab, 1975), and thus was born a new form, the "blaxploitation" film. An NAACP official condemned the transformation "to supper-nigger as just another form of cultural genocide," but black moviegoers, finding the superspade an emotionally satisfying tonic to the patient black represented by Sidney Poitier features, turned out en masse and "produced the first gold mine in years for the struggling industry" (*Newsweek,* October 23, 1972, 74).

It was Sidney Poitier's success that had brought home to filmmakers just how significant a percentage of the moviegoing public was black: in 1967 Poitier was one of the top five box office draws in the United States. According to a 1967 estimate, although blacks represented only about 15 percent of the American population, they accounted for roughly 30 percent of the moviegoing audience in the nation's cities, where the biggest movie theaters were located. As one industry executive summed up the situation, "the black population of this country comprises a much larger proportion of the movie picture audience than its proportion of our total population would indicate" (*Variety,* August 26, 1970, 5). Once the industry grasped this fact, filmmakers began to reappraise and revise their product.

The new, aggressive, and hip black audience found its first star in Jim Brown, the football star, who ironically but not surprisingly often scored macho coups at the expense of Hispanics and American Indians. In *Río Conchos* (1964), Brown refuses to repay Indian brutality in kind with the terse comment that "doing like they do, don't make it right," and in *100 Rifles* (1969) he beds Raquel Welch, who in this early example of explicit interracial sex is treated as white in the movie's promotion, but who turns out to be a half-caste Mexican in the actual production itself.

When Brown's career declined, partly due to personal problems, other black superstuds emerged, including Ossie Davis in *The Scalphunters* (1968); Roscoe Lee Browne in *The Liberation of L.B. Jones* (1969); Raymond St. Jacques in *If He Hollers Let Him Go* (1968); Godfrey Cambridge in *Cotton Comes to Harlem* (1970) and *Come Back, Charleston Blue* (1972, a sequel to *Cotton*); Melvin Van Peebles in *Sweet Sweetback's Baadasssss Song* (1971, a film that transcends the "blaxploitation" formula both in pretension and achievement); Richard Roundtree in *Shaft* (1971); *Super Fly,* directed by Gordon Parks, Jr. (1972, the most financially profitable of the genre); Calvin Lockhart in *Melinda* (1972); Fred Williamson in *Black Caesar* (1973); and many others.

The black superstud films, despite the early Jim Brown vehicles that included Westerns and war roles, such as *The Dirty Dozen,* were mostly set in the black urban milieu. The same market considerations—drawing a new ethnic group to the box office, civil rights issues, and increased Hispanic militancy in the United States affected the creation of the Hispanic macho, whose character was set in the Western genre. For example, Jorge Rivero in *Río Lobo* helps John Wayne bring Arizona land grabbers to justice with a dazzling combination of gunplay and Oriental martial arts. The Mexican-American deputy sheriff played by Burt Lancaster in *Valdez is Coming* (1971) singlehandedly defeats a brutal cattle baron and his army. The bizarre plot of *Mr. Majestyk* (1974) carries the super-Mex formula to absurd lengths. The hero, half-Mexican, half-Slavic Vincent Majestyk (Charles Bronson) keeps the Mafia out of his melon patch by hiring Mexican migrants instead of the American winos who are thrust upon him by labor racketeers.

There were sporadic examples of Hispanic avenger types during the silent period, although not usually directed against Anglos but rather against *federales* of the Mexican government. The first major appearance of the type is in the Western *The Ox-Bow Incident* (1943). Here Anthony Quinn plays a Mexican who is hanged along with two Anglos for murdering a Nevada cowboy. Of the three, he is the only one to die with his dignity and honor intact, subverting the stereotypical role of the cowardly and inept greaser. These pre-civil rights examples, however, have a quite different tone about them, primarily because they were pitched to a non-Hispanic audience. This is the case as well of the films *Death of a Gunfighter* (1969) and *The Outrage* (1964), which also depict assertive Hispanics, even though they are not part of the Hispanic exploitation model. In *Death of a Gunfighter* the aging white marshall (Richard Widmark) has become an embarrassment to a prospering Kansas town that no longer needs him. In the final, shocking scene, the shopkeepers and bankers gun him down, leaving his Chicana mistress without a husband after a last-minute wedding ceremony.

However, in the figure of Lou Trinidad (played by John Saxon) in *Death of a Gunfighter* we are confronted with a different sort, a Chicano survivor, a Mexican sheriff who knows his "place" and adopts the necessary public servility to make his way. He publicly tolerates epithets like "greaseball" and "Mex" but exacts his private physical revenge on the name-callers. Trinidad is a cautious but brave loner caught between the Anglo power structure and the oppressed Mexican populace. *The Outrage* is a remake of the classic Japanese film, *Rashomon,* and features Paul Newman as a Mexican who murders the husband and rapes the wife. Newman's character observes that if he were freed, he would wreak revenge on his oppressors; this is a direct threat to the Anglo social order that was not tolerated in earlier films, but it probably is merely an artifact of attempting to transplant a samurai story to the U.S. Southwest.

The Hispanic avenger type appears far less frequently than his black counterpart. One of the reasons is that the genre has diminished greatly since 1974, which was a bust year, and the Hispanic version got off to a much later start. Also, the Hispanic market, particularly in the late 1960s, was much smaller than the black market. An additional reason is that neither the black nor brown versions of the genre attracted white audiences, making for a limited run of this type of film. Finally, the genre itself was initially successful for its novelty value, but it soon became boring and wearing even for the black or Hispanic moviegoers to whom the films were directed.

Even with the emergence of the Hispanic avenger, which somewhat reflected the atmosphere of the civil rights movement, and the emergence of a more sexually titillating dark lady, which primarily reflected the relaxation of the Hollywood production code, the film industry continued to grind out Westerns with buffoons and bandidos. *The Sheepman* (1958) provided a comic sidekick to the Anglo played by Glenn Ford, and in *Río Bravo* (1959) we view the antics of Carlos and Consuela, a comedy couple. In *The Train Robbery* (1973), John Wayne's gun quickly turns a Mexican railroad engineer from a "¡No! ¡No!" stance to a "¡Sí! ¡Sí!"

As pointed out earlier, the role of the bandido took

Carmen Miranda.

on certain variations that reflected Hollywood's exploitation of attitudinal changes. On the one hand, we are confronted with the straight evil bandido, the continuation of the type from the earliest period, except that with the relaxation of the Hollywood morality codes this character suddenly became more "competent." Whereas the earliest version was usually a tame utterer of incomplete curses or hisses who was incapable of really delivering evil, at least on screen—he might tie the girl to the railroad track or inside a house he would set on fire, but the deed was never consummated—the new breed practiced mayhem, sadism, and sex aplenty. Anthony Quinn in *Ride Vaquero!* (1953) enjoys killing men and raping women and maims a cattleman for life in a sadistic shooting. The earlier, classic performance of Alfonso Bedoya and his gang, who brawl over their victims" boots in *Treasure of the Sierra Madre* (1947) is another of the same variety. A xenophobic variation on the same theme was John Wayne's (director and star) *The Alamo* (1961). This film, which takes egregious liberties with the facts, not only depicts Mexicans as violent and inept, but was promoted by means of a shamelessly ultrapatriotic advertising campaign. In 1969, Hollywood took another crack at the Alamo

The late Freddie Prinze.

various U.S. cultures and ethnicities primarily reflected English-speaking groups, not Spanish or other non-English-speakers. In the increased attention to multiethnicity, the Hispanic variety played a limited role. The phenomenon of increased multiculturalism in plots and acting styles combined with yet another factor to the detriment of hispanidad in film, namely, the expectation of increased sexuality on the part of actors and actresses, irrespective of their culture. In earlier decades the "carnal" tended to be the province of Hispanic Latin lovers and dark ladies. Or as Freddie Prinze once joked, "If you're Hispanic, man, they think you really *got* something downstairs" (Hadley-García, 1991, 201). While this expectation produced degrading stereotypes, it also provided considerable work for Hispanic actors and actresses, who consistently had roles exposing their "hot-blooded" nature. In contrast to the earlier traditions of Anglos and some of the other ethnicities who were expected to be aloof, glacial, dispassionate, and so on, the film expectations of the 1960s to this day cultivated unabashed carnality and hot-bloodedness on the part of all actors and actresses, whatever their national origin.

For better (reducing stereotypes) or worse (reduc-

with *Viva Max*, starring Peter Ustinov as a bumbling Mexican buffoon who retakes the historic site from the Anglos in contemporary times. This film, without a single Hispanic in any significant role, was hardly as offensive as the Wayne vehicle, and pitted inept Americans against incompetent Mexicans. In contrast to the patriotic froth associated with *The Alamo,* however, the latter film inspired minor demonstrations in several cities where it played, a good index of the progress of the civil rights movement over the 1960s.

Beginning in the 1960s and intensifying in the 1970s, changes in American society and consequently American film and television made the roles of dark lady and Latin lover considerably less important. One of these changes related to ethnicity. Particularly in the 1970s, Hollywood and other media centers rediscovered the significance of ethnicity, both from the point of view of plot and of box office. However, the primary ethnicity that was cultivated was the Italian American, and secondarily the Jewish American, Slavic, and Afro-American. This period witnessed the rise to stardom of such actors as Robert De Niro, Sylvester Stallone, Al Pacino, Barbra Streisand, and others. However, the cultivation of

Erik Estrada, star of "CHiPS."

ing acting opportunities for Hispanics), the conventions of dark lady and Latin lover waned, and in the 1970s the Hispanic community was successful in eliminating such visual media stereotypes as the Frito Bandito, a version of the film greaser, and Chiquita Banana, loosely based on the persona of Carmen Miranda. Also, Bill Dana, creator of the comic bellhop and dim-witted speaker of fractured English José Jiménez (who was the most popular Hispanic TV character of the 1960s among the general public, surpassing Desi Arnaz and Duncan Renaldo's *Cisco Kid)*, agreed at the 1970 meeting of the Congress of Mexican-American Unity to shelve this persona. In addition to eliminating stereotypes, some progress was made on television on behalf of more positive characters, notably Linda Cristal, who debuted on the series *High Chaparral* (1967). Speaking in 1982 about her role in the series as a powerful Hispana, Cristal remarked, "I was very conscious of being a role model. I received countless letters from the Spanish-speaking fans" (Hadley-García, 1990, 199). In the comic mode, the period marked the rise of Charo in a familiar role of flake and spouter of malaprops; Liz Torres, who began on variety shows featuring Melba Moore, Clifton Davis, and Ben Vereen, then did the "Phyllis" and other TV series; and the brilliant Puerto Rican comedian Freddie Prinze (who killed himself, possibly accidently, at the age of 22), who starred with Jack Albertson on *Chico and the Man.* Another Puerto Rican who got his opportunity through a TV series, "CHiPS," was Erik (Enrique) Estrada.

Actresses who achieved considerable status but were not generally known to be partially Hispanic until they appeared "as presenters or recipients on the nationally televised Golden Eagle Awards show devised by the pro-Hispanic Hollywood organization NOSOTROS" (Hadley-García, 1991, 201) were Lynda Carter of the TV series "Wonder Woman," Catherine Bach of "The Dukes of Hazard," and Victoria Principal of "Dallas" fame.

The civil rights period beginning in the 1960s also marked an important change in hiring patterns in the film industry with respect to directors, cameramen, and other production people. For the first time, an effort was made to bring Hispanics into production, and it was this cadre of professionals who were the primary group to go on to make U.S. Hispanic films (see the following section, "The Emergence of U.S. Hispanic Films"). However, the introduction of Hispanic avenger films, group Westerns, and other Hispanic-focused subgenres usually did not carry with it more work for U.S. Hispanic actors. The 1960s and 1970s were not particularly advantageous for Hispanics in acting roles, since more often than not, non-

Hispanic actors were awarded the roles of Hispanic characters. For example, George Chakiris and John Saxon got the Hispanic leading parts in *West Side Story* and *Death of a Gunfighter,* and Burt Lancaster, Charles Bronson, and Paul Newman were the respective leads in *Valdez is Coming, Mr. Majestyk,* and *The Outrage. The Young Savages* (1961), starring Burt Lancaster, was about gang war between Italians and Puerto Ricans, the latter played by non-Hispanic actors. *The Professionals* (1966) featured Claudia Cardinale as a "María" and Jack Palance as Jesús Raza, who kidnaps her and sweeps her off her feet. *Villa Rides* (1968) featured Yul Brynner as Pancho Villa and Charles Bronson, and Herbert Lom in the other significant Hispanic roles. *Che!* (1969) starred Omar Sharif and Jack Palance in the incongruous roles, respectively, of Che Guevara and Fidel Castro. *Night of the Iguana* (1964), starring Richard Burton, Deborah Kerr, and Ava Gardner all in Anglo roles, exemplified the Hollywood trend of filming on Latin location, but mostly for the purpose of local color, preferring stories reflecting non-Hispanic characters.

Despite successes in having some stereotypes eliminated, such as those described earlier, they remained abundant. in addition to the more intensive violence and sadism of Hispanic characters prevalent in the Westerns of the period, gang films also abounded during the 1960s and 1970s. *West Side Story* (1961, director, Robert Wise, with Natalie Wood, Richard Beymer, George Chakiris, Rita Moreno), the cinematic adaptation of the Broadway musical, was a major achievement of the period. Unfortunately, only one Hispanic, Rita Moreno, had a major role in the film. The updating of Romeo and Juliet had a major influence on the Broadway musical, but in drawing attention to Hispanic gangs, its greatest impact appears to have been in helping to turn the juvenile delinquent or gang film away from blacks primarily (for example, *The Blackboard Jungle,* 1955, Glenn Ford, Sidney Poitier) and also in the direction of Hispanics. It was probably a factor in a spate of either Hispanic-focused exploitation, juvenile delinquent or gang films or films with other premises that brought in Hispanic gang members for their recognition value, such as *The Pawnbroker* (1965), *Change of Habit* (1969), *Badge 373* (1973), *Assault on Precinct Thirteen* (1976, a multiethnic gang, director, John Carpenter), *Boardwalk* (1979), *Boulevard Nights* (1979, Richard Yñiguez, Danny de la Paz), *Walk Proud* (1979, featuring blue-eyed Robby Benson in contact lenses as a Hispanic), *The Exterminator* (1980), and many others. With the aid of feverish media attention dedicated to gangs, the cycle has been running strong to the present day. Other films of

The Sharks face off with the Jets in *West Side Story*.

the same general stripe did not single out Hispanics but merely included them among other various and sundry riffraff: *Dirty Harry* (1971), *The French Connection* (1971), *The New Centurions* (1972), *The Seven-Ups* (1973), *Magnum Force* (1974), and *Death Wish* (1974).

The urban violence (primarily juvenile gang) film has been exploitative of Anglo willingness to pay for explicit sex and brutality—both premeditated and mindless—and the pleasures of vicariously induced but movie-house-controlled fear of the alien. These films play upon the baser assumptions about Hispanic youth and mostly do damage to racial relations in our society. To add insult to injury, Hispanic actors do not even get the top parts in these films. *Boulevard Nights* did, however, rise above the pap. While the film is not without its defects, particularly an inaccurate understanding in some respects of Chicano mores by the Japanese-American screenwriter, Desmond Nakomo, it does have an all-Latino cast, reasonably successful use of Chicano and pachuco dialect, and a serious theme and plot development that includes Hispanic violence against Hispanics—an all-too-real phenomenon of gang life. It deserves recognition, within B movie limitations, as one of the

better Hollywood achievements in Chicano-focused film.

In *Badge 373* (1973), a minor follow-up to *The French Connection,* Robert Duvall singlehandedly fights the mafia as well as Puerto Ricans who are blamed for all sorts of evil and wrongdoing. Whatever might be thought of *Colors* (1988), also starring Duvall, it represents a major advance in the Hollywood understanding of gang psychology. (John Singleton's *Boyz in the Hood*, 1991, and Joseph Vásquez's *Hangin" With The Homeboys*, 1991, are in a class by themselves, but essentially were created outside of the Hollywood system, although Columbia distributed the former and the latter was released through New Line Cinema.) *The Warriors* (1978), although its artistry demands more respect than most of the others, primarily perpetuates the usual stereotypes.

The use of "bean," a more chic variety of the older dysphemism "beaner," came back into vogue. The World War II film *Midway* (1976) included a Hispanic character nicknamed Chili Bean. Similarly, *Freebie and the Bean* (1974) provided Alan Arkin work as the Bean; this film led to a television series with the same title, but an actual Hispanic, Hector Elizondo, got the

A scene from *Boulevard Nights*.

opportunity to play the Bean. The 1971 comedy *Bananas* is in a totally different realm. Even though it embraces every imaginable banana republic stereotype, it renders them in superb parodies, typically turning them inside out, as it does many Anglo institutions and worthies, including the court system, the FBI, television news, J. Edgar Hoover, and Howard Cosell. Wyatt Cooper describes the film this way: "*Bananas* would be unbelievable or offensive were it not so grounded in the ludicrous truth. . ..Its steady flow of jokes, sight-gags and parody make it one of the funniest pictures within memory" (Hadley-García, 1991, 218).

Revolution in Latin America became a common topic of films in the 1970s. Curiously enough, in contrast to the serious and solemn 1980s (*Salvador, Prisoner Without a Name, Cell Without a Number, Old Gringo, Latino, Missing, Under Fire, Romero,* and so on), many of these films were screwball comedies, a long-standing Hollywood genre now attached to a new environment. In addition to Woody Allen's *Bananas* (1971), there was *The In-Laws* (1979), starring Peter Falk. Both the Valdez brothers, Luis and Daniel, had parts in the Richard Pryor comedy *Which Way Is Up?* (1977). In a more common mode, *Viva*

Max! appeared in 1969, describing, in opera-buffa style, the Chicano retaking of the Alamo. When Hollywood attempted contemporary Latin American revolutionary topics or other Latin American material in a serious fashion during this period, as in *Che* (1969, Omar Sharif, Jack Palance) and *Night of the Iguana* (1964, director, John Huston, with Richard Burton, Deborah Kerr, Ava Gardner) the results were more uninspired than the comic attempts. *Iguana* was particularly disappointing in its turning of the admittedly minor Mexican characters into mere cut-out figures of sexuality.

✳ HISPANICS WHO FIGURED IN THE MOVIES OF THE 1960s AND 1970s

Anthony Quinn was one of very few Hispanic actors whose career expanded during the 1960s and 1970s. In fact, Quinn was able to move away from his Latin image of the 1950s (for example, *Viva Zapata, Ride Vaquero!*) and was permitted to do a variety of exotics. He had a role in the hit *The Guns of Navarone* (1961), played a biblical character in *Barrabas* (1961), an Arab in *Lawrence of Arabia* (1962), the title role in *Zorba The Greek* (1964), a Russian pope in *The Shoes* of the Fishermen (1968), an Italian in *The Secret of Santa Vittoria* (1969), and back to a Greek in *The Greek Tycoon* (1978). He also had Hispanic roles in *Guns for San Sebastian* (1968) and *The Children of Sánchez* (1978).

Cantinflas (Mario Moreno) played in *Pepe* as a manual laborer who pined unsuccessfully for the blonde. The film was a disaster and he returned to Mexican film. César Romero, who had a cameo role in *Pepe*, continued to obtain roles, appearing in *Seven Women from Hell* (1961), *Two on a Guillotine* (1964), *Sergeant Deadhead* (1965) and *A Talent for Loving* (1969). However, he achieved more recognition in the 1960s as the Joker in the TV "Batman" series. In the 1970s, he did two formula Disney comedies, *The Computer Wore Tennis Shoes* (1970) and *The Strongest Man in the World* (1975).

Rita Hayworth did few films in the 1960s and 1970s, none that were enduring: *The Money Trap* (1966), *Road to Salina* (1970), and *The Wrath of God* (1972), her last film.

Anthony Quinn in *The Children of Sánchez*.

Ricardo Montalbán played a European duke in *Love is a Ball* (1963), an Italian lover in *Sweet Charity* (1969), and appeared in some of the Hollywood *Planet of the Apes* sequels, but his career did not pick up until he starred in the long-running "Fantasy Island" (1978-84).

Fernando Lamas did some directing and appeared in a few less than memorable films, such as *The Violent Ones* (1967), *100 Rifles* (1969), and, the best of the lot, *The Cheap Detective* (1978), a parody of *The Maltese Falcon,* in which he had a supporting role. Gilbert Roland's best role of the 1960s was as an American Indian in John Ford's last Western and only pro-Indian film, *Cheyenne Autumn* (1963), costarring Ricardo Montalbán and Dolores del Río. In the 1970s, he appeared in *Islands in the Stream* and *The Black Pearl* (both 1977).

Martin Sheen debuted on film in *The Incident* (1967), about drunken hoods who terrorize New York subway passengers, and went on to star status, reprising his stage role in *The Subject Was Roses* (1968), about a young veteran's troubled relationship with his parents, in the anti-war film *Catch-22* (1970), and in a television landmark, the first to convey a homosexual theme, *That Certain Summer* (1972). He did another notable TV film, *The Execution of Private Slovik* (1974), about the only American soldier (World War II) executed by the American government since the Civil War, as well as *Badlands* (1974), about a killing spree in the 1950s, *The Cassandra Crossing* (1977), and the notable Vietnam War film directed by Francis Ford Coppola, *Apocalypse Now* (1979).

Hector Elizondo, who had previously won an Obie for his role as a Puerto Rican locker room attendant in the off-Broadway play *Steambath,* made his debut in 1971 with Burt Lancaster in *Valdez Is Coming*. He also did *The Taking of Pelham 1-2-3* (1974), about the hijacking of a New York City subway train, and *Cuba* (1979), an adventure/love story set against the fall of Batista.

Dolores del Río's first Hollywood role since the 1940s was the 1960 Elvis Presley film *Flaming Star*, in which she played an American Indian mother. Recalling her roles during this period, she observed that Hispanics, if they worked at all, tended to play native Americans because Westerns remained popular in the 1960s. On the other hand, "the few Hispanic characters in Hollywood were often played by Hollywood stars, even less suitable ones like Paul Newman or Janet Leigh" (Hadley-García, 1991, 168). For example, Chita Rivera played Dick Van Dyke's secretary girlfriend in the original Broadway production of *Bye Bye Birdie,* but the 1963 film featured Janet Leigh in a "Mexican wig" as the character of Rose de Leon. In addition to *Flaming Star,* Dolores del Río had roles in *Cheyenne Autumn* (1964) and *The Children of Sánchez* (1978), her last film.

Katy Jurado played character roles in *One-Eyed Jacks* (1961), starring and directed by Marlon Brando, *Barabbas* (1961), and *A Covenant With Death* (1967), subsequently moving into television films. In the 1970s she had roles in *Pat Garrett and Billy the Kid* (1973) and *The Children of Sánchez* (1978).

Rita Moreno, to date the only Hispanic actress to win an Oscar, got her award for her supporting role in *West Side Story* (1961), which unfortunately promoted the careers of mostly non-Hispanics, including Natalie Wood and George Chakiris in the roles of Hispanic characters. Moreno went on to do a supporting role in an adaptation of Tennessee Williams's *Summer and Smoke* (1961), but then courageously turned her back on the opportunity to do "looney Latina" roles, observing, "[I]t's really demeaning after you've won the Oscar to be offered the same role over and over again. They only wanted me to drag out my accent-and-dance show over and over again. And boy, I was offered them all—gypsy fortune tellers, Mexican spitfires, Puerto Ricans. . ." (Hadley-García, 1991, 174). Moreno did not play in Hollywood again until cast by Marlon Brando as the leading lady of the unsuccessful *The Night of the Following Day* (1969). She went on to appear in *Carnal Knowledge* (1971) in a cameo role in the periodic role of a Slavic hooker in "The Rockford Files" TV series, and in a memorable role of a no-talent Puerto Rican singer in the bathhouse comedy *The Ritz* (1976).

Rosenda Monteros, a Mexican actress who had been in *Villa!* (1958), had a supporting role in *The Magnificent Seven* (1960) and in *She* (1965) as second female lead to Ursula Andress. In 1969, she had a role in the film *Popi,* starring Alan Arkin as a Puerto Rican widower struggling to support his young sons. The film was able to spawn a brief TV series that starred Hector Elizondo.

Raquel Welch gained considerable attention for her role in *Fantastic Voyage* (1966) and then attained star status with such films as *One Million Years B.C.* (1966), *100 Rifles* (1969), *Myra Breckinridge* (1970), *Bluebeard* (1972), and *The Three Musketeers* (1974).

Barbara Carrera, a Nicaraguan model, made her debut in the 1970s with *The Master Gunfighter* (1975)

and went on to do *Embryo* (1976) and *The Island of Dr. Moreau* (1977).

✳ HOLLYWOOD FILMS SINCE 1980

The period from 1980 to the present has been a relatively exhilarating one for Hispanics in the film industry, especially over the last few years, primarily because of three sets of closely interrelated events or trends. The first is the increased appreciation of the importance of Hispanic culture and the Hispanic population in the United States. It became generally understood that demographics projected that Hispanics were to become the largest minority group in the United States some time early in the twenty-first century. This underlying fact of population power and consequently political, economic, and cultural importance spurred all sorts of film, television, and video initiatives for and by U.S. Hispanics. It even underlay their national promotion, as exemplified by an extended article in *Time* magazine that featured Edward James Olmos on its cover, the first time in memory that any U.S. Hispanic, much less an actor and filmmaker, had achieved such recognition.

A second factor, somewhat encouraged by the Hollywood appreciation of U.S. Hispanic box office potential, was the emergence of a considerable number of actors and filmmakers who attained star status or national recognition during the contemporary period. These included Edward James Olmos, Raúl Juliá, Andy García, and Emilio Estévez. Similarly, film figures who had labored under less recognized conditions in the 1970s also made quantum leaps with respect to their weight in the film industry, including Moctezuma Esparza, Luis Valdez, Ricardo Mestre, and Martin Sheen.

Finally, with more interest in U.S. Hispanic themes and market penetration and more power and recognition of U.S. Hispanic actors and filmmakers, came more control of product within Hollywood. For the first time, a Hispanic Ricardo Mestre of Disney, was to run a major studio. Similarly, Moctezuma Esparza coestablished Esparza/Katz Productions, raising tens of millions of dollars for a variety of projects, some but not all Hispanic-focused. Edward James Olmos, Andy García, Joseph P. Vásquez, and the comedian Paul Rodríguez all entered the film production business, with considerable diversity in their level of affiliation with or independent from traditional Hollywood sources of backing. Both the number of production outlets and either realized or pending film deals and the number of actors and other filmmakers with national recognition has never been greater, surpassing even a few "silver" years of the silent period when Latin lovers and hot-blooded

Andy García in *The Godfather, Part III*.

Latinas were in great demand, albeit with virtually no control over their acting roles. On the other hand, it should be noted that Afro-American filmmakers made even greater strides during the current period, led by Spike Lee, John Singleton, and many others.

The current period also marked the strong emergence of a phenomenon called Hispanic Hollywood by the mass media. Although Chicano films such as *Zoot Suit* had been released by the mainstream industry before, as Chon Noriega (1991a, 55) points out, between the summer of 1987 and spring 1988 Hollywood released four films that depicted the Chicano experience: *La Bamba* (The Bamba Dance, 1987), *Born in East L.A.* (1987), *The Milagro Beanfield War* (1987), and *Stand and Deliver* (1988). The Hispanic directors, producers, and writers who made these films had typically been in very junior roles in the film and television industry and then began to work as principals in the conceptualization, development, and execution of alternative, independent U.S. Hispanic films, such as *Seguín, Alambrista!* (Fence Jumper), and *Once in a Lifetime*. Now they entered the mainstream as well (although not necessarily giving up their commitments to independent, alternative films), bringing Hollywood production values to the creation of strong Hispanic images that also had (or at least were intended to have) box office appeal and arranging for distribution through mainstream outlets. The cross-pollination and collaboration inherent in the Hispanic Hollywood phenomenon ran the gamut from *The Milagro Beanfield War*—where Anglos, like Robert Redford, carried most of the picture (the script itself being based on the novel by Anglo connoisseur of New Mexican culture John Nichols) and consequently Hispanics, like Moctezuma, had secondary, although highly significant, roles—to *Stand and Deliver,* where essentially the entire film, including scripting, producing, financing, directing, and acting, was conducted by Hispanics until the point of distribution, when the appeal of the film earned it release through the industry mainstream.

Hispanic Hollywood has significantly entered the discourse of general interest, business, and industry magazines (Noriega, 1991a, 55), such as *Newsweek, Time, Advertising Age, Variety*, and other publications, focusing not only on filmic products but on the potential of the Hispanic market. For example, market studies done for the film industry estimate that the Hispanic population, estimated at about twenty-five million, approximates in its moviegoing behavior the peak audiences of the 1930s and 1940s who went to the theaters on a regular basis rather than to see a specific film.

La Bamba reprises the career of 1950s teenage rock-and-roll singer Ritchie Valenzuela (Valens), whose emerging career was cut short by a plane crash in 1959 that also killed Buddy Holly and The Big Bopper. The film has had strong appeal in diverse markets. Hispanic viewers have liked it for its stirring plot and authenticity of character, language (bilingualism), and locale, and for its theme of identity formation and family rivalry and cooperation. In many critical ways the film is eminently Chicano: the intensive use of bilingualism, the focus on Chicano characters, the evocation of the Chicano life-style, the connections it makes between Mexico and U.S. Hispanic border culture, epitomized by the song "La bamba" itself, which becomes emblematic of a Hispanic binationalism that binds those who live *aquí* and those who live *allá*. Although the film has been criticized in the Chicano community and by Anglo critics, such as Pauline Kael, as an American success film that supports an assimilationist ideology, those elements appear mostly to derive from the biography of Valens himself and are not at all imposed on the film, as was the case of the social problem examples done by Anglos in the 1930s through the 1950s. *La Bamba* is also a significant "crossover" success, appealing to teenagers of all cultures both in the United States and internationally. It features stirring music that could be related to despite much of its genuinely Hispanic nostalgia for the early rock-and-roll period, a teenage love and tragedy story that viewers could easily relate to, and psychological themes that could readily be identified with irrespective of culture. A film that rarely compromises on its Hispanicism, it also has that universal appeal that makes for an enduring work of art.

La Bamba was important not only for its artistic qualities, but because it also proved itself financially successful in the United States, not only in the English-language release, but in the Spanish one as well. A record seventy-seven Spanish-language prints were released, and the Hispanic market provided a two-to-one return over mainstream audiences on costs (Columbia allocated 5 percent of its distribution and advertising budget to the Hispanic market, which in turn accounted for 10 percent of the viewers and box office receipts).

Stand and Deliver has been both an artistic and critical triumph and a box office success. Although released theatrically by Warner Brothers, it is essentially a Hispanic film and is discussed in the following section. *Born in East L.A.* marked Richard "Cheech" Marín's debut as director and also his first film without former partner Tommy Chong. The film, based on a video parody of Bruce Springsteen's song "Born in the U.S.A.," also parodies past U.S. policies toward immigrants, including the deportation of Chicanos, most of whom were either born in the United States or legal residents. *The Milagro Beanfield War* was the least artistically realized of this group; it also was a financial failure. As Noriega (in press) points out, this beautiful film was variously seen as a "progressive fairy tale" by most Anglo reviewers and as an example of "magic realism" (associated with Latin American authors, including Nobel Prize winner Gabriel García Márquez) by some Hispanic reviewers, thus giving compelling documentation to how films are criticized not in a vacuum but from a cultural, political, or racial/ethnic point of view. However, from the point of view of character development and depth of plot, the film does succeed.

U.S Hispanics were not the only ones who helped create "Hispanic Hollywood." Norma Aleandro, the South American who was named best actress at Cannes for her wonderful performance in the Oscar-winning *The Official Story* (1985), crossed over into American films, in *Cousins* (1989), *Vital Signs* (1990), and others, even as she continued to do Spanish-language films. *The Official Story* also provided the means for Luis Puenzo, its director, to break into Hollywood with *Old Gringo* (1989), an intense, beautifully filmed epic about a young revolutionary Mexican general (Jimmy Smits), Ambrose Bierce (Gregory

Peck), and a spinster (Jane Fonda), set against the background of the Mexican Revolution of 1910. The film, based on a screenplay by Carlos Fuentes, was not financially successful, but it is a much more realistic view of Mexico and the border area than most Hollywood films. Its depiction of Pancho Villa is probably the most sophisticated that has been achieved to date by American film. Hector Babenco, noted for his direction of *Pixote* (1981), was able to leverage that Brazilian film about a child street criminal. He directed the U.S.-Brazilian coadaptation of Manuel Puig's novel *Kiss of the Spider Woman* (1985), an extraordinary movie about an apolitical homosexual, William Hurt (who won the Oscar as best actor), and a political activist, Raúl Juliá, thrown in the same prison cell. Babenco went on to do *Ironweed* (1987, Jack Nicholson, Meryl Streep) about street people in Albany, New York, during the Great Depression.

León Ichaso, who first directed *El Super* (The Super, 1979), a Spanish-language film billed as the first Cuban-American film comedy, and which is about the trials of a homesick Cuban exile who labors as a "super" in a Manhattan apartment building, represents another example of "Hispanic Hollywood." He went on to direct *Crossover Dreams* (1985), starring Panamanian Rubén Blades, which did in fact cross over to Anglo audiences. The film evokes the life of a salsa performer hoping to become a mainstream performer but whose record flops. He then finds solace in his own roots and culture.

Since 1980, several films have focused on Latin America, reflecting the political situation of the region or drug-running or both. These include *Missing* (1982), starring Jack Lemmon and Sissy Spacek during the overthrow of Salvador Allende in Chile; *Under Fire* (1983), starring Nick Nolte and Joanna Cassidy as journalists in the midst of the 1979 Sandinista revolution in Nicaragua; *Salvador* (1986), co-written and directed by Oliver Stone, featuring Jim Belushi; *Latino* (1985), directed by Haskell Wexler, about the anti-Somoza uprising; *Under the Volcano* (1984), featuring Jacqueline Bisset and Albert Finney, an adaptation of Malcom Lowry's classic novel; and *Havana* (1991), a failed movie starring Robert Redford as a gambler with a heart of gold who becomes embroiled in plots to overthrow dictator Batista in 1959. The poorly done but financially successful *Scarface* (1983), directed by Brian de Palma, starring Al Pacino, and launching Michelle Pfeiffer's career, more or less feeds at the same trough, although it also focuses on U.S. Hispanic drug runners.

A Mexican film, *Doña Herlinda and Her Son* (1986), a comedy and homosexual homage to "mother" and the first Mexican feature with a gay theme, has earned special recognition as "the best-selling-ever Mexican movie in the American market" (Hadley-García, 1991 240).

The 1980s witnessed several films dealing with the *indocumentado* (undocumented worker). Undocumented immigration from Mexico, as Greenfield and Cortés (1991, 51) have shown, became a movie theme as early as the 1932 *I Cover the Waterfront,* but the undocumented were Chinese being smuggled by sea from Mexico to San Diego. This theme continued into the 1940s; the 1941 *Hold Back the Dawn* dramatized the desperate efforts of European refugees living temporarily in Tijuana to enter the United States. Not until the post-World War II era did films like *Border Incident* (1949), *Borderline* (1950), *The Lawless* (1950), and *Wetbacks* (1956) begin to deal with Mexican immigrants, although the immigrants usually functioned as passive pawns to incite Anglo crime and Anglo crime fighting. *Border Incident* (1949, Anthony Mann, director, starring Ricardo Montalbán) is a quite violent, well-made crime story of the social problem era, also rife with the usual stereotypes, as was the original *Borderline* (1950, Fred MacMurray, Claire Trevor), with an unlikely plot featuring law enforcers each tracking down dope smugglers on the Mexican border. During the past two decades, as undocumented immigration has become a more widely debated public issue, a new wave of films has emerged: *Blood Barrier* (1979, Telly Savalas, Danny de la Paz), *Borderline* (1980, Charles Bronson), and *The Border* (1982, Jack Nicholson, Harvey Keitel, Valerie Perrine, Elpidia Carillo). Nevertheless, the theme of passive Mexican immigrants being saved by noble Anglos has continued to dominate. None of these Hollywood films has ever risen above the mediocre. The films of the 1980s have scarcely improved upon the first of the lot in terms of veracity, character development, or aesthetics. Hollywood *indocumentado* pictures have never surpassed the limitations of the social problem genre as originally conceived in the 1930s and 1940s.

In contrast to the stock characterizations of the Hollywood versions, two independently produced U.S. Hispanic works, *Alambrista!* (1979) and *El Norte* (The North, 1983), shine because of their strong and distinctive plot developments and intriguing characters. Similarly, Cheech Marín's *Born in East L.A.* (1987) shines as a Hispanic Hollywood exception to the bleakness of the rest, precisely because it combined Hispanic expertise and sensitivity to Hollywood production values.

In the area of comedy, the current period has been marked by the films of the comic team Richard "Cheech" Marín and Thomas Chong, who began by adapting their nightclub act to film in *Cheech and Chong's Up in Smoke* (1978), featuring stoned and hippy routines. The film became the highest-grossing film of the year and spurred a number of 1980s sequels, including *Cheech and Chong's Next Movie* (1980), *Cheech and Chong's Nice Dreams* (1981), *Things are Tough All Over* (1982), *Yellowbeard* (1983), and *Cheech and Chong's the Corsican Brothers* (1984).

Despite some innovations during the current period that brought Hispanic actors and filmmakers to the fore, the industry continued, as it has always done, to create more exploitative films. Among these,

The poster for *El norte*.

Salsa (1988) was a Hispanic version of *Dirty Dancing* (1987) that attempted to "outdirty" it. *The Penitent* (1988, Raúl Juliá, Julie Carmen) was a muddle that featured the eternal triangle set against the local color of New Mexican *penitentes*. *Moon over Parador* (1988, Richard Dreyfuss, Sonia Braga, Raúl Juliá) made liberal use of the usual stereotypes about Latin America and its dictators for uninspired humor. *The Believers* (1987, Martin Sheen, Jimmy Smits) abused Santería in order to make a horror/thriller. *Young Guns* (1988, Emilio Estévez, Lou Diamond Phillips, Charlie Sheen) updated the Billy the Kid cycle, having us believe that the Kid whips up the inherent violence of six young punks, including Hispanic members. *Bad Boys* (1983, Sean Penn, Esai Morales) weighs in among the newest gang films. This one, in which both Sean Penn and Morales are superb, features a personal vendetta within prison walls. Morales, who has been badly typecast merely as a Hispanic gang member, got to do his repartee also in *The Principal* (1987), featuring Jim Belushi overpowering the Hispanic youth warlord, somewhat reminiscent of the way honest Anglo do-gooders used to bring down Hispanic and other alien powerbrokers in the 1940s films. On the other hand, the gang film *Colors* (1988), directed by Dennis Hopper and starring Sean Penn, Robert Duvall, María Conchita Alonso, Rudy Ramos and Trinidad Silva, is a superior version of the genre, with the notable exception of the misuse of the Alonso romantic subplot. Trinidad Silva is excellent in this film, as he is in *The Night Before* (1988), an offbeat comedy about a young man on a senior prom who wakes up in an East Los Angeles alley.

The 1980s also marked the death of several prominent Hispanics of earlier generations, including Fernando Lamas ((1982), Dolores del Río (1983), and Rita Hayworth (1987).

✳ HISPANICS IN THE MOVIES SINCE 1980

Raúl Juliá became well known for playing Shakespearean and other classical stage roles as well as film. In 1971, he debuted in small parts in *The Organization*, *Been Down So Long It Looks Like Up to Me*, and *Panic in Needle Park*. Juliá appeared in *The Gumball Rally* (1976) and *Eyes of Laura Mars* (1978) and costarred in the notable *Kiss of the Spider Woman* (1985), from the novel by Argentine Manuel Puig. He played a political prisoner sharing a cell with an apolitical gay man, played by Willam Hurt.

Juliá has been one of the most productive Hispanic actors; he also had prominent roles in, among other films, *One from the Heart* (1982), *Compromising Positions* (1985), *The Morning After* (1986), *Florida Straits* (1986), *Trading Hearts* (1987), *The Penitent* (1988),

Raúl Juliá as Salvadoran Archbishop Oscar Romero in *Romero*.

Tango Bar (1988), *Tequila Sunrise* (1988), *Moon over Parador* (1988), *Romero* (1989), *Presumed Innocent* (1990), *A Life of Sin* (1990), and *The Rookie* (1990). Many of these productions are Hispanic-focused. Some, such as *The Penitent*, which evokes the Penitentes of New Mexico and their reenactment of Christ's crucifixion, and *Florida Straits*, an HBO production about escaping Cuba by boat, are quite obscure. Others, such as *Romero,* are likely to be enduring films. Juliá has worked in Puerto Rican productions or coproductions, including *Tango Bar* (1988) and *La gran fiesta* (1987).

Edward James Olmos debuted in *Alambrista!* (1977), an independent Chicano feature and to date one of the best of the films that evoke the U.S.-Mexican border. His first Hollywood film was a reprise of his theatrical role of the pachuco in *Zoot Suit* (1981), a critical success but box office failure. Olmos was then cast in lesser roles in *Wolfen* (1981) and *Blade Runner* (1982), in which he played a memorable part as an origami-practicing detective, and as the lead in the Chicano production *The Ballad of Gregorio Cortez* (1982, written by novelist Victor Villaseñor). He also had the role of General Santa Anna in the Chicano production *Seguín* (1982, Jesús Salvador Treviño, director). He achieved national recognition in the role of Lieutenant Martin Castillo in the television series "Miami Vice," beginning in 1984. His admirable performance in *Stand and Deliver* (1988) earned him a nomination for the Academy Award. He also acted in *The Nightingale* (1983), a fairy tale with Mick Jagger and Barbara Hershey, *Saving Grace* (1986), directed by Robert Young, about a pope incognito among Italian peasants, *Triumph of the Spirit* (1989), *Maria's Story* (1990), and *A Talent for the Game* (1991). He is currently directing and scheduled to appear in *American Me,* which evokes Chicano gang culture.

Andy García achieved star status in 1990. He had small parts in *Blue Skies Again* (1983), a baseball movie, and *The Mean Season* (1985), in which a newspaper reporter becomes a crazed killer, and he turned in an excellent performance as a villain in *8 Million Ways to Die* (1986) before earning widespread recognition as the upright FBI agent in Brian de Palma's *The Untouchables* (1987). In 1988, he did *American Roulette,* a spy thriller; was an official of the Educational Testing Service in *Stand and Deliver;* and in 1989, he played another sincere policeman in the box office failure *Black Rain.* With his appearances in *The Godfather Part III, Internal Affairs* (he cowrote the script of the latter), and *A Show of Force,* 1990 was his supreme year. *A Show of Force,* while not successful at the box office, has a significant plot. It is loosely based on the infamous Puerto Rican scandal in which two pro-independence youths (one the son of renowned Puerto Rican novelist Pedro Juan Soto) were fatally shot for political reasons.

Jimmy Smits gained wide exposure as Victor Sifuentes on the "L.A. Law" TV series. He was in the following films: *Running Scared* (1986), starring Billy Crystal and Gregory Hines as wisecracking detectives; *The Believers* (1987), a New York City voodoo cult movie starring Martin Sheen; and *Vital Signs* (1990), a medical school drama. He costarred as a Mexican revolutionary with Jane Fonda and Gregory Peck in *The Old Gringo* (1989). In 1991, he appeared in *Fire Within* and *Switch.*

Emilio Estévez, Martin Sheen's son, decided to use the original family surname, but in part because of his blond hair and blue eyes was able to secure roles in mainstream pictures. He first achieved recognition

Jimmy Smits.

in *Repo Man* (1984) and had roles in *St. Elmo's Fire* (1985), *Maximum Overdrive* (1986), *Stakeout* (1987), *Young Guns* (1988), *Men at Work* (1990), and *Young Guns II* (1990). Estévez has written several screenplays and directed two of them.

Charlie Sheen, younger brother of Emilio Estévez and son of Martin Sheen, made his first appearance as an extra in *Apocalypse Now* (1979) and attracted attention for his role as a sensitive high school jock in *Lucas* (1986). He has since emerged as one of the leading actors of his generation, best known for his roles in *Platoon* (1986), set in Vietnam, and *Wall Street* (1987), about greed and unscrupulous financial trading, also featuring Martin Sheen, both directed by Oliver Stone. His acting credits include *Red Dawn* (1984), *Ferris Bueller's Day Off* (1986), *Young Guns* (1988), *Eight Men Out* (1988), directed by John Sayles, *Men at Work* (1990), *Navy Seals* (1990), and *The Rookie* (1990).

Elizabeth Peña, while limited in her roles primarily to mothers and live-in maids, made a name for herself in the 1980s in *La Bamba* (1987), *Crossover Dreams* (1985), with Rubén Blades, *Down and Out in Beverly Hills* (1986), *Batteries Not Included* (1987), *Vibes* (1988), starring Cyndi Lauper and Jeff Goldblum, *Blue Steel* (1989), and *Jacob's Ladder* (1990). On television she was in the series "Tough Cookies" and "I Married Dora."

Lou Diamond Phillips first came to prominence as Ritchie Valens in *La Bamba.* He subsequently distinguished himself as a calculus-proficient gang member in *Stand and Deliver* (1988). His considerable credits include *Dakota* (1988), *Young Guns* (1988), *Disorganized Crime* (1989), *Renegades* (1989), *The First Power* (1990), *A Show of Force* (1990), and *Young Guns II* (1990).

Rosana de Soto appeared in the Chicano production *The Ballad of Gregorio Cortez* (1982) and subsequently crossed over into Hollywood via *La Bamba* and *Stand and Deliver.* She was Dustin Hoffman's non-Hispanic wife in *Family Business* (1989).

Rubén Blades the highly talented singer-composer-musician-lawyer and prospective future Panamian statesman, gained recognition on the screen as co-writer and star of *Crossover Dreams* (1985), and he has subsequently had a considerable number of roles, including parts in *Fatal Beauty* (1987), a bomb featuring Whoopi Goldberg, *Critical Condition* (1987), with Richard Pryor and Rachel Ticotin, *Homeboy* (1988), featuring Mickey Rourke as an aging alcoholic boxer, *Dead Man Out* (1988), in the lead as an inmate going crazy awaiting execution, *The Milagro Beanfield War* (1988), *Disorganized Crime* (1989), *The Lemon Sisters* (1989), *Mo" Better Blues* (1990), *Predator 2* (1990), and *The Two Jakes* (1990).

Rachel Ticotin made her debut in *Fort Apache, the Bronx* (1981) and played the enigmatic Melina in Arnold Schwarzenegger's *Total Recall* (1990). Her acting credits include *King of the Gypsies* (1978), *Critical Condition* (1987), and *F/X II* (1991). She was production assistant for *Dressed to Kill* (1980) and *Raging Bull* (1980).

Henry Darrow, who worked a great deal in television in the 1960s and 1970s, notably in "The High Chaparral" series, and was in *Badge 373* (1973), saw considerable action in films, usually in films about cops, convicts, and drugs, including *Attica* (1980), an excellent depiction of the prisoner uprising, *In Dangerous Company* (1988), *L.A. Bounty* (1989), and *The Last of the Finest* (1990). He also had an important role in Treviño's *Seguín* (1982).

María Conchita Alonso began her career as a beauty pageant winner (Miss Teenager of the World 1971, Miss Venezuela 1975), and she subsequently became one of South America's best-selling recording artists. She established herself in Hollywood with her role in *Moscow on the Hudson* (1984) opposite Robin Williams. Her work as an actress includes *A Fine Mess* (1986), an unsuccessful Blake Edwards comedy, *Touch and Go* (1986), *Extreme Prejudice* (1987), starring Nick Nolte in yet another undistinguished border drug film, *The Running Man* (1987), starring Schwarzenegger, *Colors* (1988), *Vampire's Kiss* (1988), and *Predator 2* (1990).

Esai Morales played Ritchie Valens's disturbed half-brother in *La Bamba* (1987) and gave a stirring performance. His first role was opposite Sean Penn in *Bad Boys* (1983), where he was superb as the sworn Hispanic enemy of the Anglo juvenile delinquent. He also has appeared in *Bloodhounds of Broadway* (1989), a Damon Runyon tale, with Madonna, and *The Principal* (1987), featuring James Belushi versus the school thugs.

Daphne Zuñiga is probably best known for her role as John Cusack's reluctant traveling companion in Rob Reiner's *The Sure Thing* (1985), an update of Frank Capra's *It Happened One Night* (1934), about two college students who do not get along and travel cross-country together. She was in Lucille Ball's first dramatic telefilm, *Stone Pillow*, played Princess

Vespa in Mel Brooks's *Spaceballs* (1987), was the leading lady in *The Fly II* (1989), and had roles in *The Dorm That Dripped Blood* (1981), *The Initiation* (1983), *Modern Girls* (1986), *Last Rites* (1988), *Staying Together* (1989), and *Gross Anatomy* (1989).

Robert Beltrán starred in Haskell Wexler's ill-fated *Latino* (1985), about the Nicaraguan war, and has had roles in *Night of the Comet* (1984), a satire about the end of the world, the Paul Bartel's comedies, *Eating Raoul* (1982) and *Scenes from the Class Struggle in Beverly Hills* (1989), the highly regarded *Gaby, A True Story* (1987), about a brilliant woman incapacitated by cerebral palsy, and *Streethawk* (1986).

Norma Aleandro, the distinguished South American actress, playwright, director, and TV performer, gained international recognition, including being named best actress at Cannes for her performance in the Academy Award-winning *The Official Story* (1985). She has had acting credits in the United States for *Gaby, A True Story*, *Cousins*, starring Ted Danson, an American version of the French *Cousin/Cousine* (1975), and *Vital Signs* (1990), a cliché-ridden medical student stint. She continues to do Spanish-language films.

Trini Alvarado debuted in pictures at the age of 11 in *Rich Kids* (1979), by Robert Young, about two kids going through puberty, and has done considerable work in television and films, including *Mrs. Soffel* (1984), starring Diane Keaton and Mel Gibson, about a woman who helps two prisoners escape, *Times Square* (1980), *Sweet Lorraine* (1987), about a small Catskill hotel past its prime, *Satisfaction* (1988), and *Stella* (1990) opposite Bette Midler in an undistinguished remake of the 1937 *Stella Dallas*.

Despite several inferior roles, Julie Carmen, an impressive actress who did well in *Gloria* (1980) and *The Milagro Beanfield War* (1988), is getting attention and plenty of work. She has done some television, including "Falconcrest" and quite a bit of film, including *Can You Hear the Laughter? The Story of Freddie Prinze* (1979), *Gloria*, a notable film starring Gena Rowlands escaping from the Mafia, *Last Plane Out* (1983), a bad rip-off of *Under Fire*, about the final days of the Somoza regime, *The Milagro Beanfield War* (1988) in a notable role, *The Penitent* (1988), *The Neon Empire* (1989), *Paint it Black* (1989), about a sculptor struggling against an unscrupulous gallery owner, and *Fright Night II* (1989).

Elpidia Carrillo attained recognition opposite Jack Nicholson in the awful potboiler *The Border* (1982), did excellent work in *Salvador* (1986), directed by

Oliver Stone and starring James Wood, and appeared in *Beyond the Limit* (1983), an undistinguished adaptation of Graham Greene's *The Honorary Consul*, and *Predator* (1987).

With respect to musical composition, Emilio Estefan, husband of Gloria Estefan, has produced the scores of numerous financially successful films, including *Top Gun* and *Three Men and a Baby*.

✳ THE EMERGENCE OF U.S. HISPANIC FILMS

Chicano Cinema

In a certain sense, the emergence of Chicano cinema has been the result of new, energetic actions on the part of the film industry to increase the participation of Chicanos and other minorities in the craft of filmmaking. In that sense, it was perhaps unexpected at least by industry executives—and due more to prodding by the courts, by certain sectors of society, such as college students, and above all by the civil rights movement. The film corporations did hire Chicanos, but for general work in the profession and not necessarily for the production of Chicano films.

During the late 1960s and early 1970s, the film industry became the target of both national and local civil rights groups. Following on the success of the NAACP in having the industry open more jobs to blacks, the League of United Latin American Citizens, the Mexican American Legal Defense and Educational Fund, ASPIRA of America, the National Council of La Raza, and others urged similar consideration for Hispanics. Also, during these years various individuals in the Los Angeles area began to coalesce and organize Chicano media activist groups, such as CARISSMA and JUSTICIA. In 1969, a group of Hispanic actors, led by Ricardo Montalbán, organized NOSOTROS, which was devoted to protesting the kinds of roles Hispanics were forced to play and to working to better the image of Hispanics in Hollywood films. At the same time that constituency-based organizations were pressing Hollywood, government statistics were confirming the extent of U.S. Hispanic underrepresentation in the industry. In 1969, a U.S. Equal Employment Opportunity Commission report found that only 3 percent of the work force at major Hollywood studios was "Spanish surnamed." Similar statistics prevailed in commercial television, and, even more amazing, public broadcasting was shown to have compiled an even worse record of less than 1 percent Mexican or Chicano employees. As Jesús Treviño observes (1982, 171), the major studios responded with token gestures to employ more Chicanos, primarily by means of internship programs;

television responded primarily through its creation of low-budget, off-hours community interest "talk" shows, and the universities (particularly the University of California, Los Angles, and the University of Southern California) participated with special admissions programs.

With respect to acting roles, beginning in the mid-1960s many Hispanics appeared in all sorts of films that were not specifically focused on Hispanics, including *The Big Fix* (1978), *Marathon Man* (1976), *Back Roads* (1980), *The Goodbye Girl* (1977), *Blume in Love* (1973), *Whose Life is it Anyway?* (1981), *Grease* (1978), *Dog Day Afternoon* (1975), *9 to 5* (1980), *Bob and Carol and Ted and Alice* (1969), *The Changeling* (1979), and many others. Unfortunately, as Carlos Cortés (1985) points out, these bit characters usually came off as nothing more than stick furniture, functioning as maids, bank tellers, secretaries, cops, a drug dealer or two, and with notable exceptions, such as the stalwart nurse in *Whose Life is it Anyway?* and the bad madam in *Back Roads,* they seldom did more than take up space, look Latin, and spout either Spanish or stereotypically accented English.

By 1978, less than ten years after the founding of NOSOTROS, the Los Angeles Chicano Cinema Coalition was founded; its philosophy had evolved from protesting Hollywood's exploitive tendencies to responding to two concerns: "the need to evolve a Chicano cinema esthetic, and the need to create an alternative to the 'commercial' influence of Hollywood film . . .." (Treviño, 1982, 167). The group had as its primary goal to promote the growth and development of a Chicano cinema aesthetic that would work on behalf of Chicano efforts toward social justice and allied concerns.

As Chicano actors, filmmakers, and other professionals began entering the industry and, particularly, receiving their apprenticeships through the production of documentaries on varied subject matter, their sensitivities inevitably turned to the Chicano experience, primarily because the *raza* story was there, beckoning and untold. As Treviño puts it. "As a by-product of this 60s activism and organizing, it became increasingly evident that if a truer story was to be told, then Chicanos would have to be the ones to tell it" (Treviño, 1982, 171).

In contrast to the actors, most of the first entries by Chicanos into production were through television, including talk shows, soap operas and other programs, such as *Canción de la raza (Song of the People)*, *¡Ahora! (Now)*, *Unidos (United)*, *Reflecciones (Reflections)*, *Acción Chicano (Chicano Action)*, *Impacto (Impact)*, *The Siesta is Over*, and *Bienvenidos (Welcome)*. The networks also did some important documentary films about Mexican Americans within the context of migrant farm workers that also provided work for Hispanics: *Harvest of Shame* (1960, CBS), *Hunger in America* (1968, NBC), and *Migrant* (1970, NBC).

The major exception to this point of entry was the case of Luis and Daniel Valdez, founders of El Teatro Campesino, who should be recognized as producers of the first Chicano film, the 1967 adaptation of the epic poem *I Am Joaquín,* by Rodolfo "Corky" Gonzales. It is quite fitting that the first Chicano film would convert the following verses into kinesis:

> They frowned upon our way of life
> and took what they could use.
> Our art,
> our literature,
> our music, they ignored—
> so they left the real things of value
> and grabbed at their own destruction
> by their greed and avarice (Gonzales, 1972, 70).

First Films

The Chicanos who entered the studios on the production side were soon producing and directing a series of politically aware documentaries on the Chicano experience. Among the most significant of these are David García's *Requiem-29* (1971), which describes the East Los Angeles riot of 1970 and the circumstances surrounding the suspicious death of Chicano reporter Rubén Salazar. Jesús Treviño's *América Tropical (1971)* is about the whitewashing of a Siquieros mural in Los Angeles. Severo Pérez's *Cristal* (1975) is about Crystal City, "Spinach Capital of the World" and birthplace of the Raza Unida party. Jesús Treviño's *Yo soy chicano* (*I Am Chicano,* 1972) was the first Chicano film to be nationally televised and to deal with the Chicano movement from its roots in pre-Columbian history to the activism of the present. José Luis Ruíz's *Cinco vidas* (*Five Lives,* 1972) glosses over the lives of five Chicanos and Chicanas of varied backgrounds and experiences. Jesús Treviño's *La raza unida* (*The United People,* 1972), covers the 1972 national convention of the Raza Unida party. Ricardo Soto's *A la brava (With Courage,* 1973), describes the condition of Chicano convicts at Soledad prison. Rick Tejada-Flores's *Sí se puede* (*Yes It Can Be Done,* 1973) records César Chávez's twenty-four day fast in Arizona to protest proposed anti-strike legislation. José Luis Ruíz's *The Unwanted* (1974) depicts the difficulties of the *indocumentado* population, and Ricardo Soto's *A Political Renaissance* (1974) examines the contemporary emergence of Chicano political power.

The earliest Chicano cinema also includes the film adaptation of one of the finest Teatro Campesino actos, *Los vendidos* (*The Sell-Outs,* 1972). Subse-

Director Jesús Salvador Treviño in 1978.

quently, this group's *La gran carpa de los rasquachis* (*The Tent of the Underdogs,* 1976) was produced for public television with critical success under the title *El corrido.* The early period also includes Jeff Penichet's *La vida* (*Life,* 1973), which describes a family of poverty-stricken Mexicans who survive by scavenging the trash left by American tourists in a small village in Baja California.

From 1975 to the present, the pace of Chicano documentary cinema has accelerated enormously. Scores of films have been produced. Following are brief notations of some of the most significant documentary productions.

Anthropological and Folkloric Films

Among the most notable documentaries of the anthropological or folkloric type are Esperanza Vázquez and Moctezuma Esparza's *Agueda Martínez* (1977), nominated for an Academy Award in 1978, and Michael Earney's *Luisa Torres* (1981). Both documentaries depict the life-styles of elderly women in northern New Mexico. Also outstanding are Les Blank's *Chulas fronteras* (*Beautiful Border,* 1976) and its sequel, *Del mero corazón* (*From the Heart,* 1979), which beautifully evoke the *norteña* or *conjunto* music prevalent in the Texas-Mexico border region and throughout the Southwest. Homer A. Villarreal's *Expression: The Miracle of Our Faith* (1978) is about the practices of *curanderismo* (faith healing) in San Antonio and elsewhere in southern Texas. Daniel Salazar's *La tierra* (*The Land,* screened at the 1981 San Antonio Cine Festival), describes the Chicano life-style in Colorado's San Luis Valley. Luis Reyes's *Los Alvarez* (*The Alvarez Family,* also screened at the 1981 San Antonio Cine Festival), depicts the hopes and dreams of a family living in California's Salinas Valley. Alicia Maldonado and Andrew Valles's *The Ups and Downs of Lowriding* (screened at the 1981 San Antonio Cine Festival) is an investigation of lowriding through the eyes of the cruisers themselves, the general public, and the police department.

Ray Téllez's *Voces de yerba buena* (*Voices of Mint,* screened at the 1981 San Antonio Cine Festival) traces the Hispanic historical foundations of the San Francisco area and evokes the contemporary Latino influence in the area today. Ken Ausubel's *Los remedios: The Healing Herbs* (screened at the 1983 San Antonio Cine festival) is a review of herbal medicine in the Southwest. Rhonda Vlasak's *Between Green and Dry* (screened at the 1983 San Antonio festival) examines the impact of accelerated economic change in the New Mexican village of Abiquiu. Paul Espinosa's *The Trail North* (1983) follows Dr. Robert Alvarez and his ten-year-old son, Luis, as they recreate the journey their familial ancestors made in immigrating to California from Baja California. Toni Bruni's *Los vaqueros* (*The Cowboys,* screened at the 1983 San Antonio festival) is about Chicano cowboys, particularly those who participate in the Houston Livestock Show and Rodeo. Rich Tejada-Flores, producer and director of *Low 'N Slow: The Art of Lowriding* (screened at the 1984 San Antonio Cine Festival), both explains the lowriding phenomenon and makes a case for it as an important form of modern industrial folk art. Jack Ballesteros, producer and director of *Mt. Cristo Rey* (screened at the 1984 San Antonio festival), has created a documentary about a priest in a small mining community near El Paso and how he erected a huge sandstone cross and statue of Christ. Toni Bruni's *Long Rider* (1986) is an English-language version of his 1983 *Los vaqueros.* Jesús Salvador Treviño and Luis Torres's *Birthwrite: Growing Up Hispanic* (1989) is a docudrama that recreates the theme of growing up and self-identity in the writing of several U.S. Hispanic writers; and *Del Valle* (*From the Valley,* 1989), directed by Dale Sonnenberg and Karl Kernbergber, evokes traditional and popular Mexican and New Mexican music performed in the central Río Grande Valley of New Mexico.

Films with Political Content

On the matter of politics and the emerging Chicano political movement, several valuable films have been produced. Marsha Goodman's *Not Gone and Not Forgotten* (screened at the 1983 San Antonio festival) depicts how the community of Pico Union in Los Angeles successfully fought the mayor, the city council, and powerful business interests in order to maintain the integrity of its neighborhood. Richard Trujillo's *Tixerina: Through the Eyes of the Tiger* (1983) is an interview with Reies López Tixerina reviewing the famous courthouse raid of 1967 in Tierra Amarilla and related events. National Education Media's *Decision at Delano* (screened at the 1982 Eastern Michigan University Chicano Film Festival), documents the historic Delano grape workers'' strike. Centro Campesino Cultural's *El Teatro Campesino* (screened at the 1982 Eastern Michigan University festival) traces the theater from its beginnings in the fields, boosting the morale of striking farm workers and winning over scabs, to its role as a theater committed to social change. Paul Espinosa and Isaac Artenstein's extraordinary documentary *Ballad of an Unsung Hero* (1984) evokes the political consciousness of an earlier era, depicting the life history of the remarkable Pedro J. González, a pioneering radio and recording star who was thrown in jail on trumped-up charges by the Los Angeles district attorney's office in the midst of the Great Depression.

Coproduced by directors Jesús Salvador Treviño and José Luis Ruíz, *Yo soy (I Am)* (1985) reviews the progress that Chicanos have made during the last two decades in politics, education, labor, and economic development and summarizes the variety of ways that Chicanos are responding to contemporary challenges. *Graffiti* (1986) by Diana Costello, producer, and Matthew Patrick, director, is about a nocturnal wall-sketcher in a militaristic South American country. *Maricela* (1986), by Richard Soto, producer, Christine Burrill, director, is the story of a thirteen-year-old Salvadoran girl who immigrates to Los Angeles with her mother seeking to find a new home and a better life. *The Lemon Grove Incident* (1986), by Paul Espinosa, producer, Frank Christopher, director, is a docudrama that examines the response of the Mexican-American community in Lemon Grove, California, to a 1930 school board attempt to segregate their children in a special school.

Watsonville on Strike (1989), by producer-director Jon Silver, describes an eighteen-month strike by cannery workers that virtually paralyzed a rural California town. Marilyn Mulford and Mario Barrera's *Chicano Park* (1989) is a compelling and moving visual history of the struggle of one community, Barrio Logan, to stake out a place for itself in the metropolis of San Diego. The film shows the process through which Logan residents begin to effect positive changes in their lives and their community by using the richness of their cultural heritage as the basis around which to educate themselves to gain political power.

Film Portrayals of Undocumented Workers and Migrant Workers

The plight of *indocumentados* (undocumented workers) and migrant labor generally has seen extensive filmic treatment during the last decade and a half, including Ricardo Soto's films *Cosecha* (Harvest, 1976), about migrant labor, *Migra* (1976), on the arrest of *indocumentados, Al otro paso* (*To Another Pass,* 1976), on the economy of the border, and *Borderlands* (1983), which once again explores the complex interrelations of the Mexican-U.S. border. F. X. Camplis's *Los desarraigados* (*The Uprooted,* 1977) is about the early problems of undocumented workers. Jesús Carbajal and Todd Darling's *Año Nuevo* (*New Year,* screened at the 1979 San Antonio Cine Festival and 1981 winner of the Eric Sevareid Award for best information program, Academy of Television Arts and Sciences) is about the nearly unprecedented court struggle by twenty-two undocumented workers against their employer, the Año Nuevo Flower Ranch. Jim Crosby's *Frank Ferree: El amigo* (screened at the 1983 San Antonio Cine Festival) depicts this man from Harlingen, Texas, known as the Border Angel, who spent most of his adult life in an untiring effort to aid the poor and dispossessed along the Texas border with Mexico. The Learning Corporation of America's *Angel and Big Jose,* an Academy Award winner for short dramatic film, starring Paul Scorvino, is an outstanding film that depicts the friendship and ultimate parting of a migrant worker youth and a lonely Anglo telephone repairman. The United Farm workers'' *The Wrath of Grapes* (1986) is a documentary that depicts the plight of California farm workers exposed to deadly pesticides. Producer-director Susan Ferris has used historical footage, clippings, interviews, and other realia to trace the history of the farm worker's union and to chronicle the experiences of Mexican farm workers in California in *The Golden Cage: A Story of California's Farmworkers* (1989). Paul Espinosa has produced and directed *Vecinos desconfiados (Uneasy Neighbors)* (1989), evoking the growing tensions between the migrant worker camps and affluent homeowners in the San Diego area.

Public Education on the Big Screen

The Chicano experience in public education has been an important topic and concern of *raza* filmmakers. Documentaries on bilingual education include the series by Adolfo Vargas, *Una nación bilingüe* (A Bilingual Nation, 1977), *Bilingualism: Promise for Tomorrow* (1978), and its sequel, *Consuelo ¿Quiénes somos?* (*Consuelo, Who Are We?* 1978), one of the best of its genre, perhaps because of the excellent screenwriting by Rudolfo Anaya. Elaine Sperber's *Overture* (screened at the 1981 San Antonio Cine Festival) uses the school setting to explore the potential for friendship and antagonism between Vietnamese and Chicanos living in a hostile urban environment. In addition, José Luis Ruíz's *Guadalupe* (1975) is a screen adaptation of the play of the same title by El Teatro de la Esperanza; it is a docudrama about conditions in Guadalupe, California, especially the deplorable educational situation. In a stirring docudrama, *Vida* (*Life,* 1980), directed by Elsie Portillo, the issue of sexual relationships, changing norms, attitudes, and behaviors, such as the use of condoms, is set against the issue of AIDS. Southwestern Bell's *America's Time Bomb: The Hispanic Dropout Rate* (1986), narrated by Edward James Olmos, is an instructive documentary on the dropout rate among Latino students. It includes an interview with then mayor of San Antonio Henry Cisneros. *At Risk* (1989), produced by Daniel Matta and directed by Warren Asa Maxey, based on an original stage play by Carlos Morton, portrays a variety of issues, prejudices, and misconceptions about AIDS.

Chicano Art, Poetry, Music, Culture, and Allied Topics

Numerous documentary films have been produced that either describe or highlight Chicano art, poetry, music, culture, and the like. Among the more notable are José Valenzuela's Chicano poetry *Segundo encuentro* (*Second Encounter,* 1978), about a gathering of writers and artists in Sacramento; Juan Salazar's *Entelequia* (*Entelechy,* 1978), which evokes the life and poetry of Ricardo Sánchez, ex-convict and current Ph.D.; and William Greaves's *In Search of Pancho Villa* and *Voice of La Raza* (both screened at the 1978 San Antonio Cine Festival), the former an interview with Mexican-American actor Anthony Quinn about the Mexican Revolution and contemporary U.S. politics and social change and the latter also with Anthony Quinn and, in addition, Rita Moreno and other vocal members of the Hispanic community concerned with issues of discrimination, culture, and language. Sabino Garza's *La llorona* (*The Crying Woman,* screened at the 1978 San Antonio Cine Festival) is a film depiction of the traditional folktale. Jeff and Carlos Penichet's *El pueblo chicano (The Chicano Peoples): The Beginnings* and *El pueblo chicano: The Twentieth Century* (both 1979) are panoramic overviews of Chicano cultural roots and contemporary issues. Chale Nafus's *Primo Martínez, santero (Primo Martínez, Saint Carver,* screened at the 1979 San Antonio Cine Festival) is about a young man in Austin, Texas, who carves statues of the Virgin Mary from wood. Francisco Torres's *Chuco (Pachuco,* 1980) and Joe Camacho's *Pachuco* (1980) treat the 1941 Zoot Suit Riots in Los Angeles through the art of José Montoya. Efraín Gutiérrez's *La onda chicana (The Chicano Wave,* screened at the 1981 San Antonio Cine Festival) is a review of a 1976 Chicano concert featuring Little Joe y la Familia, Los Chanchos, La Fábrica, and other groups. Juan Salazar's *Mestizo Magic* (screened at the 1981 San Antonio Cine Festival) is about a fantasy trip through Aztlán exploring the world of Chicano art from its ancient past through its living musicians, sculptors, painters, dancers, and writers.

Keith Kolb's *Southwest Hispanic Mission* (screened at the 1981 San Antonio Cine Festival) features noted Chicano art historian Jacinto Quirarte, who describes the technology and aesthetics of mission buildings. Teena Brown Webb's *¡Viva! la causa! (Long Live the Cause,* screened at the 1981 San Antonio Cine Festival) depicts the popular wall mural movement in Chicago. Paul Venema's *Barrio Murals* (screened at the 1983 San Antonio Cine Festival) documents the creation of the Cassiano Homes murals in San Antonio's westside. Gary Greenberg's *Dale Kranque (Crank It Up): Chicano Music and Art in South Texas* (screened at the 1983 San Antonio Cine Festival) profiles leading Texas Chicano musicians and artists. Beverly Sánchez-Padilla's *In Company of José Rodríguez* (screened at the 1983 San Antonio festival) is a visual history and conversation with the founder and artistic director of La Compañia de Teatro de Albuquerque. Director, Sylvia Morales, *Los lobos: And A Time to Dance* (screened at the 1984 San Antonio Cine Festival) is a documentary on Los Lobos, including segments of a live performance, interviews with the musicians, and montages that evoked their fusion of music forms. *Jesse Treviño: A Spirit Against All Odds* (1985) is a stirring documentary about one of San Antonio's best-known artists, who while serving in Vietnam lost a right arm and shattered his left leg, yet was still able to pursue his career.

Popol Vuh (1989), directed by Patricia Amlin, is an animated film of the Sacred Book of the Quiche Maya. Lourdes Portillo and Susana Muñoz have produced and directed *La ofrenda (The Offering): The Days of the Dead* (1989), an exploration of the pre-Hispanic roots of *El día de los muertos* (The Day of the Dead) and the social dimensions of death. *The Other Side of the Coin* (1989), by producer-director Sean Carrillo, evokes the work of three East Los Angeles visual and literary artists: Simone Gad, Marisela Norte, and Diana Gamboa.

A much earlier film, the Detroit Institute of Art's haunting *Rivera: The Age of Steel,* describes Diego Rivera's extraordinary Detroit murals of the 1930s and the equally extraordinary political reactions that this art aroused in the automobile and allied industries. A new contribution to the same topic is *Rivera in America* (1988), by producer-director Rick Tejada-Flores, who traces the artist's stay in the United States during the 1930s and examines the works he did here.

Hecho en Cuba (Made in Cuba, 1989), by Uberto Sagramoso, is a documentary on Cuban music that goes from the African rhythms that gave it birth to contemporary sounds. Graciela I. Sánchez has produced and directed *No porque lo diga Fidel Castro (Not Because Fidel Castro Says So)* (1988), which is an insightful look into gay life in Cuba, evoking both traditional and more contemporary attitudes. *The Return of Rubén Blades* (1985), by producer-director Robert Mugge, is a music documentary about the passion and commitment, art, and politics of the well-known singer, songwriter, and actor. Producer (also codirector) Eduardo Aguiar's *Federico García Lorca in New York* (1986) is an evocation of the Spanish writer's experiences and work set in New York.

Gangs, Youth, and Domestic Violence

The circumstances of gangs specifically and youth generally have been the subject of Efraín Gutiérrez's *El Juanío (Johnny,* screened at the 1979 San Antonio Cine Festival), about the drug problems (mostly paint sniffing) faced by youngsters in the barrios of San Antonio, Texas. Ray Téllez's *Joey* (1980) evokes the problems of identity and of adolescence of a sixteen-year-old Chicano youth. Terry Sweeney, S.J.'s *Streets of Anger, Streets of Hope* (screened at the 1981 San Antonio Cine Festival), is an interview documentary in which members tell what attracts them to gangs. Patt Connelly, S.J.'s *El grito de las madres dolorosas (The Scream of the Mother Dolorasas,* 1981) is one of the most moving accounts of gang violence (in unincorporated East Los Angeles) and what a church brother teamed together with a group of concerned mothers attempted to do about it. Director Bill Jersey's, *Children of Violence* (screened at the 1984 San Antonio Cine Festival) treats four brothers in the Oakland, California, barrio, and *Dolores* (1989), produced and directed by Pablo Figueroa, portrays the problem of domestic violence within the Latino community. Jesús Salvador Treviño won the Director's Guild of America Award (1989) in the dramatic daytime show category for his CBS special, *Gangs*.

Chicana Studies

In the area of Chicana studies, Conchita Ibarra Reyes's *Viva: Hispanic Woman on the Move* (screened at the 1979 San Antonio Cine Festival) looks at the recent successes and the continuing struggles of Hispanic women. Julio Rosetti's *La mujer, el amor y el miedo* (*Woman, Love and Fear*, screened at the 1981 San Antonio Cine Festival) is concerned with the needs of battered *raza* women. Barbara Wolfinger's *Chile pequín* (*Peguin Chile Pepper*, screened at the 1983 San Antonio Cine Festival) is about a college-educated Chicana whose values clash with the more traditional ones of her family hometown. Sylvia Morales's *Chicana* (1979) traces the traditional, historically imposed, and emerging roles of Mexicanas and Chicanas from pre-Columbian times to the present. Elvia M. Alvarado's *Una mujer* (*A Woman*, screened at the 1984 Eastern Michigan University Chicano Film Festival) is an interview with a Chicana in Los Angeles who speaks out about rape and sexual assault.

World War II

Memories of Hell (screened at the 1983 San Antonio Cine Festival) describes the suffering of some 1,800 New Mexican soldiers who fought in the Philippines, many of them survivors of the 1941 Bataan death march. Alfredo Lago's *The Men of Company E* (screened at the 1983 San Antonio festival) recounts the bravery and tragedy in Italy during World War II of the all-Latino unit of the U.S. Fifth Army from El Paso, Texas. *Hero Street U.S.A.* (1985), produced and directed by Mike Stroot, is a dramatic story of how, beset by unrelenting discrimination, the Mexican-American community of twenty-two families in the town of Silvis, Illinois, set out to establish itself firmly as all-American and in the process contributed eighty-seven sons to war, eight of whom died in battle. *Valor* (1989), produced and directed by Richard Parra and narrated by Ricardo Montalbán, relates the contributions of Al Ramírez (awarded four Bronze Stars) and other Mexican Americans during World War II, as well as the discrimination that they experienced that provides background for the establishment of the American GI Forum.

Other Chicano Films

Other significant documentaries relating to various aspects of the Chicano community include Mercedes Sabio's *Wealth of a Nation—Hispanic Merchants* (two parts, both screened at the 1981 San Antonio Cine Festival), about Hispanic businesses both in the barrio and outside Hispanic neighborhoods, and Dale Sonnenberg and Joseph Tovares" *Barbacoa, Past, Present, Future* (screened at the 1983 San Antonio Cine Festival), on how this food is produced, distributed and consumed.

Chicano Features. A significant and growing number of Chicano features have been produced since the distribution of what might be considered the first Chicano feature, *Los vendidos* (*The Sellouts*, 1972), a film adaptation of one of the finest of El Teatro Campesino's actos. On the other hand, some of what has been produced, such as the works of Efraín Gutiérrez, have fallen into complete obscurity. If we include some of the dramatic films that were aired on television (for example, *Seguín*) or originally planned for television (*Stand and Deliver*), in addition to the films made for theatrical distribution, the Chicano features include the following, directors noted: *La Vida* (1973, Jeff Penichet), *Please Don't Bury Me Alive! (Por favor ¡No me entierren vivo!*, 1977, Efraín Gutiérrez), *Alambrista!* (1977, Robert M. Young), *Amor Chicano es para siempre* (*Chicano Love Is Forever*, 1978, Efraín Gutiérrez), *Only Once in a Lifetime* (1978, Alejandro Grattan), *Raíces de sangre* (Roots, 1978, Jesús Salvador Treviño), *Run, Junkie (Tecato, Run)*, (1979, Efraín Gutiérrez), *Zoot Suit* (1981, Luis Valdez), *The Ballad of Gregorio Cortéz* (1982, Robert M. Young), *Seguín* (1982, Jesús Salvador Treviño), *Heartbreaker* (1983, Frank Zúñiga), *El Norte* (1983, Gregory Nava), *Stand and Deliver* (1988, Ramón Menéndez), *Break of Dawn* (1988, Isaac Artenstein), and Puerto Rican filmmaker Joseph B. Vásquez's *Hangin" With the Homeboys* (1991). The Hispanic Hollywood films (combining Hispanic expertise and often control with Hollywood production values and distribution) usually are more closely affiliated with Chicano independent film than with the average Hollywood production that makes use of Chicano material. This is certainly the case of *La Bamba* (1987) and *Born in East L.A.* (1987).

Chicano feature films have contrasted greatly with contemporaneous films about Chicanos made by Hollywood directors and producers, even as they have shared some themes, situations or genres, such as the problems at the U.S.-Mexican border, the Western genre, or teenage groups. Some salient characteristics of Chicano film not usually seen in the Hollywood product have been a meticulous attention to the authentic cultural and social conditions of Chicano life, the use of Spanish to produce a bilingual film with considerable switching between languages, the recuperation of Chicano history (in period pieces), close attention to the political dimensions of the topics that are cultivated on screen, commitment to dealing with issues above considerations of box office, and a willingness to employ considerable numbers of Hispanic actors and Hispanic production people. Chicano pictures feature plots that may or may not appeal to the mainstream audience, but are definitely designed for Chicano filmgoers. They feature Hispanic actors in genuine situations, usually filmed on location in authentic settings and speaking or singing in a natural, often bilingual environment.

In contrast to the conventional Hollywood pap of the border, Chicano productions such as *Raíces de Sangre* (Roots [of Blood], 1977, Jesús Treviño), *Alambrista!* (1977, Robert Young and Moctezuma Esparza), *El Norte* (*The North*, 1983, Gregory Nava), and *Break of Dawn* (1988, Isaac Artenstein), about a radio announcer and singer deported to Tijuana, have all evoked the situation at the border with sociological depth and creative distinction. The quality of verisimilitude, heightened by the bilingual (or in the case of *El Norte,* trilingual) script, have caused these movies to stand head and shoulders above their Hollywood contemporaries, such as *Blood Barrier, The Border,* and *Borderline.*

Chicano "Westerns" have differed markedly from the Hollywood version. Both *Seguín* (1981, Jesús Treviño) and *The Ballad of Gregorio Cortez* (1982, directed by Moctezuma Esparza and Robert Young, written by novelist Victor Villaseñor) have been fundamentally involved with the recuperation of lost (or rather, suppressed) aspects of Chicano history and have evoked politically charged elements of that history. *The Ballad,* about social hero Gregorio Cortez, wrongly accused of stealing a horse, is also a stirring evocation of false assumptions and cultural and linguistic misunderstandings, since the fatal encounter with Anglo law enforcers arises out of their misunderstanding of the difference between *caballo* (stallion) and *yegua* (male).

Seguín is the first Chicano version of the Alamo story in the history of the cycle, which dates to as early as 1911. The 1911 *The Immortal Alamo* and the 1915 *The Martyrs of the Alamo* began this cycle of films, generally presenting Mexicans as ineffective fighters, able to triumph only through vast superiority of numbers, certainly not skill. With the 1953 *The Man from the Alamo,* the 1955 *The Last Command,* the 1960 *The Alamo,* and the 1986 television docudrama, *The Alamo: 13 Days to Glory,* the basic view remains of heroic Anglos killing masses of Mexicans before succumbing to overwhelming odds. In contrast, *Seguín* depicts a *tejano* who out of complex social circumstances fights at the Alamo with the Anglos against the Mexicans, leaves before the final siege, becomes mayor of San Antonio during the early days of the Texas republic, is discriminated against by Anglos, and subsequently fights with Santa Anna on the side of the Mexicans in the Mexican-American War.

Luis Valdez's productions *Zoot Suit* (1981) and *La Bamba* (1987), as well as *Stand and Deliver* (1988, Ramón Menéndez, Tom Musca and Edward James Olmos) and *Hangin' With the Homeboys* (1991), all deal with various aspects of Chicano or Puerto Rican juvenile and domestic life in the United States. Valdez's works, both of which have an important historical dimension, are fine examples of Chicano filmmaking, with Hollywood support and distribution. The Chicano juvenile films are light-years ahead of Hollywood products such as *Streets of L.A.* (1979) and *Walk Proud* (1981). The Hollywood films are invariably exploitive in their approach. Whether the Chicanos in these films are a menace to whites or to themselves, it is strictly the prospect of violence and its description on screen that carries these Hollywood juvenile films. In contrast, *Stand and Deliver* is a stirring story that barely even evokes gang violence. It is primarily about an extraordinary Bolivian mathematics teacher who helps Hispanic high school students in East Los Angeles learn college-level calculus and get admitted into selective universities. *Hangin" With the Homeboys* (1991), by Puerto Rican director-writer Joseph P. Vásquez, the most recent contribution to the cycle, was the cowinner of a screenwriting award at the Sundance Film Festival. *Homeboys* evokes the coming of age of four young male friends, two Puerto Rican, two Afro-American, out on the town during a night in which their futures and relationships with each other are tested.

Puerto Rican Films

Both the film industry in Puerto Rico and Puerto Rican films deserve considerably more attention than they have been given to date. Puerto Rican film dates at least from 1916, with the establishment of the Sociedad Industrial Cine Puerto Rico by Rafael J. Colorado and Antonio Capella (in 1912 Juan Emilio Viguié Cajas took the first known shots in Puerto Rico, of Ponce). This production company's first work had a *jíbaro* (Puerto Rican rural highlander) focus and was titled *Por la hembra y el gallo* (*For Women and Fighting Cocks*; 1916), which was followed by *El milagro de la virgen (The Miracle of the Virgin,* 1916) and *Mafia en Puerto Rico (The Mafia in Puerto Rico,* 1916). Because of lack of funds and competition from U.S. film, the Sociedad Industrial was bankrupted, and no prints of its films are known to exist, although there are still photographs of *Por la hembra y el gallo.*

In 1917, Tropical Film Company was organized with the participation of such well-known Puerto Rican literary figures as Luis Lloréns Torres and Nemesio Canales. Although its existence terminated with the entry of the United States into World War I, it did produce *Paloma del monte (Mountain Dove),* directed by Luis Lloréns Torres. In 1919, the Porto Rico Photoplays company was organized and produced *Amor tropical* (Tropical Love, 1920) with American actors Ruth Clifford and Reginald Denny, a melodrama produced for the North American market, but which failed to penetrate that distribution system, causing the company to go bankrupt.

Juan Emilio Viguié Cajas purchased the equipment of Photoplays and began a long and productive filmmaking career in Puerto Rico, primarily doing newsreels for continental U.S. enterprises, such as Pathé, Fox Movietone, and MGM. Among his work was a film on Charles A. Lindbergh's trip to Puerto Rico in 1927 and another on the San Ciriaco hurricane of 1928. He did many documentaries for private entities and for the government, the first of which, in 1920 was *La colectiva* (*The Collective*), about the tobacco industry. His film *Romance tropical* (*Tropical Romance,* 1934) was the first Puerto Rican feature of the sound period. Written by the poet Luis Palés Matos, it depicts a lovesick young musician who attempts to seek his fortune at sea in a tiny boat.

No copies of *Romance tropical* remain; it debuted at the Paramount in Santurce but was not financially successful. It was the only feature that Cajas did. On the other hand, Rafael Ramos Cobián, who owned the largest chain of movie theaters in Puerto Rico, backed some production, mostly in Mexico, including *Mis dos amores* (*My Two Loves,* 1938), with Puerto Rican actress Blanca de Castejón and Mexican Tito Guízar, and *Los hijos mandan* (*The Children Rule,* 1939), with Blanca de Castejón again and Arturo de Córdova.

With the exceptions described above, film languished in Puerto Rico until 1949 when the government established a production facility in Old San Juan. Administered by the División de Educación de la Comunidad (which was part of the Departamento de Instrucción Pública), this unit was able to produce sixty-five shorts and two features by 1975, the year of publication of its last catalog. It counted on the cooperation of many of the best Puerto Rican graphic artists (Homar, Tony Maldonado, Eduardo Vera, Rafael Tufiño, Domingo Casiano, and so on) and writers (René Marqués, Pedo Juan Soto, Emilio Díaz Valcárcel, Vivas Maldonado, for instance). The unit also made considerable use of North American expertise, particularly screenwriter Edwin Rosskam; director Jack Delano, a longtime resident of Puerto Rico, cameraman Benji Donniger, and director Willard Van Dyke. Because these films were produced by a unit of government responsible for education, they generally had a pedagogical or didactic quality. *Los peloteros* (*The Ballplayers,* 1951) is generally thought to be the best film from this period. Directed by Jack Delano, it is based on a script by Edwin Rosskam and features Ramón Ortiz del Rivero (the celebrated comedian Diplo) and Miriam Colón. The premise revolves around a group of children raising money to buy baseball uniforms and equipment.

Viguié Film Productions, founded in 1951 by Juan Emilio Viguié Cajas, Jr., and the journalist Manuel R. Navas, became the first large Puerto Rican film producer. In 1953, the writer Salvador Tió became a partner of the company, which had its own studio and laboratory in Hato Rey. Many filmmakers received their training here or with the División de la Educación de la Comunidad. The company produced both commercials and documentaries for the government and private firms. In 1962, the company was associated with the brothers Roberto and Marino Guastella, and what emerged ultimately in 1974 was Guastella Film Producers, currently the largest producer in Puerto Rico. Unfortunately, no film laboratory currently exists in Puerto Rico, so footage is sent to New York.

Beginning in the 1950s, the production of film features accelerated somewhat. A group of investors and actors headed by Víctor Arrillaga and Axel Anderson produced a few films under the Producciones Borinquen. *Maruja* (1959) was the most successful, premised on the love life of a barber's wife and starring Marta Romero and several well-known actors and actresses from Puerto Rican television. A few films were produced in Puerto Rico by North American filmmakers for the continental market. *Machete,* 1958, is the best known, primarily for its sexuality. Coproduction with Mexican interests began during the 1960s, but led to no more than the repetition of old Mexican formula films with Puerto Rican settings. Among the films produced were *Romance en Puerto Rico* (1961, which has the distinction of being the first Puerto Rican color film), *Bello amanecer* (*Beautiful Dawn,* 1962), *Lamento borincano* (*Puerto Rican Lament,* 1963), *Mientras Puerto Rico duerme* (*While Puerto Rico Sleeps,* 1964, about the drug problem), *El jibarito Rafael* (1966, about Rafael Hernández), and *Fray Dollar* (*Brother Dollar,* 1970). Most of the major actors and directors were not Puerto Rican, but of Mexican or other Latin American nationality.

In 1964, Pakira Films was organized, led by the television producer Paquito Cordero and with financial backing from Columbia Pictures. It made several films based on the appearances of the television comedian Adalberto Rodríguez (Machuchal). These films were financially successful, including *El alcalde de Machuchal* (*The Mayor of Machuchal*, 1964), *Millionario a-go-go* (*Millionaire A-Go-Go*, 1965), *El agente de Nueva York* (*The New York Agent*, 1966), and *El curandero del pueblo* (*The Town Healer*, 1967). The company also produced its own Mexican formula films, called churros by the Mexican industry, such as *En mi viejo San Juan* (*In Old San Juan*, 1966), *Luna de miel en Puerto Rico* (*Honeymoon in Puerto Rico*, 1967), and *Una puertorriqueña en Acapulco* (*A Puerto Rican Girl in Acapulco*, 1968).

Another type of film based on criminals who had captured the popular imagination was produced by Anthony Felton, a Puerto Rican resident of New York. Popular for a while, the public eventually tired of these films with very low budgets and production values and earthy language and titillating situations: *Correa Coto, ¡así me llaman!* (*Correa Coto, That's What They Call Me!*, 1968), *La venganza de Correa Coto* (*The Revenge of Correa Coto*, 1969), *Arocho y Clemente* (*Arocho*, 1969), *La palomilla* (*The Gang*, 1969), and *Luisa* (1970).

In the 1970s, the number of Mexican coproductions declined significantly, primarily because of political changes in the film industry (Treviño, 1982). Among the few that were done were *Yo soy el gallo* (*I Am the Rooster*, 1971), featuring Puerto Rican singer José Miguel Class, *La pandilla en apuros* (*The Gang in Trouble*, 1977), *¡Qué bravas son las solteras!* (*Single Women Are Brave*), featuring *vedette* Iris Chacón, and *Isabel La Negra* (*Black Isabel*, 1979), by Efraín López Neris, the first superproduction by Puerto Rican standards, featuring José Ferrer, Henry Darrow, Raúl Juliá, and Miriam Colón. This last film is about a notorious madam of a Ponce brothel and is recorded in English. However, the production was both an artistic and financial failure.

While the number of features declined, the number of documentaries increased greatly in the 1970s, spurred in part by the intense political climate of Puerto Rico. A number of *talleres cinematográficos* (movie workshops) were established. Notable among them was Tirabuzón Rojo, which produced *Denunica de un embeleco* (*Charges Filed Against a Madman*, director, Mario Vissepó), *Puerto Rico* (1975, Cuban Film Institute and Tirabuzón Rojo), a socioeconomic analysis of present-day Puerto Rico from a nationalist point of view, and *Puerto Rico: paraíso invadido* (*Puerto Rico: Paradise Invaded*, 1977, Alfonso Beato, director), an examination of the history and present-day reality of Puerto Rico from a nationalist perspective. Independent filmmakers produced *The Oxcart* (1970, director, José García Torres), a short (twenty-minute) portrayal of the migration of a Puerto Rican

family that is based on the famous play by René Marqués; *Culebra, el comienzo* (*Island of Culebra, the Beginning*, 1971, director, Diego de la Texera), *La carreta* (1972, José García, Spanish-language version of *The Oxcart*); *Los nacionalistas* (*The Nationalists*, 1973, José García Torres, director), which surveys the activities of the Puerto Rican Nationalist party during the 1950s with a special focus on Don Pedro Albizu Campos; *La vida y poesía de Julia de Burgos* (*The Life and Poetry of Julia de Burgos*, 1974); *Destino manifiesto* (*Manifest Destiny*, 1977); *A la guerra* (*To War*, 1979, Thomas Sigel, director), an ode to the Puerto Rican community's war against cultural and racial discrimination in the form of a poem read by its author, Bimbo Rivas; and *The Life and Poetry of Julia de Burgos* (1979, José García Torres, director, Spanish-language version in 1974), a docudrama on the life and work of the great Puerto Rican poet.

In the 1980s, several features were produced including, *Una aventura llamada Menudo* (*An Adventure Called Menudo*, 1983, Orestes Trucco, director), featuring the famous young musical group. This film was one of the biggest box office successes in Puerto Rican history; however, its sequel, *Operación Caribe* (*Operation Caribbean*, 1984) with another very popular juvenile group, Los Chicos, was a financial flop. Also produced, all in 1986, were *Reflejo de un deseo* (*Reflection of a Desire*, Ivonne María Soto, director), about the director's mother, a poet; *Nicolás y los demás* (*Nicolás and the Others*, Jacobo Morales, director), a variation on the eternal triangle theme; and *La gran fiesta* (*The Great Fiesta*, Marcos Zurinaga, director). The first two were low-budget vehicles, done in sixteen millimeters and blown up to thirty-five. They were not financially or artistically successful. On the other hand, *La gran fiesta* was a watershed in Puerto Rican film. Produced with a high budget by local standards (about one million dollars) and boasting excellent production values, this period piece with strong political dimensions evokes the handing over of the San Juan Casino to the U.S. military in 1942 amidst considerable turmoil about the possibility of a Nazi invasion, the status of Puerto Rico, and changing attitudes among the upper classes, particularly growers and merchants. This financially successful film was also the first to be produced under the new Ley de Sociedades Especiales (Law of Special Societies, Ley 8, July 19, 1985), which was designed to spur filmic production.

Among independent filmmakers, primarily with financial support of the Fundación Puertorriqueña de las Humanidades (Puerto Rican Humanities Foundation), the number of documentaries were on the increase in the 1980s. *Retratos* (*Pictures*, 1980, Stewart Bird, director) chronicles the life stories of four individuals from New York's Puerto Rican community in their attempts to adjust to life in the United States. *Puerto Rico: Our Right to Decide* (1981, Stanley Nelson, director) features interviews with people from various walks of life on Puerto Rico's current problems and aspirations for its political future. *Puerto Rico: A Colony the American Way* (1982, Diego Echeverría, director), examines the island's economic relationship with the United States. *La operación (The Operation*, 1982, Ana María García, director) studies the sterilization of Puerto Rican women. *El arresto (The Arrest*, 1982, Luis Antonio Rosario Quiles, director) dramatizes a major event in the history of the Puerto Rican independence movement. *Ligía Elena* (1983, Francisco López, director), is a color animation that criticizes consumerism, snobbery, and racism, set to a salsa song by Rubén Blades. *Manos a la obra (Let's Get To Work): The Story of Operation Bootsrap* (1983, Pedro Rivera and Susan Zeig, directors) is an examination of the economic development plan undertaken in the 1950s called Operation Bootstrap. *La herencia de un tambor (The Heritage of a Drum*, 1984, Mario Vissepó, director is about Afro-Caribbean music, *Luchando por la vida (Fighting for Life*, 1984, José Artemio Torres, director) is about Puerto Rican tobacco workers, *Luis Muñoz Marín* (1984, Luis Molina, director) is a biography of the noted governor, and *Correjer* (1984, Antonio Segarra, director) is a portrait of the noted poet and politician.

La batalla de Vieques The Battle of Vieques, 1986, Zydnia Nazario, director) examines the U.S. Navy's control and use of the small island of Vieques. *Tufiño* (1986, Ramón Almodóvar, director) evokes the life and work of this painter. *Raíces eternas (Eternal Roots*, 1986, Noel Quiñones, director) describes the history of Puerto Rico since the discovery. *Cimarrón (Cimarron*, 1986, Juis Antonio Rosario, director) is a short fiction about a black slave who escapes his owner's manor and searches for his wife and child in Puerto Rico. *Machito* (1986 Carlos Ortiz, director) is an excellent biographical film that follows salsa musician Machito's career as well as the evolution of Latin jazz from the Cuba of the 1920s to contemporary New York City. *Una historia de los Reyes Magos (A History of the Three Wise Men*, 1988, Producciones Rodadero) is an animation that brings to life a Puerto Rican story inspired by the tradition of the magi. *Sabios árboles, mágicos árboles (Wise Trees, Magic Trees*, 1988, Puerto Rico Conservation Trust) is an animation that deals with the importance of trees and with man's relationship to nature. *Las plumas del múcaro (The Feathers of the Múcaro*, 1989, Puerto Rico Animation Workshop) is an animated Puerto Rican folktale from the oral tradition.

✳HISPANICS IN FILM: FUTURE DIRECTIONS

What lies ahead for U.S. Hispanic film? Several factors will come into play. Prime among them is the growing constituent power of U.S. Hispanics and the growing understanding of this power. Hollywood now understands that Hispanics go to the movies and that there are many Hispanics. It also realizes that there is a growing fear of the Hispanic presence among Anglos and even other minorities. The first Hollywood inclination will be to create films that exploit these features, even simultaneously if at all possible. Most Hollywood films will continue to capitalize on the inherent habits of secret wish-fulfillment, projection of one's hostility on out-groups, and anticipation of ethnic group violence that has been inculcated into the American viewing public from the very emergence of narrative film. If Hollywood can do that in a way that will simultaneously bring in the Hispanic audience as well, all the better. This has been the design of gang films, successfully realized in such films as *Walk Proud,* where young Hispanics come to the film to see it for its novelty value (there being so little about Hispanics of any sort), while Anglos come for the intermixed violence and sexuality. If anything, Hispanic exploitation films intended for Anglo sensibilities will be accelerated, if only because this minority group will become the largest early in the twenty-first century, and therefore, possibly overtake blacks as the most menacing. However, Hollywood will attempt to update the stereotypes and even disguise them ever so delicately, possibly with subplots that provide something for the Hispanic viewer as well.

The first trend of increased Hispanic population and audiences represents a constant, so it will continue. Nevertheless, what is new is the parallel development of a "Hispanic Hollywood." To better understand this trend one must realize that the studio system has long been subverted and the power of studios themselves over film content has been on the decline now for decades. Currently, even the largest studios, such as Universal (itself a subsidiary of one of the largest corporations in the world, Matsushita), have farmed out their facilities to independent producers or other studios. Conversely, and particularly since stars still are luminaries in the system, we have witnessed the rise of powerful production companies headed by leading Hollywood figures. Many of these leaders, actors and actresses such as Robert Redford, Jane Fonda, or, among Hispanics, Edward James Olmos, Raúl Julia, Martin Sheen, Emilio Estévez, Paul Rodríguez, "Cheech" Marín, and producers and directors such as The Zanuck Corporation, Esparza/Katz, and so on, are going into production, including conceptualization, scripting, actual film production, and arrangement through the studios for distribution. The Hispanic Hollywood phenomenon has tended to emerge from a partnership between superstars, such as Robert Redford or Jane Fonda, for whom additional money is no longer a primary concern but for whom movies of high artistic promise and progressive sensibilities are. And if such vehicles provide them the satisfaction of directorial or acting roles as well, all the better. Similar kinds of motivations, albeit without the presumption of the type of command of resources and industry clout embodied in a Fonda or Redford, inspire such well-recognized Hispanics as "Cheech" Marín, Raúl Juliá, and Edward James Olmos.

Given the vast changes in the control of artistic content at Hollywood, the existence of Hispanic expertise to make genuine Hispanic films, the progressive sensibilities and interests in film as an art form among a distinct but influential minority of Hollywood figures, and the precedents of films like *La Bamba* and *Stand and Deliver* that were financially and artistically successful, one would expect continued and accelerated Hispanic Hollywood productions.

Finally, the prospects of the independent U.S. Hispanic film movement are good, but without any perceived fundamental changes in the budgetary and distribution limitations of these films. Independent U.S. Hispanic filmmakers will enjoy most of the benefits of the trends previously described, including more Hispanic viewers and more awareness of the importance of U.S. Hispanic culture; the decline in power and control of market of the film studios and more recently of the television networks; more diversity in distribution, particularly through television; the existence of a small, influential number of benefactors with money or other substantive resources; and perhaps, most of all, the growing number of well-trained and recognized Hispanic production people and actors and actresses who may not want to make a career out of low-budget productions but are willing to cross over to the independent side periodically.

The outlook is relatively good for U.S. Hispanic cinema. Both the Hispanic Hollywood and the independent U.S. Hispanic film movement will expand, and their productions will tend to be more comparable to each other than to the exploitive films that will also continue to be ground out by the Hollywood film carnival industry. The cadre of hispano talent will continue to expand, fostered by all elements of the film, television and video industries, even the most crass sectors. However, once these individuals have been initiated into the field and develop their skills, they will be qualified and eager to produce, at least

from time to time, a "real" movie about some aspect of U.S. Hispanic people.

✳OUTSTANDING HISPANICS IN THE FILM INDUSTRY

Norma Aleandro (1941-)

An actress, playwright, and director born in Argentina, Norma Aleandro is known best for her performance in the Academy Award-winning *The Official Story* (1985), for which she was named best actress at Cannes. She has also acted in *Gaby—A True Story* (1987), *Cousins* (1989), and *Vital Signs* (1990) and continues to do Spanish-language film.

Néstor Almendros (19?-)

A photography director born in Havana, Cuba, Néstor Almendros worked as a cameraman or director on several documentaries of the early Castro era, then moved to France where he worked for television and on film shorts. In the mid sixties he began collaborating regularly with director Erich Rohmer and later director Franscois Truffaut. He won the Academy Award for cinematography for the 1978 film *Days of Heaven*. Included among his films are *The Wild Racers* (1968), *Gun Runner* (1968), *Ma nuit chez Maud (My Night at Maud's,* 1969), *L'enfant sauvage (The Wild Child,* 1970), *Le genou de Claire (Claire's Knee,* 1971), *L'amour l'après-midi (Chloe in the Afternoon,* 1972), *L'histoire d'Adele (The Story of Adele H.,* 1975), and *Days of Heaven* (1978).

Pedro Armendáriz (1912-1963)

Born May 9, 1912, in Mexico City, Pedro Armendáriz was one of Mexico's most successful film stars, appearing in over forty films, many directed by Emilio "El Indio" Fernández. He was internationally recognized for *María Candelaria* (1943) and his work

The late Academy-Award-winning cinematographer, Néstor Almendros.

with major directors, including Luis Buñuel and John Ford. His son, Pedro Armendáriz, Jr., is also an actor. Included among his films are *María Candelaria* (1943), *La Perla (The Pearl*, (1945), *Fort Apache* (1948), *Three Godfathers, We Were Strangers, Tulsa* (1949), *Border River* (1954), *The Littlest Outlaw* (1955), *The Wonderful Country* (1959), *Francis of Assisi* (1961), and *Captain Sinbad* (1963).

Armida (1913-)

Born in 1913 in Sonora, Mexico, Armida became a stereotypical Latin lady of Hollywood B pictures of the 1930s and 1940s. Included among her films are *Under a Texas Moon, Border Romance* (1931), *Border Café* (1940), *Fiesta* (1941), *The Girl from Monterey* (1943), *Machine Gun Mama* (1944), *South of the Rio Grande* (1945), and *Bad Men of the Border* (1946).

Desi Arnaz (Desiderio Alberto Arnaz y de Acha III) (1917-)

The funny actor-musician Desi Arnaz was born on March 2, 1917, in Santiago, Cuba. In the United States from age 16, he became a popular singer and drummer, in 1940 marrying Lucille Ball, his costar in *Too Many Girls,* his screen debut. The 1950s television series "I Love Lucy," in which he and Lucille Ball starred, was enormously popular. (He and Ball were divorced in 1960; their son, Desi Arnaz, Jr., born in 1953, is also an actor). Included among his films are *Too Many Girls* (1940), *Father Takes a Wife* (1941), *The Navy Comes Through* (1942), *Bataan* (1943), *Cuban Pete* (1946), *Holiday in Havana* (1949), *The Long Long Trailer* (1954), and *Forever Darling* (1956).

Alfonso Bedoya (1904-1957)

Born in Vicam, Mexico, Bedoya developed a considerable career as a character actor in Mexican films. He made a notable American film debut in 1948 in John Huston's *The Treasure of the Sierra Madre* as a treacherous, smiling, and mocking stereotypical Mexican bandit. His performance is both recognized and parodied in Luis Valdez's notable play *I Don't Have to Show You No Stinking Badges.* Included among his films are *La perla (The Pearl,* 1945), *The Treasure of the Sierra Madre* (1948), *Streets of Laredo, Border Incident* (1949), *Man in the Saddle* (1951), *California Conquest* (1952), *Sombrero, The Stranger Wore a Gun* (1953), *Border River* (1954), *Ten Wanted Men* (1955), and *The Big Country* (1958).

Rubén Blades (1948-)

Actor, musician, composer, and lawyer Rubén Blades was born in Panama City, July 16, 1948. Known as a leading salsa musician, in 1985 Blades was recognized as cowriter and star of *Crossover Dreams* and has gone on to do several film performances, including the role of the sheriff in *The Milagro Beanfield War* (1988). Among his other films are *Critical Condition* (1987), *Fatal Beauty* (1987), *Disorganized Crime* (1989), *The Lemon Sisters* (1989), *The Heart of the Deal* (1990), *Mo" Better Blues* (1990), *Predator 2* (1990), *The Two Jakes* (1990), and *From the Heart* (1991).

Leo Carrillo (1880-1961)

Born in Los Angeles to an old California family, Leo Carrillo began as a cartoonist before becoming a dialect comedian in vaudeville and later on the stage. Debuting in Hollywood in the late 1920s, he became one of Hollywood's busiest character actors of the 1930s and 1940s. In the early 1950s, he played Pancho, Duncan Renaldo's sidekick in "The Cisco Kid" TV series. His films include *Mister Antonio* (1929), *Girl of the Rio* (1932), *Villa Villa!, Manhattan Melodrama, The Gay Bride* (1934), *In Caliente* (1935), *The Gay Desperado* (1936), *Manhattan Merry-Go-Round* (1937), *The Girl of the Golden West* (1939), *Captain Caution* (1940), *Horror Island* (1941), *Sin Town, American Empire* (1942), *Gypsy Wildcat* (1944), *Crime Incorporated* (1945), *The Fugitive* (1947), *The Girl from San Lorenzo* (1950).

Linda Cristal (Victoria Moya) (1935-)

Born in 1935 in Buenos Aires and orphaned at 13, Linda Cristal played leads in Mexican films from age 16 and debuted in Hollywood in the mid-1950s in both films and television ("High Chaparral") as a leading lady. Her U.S. films include *Comanche* (1951), *The Perfect Furlough* (1958), *Cry Tough* (1959), *The Alamo* (1960), *Two Rode Together* (1961), *Panic in the City* (1968), *Mr. Majestyk* (1974), and *Love and the Midnight Auto Supply* (1978).

Henry Darrow (1933-)

Born on September 15, 1933, in New York City, Henry Darrow starred in "The High Chaparral" TV series (1967-71); had the role of Alex Monténez (1973-74) on "The New Dick Van Dyke Show"; was Detective Lieutenant Manny Quinlan (1974-75) on "Harry-O," a TV drama series; played Don Diego de la Vega (Zorro SR.) on "Zorro and Son," a TV comedy (1983); and was Lieutenant Rojas on "Me and Mom," a TV drama series (1985). His film credits include *Badge 373* (1973), *Attica* (1980), *Seguín* (1982), *In Dangerous Company* (1988), *L.A. Bounty* (1989), and *The Last of the Finest* (1990).

Pedro de Córdoba (1881-1950)

Born September 28, 1881, in New York to Cuban-French parents, Pedro de Córdova began as a stage actor and later played character parts in numerous silent and sound films, usually as either a benevolent or malevolent Latin aristocrat. His films include *Carmen, Temptation* (1915), *Maria Rosa* (1916), *The New Moon* (1919), *When Knighthood Was in Flower* (1922), *The Bandolero* (1924), *Captain Blood* (1935), *Rose of the Rancho, Anthony Adverse, Ramona* (1936), *Juárez* (1939), *The Mark of Zorro* (1940), *Blood and Sand* (1941), *For Whom the Bell Tolls* (1943), *The Keys of the Kingdom* (1945), *Samson and Delilah* (1949), *Comanche Territory,* and *Crisis* (1950).

Arturo de Córdova (Arturo García) (1908-1973)

Born on May 8, 1908, in Merida, Yucatán, Mexico, Arturo de Córdova made his debut in Mexican films in the early 1930s and played Latin lovers in Hollywood during the 1940s, thereafter returning to Spanish-language film. His films include *Cielito lindo* (1936), *La zandunga* (1937), *For Whom the Bell Tolls* (1943), *Masquerade in Mexico, A Medal for Benny* (1945), *New Orleans* (1947), and *Adventures of Casanova* (1948).

Dolores del Río (Lolita Dolores Martínez Asunsolo López Negrete) (1905-1983)

Born on August 3, 1905, in Durango, Mexico, Dolores del Río was educated in a convent. By age 16, she was married to writer Jaime del Río. Director Edwin Carewe was struck by her beauty and invited her to Hollywood where she appeared in *Joanna* in 1925. She became a star in many silent films, but her career suffered from frequent typecasting in ethnic and exotic roles, particularly after the advent of sound. Dissatisfied with Hollywood, she returned to Mexico in 1943 to do many important films of the 1940s, including *María Candelaria* (1943) and John Ford's *The Fugitive* (1947, filmed on location in Mexico). She finally returned to Hollywood in character parts in the 1960s. Her films include *Resurrection, The Loves of Carmen* (1927), *Ramona, Revenge* (1928), *Evangeline* (1929), *The Bad One* (1930), *The Girl of the Rio* (1932), *Flying Down to Rio* (1933), *Madame Du Barry* (1934), *In Caliente* (1935), *Devil's Playground* (1937), *Doña Perfecta* (1950), *La cucaracha (The Cockroach,* 1958), *Flaming Star* (1960), *Cheyenne Autumn* (1964), and *The Children of Sánchez* (1978).

Moctezuma Esparza (19?-)

Producer and director and one of the best-known Chicano figures in the film industry, Moctezuma Esparza has been involved in feature, documentary,

Producer-Director Moctezuma Esparza.

and educational filmmaking since 1973. He has formed a production company, Esparza/Katz, which has raised considerable funds to produce feature-length motion pictures with Latino themes, including an adaptation of the Rudolfo Anaya novel *Bless Me Ultima* (written and to be directed by Luis Valdez) and *Angel's Flight* (written by first-time feature scripter Jill Isaacs and scheduled for direction by Luis Valdez), about a Hispanic detective embroiled in a major plot to bankrupt Los Angeles's mass transit rail system to clear the way for freeways. His films include *Only Once in a Lifetime* (1978, producer), *The Ballad of Gregorio Cortez* (1983, producer), *The Milagro Beanfield War* (1988, coproducer), and *Radioactive Dreams* (1986, producer).

Paul Espinosa (1950-)

Long affiliated with KPBS Television, San Diego, California, Paul Espinosa has produced and directed exceptional documentaries and docudramas, including *Los mineros (The Miners,* 1990, Héctor Galán, coproducer), a stirring view of the history of the labor struggle by Arizona Mexican-American miners from the turn of the century to the present. He is the producer for the "American Playhouse" TV drama series of a dramatic adaptation of Tomás Rivera's masterpiece, *And the Earth Did Not Part* (1992, Severo Pérez, director-writer). Others films by Espinoza are *Ballad of an Unsung Hero (1983),* about a scandalous case of discrimination and deportation of a well-known Chicano radio figure, and *The Lemon Grove Incident* (1985), about separate and unequal education of Chicanos in California.

Emilio Estévez (1962-)

Actor, director, and screenwriter Emilio Estevez was born May 12, 1962, in New York City and is the son of Martin Sheen and brother to Charlie Sheen. Estévez decided to use the original family surname. With his blond hair and blue eyes, he has been able to secure roles in mainstream pictures. His accomplishments as an actor are many and varied; much of the work has been highly recognized for its excellence. He first achieved recognition in *Repo Man* (1984) and had acting roles in *St. Elmo's Fire* (1985), *Maximum Overdrive* (1986), *Stakeout* (1987), *Young Guns* (1988), *Men at Work* 1990), and *Young Guns II* (1990). Estévez has written several screenplays and directed two of them. His other films include *Tex* (1982), *Nightmares* (1983), *The Outsiders* (1983), *The Breakfast Club* (1985), *That Was Then . . . This is Now* (1985), *Wisdom* (1986), and *Nightbreaker* (1989).

Emilio "El Indio" Fernández (1904-1986)

The famous director and actor, Emilio Fernández was born on March 26, 1904, in El Seco, Coahuila, Mexico. One of the most important figures of Mexican cinema, he was born to a Spanish-Mexican father and Indian mother (hence the nickname El Indio). At 19, he took part in the Mexican Revolution and in 1923 was sentenced to twenty years" imprisonment, but escaped to California where he played bit parts and supporting roles until returning to Mexico, first as an actor, debuting in the role of an Indian in *Janitizio* (1934), and then as Mexico's most prominent director. His film *María Candelaria* (1943) won Grand Prize at Cannes, and *La Perla (The Pearl,* 1946) won the International Prize at San Sebastián (Spain). As a Hollywood actor, he had a few notable parts in Sam Peckinpah films. Among the films he directed are *Soy puro mexicano* (*I Am Full-Blooded Mexican,* 1942), *Flor silvestre (Wildflower), María Candelaria* (1943), *Bugambilla (Bougainvillea,* 1944), *La perla (The Pearl,* 1946), *El gesticulador (The Gesticulator,* 1957), and *A Loyal Soldier of Pancho Villa* (1966). His films as an actor include *The Reward* (1965), *The Appaloosa, Return of the Seven* (1966), *A Covenant with Death, The War Wagon* (1967), *The Wild Bunch* (1969), *Pat Garrett and Billy the Kid* (1973), *Bring Me the Head of Alfredo García* (1974), *Lucky Lady* (1975), *Under the Volcano* (1984), and *Pirates* (1986).

Mel Ferrer (Melchior Gastón Ferrer) (1917-)

Actor, director, and producer, Mel Ferrer was born on August 25, 1917, in New York to a Cuban-born surgeon and a Manhattan socialite. He attended Princeton University but dropped out to become an actor, debuting on Broadway in 1938 as a chorus dancer. He made his screen acting debut in 1949 and appeared in many films as a leading man. His third (1954-68) of four wives was actress Audrey Hepburn, whom he directed in *Green Mansions* (1959). His films as actor include *Lost Boundaries* (1949), *The Brave Bulls* (1951), *Rancho Notorious, Scaramouche* (1952), *Lili* (1953), *War and Peace* (1956), *The Sun Also Rises* (1957), *The World, the Flesh and the Devil* (1959), *Sex and the Single Girl* (1964), *Eaten Alive* (1977), *Guyana: Cult of the Damned* (1979), and *City of the Walking Dead* (1980). The films he directed include *The Girl of the Limberlost* (1945) and *Green Mansions* (1959).

Gabriel Figueroa (1907-)

Photography director, Gabriel Figueroa was born on April 24, 1907, in Mexico. An orphan, as a boy he was forced to seek work, yet was able to pursue painting and photography on his own. In 1935, he went to Hollywood to study motion picture photography and returned to Mexico the following year, and began a prolific career as the cameraman of over one hundred films. He worked for Buñuel, John Ford, and Emilio Fernández and ranks among the leading directors of photography in world cinema. His films (primarily Mexican) include *Allá en el rancho grande* (*Out on the Big Ranch,* 1936), *Flor silvestre (Wildflower), María Candelaria,* (1943), *Bugambilla* (*Bougainvillea,* 1944), *La perla* (*The Pearl,* 1946), *The Fugitive* (1947), *Los olvidados* (*The Forgotten,* 1952), *La cucaracha* (*The Cockroach,* 1958), *Nazarín* (1959), *Macario* (1960), *Animas Trujano* (1961), *El angel exterminador* (*The Exterminating Angel,* 1962), *The Night of the Iguana* (1964), *Simón del desierto* (*Simon in the Desert,* 1965), *Two Mules for Sister Sara* (1970), *The Children of Sánchez* (1978), and *Under the Volcano* (1984).

Andy García (Andrés Arturo Garci-Menéndez) (1956-)

Born in Havana, García worked as an actor in regional theater in the early 1960s. In *8 Million Ways to Die* (1986) he turned in a superb performance as a villain, and in 1987 in Brian De Palma's *The Untouchables* he achieved widespread recognition as an earnest FBI agent. In 1990, he achieved star status as the good cop in *Internal Affairs* and as the illegitimate nephew of Don Corleone in *The Godfather Part III*. His other films include *Blue Skies Again* (1983), *The Mean Season* (1985), *American Roulette* (1988), *Stand and Deliver* (1988), *Black Rain* (1989), and *A Show of Force* (1990).

Rita Hayworth (Margarita Carmen Cansino) (1918-1987)

Rita Hayworth was born October 17, 1918, in Brooklyn, New York, to Spanish-born dancer Eduardo Cansino and his Ziegfeld Follies partner Volga Haworth. Hayworth danced professionally by age 13 in Mexican nightspots in Tijuana and Agua Caliente, where she was eventually noticed by Hollywood. She made her screen debut in 1935, playing bit parts under her real name. In 1937, she married Edward Judson, under whose guidance she changed her name and was transformed into an auburn-haired sophisticate. For the remainder of the 1930s, Hayworth was confined to leads in B pictures, but through much of the 1940s she became the undisputed sex goddess of Hollywood films and the hottest star at Columbia Studios. Her tempestuous personal life included marriages to Orson Welles, Aly Khan, and singer Dick Haymes. As Rita Cansino, her films included *Under the Pampas Moon, Charlie Chan in Egypt,* and *Dante's Inferno* (1935), *Meet Nero Wolfe* (1936), *Trouble in Texas, Old Louisiana,* and *Hit the Saddle* (1937). As Rita Hayworth, she acted in *The Shadow* (1937), *Angels Over Broadway* (1940), *The Strawberry Blonde, Blood and Sand* (1941), *Cover Girl* (1944), *Gilda* (1946), *The Lady from Shanghai, The Loves of Carmen* (1948), *Salome, Miss Sadie Thompson* (1953), *Pal Joey* (1957), *Separate Tables* (1958), *They Came to Cordura* (1959), *The Happy Thieves* (1962), *The Money Trap* (1966), *The Wrath of God* (1972), and *Circle* (1976).

Raúl Juliá (1940-)

Born on March 9, 1940, in San Juan, Puerto Rico, Raúl Juliá has become one of the best-known Hispanic actors for his Shakespearean and other classical stage roles and for musicals as well as film. In 1971, he debuted in small parts in *The Organization, Been Down So Long It Looks Like Up to Me,* and *Panic in Needle Park*. Juliá appeared in *The Gumball Rally* (1976) and *Eyes of Laura Mars* (1978) and achieved national attention as the costar in the notable *Kiss of the Spider Woman* (1985), adapted from the novel by Argentine Manuel Puig. His other films include *One from the Heart* (1982), *Tempest* (1982), *Compromising Positions* (1985), *The Morning After* (1986), *Florida Straits* (1986), *Trading Hearts* (1987), *The Penitentes* (1988), *Tango Bar* (1988), *Tequila Sunrise* (1988),

Moon over Parador (1988), *Romero* (1989), *Mack the Knife* (1989), *Presumed Innocent* (1990), *A Life of Sin* (1990), and *The Rookie* (1990).

Katy Jurado (María Cristina Jurado García) (1927-)

Born in 1927 in Guadalajara, Mexico, Katy Jurado began her Hollywood career as a columnist for Mexican publications following a Mexican film career. In Hollywood she played dark lady roles in a variety of films, most memorably *High Noon* (1952) and *One-Eyed Jacks* (1961). She was nominated for an Oscar for her supporting role in *Broken Lance* (1954). Between 1959 and 1964, she was wed to actor Ernest Borgnine. Her other films include *The Bullfighter and the Lady* (1951), *Arrowhead* (1953), *Trapeze, The Man from Del Rio* (1956), *Barabbas* (1961), *Pat Garrett and Billy the Kid* (1973), *El recurso del método* (*The Method's Resource,* 1978) and *The Children of Sánchez* (1978).

Fernando Lamas (1915-1982)

Born on January 9, 1915, in Buenos Aires, Fernando Lamas became a movie star in Argentina. Lamas was imported to Hollywood by MGM and typecast as a sporty Latin lover in several lightweight films, some of which featured his singing. He married Arlene Dahl (1954-60) and Esther Williams (since 1967). His films include *The Avengers* (1950), *The Merry Widow* (1952), *The Diamond Queen* (1953), *Jívaro, Rose Marie* (1954), *The Violent Ones, Kill a Dragon* (1967), *100 Rifles, Backtrack* (1969), and *The Cheap Detective* (1978).

Adele Mara (Adelaida Delgado) (1923-)

Born on April 28, 1923, in Highland Park, Michigan, Adele Mara began as a singer-dancer with Xavier Cugat's orchestra. In Hollywood she played dark lady/other woman parts in scores of low-budget films in the 1940s and 1950s, including *Navy Blues* (1941), *Alias Boston Blackie* (1942), *Atlantic City* (1944), *The Tiger Woman, Song of Mexico* (1945), *The Catman of Paris* (1946), *Twilight on the Rio Grande, Blackmail, Exposed* (1947), *Campus Honeymoon, Wake of the Red Witch, Angel in Exile* (1948), *Sands of Iwo Jima, The Avengers, California Passage* (1950), *The Sea Hornet* (1951), *Count the Hours* (1953), *Back from Eternity* (1956), and *The Big Circus* (1959).

Margo (Marie Marquerita Guadalupe Teresa Estela Bolado Castilla y O'Donnell) (1917-)

Born on May 10, 1917, in Mexico City, Margo was coached as a child by Eduardo Cansino, Rita Hayworth's father, and she danced professionally with her uncle Xavier Cugat's band in Mexican nightclubs and at New York's Waldorf-Astoria, where they triumphed in introducing the rumba. From 1934, she became known as a dramatic actress, mostly typecast as a tragic, suffering woman. She has been married to Eddie Albert since 1945 and is the mother of actor Eddie Albert, Jr. In 1974, she was appointed commissioner of social services for the city of Los Angeles. Her films include *Crime Without Passion* (1934), *Rumba* (1935), *The Robin Hood of Eldorado, Winterset* (1936), *Lost Horizon* (1937), *Behind the Rising Sun* (1943), *The Falcon in Mexico* (1944), *Viva Zapata!* (1952), *I'll Cry Tomorrow* (1955), *From Hell to Texas* (1958), and *Who's Got the Action?* (1962).

Richard ("Cheech") Marín (1946-)

Renowned comic, actor, and writer Richard Marín was born July 13, 1946, in Los Angeles. Marín began in show business as part of the comedy team Cheech and Chong in 1970, bringing stoned and hippy routines to the screen with *Cheech and Chong's Up in Smoke* (1978), which was the highest-grossing film of the year. Following the split-up of the duo in 1985, Cheech continued to appear in films and wrote, directed, and starred in *Born in East L.A.* (1987). His films include *Cheech and Chong's Next Movie* (1980), *Cheech and Chong's Nice Dreams* (1981), *Things are Tough all Over* (1982), *Yellowbeard* (1983), *Cheech and Chong's the Corsican Brothers* (1984), *Ghostbusters II* (1989), *Rude Awakening* (1989), *Troop Beverly Hills* (1989), and *The Shrimp on the Barbie* (1990).

Mona Maris (María Capdevielle) (1903-)

Born in 1903 in Buenos Aires and convent-educated in France, Mona Maris acted in several British and German films before embarking on a Hollywood career in the late 1920s and the 1930s in the usual sultry, exotic-type role. Her films include *Romance of the Rio Grande* (1929), *Under a Texas Moon, The Arizona Kid, A Devil With Women* (1930), *The Passionate Plumber, Once in A Lifetime* (1932), *Flight From Destiny, Law of the Tropics* (1941), *My Gal Sal, Pacific Rendezvous, I Married an Angel, Berlin Correspondent* (1942), *The Falcon in Mexico* (1944), *Heartbeat* (1946), and *The Avengers* (1950).

Chris-Pin (Christopher) Martin (Ysabel Ponciana Chris-Pin Martin) (1893-1953)

Born on November 19, 1893, in Tucson, Arizona, of Mexican parentage, he provided comic relief in the Cisco Kid series (as Pancho or Gordito) and many other Westerns. His films include *The Rescue* (1929), *Billy the Kid* (1930), *The Cisco Kid* (1931), *South of Santa Fe* (1932), *Bordertown* (1935), *The Gay Desper-*

ado (1936), *The Texans* (1938), *Stagecoach, The Return of the Cisco Kid* (1939), *Lucky Cisco Kid, Down Argentine Way, The Mark of Zorro* (1940), *Weekend in Havana* (1941), *Tombstone* (1942), *The Ox-Bow Incident* (1943), *Ali Baba and the Forty Thieves* (1944), *San Antonio* (1945), *The Fugitive* (1947), *Mexican Hayride* (1948), *The Beatiful Blonde From Bashful Bend* (1949), and *Ride the Man Down* (1952).

Ricardo Montalbán (1920-)

Born on November 25, 1920, in Mexico City, Ricardo Montalbán first played bit roles in several Broadway productions before debuting on the screen in Mexico in the early 1940s and subsequently being recruited as a Latin lover type by MGM in 1947. He was eventually given an opportunity to demonstrate a wider acting range on television, including roles in segments of "The Loretta Young Show." He has been a strong force in Hollywood for the establishment of better opportunities for Hispanics. His films include *Fiesta* (1947), *The Kissing Bandit* (1948), *Neptune's Daughter, Border Incident* (1949), *Right Cross, Two Weeks With Love* (1950), *Across the Wide Missouri, Mark of the Renegade* (1951), *Sombrero, Latin Lovers* (1953), *The Saracen Blade* (1954), *A Life in the Balance*

Ricardo Montalbán in the T.V. series, "Fantasy Island."

(1955), *Sayonara* (1957), *Let No Man Write My Epitaph* (1960), *Cheyenne Autumn* (1964), *The Money Trap, The Singing Nun* (1966), *Sweet Charity* (1969), *Escape from the Planet of the Apes* (1971), *Conquest of the Planet of the Apes* (1972), *The Train Robbers* (1973), *Joe Panther* (1976), and *Star Trek II: The Wrath of Khan* (1982).

María Montez (María Africa Vidal de Santo Silas) (1920-1951)

Born on June 6, 1920, in Barahona, Dominican Republic, Maria Montez became one of the most notable, exotic dark ladies. Affectionately called The Queen of Technicolor, she started her screen career in 1941 doing bit parts in Universal films. Although inordinately unskilled at acting, she nevertheless became immensely popular in a string of color adventure tales, often costarring with fellow exotics Jon Hall, Sabu, and Turhan Bey. She remains the object of an extensive fan cult thirsting for nostalgia and high camp. Her films include *Lucky Devils, That Night in Rio, Raiders of the Desert, South of Tahiti* (1941), *Bombay Clipper, Arabian Nights* (1942), *White Savage* (1943), *Ali Baba and the Forty Thieves, Cobra Woman, Gypsy Wildcat, Bowery to Broadway* (1944), *Sudan* (1945), *Tangier* (1946), *The Exile*, and *Pirates of Monterey* (1947).

Sylvia Morales (19?-)

One of the best-recognized Chicana directors, Sylvia Morales has directed the short film *Chicana* (1979), about the changing roles of women in Hispanic/Chicano society from pre-Columbian times to the present; *Los Lobos: And A Time to Dance* (1984), a short musical special produced for PBS that profiles the musical group Los Lobos; *Esperanza*, a one-hour narrative drama directed under the Women Filmmakers Program at the American Film Institute, about the story of a young immigrant girl whose mother is arrested and who has to cope on her own; *SIDA Is AIDS*, a one-hour video documentary for PBS, broadcast in both Spanish and English; *Values: Sexuality and the Family*, a half-hour documentary on health issues affecting the Latino community, broadcast in Spanish and English; and *Faith Even to the Fire*, a one-hour video documentary for PBS profiling three nuns whose conscience motivated them to speak out on issues of social justice, sexism, racism, and classism within the Catholic church.

Silvia Morales, director-cinematographer.

Antonio Moreno (Antonio Garride Monteagudo) (1887-1967)

Born on September 26, 1887, in Madrid, Antonio Moreno played a dapper Latin lover in numerous Hollywood silent films. He began his career in 1912 under D. W. Griffith and was quite popular during the 1920s, when he played leads opposite such actresses as Gloria Swanson, Greta Garbo, Pola Negri, and Bebe Daniels. His foreign accent limited his career in talkies, where he was seen mainly in character roles. He appeared in hundreds of films, including *Voice of the Million, The Musketeers of Pig Alley* (1912), *The Song of the Ghetto, The Loan Shark King, In the Latin Quarter, Sunshine and Shadows* (1914), *The Quality of Mercy, The Gypsy Trail* (1915), *My American Wife, The Spanish Dancer* (1923), *One Year to Live* (1925), *Mare Nostrum, The Temptress* (1926), *Venus of Venice, The Whip Woman* (1928), *Romance of the Rio Grande* (1929), *One Mad Kiss* (1930), *The Bohemian Girl* (1938), *Rose of the Rio Grande* (1938), *Seven Sinners* (1940), *Notorious* (1946), *Captain from Castille* (1947), *Crisis, Dallas* (1950), *Wings of the Hawk* (1953), *Creature From the Black Lagoon* (1954), and *The Searchers* (1956).

Rita Moreno (Rosita Dolores Alverio) (1931-)

An actress, dancer, singer, Moreno was born on December 11, 1931 in Humacao, Puerto Rico. A dancer from childhood, she reached Broadway at thirteen and Hollywood at fourteen. She won a 1962 Academy Award as best supporting actress for *West Side Story* and has been in several films important for understanding the Hollywood depiction of Hispanics, including *A Medal for Benny*, (1954), *The Ring* (1952), and *Popi* (1969). Her other films include *Pagan Love Song* (1950), *Singin" in the Rain* (1952), *Latin Lovers, Fort Vengeance* (1953), *Jivaro, Garden of Evil* (1954), *The King and I, The Vagabond King* (1956), *The Deerslayer* (1957), *Summer and Smoke* (1961), *Marlowe* (1969), *Carnal Knowledge*, (1971), *The Ritz* (1976), *The Boss" Son* (1978), *Happy Birthday, Gemini* (1980), *The Four Seasons* (1981), and *Life in the Food Chain* (1991).

Barry Norton (Alfedo Birabén) (1905-1956)

Born on June 16, 1905, in Buenos Aires, Barry Norton became a romantic lead in Hollywood's late silent and early sound films. He later appeared in Hollywood-made Spanish-language or Mexican productions, sometimes directing his own films. His Hollywood films include *The Lily, What Price Glory* (1926), *Ankles Preferred, The Wizard, The Heart of Salome, Sunrise* (1926), *Mother Knows Best, Legion of the Condemned, Four Devils* (1928), *The Exalted Flap-*

Rita Moreno receives her second Emmy in 1978.

per (1929), *Lady for a Day* (1933), *Nana* (1934), *The Buccaneer* (1938), *Devil Monster* (1946), and *Around the World in Eighty Days* (cameo, 1956).

Ramón Novarro (Ramón Samaniegos) (1899-1968)

Born on February 6, 1899, in Durango, Mexico, he became a romantic idol of Hollywood silents of the 1920s. He began his career as a singing waiter and vaudeville performer before breaking into films as an extra in 1917. By 1922, he had become a star Latin lover and was overshadowed only by Rudolph Valentino in that role. He soon sought a broader range and less exotic image. His most famous part was the title role of the 1926 *Ben-Hur*. He was found beaten to death by intruders on October 31, 1968. His films include *A Small Town Idol* (1921), *The Prisoner of Zenda* (1922), *Scaramouche* (1923), *The Arab, Thy Name is Woman* (1924), *A Lover's Oath* (1925), *The Student Prince* (1927), *The Pagan* (1929), *In Gay Madrid* (1930), *Call of the Flesh* (1930), *Son of India, Mata Hari* (1931), *The Barbarian* (1933), *The Sheik Steps Out* (1937), *The Big Steal* (1949), *The Outriders* (1950), and *Heller in Pink Tights* (1960).

Edward James Olmos (1947-)

Actor, composer, producer, and director, Edward James Olmos was born on February 24, 1947, in Los Angeles. He began his career as a rock singer and earned a Los Angeles Drama Critics Circle Award for his performance in Luis Valdez's musical play *Zoot Suit*, which he reprised on Broadway and in the 1981 film version. He became nationally known as Lieutenant Castillo on television's "Miami Vice" (1984-89) and was nominated for an Oscar for best actor for his lead as a committed Latino teacher of calculus to East Los Angeles high school students in *Stand and Deliver* (1988). The film also helped propel him to the cover of *Time* magazine, perhaps the only Chicano to have attained that recognition. Additional films include *Wolfen* (1981), *Blade Runner* (1982), *The Ballad of Gregorio Cortez* (1983), *Saving Grace* (1986), *Triumph of the Spirit* (1989), *Maria's Story* (1990), and *A Talent for the Game* (1991).

Anthony Quinn (1915-)

Born on April 21, 1915, in Chihuahua, Mexico, of Irish-Mexican parentage, Anthony Quinn has lived in the United States from childhood. He entered films in 1936 and the following year married Cecil B. deMille's adopted daughter, Katherine (they are now divorced), but his father-in-law did nothing to advance Quinn's career, which did not attain star status until 1952 with his Academy Award-winning role as Zapata's brother in *Viva Zapata!* Quinn went on to win a second Academy Award for *Lust for Life* (1956), and he began playing leads that emphasized his earthy and exotic qualities. He has appeared in over one hundred films and has written his autobiography, *The Original Sin* (1972). Among his many films are *Parole!* (1936), *The Buccaneer, King of Alcatraz* (1938), *Texas Rangers Ride Again* (1940), *Blood and Sand* (1941), *The Ox-Bow Incident, Guadalcanal Diary* (1943), *Back to Bataan* (1945), *California, Sinbad*

Edward James Olmos.

the Sailor, Black Gold (1947), *The Brave Bulls* (1951), *Against All Flags* (1952), *Ride Vaquero* (1953), *Man From Del Rio* (1956), *The Black Orchid* (1958), *The Guns of Navarrone, Barabbas* (1961), *Requiem for a Heavyweight, Lawrence of Arabia* (1962), *Zorba the Greek* (1964), *A High Wind in Jamaica* (1965), *The Shoes of the Fisherman, The Magus* (1968), *The Secret of Santa Vittoria* (1969), *The Greek Tycoon, The Children of Sánchez* (1978), *The Salamander* (1981), *Ghosts Can't Do It* (1990), and *Revenge* (1990).

Duncan Renaldo (1904-)

A foundling thought to have been born in Spain on April 23, 1904, Duncan Renaldo arrived in the United States in the early 1920s and was a Hollywood leading man and supporting player. He debuted with MGM in 1928 and by the early 1940s had found a niche in Westerns as one of the Three Mesquiteers and subsequently as the screen's fourth Cisco Kid. His films include *Clothes Make the Woman* (1928), *The Bridge of San Luis Rey* (1929), *Trapped in Tia Juana* (1932), *Zorro Rides Again* (serial, 1937), *Rose of the Rio Grande* (1938), *The Long Ranger Rides Again* (serial), *The Kansas Terrors* (1939), *Down Mexico Way* (1941), *For Whom the Bell Tolls* (1943), *The Cisco Kid Returns* (1945), *The Gay Amigo, The Daring Caballero* (1949), and *Zorro Rides Again* (1959).

Gilbert Roland (Luis Antonio Dámaso de Alonso) (1905-)

Born in Júarez, Mexico, on December 11, 1905, the son of a bullfighter, Gilbert Roland trained for the *corrida* (bullfight), but chose a career in film instead after his family moved to the United States. He debuted as an extra at age 13 and subsequently played a Latin lover on both the silent and sound screens. His films include *The Plastic Age* (1925), *The Campus Flirt* (1926), *Camille, Rose of the Golden West* (1927), *The Dove* (1928), *The Last Train from Madrid* (1937), *Júarez* (1939), *The Sea Hawk* (1940), *Captain Kidd* (1945), *The Gay Cavalier, Beauty and the Bandit* (1946), *The Bullfighter and the Lady, Mark of the Renegade* (1951), *Bandido* (1956), *Cheyenne Autumn* (1964), *Islands in the Stream, The Black Pearl* (1977), and *Barbarosa* (1982).

César Romero (1907-)

Born on February 15, 1907, in New York City and of Cuban parentage, César Romero played a Latin lover in Hollywood films from the 1930s through the 1950s and later did suave supporting character roles. He played the Cisco Kid in the late 1930s and early 1940s. His films include *The Thin Man* (1934), *Clive of India, Cardinal Richelieu* (1935), *The Cisco Kid and the Lady*

(1939), *Viva Cisco Kid, The Gay Caballero, Romance of the Rio Grande* (1940), *Ride on Vaquero, Weekend in Havana* (1941), *Captain from Castile* (1948), *Vera Cruz* (1954), *Villa!* (1958), *Batman* (1966), and *The Strongest Man in the World* (1975).

Martin Sheen (Ramón Estévez) (1940-)

Born on August 3, 1940, in Dayton, Ohio, to a Spanish immigrant father and an Irish mother, Martin Sheen began at the New York Living Theater and debuted on the screen in 1967. He was named as best actor at the San Sebastián (Spain) Film Festival for his role in *Badlands* (1973). His other films include *The Incident* (1967), *The Subject Was Roses* (1968), *Catch-22* (1970), *The Cassandra Crossing* (1977), *Apocalypse Now* (1979), *That Championship Season* (1982), *Gandhi* (1982), *The Guardian* (1984), *Siesta* (1987), *Wall Street* (1987), *Da* (1988), and *Beverly Hills Brats* (1989).

Jesús Salvador Treviño (?-)

Director, producer, and writer, Jesús Treviño is one of the best-known Chicano filmmakers. His credits include directing episodes of the ABC series "Gabriel's Fire," the NBC series "Lifestories," and the PBS series "Mathnet." His films include *Raíces de sangre* (*Roots [of Blood]*, 1977, with Richard Yñiguez), which evokes border life and the *maquiladoras* (twin manufacturing plants); *Seguín* (1982, with Henry Darrow and Edward James Olmos), a Hispanic perspective on the Alamo; and documentaries and docudramas, including *Salazar Inquest* (1970), *Chicano Moratorium* (1970), *America Tropical* (1971), *La Raza Unida* (1972), *Yo soy chicano* (*I Am Chicano*, 1972), *Have Another Drink, Ese* (1977), *One out of Ten* (1979), and *Yo soy* (*I Am*) (1985).

Luis Valdez (1940-)

See Chapter 19.

Lupe Vélez (María Guadalupe Vélez de Villalobos) (1908-1944)

Born on July 18, 1908, in San Luis Potosí, Mexico, Lupe Vélez became one of the most famous Hispanic screen actresses of all time. Originally a dancer, she debuted in film in 1926 under Hal Roach's direction and became a star the following year as the leading lady in *The Gaucho* opposite Douglas Fairbanks. Known as a fiery leading lady, both in silent and sound films, she later made positive use of her Spanish-accented English to reposition herself as a comedienne in the Mexican Spitfire series. Her volatile personal life, including a romance with Gary Cooper and marriage to Johnny Weismuller, ended in sui-

cide. Her films include *Stand and Deliver* (1928), *Lady of the Pavements* (1929), *The Squaw Man, The Cuban Love Song* (1931), *Hot Pepper* (1933), *The Girl from Mexico* (1939), *Mexican Spitfire* (1940), and *Redhead from Manhattan* (1943).

Raoul Walsh

Raoul Walsh was given his first directorial assignment by D. W. Griffith at Biograph, which was, in collaboration with Christy Cabanne, *The Life of General Villa* (1914), a seven-reel mixture of staged scenes and authentic footage of Pancho Villa's military campaign starring the Mexican bandit himself. Walsh's most notable appearance as an actor was in the role of John Wilkes Booth in Griffith's *The Birth of a Nation* (1915). He subsequently appeared in occasional films but largely devoted himself to a career as a director.

Raquel Welch (Raquel Tejada) (1940-)

Raquel Welch was born on September 5, 1940, in Chicago to a Bolivian-born engineer and a mother of English background. Despite a very difficult and inauspicious beginning, and thanks to a phenomenally successful 1963 publicity tour in Europe devised by her second husband, former child actor Patrick Curtis, and herself, she became a major international star without having appeared in a single important film. Known first as a voluptuous sex goddess, subsequently she also made a name as a comedienne. Her films include *A Swingin" Summer* (1965), *One Million Years B.C.* (1966), *The Biggest Bundle of Them All, Bandolero!* (1968), *100 Rifles* (1969), *Myra Breckinridge* (1970), *Kansas City Bomber* (1972), *The Three Musketeers* (1974), and *Mother, Jugs, and Speed* (1977).

References

"Authentic Pachuco." *Time* (10 July 1944): 72.

Barry, Iris. *D. W. Griffith: American Film Master*. New York: Museum of Modern Art, 1965.

Biberman, Herbert. *Salt of the Earth: The Story of a Film*. Boston: Beacon Press, 1965.

Bowser, Eileen, ed. *Film Notes*. New York: Museum of Modern Art, 1969.

Candelaia, Cordelia. "Film Portrayals of La Mujer Hispana," *Agenda* (June 1981): 32-36.

Cárdenas, Don, and Suzanne Schneider, eds. *Chicano Images in Film*. Denver, Colo.: Denver International Film Festival, 1981.

Cortés, Carlos E. "Chicanas in Film: History of an Image." In *Chicano Cinema: Research, Review, and Resources*, edited by Gary D. Keller, 94-108. Binghamton, N.Y.: Bilingual Review/Press, 1985

———. *"The Greaser's Revenge to Boulevard Nights: The Mass Media Curriculum on Chicanos." In History, Cul-*

ture, and Society: Chicano Studies in the 1980s. Ypsilanti, Mich.: Bilingual Press, 1983.

———. "The History of Ethnic Images in Film: The Search for a Methodology." In *Ethnic Images in Popular Genres and Media* Special issue. *MELUS, The Journal of the Society for the Study of the Multi-Ethnic Literature of the United States* 11, no. 3 (Fall 1984): 63-77.

———. "The Immigrant in Film: Evolution of an Illuminating Icon." In *Stock Characters in American Popular Film,* edited by Paul Loukides and Linda K. Fuller, 23-24. Vol. 1 of *Beyond the Stars.* Bowling Green, Ohio: Bowling Green State University Popular Press, 1990.

———. "The Role of Media in Multicultural Education." *Viewpoints in Teaching and Learning* 56, no. 1 (Winter 1980): 38-49.

Croy, Homer. *The Story of D. W. Griffith.* New York: Duell, Sloan and Pearce, 1959.

D.W. Griffith: The Years at Biograph. New York: Farrar, Straus and Giroux, 1970.

Delpar, Helen. "Goodbye to the 'Greaser': Mexico, the MPPDA, and Derogatory Films, 1922-1926," *Journal of Popular Film and Television* 12 (1984): 34-41.

Farber, Stephen. "Peckinpah's Return," *Film Quarterly* 23 (Fall 1969): 2-11.

Fregoso, Rosa Linda. "*Born in East L.A.* and the Politics of Representation." *Cultural Studies* 4, no. 3 (October 1990): 264-80.

García, Juan R. "Hollywood and the West: Mexican Images in American Films, 1894-1983." In *Old Southwest, New Southwest,* edited by Judy Nolte Lensink. Tucson Ariz.: Tucson Public Library, 1988.

Geduld, Harry M. *Focus on D. W. Griffith.* Englewood Cliffs, N.J.: Prentice-Hall, 1971.

Gonzales, Rodolfo. *Yo Soy Joaquín/I Am Joaquín.* Denver: La Causa, 1972. Graham, Cooper C., Steven Higgins, Elaine Mancini, and Joao Luiz Vieira. *D. W. Griffith and the Biography Company.* Metuchen, N.J.: Scarecrow Press, 1985.

Greenberg, Bradley S., and Pilar Baptista-Fernández. "Hispanic American—The New Minority on Television." In *Life on Television: Content Analysis of U.S. TV Drama,* edited by Bradley S.Greenberg, 3-12 Norwood, N.J.: Ablex; 1980.

Greenfield, Gerald Michael, and Carlos E. Cortés. "Harmony and Conflict of Intercultural Images: The Treatment of Mexico in U.S. Feature Films and K-12 Textbooks." *Estudios Mexicanos* 7, no. 2 (1991) 45-56.

Griffith, Albert J. "The Scion, The Señorita, and the Texas Ranch Epic: Hispanic Images in Film." *Bilingual Review/Revista Bilingüe.* In press.

Gunning, Tom, "Weaving a Narrative: Style and Economic Background in Griffith's Biograph Films," *Quarterly Review of Film Studies* (Winter 1981): 11-21.

Hadley-García, George. *Hollywood hispano: Los latinos en el mundo del cine.* Secaucus, NJ: Carol Publishing Group, 1991.

Haskell, Molly. *From Reverence to Rape. The Treatment of Women in the Movies.* New York: Holt, Rinehart and Winston, 1974.

Henderson, Robert M. *D. W. Griffith: His Life and Work.* New York: Oxford University Press, 1972.

Jacob Lewis. *The Rise of the American Film: A Critical History.* New York: Harcourt Brace and Company, 1939.

Kazan, Elia. "Letters to the Editor." *The Saturday Review* 35 (5 April, 1952): 22.

Kearney, Jill. "The Old Gringo." *American Film* 13, no. 5 (March 1988): 26-31, 67.

Keller, Gary D., *Chicano Cinema: Research, Reviews, and Resources.* Binghamton, N.Y.: Bilingual Review/Press, 1985.

———. *Cine chicano.* México City: Cineteca Nacional, 1988.

Kitses, Jim. *Horizons West: Anthony Mann, Budd Boetticher, Sam Peckinpah: Studies in Authorship within the Western.* Bloomington: Indiana University Press, 1969.

Lamb, Blaine P. "The Convenient Villain: The Early Cinema Views the Mexican American," *Journal of the West* 14 (October 1975): 75-81.

Latino Film and Video Images. Special issue, *Centro,* 2, no. 8 (Spring 1990). [Centro de Estudios Puertorriqueños, Hunter College/CUNY.]

Latinos and the Media. Special Issue. *Centro,* 3, no. 1 (Winter 1990-91). [Centro de Estudios Puertorriqueños, Hunter College/CUNY.]

Leab, Daniel J. *From Sambo to Superspade: The Black Experience in Motion Pictures.* Boston: Houghton Mifflin, 1975.

Levine, Paul G. "Remember the Alamo? John Wayne Told One Story. PBS's Seguçn Tells Another." *American Film* (January-February 1982): 47-48.

Maciel, David R. "Braceros, Mojados, and Alambristas: Mexican Immigration to the United States in Contemporary Cinema," *Hispanic Journal of Behavioral Sciences* 8 (1986): 369-85.

———. *El Norte; The U.S.-Mexican Border in Contemporary Cinema.* San Diego, Calif.: Institute for Regional Studies of the Californias, San Diego State University, 1990.

Miller, Jim. "Chicano Cinema: An Interview with Jesús Treviño." *Cineaste* 8, no. 3 (1978).

Miller, Mark Crispin. "In Defense of Sam Peckinpah." *Film Quarterly* 28 (Spring 1975): 2-17.

Miller, Randall M., ed. *The Kaleidoscopic Lens: How Hollywood Views Ethnic Groups.* Englewood Cliffs, N.J.: Jerome S. Ozer, 1980.

Mindiola, Jr., Tatcho. "El corrido de Gregorio Cortez: The Challenge of Conveying Chicano Culture Through the Cinematic Treatment of a Folk Hero." *Tonantzin* (November 1986): 14-15.

Monsiváis, Carlos. "The Culture of the Frontier: The Mexican Side." In *Views Across the Border: The United States and Mexico,* edited by Stanley R. Ross, Albuquerque: University of New Mexico Press, 1978.

Mora, Carl J. *Mexican Cinema: Reflections of a Society, 1896-1980.* Berkeley: University of California Press, 1982.

Morsberger, Robert E., ed. *Viva Zapata! (The Original Screenplay by John Steinbeck).* New York: Viking Press, 1973.

Niver, Kemp R. *D. W. Griffith: His Biograph Films in Perspective.* Los Angeles: John D. Roche, 1974.

Noriega, Chon. *Chicano Cinema and the Horizon of Expectation: a Discursive Analysis of Recent Reviews in the Mainstream, Alternative and Hispanic Press.* (SCCR Working Paper No. 30). Stanford, Calif.: Stanford Center for Chicano Research, 1990.

———. ed. *Chicanos and Film: Essays on Chicano Representation and Resistance.* New York: Garland. In press.

———. "Citizen Chicano: The Trials and Titillations of Ethnicity in the American Cinema, 1935-1962." *Social Research* 58, no. 2 (Summer 1991): 413-38.

———. "In Aztlán: The Films of the Chicano Movement, 1969-79." *Whitney Museum of American Art.* No. 56 (pamphlet). January 9-27, 1991.

———. *Working Bibliography of Critical Writings on Chicanos and Film.* Working Bibliography Series, no. 6. Stanford, Calif.: Mexican-American Collections, Stanford University Libraries, 1990.

O'Connor, John. "TV: Seguín: True Tale of the Texas Revolution." *New York Times* (26 January 1982).

O'Dell, Paul. *Griffith and the Rise of Hollywood.* New York: The International Film Guide Series, 1970.

Pettit, Arthur G. *Images of the Mexican American in Fiction and Film.* College Station: Texas A&M University Press, 1980.

———. "Nightmare and Nostalgia: The Cinema West of Sam Peckinpah," *Western Humanities Review* 29 (Spring 1975): 105-22.

Ramírez Berg, Charles. "Stereotyping in Film in General and of Hispanics in Particular." *Howard Journal of Communications* 2.3 (Summer 1990): 286-300.

Reyes, Luis. "The Mexican's Turn to Remember the Alamo." *Los Angeles Times* (24 August 1982): 1.

Roeder, Jr. George H. "Mexicans in the Movies: The Image of Mexicans in American Films, 1894-1947." Unpublished manuscript, University of Wisconsin, Madison, 1971.

Roffman, Peter, and Jim Purdy. *The Hollywood Social Problem Film.* Bloomington: Indiana University Press, 1981.

Rosen, Marjorie. *Popcorn Venus: Women, Movies and the American Dream.* New York: Coward, McCann and Geoghegan, 1973.

Rosenfelt, Deborah Silverton. *Salt of the Earth.* Old Westbury, NY: Feminist Press, 1978.

Saragoza, Alex M. " The Border in American and Mexican Cinema." *In Cultural Atlas of Mexico-United States Border Studies*, edited by Raymond Paredes. Los Angeles: UCLA Latin American Center Publications, 1990.

———. "Mexican Cinema in the United States, 1940-1952." In National Association for Chicano Studies, *History, Culture and Society: Chicano Studies in the 1980s.* Ypsilanti, MI: Bilingual Press, 1983.

Schickel, Richard. *D. W. Griffith: An American Life.* New York: Simon and Schuster, 1984.

Sklar, Robert. *Movie-Made America: A Cultural History of American Movies.* New York: Random House, 1975.

Slide, Anthony. *The Griffith Actresses.* South Brunswick, NJ and New York: A. S. Barnes, 1973.

Taylor, Frank J. "Leo the Caballero." *Saturday Evening Post* (6, July 1946): 26.

Treviño, Jesús Salvador. "Chicano Cinema." *New Scholar* 8 (1982): 167-73.

Valle, Victor. "Latino: Hollywood Opens Door as 'La Bamba' Leads Way." *Mesa* (Arizona) *Tribune*, (6, April, 1988): D2.

Vanderwood, Paul. "An American Cold Warrior: *Viva Zapata!*" In, *American History/American Film: Interpreting the Hollywood Image,* edited by John E. O'Connor and Martin A. Jackson, 183-201. New York: Frederick Ungar, 1979.

Whitney, John. "Image Making in the Land of Fantasy." *Agenda, A Journal of Hispanic Issues* 8, no. 1 (January-February 1978).

Williams, Linda. "Type and Stereotype: Chicano Images in Film." *Frontiers: A Journal of Women's Studies* 5, no. 2 (Summer 1980): 14-17.

Williams, Martin. *Griffith: First Artist of the Movies.* New York: Oxford University Press, 1980.

Woll, Allen L. "Hollywood's Good Neighbor Policy: The Latin American Image in American Film, 1939-1946," *Journal of Popular Film* 3 (Fall 1974a): 283-85.

———. *The Latin Image in American Film.* Los Angeles: LatinAmerican Center, University of California, 1977.

———. "Latin Images in American Films," *Journal of Mexican History* 4 (1974):28-40. Wong, Eugene Franklin: "On Visual Media Racism: Asians in the American Motion Pictures." Ph.D. diss., Graduate School of International Studies, University of Denver, 1977, Reprint. New York: Arno Press, 1978.

Yacowar, Maurice. "Aspects of the Familiar: A Defense of Minority Group Stereotyping in Popular Film." *Film Literature Quarterly* 2, no. 2 (Spring 1974): 129-39.

Zinman, David. *Saturday Night at the Bijou.* New Rochelle, NY: Arlington House, 1973.

Gary D. Keller

Music

✹ The Corrido and Canción-Corrido ✹ Música Norteña (The Mexican-Texan Conjunto)
✹ The Mexican-American Orquesta ✹ Salsa ✹ Latin Jazz/Rock ✹ Música Tropical
✹ Selected Discography

Music is a form of cultural communication. As such, it speaks in a symbolic way about the thoughts and feelings of people, which means that it makes associations that people understand between the particular musical sounds and their own particular thoughts, actions, and experiences. Music can thus transmit shared feelings and values, and, when words are added, it can be the ideal vehicle for communicating ideologies, or certain ways of thinking and acting, that those who subscribe to the musical message believe are appropriate guides for living.

Normally, the most strongly symbolic or cultural musical forms connected to a people's deepest sentiments about their way of life. Such musical forms are considered to be "strong" symbols that are, moreover, "organically" link ed to a people's everyday thoughts and actions. They express the most profound feelings that those people have about their sense of identity and their everyday life rhythms. Most important, organic, culturally powerful music is generally "homegrown," in the sense that it is created by and belongs to the communities that perform. Thus, unlike pop music, for example, which is intended to appeal to the largest possible audience and is created for financial gain, organic, homegrown music usually has deep roots within smaller, tightly knit communities, and this is what makes such music a powerful cultural expression.

Of course, the for-profit motive that drives pop music production does not completely strip it of its cultural message. Often it does communicate to young people a "hip" life-style, as opposed to the more conservative tastes of older generations. But pop commercial music can never be a "strong" cultural symbol. Cultural music—the Puerto Rican *salsa* and the Mexican-Texan *norteño*, for example—speak to the innermost feelings, desires, and conflicts

of specific Hispanic groups in the United States, and they bring into play a whole array of social, political, economic, and cultural factors that form the basis for a collective identity. At best, meanwhile, commercial pop music can only provide a sense of momentary escape into youthful fantasies.

Among Latinos in the United States, several musical forms and styles fall into the category of organic, homegrown musical communication. They symbolize the most powerful cultural beliefs and ways of doing things for specific segments of the Latino community. They speak, both directly and indirectly, to challenges and problems that confront the various segments of the Latino community in the United States. Over the span of many years, these musical forms and styles have developed into cultural traditions that enjoy deep and widespread popularity among their respective audiences. *Música norteña*, the Mexican-American *orquesta*, and *salsa* are excellent examples. These traditions have all contributed in important, "organic" ways toward the cultural life of the Latino groups with which they are historically associated. They represent major musical developments whose cultural power is linked to fundamental forces—social, economic, and ideological—among the various segments of the Latino community. These and other musical forms and styles speak symbolically to such issues as acculturation, intercultural conflict, and socioeconomic differences within the Latino communities.

Latinos in the United States have been witness to a multitude of styles and performers, but not all have equal cultural value. Some are fleeting expressions that leave little trace behind. On the other hand, some homegrown creations—mostly in the form of musical ensembles, their styles, and repertoires—have achieved great popularity and widespread dis-

Mexican musicians in the 1890s in California (Courtesy of the Huntington Library, San Marino, California).

tribution, and these are the ones earmarked for study here.

Among the most important Latino musical creations are two ensembles that originated among the Mexicans in Texas. These are *música norteña*, known among Mexican Texans , or tejanos, as *conjunto*, and *orquesta tejana*, or simply *orquesta*. Both of these musical styles originated in the first half of the twen-

tieth century, and both should be seen as musical responses to important economic, social, and cultural changes that take place among the Mexican Texans beginning in the 1930s. Both conjunto and orquesta had become major musical styles by the 1950s, and their influence had spread far beyond the Texas borders by the 1970s.

A type of Afro-Caribbean music that came to be known in the 1970s as *salsa* is another major style of Latino music in the United States. Just as conjunto and orquesta are homegrown Mexican-Texan styles, salsa likewise is the unique music of Afro-Hispanics from Puerto Rico, Cuba, and the Dominican Republic. It too is organically linked to the people who created it, and, despite its heavy commercialization in the last thirty years by the recording industry in the United States, it continues to occupy a central position in the musical life of Afro-Hispanic people in the United States.

Two cousins of salsa, Latin jazz and Latin rock, are also important enough to be included here. Although neither has the kind of organic links that salsa, orquesta tejana, or conjunto have to specific segments of the Latino population, both of these related forms have produced their share of gifted performers.

Xavier Cugat and his orchestra in the 1940s.

Augusto Coen and his Golden Orchestra, ca. 1930s-1940s. Postcard. (José A. Martí Collection. Courtesy of the Center for Puerto Rican Studies Library, Hunter College, CUNY.)

These performers see themselves as members of the Latino community, and they perceive their music as a contribution to the life and culture of this population.

Two important types of vocal music are the Mexican *corrido* (ballad) and a hybrid between the *corrido* and the *canción* (song). These occupy a special place in the musical life of Mexican-Americans, especially those living in the southwestern states of Texas, New Mexico, Arizona, and California. The corrido and the canción-corrido hybrid emerged as powerful cultural expressions in the Hispanic Southwest during the twentieth century, especially the years leading up to World War II. Through their lyrics, the corrido and canción-corrido address more directly than any of the ensemble styles (salsa, conjunto, orquesta) the social and ideological issues which Latinos face in their often difficult adjustment to American life. The graphic manner in which the corrido and canción confront such issues places them high on the scale of cultural significance.

Finally there is also a musical ensemble that has made a powerful, although largely unrecognized, impact on a large segment of the Mexican population in the United States—the Mexican immigrants, many of them undocumented, who have been coming to the United States in increasing numbers since the 1960s. This ensemble goes by several names—*grupos cumbieros, grupos tropicales, grupos modernos*—but it may best be defined as a Mexican working-class variant of so-called *música tropical*. Música tropical has a long history in Mexico and Latin America, but this ensemble has a history that coincides with the massive emigration that began in Mexico in the 1960s. Since that time, the grupo tropical/moderno has become an everyday music in the lives of many Mexicans in the American Southwest.

THE CORRIDO AND CANCIÓN-CORRIDO

Historically, the *corrido* and *canción* are two distinct genres or musical forms. However, in the Hispanic Southwest they have at times experienced considerable overlap, especially since the 1920s. The overlap occurs when, on the one hand, the corrido sheds some of its most familiar features, such as the call of the *corridista* to his audience and mention of the date, place, and cast of characters. At the same time, many canciones composed during and after the 1920s abandon that genre's most recognizable feature—its lyrical quality—and assume a seminarrative form, thus moving them in the direction of the *corrido*. The result is a convergence of the two genres. Of course, this convergence is never complete; some corridos retain enough of their "classical" narrative features to stamp them unmistakably as corridos, while most canciones remain purely lyrical expressions, usually about love.

In any case, beginning in the 1920s a number of canción-corrido hybrids made their appearance in the Hispanic Southwest. Not coincidentally, it was at this time that the large American recording labels, such as Columbia and RCA, first moved into the Southwest and began to commercially exploit Mexican-American music in all its variety. Not coincidentally, either, the first of the famous Mexican-American troubadors—singers of the canción and corrido—attained widespread popularity throughout the Southwest during the 1920s. Many of these troubadors were composers of the canción-corrido, as well. From the 1920s, through the 1940s, they produced a steady flow of canciones-corridos that depicted life in the Hispanic Southwest with great feeling and accuracy, describing in vivid detail both the sadness and the humor of life in the borderlands. Especially moving are those compositions that address the long-standing conflict between Anglos and Mexicans and the oppression endured by the latter.

The rising popularity of the Mexican-American troubadors was not a spontaneous event, however. It is true that the intervention of the major recording labels energized musicians and propelled a number of musical traditions to a higher level of innovation, and until the arrival of the wax disk, singers and their songs tended not to attain recognition beyond their immediate locale. Some of the ancient songs had, indeed, spread throughout the Southwest over the previous centuries, but newly composed songs, as well as their composer-performers, were usually confined to their immediate point of origin.

The major labels changed all that. In 1926, RCA, Columbia, Decca, and Brunswick began setting up makeshift studios in rented hotel rooms in cities like Dallas, San Antonio, and Los Angeles, and with the help of local entrepreneurs who knew the pool of musicians available, they began to record commercially a wide variety of musical forms, including the then evolving música norteña, various orquestalike ensembles, and, of course, the canción and the corrido. Women made their impact on Mexican American music at this time, with one female troubador in particular attaining immense popularity throughout

the Southwest—the venerable Lidia Mendoza. Other popular troubadors of the period who made a lasting impact on the emerging canción-corrido form include Los Hermanos Bañuelos (The Bañuelos Brothers, the first to record with the major labels, in 1926) and Los Madrugadores (The Early Birds), both groups from Los Angeles, as well as Los Hermanos Chavarría (The Chavarría Brothers) and Gaytán y Cantú (Gaytán and Cantú), from Texas.

These troubadors and others left a rich legacy of canciones-corridos, a legacy that attests to the creative energy the Mexican Americans devoted to a music that could document the harshness of their daily life. This music was so poetically charged that its cultural power can be felt to this day. The number of canciones-corridos preserved on wax is large (see Arhoolie/Folklyric Records, volumes 2, 3, 6-9, 14, 15), but the following excerpts should be enough to provide a feel for the range of topics. The first example is from "El deportado" ("The Deported One"), a canción-corrido recorded by Los Hermanos Bañuelos in the early 1930s. *El deportado* depicts the bitter experiences of a Mexican immigrant in his encounter with the cold, exploitive system of American capitalism. (All English translations are the author's):

> I'm going to sing to you, gentlemen,
> I'm going to sing to you, gentlemen
> all about my sufferings,
> since I left my country,
> since I left my country
> to come to this nation [the U.S.].
>
> We arrived at Juarez at last,
> we arrived at Juarez at last,
> there I ran into trouble.
> "Where are you going, where do you come from?
> How much money do you have to enter this country?"
> "Gentlemen, I have money,
> gentlemen I have money,
> so that I can emigrate."
> "Your money is worth nothing,
> your money is worth nothing,
> we have to bathe you."
>
> The white men are very wicked,
> the white men are very wicked,
> they take advantage of the occasion.
> And all the Mexicans,
> and all the Mexicans
> they treat without compassion. (Arhoolie/Folklyric, 1975)

Lidia Mendoza (center) with Marcelo, comic Tin Tan and Juanita Mendoza in Chicago in the 1950s.

Another canción-corrido hybrid, "El lavaplatos" ("The Dishwasher"), also recorded by Los Hermanos Bañuelos (reissued by Archoolie/Folklyric, 1975), recounts in more humorous language the adventures of a poor Mexican who immigrates to the United States in search of the glamorous life of Hollywood, only to find himself drifting from one backbreaking job to another. The following stanzas are representative of the narrative tone:

One day very desperate,
because of so much revolution,
I came over to this side [of the border]
without paying the immigration.
Oh, what a fast one,
Oh what a fast one,
I crossed without paying anything.
On arriving at the station,
I ran into a friend,
who gave me an invitation
to work on *el traque*.
I supposed *el traque*
would be some kind of warehouse,
but it was to repair the track
where the train ran.

Oh what a friend,
oh what a friend,
how he took me to the track.
When I got tired of the track,
he invited me again,
to pick tomatoes and thin beets.
And there I earned indulgences
walking on my knees;
about four or five miles
they gave me for penance. (Arhoolie/Folklyric, 1975).

As can be seen from these examples—and many more could be provided—composers of the 1920s through them 1940s were exceptionally committed to documenting the enduring hardships of life for Mexicans in the Southwest. For this they utilized the canción-corrido extensively. But the corrido itself, in its more or less pure form, plays an even more central role in the music culture of Mexican Americans, one that dates back to the nineteenth century.

Merle E. Simmons (1957) observed that the Mexican *corrido* plays an important historical role in articulating the sociopolitical position of the Mexican folk vis-á-vis the dominant classes. The folklorist

A working-class *orquesta*, circa 1930 (Courtesy of Thomas Kreneck).

Américo Paredes has argued the same for the corrido on this side of the border and, in fact, advances the proposition that the Mexican corrido actually originated along the Texas-Mexico border, since the earliest corrido collected in complete form comes from Texas—"El corrido de Kiansis" ("The Ballad of Kansas"), dating from the 1860s. For Paredes, the climate of intercultural conflict that grew out of the Anglo invasion and subsequent annexation of what became the American Southwest at the end of the Mexican-American War (1848) was the ideal setting for the birth of an expressive culture that would key in on this conflict.

It was at this point, between 1848 and 1860, that the modern corrido emerged out of an ancient musico-literary form that had been introduced from Spain in the sixteenth century—the romance. And it was evidently in Texas, and not in Michoacán, Durango, or Jalisco, as once thought, that the first corridos were composed (Paredes 1958a). One of these was "Kiansis," a corrido that documents the epic cattle drives from Texas to the Kansas stockyards. More important, we see in Kiansis subtle indications of the intercultural conflict that attended Anglo-Mexican relations at the time. For that reason, Paredes has

proposed "Kiansis" as the first of what he labels corridos of intercultural conflict (1976). This conflict is subtly captured in the following stanzas:

Five hundred steers there were,
all big and quick;
Then five Mexicans arrive,
all of them wearing good chaps;
and thirty Americans
couldn't keep them together.
and in less than a quarter-hour
they had the steers penned up.

As Paredes notes, "There is intercultural conflict in 'Kiansis,' but it is expressed in professional rivalries rather than in violence between men" (1976, 26). That violence, however, is present in another corrido from the late nineteenth century, titled "El corrido de Juan Cortina." This corrido details in stronger language the resentment that Mexicans on the border felt toward the Americans:

That famed General Cortinas
is quite sovereign and free,
the honor due him is greater

for he saved a Mexican's life.
The Americans made merry,
they got drunk in the saloons,
out of joy over the death
of the famed General Cortinas.

The corrido celebrates the exploits of Juan Nepomuceno Cortina, a Mexican from south Texas who, according to Paredes, "was the first man to organize Texas-Mexican protest against abuses on the part of the Anglos who controlled /the . . . power structure [in South Texas] after 1848" (Parades, 1976, 22). Cortina, a member of a wealthy landowning family with deep roots in the Texas-Mexico border region, came to resent the arrogant attitude of the Anglo newcomers, especially the fortune makers. After an incident in which he accosted a town marshal who was pistol-whipping a *vaquero* (cowboy) who worked on his mother's ranch, Cortina was declared an outlaw, and thereafter he dedicated his life to guerrilla warfare, until he was driven out of Texas by the U.S. cavalry.

"El Corrido de Juan Cortina" ushered in what has been called the hero corrido period (Peña 1982), when the prevalent type was the corrido of intercultural conflict (Paredes 1976). This type of corrido invariably features a larger-than-life Mexican hero who single-handedly defies a cowardly, smaller-than-life gang of Anglo-American lawmen. The hero either defeats the Anglos or goes down fighting "with his pistol in his hand" (Paredes 1958b). In this way, the protagonist gains heroic status in the Mexican-American community, becoming, in effect, a kind of redeemer for the collective insults suffered by his people at the hands of the Anglos.

Hero corridos were written until the 1920s, in Texas and elsewhere, including such classics as "Joaquín Murrieta and Jacinto Treviño," but perhaps the most memorable is "El corrido de Gregorio Cortez," immortalized by Américo Paredes in his book *"With His Pistol in His Hand"* (1958b, which served as the basis for the film *The Ballad of Gregorio Cortez,* released in 1982). The corrido documents the odyssey of a Mexican Texan who fled for his life after he killed an Anglo sheriff in self-defense, because of a linguistic misunderstanding over some stolen horses.

"Gregorio Cortez" is the ideal example of the hero corrido. As a symbol of his people's hopes for deliverance, the hero achieves his revenge through the process of "status reversal" (Turner 1969), wherein the hero, who personifies the collective will, defeats or at least defies the American lawmen, who personify the dominant Anglos. Thus, through the exploits of the hero, the Mexican Americans of the Southwest symbolically invert the real world, assuming in vicarious

fashion a dominant position over their oppressors and in this way achieving a sense of deliverance.

The following stanzas from "Gregorio Cortez" illustrate the contrastive opposition between heroic Mexican and cowardly Anglo:

The Americans came,
whiter than a dove,
from fear they had
Gregorio Cortez left,
of Cortez and his gun.
he left heading for Laredo;
they refused to follow him,
because they were afraid of him.

The hero corrido was most prevalent during the early period of Anglo-Mexican contact, when relations between the two groups were characterized by what Paredes (1966) has called the open hostility stage of Mexican-American folklore. This period spans the years from about 1848 to the early 1900s—a period during which Mexicans still entertained hopes, albeit diminishing with time, that they could still defeat the Anglos and drive them out of their territory. However, the hero corrido continued to enjoy prominence until the 1930s, when a new type emerged.

The new corridos, prevalent since the end of World War II, have been labeled victim corridos (Peña 1982). The new corridos demonstrate sharp differences in subject matter from those of the earlier period. Foremost is the disappearance of the larger-than-life hero. In his place a new protagonist emerges, one who is usually portrayed as a helpless victim of Anglo oppression. This shift in the corrido of intercultural conflict from hero to victim is too fundamental to be considered a random event. In fact, it coincides with equally fundamental changes in Mexican-American society. It thus happens that the newer corridos appeared at the precise moment when Mexican-Americans initiated a wholesale movement from rural to urban, from folk to modern, from a monocultural to a bicultural life-style, and from proletarian status to a more diversified social organization.

After World War II, in this climate of emergent political and economic diversification, new cultural directions and new modes of interpreting the Mexican-American experience were being charted. Fully conscious of their newfound power, the postwar Mexican Americans began to rethink their relationship with the dominant Anglo majority and to demand more economic and political equality (as well as acceptance). However, despite the tentative beginnings of an interethnic accommodation, the Anglos were not yet ready to accept the Mexicans as equal, and the intercultural friction persisted. This friction at times forced Mexican Americans to put aside growing internal class differences, as they closed ranks to fight racial discrimination. In this atmosphere of heightened political awareness, the corrido continued to play an important role. As this writer observed in an article on the corrido of intercultural conflict, "Chicanos [Mexican Americans], having developed more effectively organized political machinery to challenge Anglo supremacy, relied less on their *corridos* to uplift a battered cultural image and more to rally support for active political causes. The reasoning seems self-evident: a *corrido* is more likely to elicit an active response, i.e., outrage and group mobilization, if it depicts a helpless victim rather than a potent, larger-than-life hero. In a sense, the two types of *corrido* are antithetical—one reflecting pent-up frustration and powerlessness, the other active resistance" (Peña 1982, 38).

Several well-known victim corridos have been written since World War II. Among them is "Discriminación a un mártir" ("Discrimination Against a Martyr"), one of the first and an outstanding example of the genre. Written in 1949, it documents the case of Private Félix Longoria, a soldier killed in action during World War II. A native of Three Rivers, Texas, Longoria was drafted into the army in 1944, and early in 1945 he was assigned to the war in the Pacific theater, where the Allies were engaged in heavy combat against the Japanese. Longoria was killed during one of the final assaults. Like many men killed in action, Private Longoria was temporarily buried in the Philippines. When his remains were finally exhumed, in 1949, and flown to his relatives in Texas, the local funeral home refused to provide funeral services, citing the past practice against funerals for Mexicans (Peña 1982, 18-23).

The Mexican-American community was shocked and outraged by the funeral home's callous act of discrimination. Led by Héctor García, president of a political action group known as the G.I. Forum, the community applied pressure on authorities until Lyndon B. Johnson, then senator for the state of Texas, yielded to the Mexican Americans" demands for justice and had the remains of Private Longoria flown to Arlington National Cemetery for burial there.

"*Discriminación*" was composed and recorded commercially not long after the incident to celebrate the moral victory the Hispanics had won. Like other postwar corridos, this one focused on the victimization of the protagonist and the community's intervention. The following stanzas convey the basic theme of moral outrage:

When the body of the soldier
with his next-of-kin,
The mortuary in his hometown
denied him a funeral.
That is discrimination arrived
against a poor human being;
not even in a cemetery
do they admit a Mexican.

"El 29 de Agosto" ("August 29"), a well-known corrido written by the legendary folksinger-composer Lalo Guerrero, presents an interesting variation on the victim theme. This corrido describes the events surrounding the Chicano Moratorium of August of 1970, when a massive demonstration was organized in Los Angeles to protest against the disproportionate numbers of Chicanos being killed in Vietnam. As in other victim corridos, "El 29" celebrates the resolute actions of the Chicano masses as they protest the perceived victimization of Mexican Americans in the form of an unfair draft. But an interesting twist develops, one related to the suspicious killing of Rubén Salazar, a popular television reporter, on the day of the demonstration.

After having covered the demonstration, Salazar was sitting in a bar when police approached, ostensibly to seek out a man reported to be carrying a rifle. While the accounts of police officers and other witnesses conflict, the police apparently fired a rifle-powered tear gas canister into the bar without warning, hitting Salazar in the head and killing him instantly. According to historian Rodolfo Acuña, there is evidence that Los Angeles police were out to "get" Salazar for news coverage that was critical of police actions against the Mexican community (Acuña 1972, 261).

No action was ever taken against the officers who killed Salazar. Authorities concluded that his death was accidental, although, according to Acuña, many in the Chicano community remained convinced that the police had murdered Salazar by way of getting even for his critical reporting.

In "El 29 de Agosto," composer Guerrero deftly combines the defiant actions of the demonstrators with the death of reporter Salazar to transform a song about mass protest into a victim *corrido*. The following stanzas effect this transformation:

Cuando vino la policía
violencia se desató;
el coraje de mi raza
luego se desenlazó;
por los años de injusticia
el odio se derramó;
y como huracán furioso

su barrio lo destrozó.
En un edificio cercano
desgracia vino a caer
un gran hombre y buen humano:
periodista mexicano
de fama interancional;
fino padre de familia
voz de la comunidad.
When the police arrived
violence was unleashed;
the wrath of my people
uncoiled from within;
Against years of injustice
hate spilled out;
and like a ferocious hurricane
its barrio it destroyed.
In a nearby building
y misfortune came to fall
a great man and human being
él fue Rubén Salazar,
he was Rubén Salazar,
Mexican newspaperman
of international fame;
a fine father and husband
spokesman for the community.

Many corridos of this type have been composed since the end of World War II. In the typical victim corrido, the Anglos openly abuse the basic rights of a Mexican victim (or victims), and the Mexican community responds vigorously to defend the victim(s). The corrido draws attention to the community's forceful actions in protesting Anglo injustice, and when the outcome permits it (as in "Discriminación"), the corrido celebrates the community's victory. In any case, the Anglos are portrayed in a negative light, while the Mexicans are seen as a proud people fighting for their civil rights.

Both the hero and victim corridos of intercultural conflict have a long and auspicious history in the Mexican-American oral music tradition. As indicated, the former was prevalent at a time when conflict between Anglo and Mexican was rampant and undisguised. The hero corrido peaked in the early twentieth century, when the Mexican Americans reached the lowest point in their history of oppression in the United States. As they climbed out of their wretched state, during and after World War II, the victim corrido appeared and gained ascendancy. Both types of corrido have survived into the late twentieth century, but their presence in the musical repertory of Mexican Americans today is sporadic. They tend to surface only during moments of intercultural crisis—usually when the still-dominant Anglos commit a blatant act of discrimination.

✳ MÚSICA NORTEÑA (THE MEXICAN-TEXAN CONJUNTO)

Of all the musical creations of the Latino community in the United States, *música norteña* (also known as the Mexican-Texan *conjunto*) is unquestionably one of the most culturally powerful. Anchored by the diatonic button accordion, this folk tradition had grown deep roots among the Mexicans living along the Texas-Mexico border by the early twentieth century. And, thanks to the commercialization introduced by the major American recording labels in the 1920s, it eventually spread far beyond its origins in south Texas and northern Mexico. By the late twentieth century, música norteña had been adopted by millions of Mexicans in both Mexico and the United States.

How a music of such humble folk origins could develop into a powerful artistic expression with such widespread appeal is a provocative question. The answer lies in its beginnings along the Texas-Mexico border. The diatonic button accordion, which is the heart of música norteña, was evidently introduced into northeastern Mexico sometime in the middle of the nineteenth century—perhaps by German immigrants who settled in the Monterrey, Nuevo León, area of northeastern Mexico in the 1860s. Since the Mexican-Texans of this period maintained close cultural links with Mexican *norteños* (northerners), it is likely that the instrument quickly spread into south Texas (Peña 1985a). It is possible, however, that the accordion was introduced to the tejanos (Mexican-Texans) by way of the German, Czech, and Polish settlers who had migrated to south central Texas beginning in the 1840s. Since intense conflict, marked by overt discrimination against Mexicans, was the norm between tejanos and the latter groups, it is less likely that the interchange occurred on that front. In any case, the exact identity of the donor culture may never be known.

What we do know is that by the late nineteenth century the accordion, coupled with one or two other instruments—the *tambora de rancho* (ranch drum) and the *bajo sexto* (a twelve-string guitar)—had become the norm for music-and-dance celebrations in south Texas. The tambora was a primitive folk instrument fashioned out of native materials. It was usually played with wooden mallets, their tips covered with cotton wrapped in goatskin. The bajo sexto apparently originated in the Guanajuato-Michoacán area in Mexico; it is a twelve-string guitar tuned in double courses. How it migrated to and established itself in the border area is a mystery. But in its new locale it became an indispensable companion to the accordion, especially after 1930, when it and the accordion emerged as the core of the evolving ensemble.

The conjunto norteño, or conjunto, as it came to be known in Texas, thrived from early on. It soon became the preferred ensemble for the rural working-class folk who adopted it and eventually molded it into a genuine working-class expression. In its early days it relied on the salon music introduced from Europe in the eighteenth and nineteenth centuries and popularized first among the genteel city dwellers, then passed on to the masses later. The principal genres were the polka, the *redowa,* and the *schottishe,* although the mazurka was also current. Rounding out the repertoire was the *huapango,* culturally important because it was native to the Gulf Coast region of Tamaulipas and northern Vera Cruz, and thus represented a regional contribution. The huapango is more frequently associated with the music of the *huasteca* region of southern Tamaulipas, Mexico, where it has a ternary pulse built around a 3/4 meter. As performed by norteños, however, the huapango early on acquired a binary pulse built around the triplets of 6/8 meter.

Despite the presence everywhere of the accordion in the musical celebrations of the tejanos/norteños, the conjunto did not achieve dominance until the 1930s. Prior to this time it was still an improvised ensemble with little stylistic development and plenty of competition from other types of (also improvised) ensembles. In fact, the history of the Mexican-Texan conjunto can be divided into three distinct stages (Peña 1985a). The first, to the late 1920s, is the formative, when the ensemble was strictly improvisational and the accordion was still played either solo, with guitar or bajo sexto, or with the tambora de rancho. The technique used to play the accordion itself owed much to that of the Germans who had originally introduced the instrument to the Mexicans. This included the heavy use of the left-hand bass-chord buttons, a technique that lent the instrument a distinctive sound and articulation. As noted, this embryonic ensemble was common to Mexicans on both sides of the border.

The second stage begins in the mid-1930s, when the Mexican-Texan conjunto began to move beyond its counterpart across the border—gradually at first, radically after World War II. The sudden development of the conjunto during the second stage is undoubtedly linked to intervention of the large American recording labels, which began in earnest in the early 1930s. At this time RCA Victor (through its Bluebird subsidiary), Columbia, and Decca moved into the Southwest and began commercially exploiting the variety of music then flourishing in the region. But the rapid development of the conjunto cannot be explained simply in terms of its commercialization, which, in any case, was never as massive as that of mainstream American pop music. On the other hand, the ethnic/class dichotomy which came to dominate the political culture of Mexican-Texans after the 1930s was certainly a powerful catalyst (Peña 1985a).

Thus, by the mid-1930s, when accordionist Narciso Martínez began his commercial recording career, the first steps had been taken toward cementing the core of the modern conjunto—the accordion-bajo sexto combination. These two instruments would become inseparable after this time. Meanwhile, Martínez, who is acknowledged as the "father" of the modern conjunto, devised a new technique for the instrument, one that differed radically from the old Germanic style. He stopped using the left-hand bass-chord buttons, leaving the accompaniment to the bajo sexto, which was very capably played by his partner Santiago Almeida.

The resulting sound was dramatically novel—a clean, spare treble, and a staccato effect that contrasted sharply with the Germanic sound of earlier norteño accordionists. The Martínez style quickly took hold and became the standard that younger accordionists emulated, particularly those who established themselves after World War II.

In fact, the years immediately following the war ushered in the third stage in the conjunto's development. A younger group of musicians began charting a new direction for the rapidly evolving style. Foremost among these was accordionist Valerio Longoria, who was responsible for several innovations. Among these were two elements of the modern conjunto that Longoria introduced—the modern trap drums and the canción ranchera, the latter a working-class subtype of the Mexican *ranchera,* which dates from the 1930s. Obsessed with abandoned men and unfaithful women, the canción ranchera has always had special appeal for male patrons of conjunto music. Since it was often performed in the 2/4 meter of the traditional polka favored by Mexican-Texans, the ranchera quickly replaced the polka itself as the mainstay of the modern conjunto. Longoria's introduction of the drums and ranchera earned him a special leadership position in the unfolding style, and several younger conjunto musicians have cited his example as the source of their inspiration—Paulino Bernal and Oscar Hernández, to name two of the best.

Paulino Bernal is himself a major figure in the development of the modern ensemble. His conjunto is hailed as the greatest in the history of the tradition, an honor based on the craftsmanship and the number of innovations attributable to El Conjunto Bernal.

The latter include the introduction of three-part vocals and the addition of the larger chromatic accordion. El Conjunto Bernal's greatest distinction, however, lies in its ability to take the traditional elements of the conjunto and raise them to a level of virtuosity that has not been matched to this day. Bernal had accomplished all of this by the early 1960s.

Meanwhile, after about 1960 the *conjunto* and the older norteño ensemble across the Rio Grande began to converge, as the norteños came under the influence of their tejano counterparts. Especially responsible for this convergence was Los Relámpagos del Norte (The Northern Lightning Bolts), a group led by accordionist Ramón Ayala and bajo sexto player Cornelio Reyna. Ayala and Reyna were strongly influenced by El Conjunto Bernal, in particular. In fact, Los Relámpagos was "discovered" by Paulino Bernal in 1964 while he was on a scouting trip to Reynosa, Tamaulipas, across the border from McAllen, Texas, in search of talent for a new recording label he had recently started.

Los Relámpagos began recording for Bernal's Bego label in 1965, and within two years had risen to unparalleled fame on both sides of the border. The group remained unchallenged until the mid-1970s, when Ayala and Reyna went their separate ways. Ayala shortly organized his own conjunto, Los Bravos del Norte (The Northern Brave Ones), and that group went on to dominate the *norteño* market for at least a decade.

Since the innovations of the 1960s, the conjunto has turned decidedly conservative, with both musicians and patrons choosing to preserve the elements of the style as these were worked out in the 1940s through the 1960s. Despite its conservatism, the tradition has expanded phenomenally, in the 1970s to 1990s spreading far beyond its original base along the Texas-Mexico border. In the last few years, the music has taken root in such far-flung places as Washington, D.C., California, and the Midwest, as well as the entire tier of northern Mexican border states and even in such places as Michoacán and Sinaloa. In its seemingly unstoppable expansion, conjunto music has always articulated a strong Mexicanized, working-class life-style, thus helping to preserve Mexican culture wherever it has taken root on American (and Mexican) soil.

The rapid rise and maturation of conjunto music is a remarkable phenomenon in itself, but more important from an anthropological perspective is its cultural significance, its strong "organic" connection to working-class Mexicans in the United States. Clearly, the music is anything but a casual item of entertainment among its supporters. In fact, as a musical expression the conjunto has become a symbolic emblem of Mexican working-class culture—those people employed in farm labor and other unskilled and semiskilled occupations found mostly in service industries. And, the conjunto's alliance with that class was cemented during its rapid evolution between the years 1936 and 1960 (Peña 1985a).

Beyond this identification with the working class, in the years following World War II the conjunto became linked to the cultural strategies of Mexican Texans, in particular, as these proletarian workers faced continuing prejudice from a hostile Anglo population, as well as antagonism from a new class of upwardly mobile, acculturated Mexican Texans, who sought to put some distance between themselves and the more Mexicanized common workers. The attitude of middle-class Mexican Texans was cogently summarized by the owner of Falcon Records, Arnaldo Ramírez, who recalled that in the 1930s to 1950s "to mention the accordion to people of position was like calling their mother a name" (pers. com. March 27, 1980).

In the end, conjunto music came to symbolize the struggle of the workers to maintain a sense of social solidarity and cultural uniformity against the upwardly mobile Mexican Americans, who espoused a different musical ideal, in the form of the orquesta or big band (discussed later), and who viewed conjunto music as the expression of a vulgar, unassimilatable class of people. This quality of conjunto—its strong endorsement by the common workers and repudiation by more affluent people—was particularly evident in its Mexican Texan home base, but it was carried over to new locales, such as Arizona, where it was derisively called *catachún* music, and California, where it was universally considered cantina "trash."

It is against this politico-cultural background that the words of Paulino Bernal, one of conjunto's most innovative performers, may best be appreciated: "There was always among *la raza*, among Chicanos, what we used to call, "No man, you think you're really high society." That is, there was one class of people among Chicanos that was higher, and they wanted to live like the American, and live better. Of course, they had already reached a higher position economically, and there was still a lot of *raza* [Mexican people] that was just arriving, and with a lot of . . . truggling all the way. So there *was* a division; and that is where not only the social or economic position was divided, but the music was divided as well—that of orquesta and that of conjunto (pers. com. May 9, 1980).

❋THE MEXICAN-AMERICAN ORQUESTA

Paulino Bernal's comments on the socioeconomic difference between conjunto and orquesta serves as a suitable introduction to the orquesta, which has a fascinating history in the music of the Hispanic Southwest (Peña 1985b; 1989). Actually, three types of orquestas have been present in the Southwest at different periods in the last century. The earliest type is one that existed during the nineteenth century and the early part of the twentieth. This early ensemble, built primarily around the violin, was hardly an "orquesta." It was for the most part an improvised ensemble, one dependent on the availability of musicians and scarce instruments for composition.

The rudimentary nature of this early orquesta is linked to the marginalization of the Mexicans of the Southwest—their having been stripped of all political and economic stability by the Anglo-Americans who invaded the territory and eventually annexed it to the United States. Having become American citizens by default, the new Mexican Americans found themselves at a decided disadvantage—as did all Mexican immigrants who came after them. The original settlers were gradually dispossessed of all their lands and forced into a state of subordination, setting a pattern that would apply to all those who migrated to the Southwest in the twentieth century. José Limón, the noted Mexican-American folklorist, has summarized developments in the Southwest following the American invasion: "Between 1848 and 1890, an Anglo ranching society established itself among the native (also ranching) Mexican population, living with them in a rough equality. However, beginning in the 1890s, a clear racial-cultural stratification and subordination began to emerge, as a new wave of Anglo-American entrepreneurs and farming interests established a political and economic hegemony over the native population as well as the thousands of Mexican immigrants entering the area after 1910. . . . With few exceptions, this total population . . . became the victim of class-racial exploitation and mistreatment" (Limón 1983, 216-117).

Given their precarious social organization as a subordinate group in the new social order that was created in the Southwest, the resident Mexicans (now Mexican Americans) and all those who came afterward found it difficult to maintain any but the most rudimentary of musical traditions. To be sure, the norteños had never enjoyed the best of facilities for

An *orquesta típica* in Houston (Courtesy of Thomas Kreneck).

any kind of education, musical or otherwise. Throughout the Spanish colonial era and the period of Mexican independence, life in the north had been of a peasant, agrarian nature, with few of the amenities that Mexicans in more centralized and urban areas enjoyed. Despite their relative isolation, the norteños managed to keep up with musical developments in Mexico and, as early chroniclers have documented, were able to maintain reasonably equipped ensembles (Robinson 1925).

With the American invasion and the subsequent oppression of the native Mexicans, the opportunities for musical training all but disappeared, except in urban areas along the border, where the Mexicans preserved a degree of political and economic integration, even after the annexation of the Southwest by the United States. Thus, cities like Brownsville, Laredo, and El Paso managed to support modest resources for the training and equipping of musical groups. But in general, the American invasion reduced an orquesta tradition inherited from Greater Mexico to its bare and often improvised essentials—a violin or two plus guitar accompaniment, with other instruments added on an ad hoc basis.

Despite its impoverished character, the early orquesta of the Hispanic Southwest nonetheless enjoyed great prominence in the musical affairs of the Mexican communities across the territory—even in Texas, where the emergent conjunto offered strong competition. As sources from the nineteenth and early twentieth centuries confirm (Dinger 1972; Robinson 1925), small orquestas were enlisted for all kinds of celebrations, which ran the gamut from private weddings and birthdays to public multievent celebrations known as *funciones*. Again, almost without exception, these orquestas were of variable composition, although they seldom included more than the minimum instruments mentioned before—a violin or two with guitar accompaniment.

The 1920s saw the emergence in the urban areas of better-organized orquestas, built, again, around the violin. This was the so-called *orquesta típica* (typical orchestra). The first típica was organized in Mexico City in 1880, and it was supposedly modeled after an earlier folk orquesta common in Mexican rural areas throughout the nineteenth century (also known as típica) and apparently similar in instrumentation to the folk *orquestas* of the Hispanic Southwest (Mayer-Serra 1941, 116; Baqueriro-Foster 1964, 532). The self-styled orquestas típicas of urban origin were clearly expressions of what is known as *costumbrismo*, a type of romantic nationalism in which the dominant groups find it appealing to imitate certain elements of the folk, or peasant classes. As such, these orquestas were given to wearing "typical" *charro* (cowboy)

outfits similar to those worn by the Mexican mariachi, in an effort to capture in vicarious fashion some of the flavor of Mexican pastoral life.

In the United States, the first típica was probably organized in El Paso or Laredo sometime in the 1920s. In any case, these orquestas were strongly reminiscent of the modern mariachi, whose historical roots they may well share. The basic instrumentation of the orquesta típica consisted of violins, guitars, and psalteries, although in the Southwest other instruments were often added in ad hoc fashion. The size of the típica could vary from four or five musicians to as many as 20.

Típicas were enlisted for almost any occasion, although they were ideally suited for patriotic-type celebrations, such as *cinco de mayo* (5th of May, when the Mexican general Ignacio Zaragoza postponed the French invasion of Mexico by defeating General Laurencez at Puebla) and *dieciseis de septiembre* (16th of September, Independence Day), two dates of special significance for Mexican people. The repertoire of orquestas típicas consisted of *aires nacionales*—tunes that over the years had acquired status as "national airs," such as "El Jarabe Tapatío" ("The Jalisco Dance"), "La Negra" ("The Dark Beauty"), "Pajarillo Barranqueño" ("Little Bird of Barranca"), and others. Típicas seem to have fallen out of favor among Mexican Americans during the Great Depression of the 1930s. They disappeared from the musical scene in the Southwest during World War II.

On the other hand, the 1930s saw the emergence of the third and most important type of orquesta, this one a version of the modern dance bands that swept through the urban landscapes of both Mexico and the United States during the 1920s and 1930s. The modern orquesta clearly represented a musico-cultural departure from earlier ensembles. In fact, it is tied to the fortunes of a new group of Mexican Americans who began to make an impact on Hispanic life in the United States during the 1930s and 1940s. Historian Mario García has aptly labeled this group The Mexican American Generation (García 1984). This was the first generation of Americans of Mexican descent to aspire for inclusion in Anglo-American life. Consequently, it advocated the ideology of assimilation, an ideology based on the notion that Mexican Americans should detach themselves from their Mexican heritage and begin thinking like Americans. However, the persistent conflict with the Anglos and their continuing discrimination against Mexicans ultimately forced The Mexican American Generation to modify its ideology of assimilation and adopt a more biculturalist stance—to be both Mexican and American.

The modern orquesta played a prominent role in

accommodating The Mexican American Generation's biculturalist strategy. In the bimusical repertoire it adopted, the orquesta catered to the generation's bicultural nature. By performing music traditionally associated with Mexico and Latin America, it kept alive the Mexican Americans'' ethnic roots; by performing music associated with American big bands, it satisfied The Mexican American Generation's desire to assimilate American culture. Thus, from Mexico and Latin America came the *danzón*, *bolero*, *guaracha*, *rumba*, and other dance genres; from the United States came the boogie, swing, fox-trot, and so on.

Very quickly, however, the Mexican-American orquesta began to experiment with various bimusical combinations—especially the orquestas in Texas, which, like the conjunto, assumed a leadership role in music developments in the Hispanic Southwest after World War II. As a result of their increasing exposure through commercial recordings (Texas had the biggest Hispanic recording companies), the most professional orquestas típicas became the models that others around the Southwest imitated. Coincident with this professionalization was the appearance and popularization of the public ballroom dance, which allowed the most successful orquestas to rely exclusively on performance for full-time employment.

Thus, ever since the birth of the modern Mexican-American orquesta, the most renowned names have come from Texas. There was, for example, Beto Villa, from Falfurrias, Texas, sometimes called the "father" of the Mexican-American orquesta (Peña 1985b). Acclaimed for a folksy, ranchero polka that took the Southwest by storm, Villa deftly juxtaposed this "country" style polka, which came to be known as Tex-Mex, against more sophisticated genres drawn from Latin America and the United States—*danzones*, *guarachas*, former, fox-trots, and swings.

Villa's influence on orquestas throughout the Hispanic Southwest was enormous during the 1940s and 1950s, and he inspired many imitators. A notable successor to the Tex-Mex tradition Villa inaugurated was Isidro López, also from Texas. A singer-saxophonist, López deliberately emphasized the ranchero mode of performance in an attempt to attract a larger share of the common workers, who were otherwise more faithful to the ever more powerful (and more ranchero) conjunto. López was thus the first orquesta leader to add the working-class *canción ranchera* to the orquesta repertoire. But he added his own touch to the ranchera, embellishing it with a blend of mariachi and Tex-Mex that López himself dubbed Texachi.

There were at least two other orquestas of note during the 1940s and 1950s—Balde González's, from Victoria, Texas, and Pedro Bugarín's, from Phoenix, Arizona. The former specialized in a smoother, more romantic delivery that appealed in particular to those upwardly mobile tejanos who were seen by working-class people as snobbish and who were derisively known as *jaitones* (from high tone). As such, Balde González, a pianist-singer, was best known for the smooth delivery of the romantic and sophisticated *bolero*, although he often turned as well to the American fox-trot, which he transformed by adding lyrics in Spanish. Bugarín pursued a more eclectic approach, one that included the full gamut of bimusical performance, from rancheras to fox-trots.

In the Los Angeles area, meanwhile, a number of orquestas operated during the maturating years of the Mexican-American *orquesta*—the 1940s and 1950s. Most of these took their cue from music developments in Latin America (including the Afro-Caribbean) and were less influenced by developments in the Tex-Mex field. One noteworthy exception was the orquesta that the legendary Lalo Guerrero fronted for a time. As Guerrero himself admitted, he "mixed it all up," combining Tex-Mex with boogie and Latin American, including salsa. But Guerrero was best known for his unique bimusical tunes, which fused music and linguistic elements from swing, rhumba, and *caló*, a folk dialect popular among working-class youth in the Southwest and elsewhere. Most of these tunes were written by Guerrero himself. Some achieved immortality through the movie *Zootsuit*, produced in 1982 by the Chicano filmmaker and erstwhile activist Luis Valdez (for example, the tune "Marihuana Boogie").

But the most influential orquestas continued to originate in Texas. In the 1960s and 1970s, which may well have been the peak years for the Mexican-American *orquesta*, several groups emerged from the active tradition established in the Lone Star State. Foremost among these was Little Joe and the Latinaires, renamed Little Joe y la Familia in 1970. La Familia exploited the Tex-Mex ranchero sound fashioned by Isidro López to its utmost, fusing it to American jazz and rock *within the same musical piece* to achieve a unique bimusical sound that came to be known as La Onda Chicana (The Chicano Wave).

Little Joe first experimented with the fusion of Mexican ranchero and American jazz/rock in a hugely successful LP titled *Para la Gente* (*For the People*), released in 1972 by Little Joe's own company, Buena Suerte Records. On this album, Little Joe and his brother Johnny combined their voices duet-fashion to create a style of ranchera so appealing to Mexican Americans that La Familia was catapulted to the very top of La Onda Chicana. Backing Little Joe and Johnny was the usual complement of instru-

Beto Villa y su Orquesta, circa 1946 (Courtesy of Chris Strachwitz).

ments found in the best-organized Mexican-American orquestas—two trumpets, two saxophones, a trombone, and a rhythm section of bass, electric guitar, drums, and keyboards.

The music selections on the landmark LP varied from the hard, brash sounds of traditional Tex-Mex rancheras, like "La Traicionera" ("The Treacherous Woman"), to the lush, big-band sounds of the Mexican fox-trot, as in "Viajera" ("Traveler"), to an interesting arrangement of an old folk song, "Las Nubes" ("The Clouds"). The last tune mentioned seemed to capture the cultural essence of La Onda Chicana and its obvious link to the cultural revivalism of the Chicano political and cultural movement that swept through the Mexican-American community in the late 1960s and early 1970s. Thanks, at least in part, to the nationalistic climate fostered by the Chicano movement, "Las Nubes" became a sort of anthem for Chicano music celebrations everywhere.

Many of the arrangements on the *Para la Gente* album were augmented with strings borrowed from the Dallas Symphony—a great novelty in itself—but most effective of all was the strategic interlacing of jazz riffs within the rancheras. The effects were stunning and captured the music sentiments of bicultural Mexican Americans everywhere. The impact of this trailblazing LP was so great that in the early 1990s, almost twenty years from the time it appeared, several of its tunes still formed part of the basic repertory of semiprofessional weekend dance orquestas still to be found in the Southwest.

As fashioned by Little Joe y la Familia, La Onda Chicana spread rapidly throughout the Southwest and beyond. Other orquestas followed La Familia's lead, as more and more efforts were directed at creating a synthesis of ranchera and jazz/rock. Many of these efforts were remarkable for their effect, with particularly successful results being achieved by the orquestas of Sunny and the Sunliners, Latin Breed, and Tortilla Factory, all from Texas.

By the mid-1980s, La Onda Chicana had receded from its watershed years, with the orquesta tradition generally suffering a noticeable decline. Not only did further innovation come to a stop, but the style suffered a retreat from its golden years of the 1960s and 1970s. The most notable sign of decline was the substitution, beginning in the early 1980s, of the horn section for synthesized keyboards. At first, these tried to imitate, synthetically, the sound of the trumpets, saxes, and trombone, but eventually the keyboards

Alonzo y su Orquesta, a typical orchestra, circa 1950. (Courtesy of Thomas Kreneck).

developed their own synthesized sound, one closer in spirit to the conjunto, and this became the norm after about 1985.

The reasons for the decline of the orquesta are not entirely clear, but they evidently have to do with the aging of the population that originally gave impetus to the orquesta tradition—the strongly bicultural Mexican American Generation and its immediate successors, the baby boomers born in the late 1940s and early 1950s. Except in Texas, where an entrenched tradition survived into the 1990s, Mexican Americans growing up in more recent years have been less attracted by the old-fashioned orquesta. The lack of support can be seen in the declining number of semiprofessional orquestas throughout the Southwest, as DJs and the smaller synthesizer-dependent groups have replaced the orquesta in most public and domestic celebrations.

The popularity of the Mexican-American orquesta, as well as its social power, is directly linked to the cultural economy of The Mexican American Generation and its immediate successors. From the outset, orquesta served as a link between the generation's ideology and its political economy. That is, to the extent that this bloc of people aspired "toward life goals which include[d] equality with Anglos," as well as "regular income derived from 'clean,' non-agricultural employment" (Rubel 1966, 12), it adopted musical expression that would bring its cultural life into conformity with its economic status. Orquesta music fulfilled this need perfectly.

Thus, unlike conjunto, which early on became a mirror for working-class life and the workers" resistance to the pressures of acculturation, orquesta was as culturally flexible as its clientele. In it early years, however, especially the 1940s and 1950s, the orquesta was rather tentative in its approach to bimusical performance—the mixing of American and Mexican styles. At a time when his clientele was still unaccustomed to its newfound prosperity and biculturalism, a Beto Villa could at best choose between one or the other: he could play a Tex-Mex polka or an American swing, but never the two simultaneously. In time, as the Mexican Americans adapted to their bicultural reality and even succeeded in synthesizing the two cultures into one "compound biculturalism" (Peñalosa 1980, 47), orquesta performed a parallel synthesis—what we might call "compound bimusicality (Peña 1989a; see also Ervin and Osgood 1954; Vaid 1986).

Octavo García y sus GGs, circa 1952 (Courtesy of Octavio García).

By the 1970s, this "compound bimusicality" had reached full expression in the orquestas" mastery of the art of musical code switching. Similar to the "compound bilingual," who code switches from one language to another within the same sentence, orquesta had learned to switch musical languages within the same musical "sentence," that is, within the same musical piece. This is what Little Joe truly accomplished for the first time in his landmark album, *Para la Gente*. He succeeded in fusing two musical systems under one code of performance. This feat was repeated with equal success by many other orquestas in the succeeding years.

But the musical code switching of the Mexican-American orquesta was even more subtle than the linguistic code switching of its supporters, in that it took place on two distinct but overlapping planes. One switch occurred at the level of ethnicity, the other at the level of class. At the level of ethnicity, the switch was signified by the interlacing of jazz riffs within the flow of an otherwise Mexican ranchera. At the same time, this switch was mediated by parallel shifts occurring at another level of acoustic discrimination—class stylistics, or what Mexican-Texans used to distinguish between a *jaitón* (high-tone) ver-

sus a ranchero style (Peña 1985b). The former was a marker for alleged (or contrived) musical sophistication, but above all it was an index for "high class" snobbery. Ranchero, on the other hand, was a token for the simple, unpretentious life of the country and the barrio—a token The Mexican American Generation was reluctant to renounce.

Above all, in its bimusicality the Mexican-American orquesta represents the dialectical synthesis of two sets of opposed cultures—Mexican and American on the one hand, working and middle class on the other. This synthesis was masterfully articulated by the bimusical orquesta. The best were perfectly adept at this double code switching, as they moved effortlessly from ranchero to jaitón and from Mexican to American (Peña 1985b). At their very best, orquestas achieved a seamless stream of bimusical sound that found a fitting label—La Onda Chicana.

✺SALSA

Salsa is Spanish for "sauce"—in this case a term that refers to the hot, spicy rhythms of Afro-Caribbean music. When people talk about salsa music, however, they are actually referring to a generic term that includes a number of distinct types of Afro-Caribbean music, although one in particular, the *son guaguancó*, has predominated since the 1960s. As Jorge Duany wrote, "*Salsa* is neither a musical style nor a particular rhythm, but rather a hybrid genre ..." (1984, 187). According to Duany, the word "salsa" was first used to refer to this hybrid genre in the 1960s, but it did not gain universal recognition until 1975, when it was used as the title for a popular movie. Whatever the origins of the term "salsa," the music has deep, even sacred, roots in its Afro-Caribbean context.

Salsa as a Cultural Expression

In a fine study of a religious musical ritual in the Dominican Republic called *salve*, Martha Ellen Davis informs us that the salve is a bimusical expression that, as usually performed, progresses from a purely Hispanic section (the *salve sagrada*) to a more intense, spontaneous, and Africanized section (the *salve secular*) (Davis 1981, 63 ff.). The latter section incorporates many of the rhythms (and polyrhythms) of a generalized Afro-Caribbean music that we eventually distilled in the United States into what is now commonly known as salsa. Davis interprets the bicultural nature of the salve as the logical result of the syncretization of two radically different cultures in a historical relationship of domination/subordination—Hispanic and African (ibid: 76 ff.).

What is most important about Davis's analysis of the salve is her conception of this ritual as a key symbol of Afro-Caribbean culture, specifically, its location at the center of the Afro-Dominicans" musical universe. As an expression of an Afro-Caribbean music that is rooted deep within the practice of everyday culture, the salve provides a powerful example of the essentially sacred origins of Afro-Caribbean music. This is a sacredness that Americans of Afro-Carib-

An outdoor *salsa* concert in Houston, Texas (Courtesy of the Arte Público Press archives).

bean descent who subscribe to various offshoots of that music—including salsa—have been reluctant to give up.

Thus, in his study of the ritual aspects of Afro-Cuban music among Cubans and Puerto Ricans of New York City, Morton Marks (1974) argues that despite the commercialization of the music, strong elements of African Yoruba religion have survived in at least some of its development in urban areas such as New York City. In Cuba, these Yoruba elements were syncretized early on with Catholicism to create the Lucumí religious cults, while in New York, Yoruba religion survives in the Santería cults, which, again, combine in their worship deities from both Catholic and Yoruba religion. For Marks, moreover, the interplay of musical styles, as they unfold within a given song (like the salve, usually progressing from a Hispanic form of communication to an African one), is the centrally defining characteristic. Thus, in analyzing the songs "Alma con Alma" ("Soul with Soul"), by the great salsa singer Celia Cruz, and "El Santo en Nueva York" ("The Saint in New York"), by La Lupe, a Cuban vocalist, Marks proposes that "the process of 'Africanization' underlies the performance, with the musical form proceeding from a strongly North American-influenced dance band style, into an *emically* named Yoruba and Lucumí praise song style known as kasha" (1974, 85).

The transformation described by Marks is, in fact, the hallmark of most salsa music since the 1960s. In piece after musical piece, particularly the vast majority that utilize the son guaguancó, the music begins with a standardized Hispanic section whose lyrics are divided into an "A" part, followed by a "B," then returning to the "A" part (ABA form). Meanwhile, the musical background, usually provided by brass instruments (trumpets and/or trombones) in obbligato mode, displays the strong influence of American jazz. Once this section is completed (often it is the shortest section of the tune), the *son montuno* section begins. It is in this section that the African style predominates, particularly through the call-and-response pattern, in which a solo and chorus keep alternating phrases.

Afro-Caribbean music, then, has dual roots, Hispanic and African, which in the United States have undergone further development with the infusion of jazz elements as articulated in the horn obbligatos. In its duality, the music richly displays the process of syncretization, although it has also maintained a dialectical relationship to its twin roots—a relationship that enables the participants in musical events to juxtapose one cultural domain against the other with dramatic effects. This is the point that both Marks and Davis are at pains to demonstrate. In the

Celia Cruz at the Hollywood Palladium.

logical study of culture, expressions that are deeply embedded within the social life of a particular community are sometimes called "summarizing symbols" (Ortner 1973) or "root metaphors" (Turner 1969), in that they sum up, embody, or represent the core or root of the given community's cultural identity. Needless to say, the group cherishes such expressions, singling them out as special markers for whatever it considers to be unique about its culture.

Clearly, for people of Afro-Caribbean descent—Puerto Ricans, Cubans, Dominicans, and others—what is now called salsa has that kind of summarizing power. Salsa stands preeminently for their special sense of Afro-Hispanic "Caribbeanness." But salsa obviously has an audience that extends far beyond its core Caribbean setting. As a cultural symbol, it spreads out with diminishing influence toward audiences whose contact with the music's cultural roots is at best casual. Among these audiences the music's symbolic power is highly diluted or even nonexistent.

Music such as salsa, which has variable significance among diverse audiences, is either a strong or weak symbol depending on the context in which it is performed. As an artistic expression with both commercial and ritual contexts, salsa lends itself particularly well to this strong versus weak concept. This concept can be visually illustrated through a series of concentric circles, where the strong or summarizing symbols—those linked with the most sacred cultural practices—revolve around the innermost circle. Weaker symbols, meanwhile—those connected only casually with the listeners" cultural practices—occupy the outermost circle. Symbols of intermediate strength circulate between these two extremes.

A specific example of salsa as a strong cultural symbol is its role in Santería rituals, where it functions as a powerful icon that is organically linked to Santería practitioners as a root metaphor that defines their deepest sense of cultural and religious identity. In this context, the music resists the riffing or "watered-down" effects that commercialization introduces into any music. Occupying the innermost circle in this example, ritual salsa remains an organic part of Afro-Caribbean culture.

On the other hand, as a musical expression that people of non-Afro-Caribbean background have come to enjoy through commercial exposure, the music begins to lose its organic connection to the powerfully defining rituals of its indigenous cultural setting. It becomes a more casual symbol—for example, one that defines a vague feeling of pan-Latino solidarity among individuals who have otherwise lost an identification with their own musical roots. This is the case with some young Chicanos (Mexican Americans), who have no particular allegiance to their

United States, meanwhile, Afro-Caribbean music has preserved much of this duality, despite the jazz accretions and heavy commercialization. Here, too, among initiates of Santería cults the music retains the ritual qualities and the dialectical movement between two cultures that are associated with sacred performances in the homeland.

It is appropriate at this point to propose a theoretical model that has application to musical culture in general but would seem to be particularly suited to an analysis of Afro-Caribbean music. In the anthropo-

ancestral music (for instance, *norteño*) but who develop an intense feel for salsa. To these individuals the music is at best a symbol of intermediate strength, since it can never occupy in their lives the position that it does in Santería cults.

Dual origins of Salsa recall that its antecedents are hybrid or syncretic expressions that draw from two cultures Hispanic and African. Modern salsa owes its greatest debt to the musical culture of Cuba, although Puerto Rico and, to a lesser extent, the Dominican Republic are also contributing cultures. Two Puerto Rican musical genres, in particular, are legitimate antecedents of modern salsa—the *bomba* and the *plena*. According to ethnomusicologists Singer and Friedman, both emerged in the coastal towns of Puerto Rico, where "large communities of black workers gathered around the sugarcane mills" (1977, 1). Moreover, "*Bomba* is an entertainment form . . . generally performed at social gatherings. It is a couple dance in which the woman performs relatively fixed dance steps while her partner is free to exhibit his dancing skills. . . . *Bomba* texts are usually topical themes relating to everyday life in the community, such as social relationships, work, or historical events. . . . The musical form of *bomba* consists of alternation between solo singer and chorus in a call-and-response pattern" (ibid.).

"The plena is more heavily influenced by European musical culture than the bomba. According to Singer and Friedman, "*Plena* began as a street music, but as it moved into the bars and nightclubs it came to be associated with night life and the underworld. . . . *Plena* texts are on contemporary or historic events . . ." (ibid.).

Both the plena and the bomba were once integral elements in the life of Puerto Rican blacks. They are still performed on the island, though with decreasing frequency. In the United States, however, plena and bomba have undergone some transformation. Adopted (and adapted) by small salsa conjuntos (such as Julito Collazo and his Afro-Cuban Group), bomba and plena are reaching larger audiences, even as some of their elements are absorbed by salsa itself.

Cuba is the indisputable cradle of modern *salsa*, although in the United States the music is more intimately associated with Puerto Ricans. In Cuba, Africans established strong enclaves that carried on many of the musico-ritualistic traditions from the homeland, specifically those attached to the Lucumi cults mentioned earlier. As the anthropologist William Bascom wrote, "African traditions are actually strongest and purest in the larger urban centers of Cuba" (1951, 19). Secularized and made popular commercially in the twentieth century, Afro-Cuban music attached to the Lucumi/Santería cults underwent

further hybridization with Western musical forms. In its hybrid form, this music acquired strong stylistic features that came to appeal to millions of people outside the original cultural core.

It was out of this hybridization process that salsa emerged. However, salsa represents the end stage of this process. Earlier Afro-Cuban forms enjoyed their own moments of glory, as the pace of hybridization accelerated in the middle part of the twentieth century. In this, Cuba again took center stage. John Storm Roberts has described this hybridization as follows: "Taken as a whole, Cuban music presents a more equal balance of African and Spanish ingredients than that of any other Latin country except Brazil. Spanish folklore enriched the music of the countryside, of the city, and of the salon. At the same time—aided by an illicit slave trade that continued right through the nineteenth century—the pure African strain remained stronger in Cuba than anywhere else. . . . As a result, Western African melody and drumming . . . were brought cheek by jowl with country music based on Spanish ten-line *décima*.'" (1979, 4).

It should come as no surprise that Cuba is the

The Joe Cuba Sextet, one of the first groups to record *salsa* in English.

A Machito album cover.

source of many of the musical genres that precede salsa—genres that in fact make up the tapestry of its sounds. Thus, important salsa antecedents such as the *dazón, rumba-guaguancó, charanga, mambo, guaracha, son, bolero,* and *cha cha cha* all originate in Cuba. The mambo and cha cha cha had an enormous impact in and of themselves, of course, but the two genres that most influenced modern salsa directly are the son and the rumba. As ethnomusicologist Peter Manuel has correctly pointed out, "Of the various types of *rumba,* the *guaguancó* was the most influential, as its more westernized successors, *son* and *salsa,* have incorporated and retained its formal structure (introductory *diana,* litany-like *canto,* and call-and-response *montuno*) and most of its basic rhythm patterns" (1985, 252).

As Manuel implies, the rumba is actually a generic term for more specific Afro-Cuban genres—the *yambú, cumbia,* and guaguancó (Singer and Friedman 1977). Again, of these three, it is the guaguancó that is most closely identified with salsa. All, however, have common African characteristics—complex polyrhythms and alternating sections of solo voice and call-and-response. Originally, the rumba was played with African or Africanized instru-

ments of the drum family—the *quinto, segundo,* and *tumba,* reinforced by *cáscara* (a pair of sticks struck against each other) and *claves* (a pair of smooth, cylindrical hardwood sticks struck against each other). Today the drum rhythms are executed on conga drums, but the clave effects remain essentially unchanged in modern salsa.

The son, meanwhile, describes more of a feeling than an actual musical form. It is, however, identifiable by the strong rhythmic patterns associated with it. Most notable among these is the anticipated bass, which is unique to Afro-Cuban music generally, and salsa in particular (Manuel 1985). The son emerged among Africans in the Cuban countryside and spread to the urban areas early in the twentieth century. It was in the latter areas that the son combined with European instruments to create its modern hybrid form. Earlier Africanized instruments were replaced by such European ones as the contrabass, trumpet, and guitar, although the basic percussion was necessarily retained—the bongos, claves, and the guitarlike *tres.* One of Cuba's greatest popular musicians, and the "father" of modern salsa, Arsenio Rodríguez, is credited with further upgrading the son ensemble in the 1930s. He did this by adding a second trumpet, conga drums, and, most important, a piano.

Rodríguez also anticipated some of the greatest modern *salseros* (salsa musicians) by moving away from the romantic themes of earlier *sones* and incorporating texts that addressed nationalist and social issues. Other important figures from the early period of Afro-Cuban music include Ernesto Lecuona, whose group, the Lecuona Cuban Boys, recorded for Columbia, and Arcano y sus Maravillas (Arcano and His Marvels), a charanga orchestra that was responsible for africanizing this erstwhile Europeanized ensemble.

The orquesta charanga is an interesting phenomenon in Afro-Cuban music history. Until the 1930s, this group espoused a genteel, Europeanized sound that appealed to middle-class whites. Its instrumentation consisted of lead flute and violins. Arcano moved to make his group conform more to an African style by adding percussion, such as the bongo and conga drums. Loza (1979) has suggested that Arcano y sus Maravillas actually led the way in the emergence of the phenomenally popular cha cha cha. The king of that genre, however, was La Orquesta Aragón (The Aragón Orchestra), a group popular from the 1940s through the 1960s, whose incomparable style of cha cha cha endeared the music to millions of Latinos across Latin America and the United States.

Meanwhile, several individuals who later went on to make their mark on modern salsa music actually played with charanga groups in the 1940s and 1950s.

These included such well-known figures as Charlie Palmieri, Johnny Pacheco, and Ray Barreto. Along with a host of other salseros, these individuals brought a vitally evolving musical tradition to the United States, where both African- and European-oriented groups experienced a strong cross-fertilization with jazz-a fertilization that resulted in the final emergence of salsa.

Thus, by the late 1950s key performers, such as Tito Rodríguez, Tito Puente, and Machito, had laid the stylistic framework for the modern sound. In fact, when we listen to Tito Rodríguez's recordings from the late 1950s, we cannot but be impressed with how similar his rumbas and guaguancós are to latter-day salsa, even though the music was not recognized as such until the 1970s. Meanwhile, the style and instrumentation was further strengthened in the 1960s and 1970s by a host of great performers, which included such memorable names as Willie Colón, Eddie Palmieri, El Gran Combo (The Great Combo), as well as vocalists like Héctor Lavoe, Celia Cruz, and Rubén Blades. The last is particularly recognized for the poignant social themes that his lyrics often contained (Duany 1984).

By the mid-1960s, the modern salsa sound had pretty much crystallized. And, its most basic genre remained the son/rumba/guaguancó complex, as it had been synthesized by Tito Rodríguez and others in the 1950s. Since the 1960s, this amalgamation of genres, which goes by the label "salsa," has served as the core for numerous explorations that have expanded the parameters of the music. Thus, as Jorge Duany wrote, "The main pattern for *salsa* music remains the *son montuno*, built on the alternation between soloist and chorus" (1984, 198). Moreover, like the son, "[salsa's] characteristics are a call-and-response song structure; polyrhythmic organization with abundant use of syncopation; instrumental variety with extensive use of brass and percussion and strident orchestral arrangements . . . and, above all, a reliance on the sounds and themes of lower-class life in the Latin American *barrios* of U.S. and Caribbean cities" (Duany 1984, 187).

All these elements had been worked out by Tito Rodríguez and other Afro-Caribbean performers by the late 1950s. Since that time, at its most basic level the music has remained faithful to those elements. And, as always, in its most intimate contexts the music still evokes strong feelings of African identification among its most devoted followers—some of whom belong to Santería cults. At the very least, the music provokes feelings of nationalist pride, a strong identity with the people whose culture it symbolizes. As salsa pianist Oscar Hernández observed, "There's a nationalistic sense of pride when people hear *salsa*.

A Tito Puente album cover.

They say, "that's *our* music." It gives people a sense of pride in their Ricanness and Latinoness" (Singer 1983, 184). And, at a more general level, salsa serves as a kind of pan-Latino link that unites many Hispanics under one musical banner—in the words of Félix Padilla, "a medium through which the different Latino life circumstances [can] be spoken to" (1990, 100).

Eddie Palmieri.

✳LATIN JAZZ/ROCK

Two important musical cousins of salsa are Latin jazz and Latin rock. The former is closely associated with the development of salsa music in the United States, although it represents a more self-conscious effort to link Afro-Caribbean with Afro-American music. One can argue, however, that Latin jazz possesses neither the cultural breadth nor depth of salsa, although it clearly represents some of the most experimental efforts in the whole field of Latino music. Outstanding among these efforts are those of Cuban *conguero* (conga player) and vocalist Chano Pozo, whose association with American jazz trumpetist Dizzy Gillespie produced such Latin jazz gems as "Algo Bueno" ("Something Good"), "Afro-Cuban Suite," and "Manteca" ("Lard"), the latter a piece that received high marks for its successful blend of Afro-Caribbean and Afro-American styles (Loza 1979, 106).

More recent standouts in the Latin jazz/rock movement include Chick Corea, who apprenticed with Afro-Cuban greats Mongo Santamaría and Willie Bobo. Meanwhile, Latin jazz's relative, Latin rock, has also had considerable impact on Latinos in the United States. Carlos Santana, the indisputable king of Latin rock since the 1960s, has continued to exploit a wide array of Afro-Cuban rhythms, fusing them to American rock to create a highly innovative style. Santana has inspired many imitators over the years, especially in California, where his music has had exceptional influence on young Chicanos.

Again, it can be argued that Latin jazz and rock lack the cultural power of salsa, norteño, or orquesta. Fundamentally, they are creations of the commercial market, hence must be considered "superorganic" or "second-order" expressions, as opposed to salsa's organic, first-order links to the Afro-Caribbeans. Nonetheless, the contributions of the individuals mentioned, as well as those by such noted figures as José Feliciano, Cal Tjader, and others, cannot be underestimated. In sum, although offshoots of salsa, Latin jazz and rock lack the status of a strong symbol like that of *salsa*, which emanates from the deepest levels of Afro-Caribbean culture. Neither Latin jazz nor rock can make that claim, of course; they are not "wired" into the core of any particular culture. For this, however, they should not be dismissed as transitory. Despite their cultural limitations, the degree of innovation in both Latin jazz and rock has been remarkable, and at times the popularity of Latin rock, especially, has had considerable impact on mainstream American music.

✳MÚSICA TROPICAL

The term "música tropical" has been used historically to refer to any music with a "tropical" flavor, that is, any music identified with the tropics, usually the Afro-Caribbean rim. In the present instance, it is not an entirely accurate label, since the ensemble that represents this type of music—the grupo tropical/moderno—is not necessarily "tropical" in character. Aside from the fact that one of its musical mainstays is the *cumbia*, a dance originally from the tropics of Colombia, the grupo tropical/moderno need not feature any of the percussion instruments normally associated with tropical, that is, Afro-Caribbean, music. And, in fact, the *grupo tropical* is known today as much for its emphasis on another popular genre, *música moderna* (or *romántica*), as it is for the cumbia.

As it has evolved in recent years (the group was originally more "tropical" in that it featured instruments such as the conga drums and the *güiro,* or scrapergourd), the grupo tropical/moderno often features four instruments—keyboard (originally an electric organ, later synthesizer), electric guitar and bass, and trap drums. It originated in Mexico in the 1960s and then spread to the United States via the heavy Mexican immigration that has occurred during the last twenty-five years or so.

The grupo tropical's mainstay, the cumbia, was originally a Colombian folk dance that in the twentieth century became urbanized and diffused commercially throughout Latin America. Upon reaching Mexico in the mid-1960s, the cumbia was appropriated by the working-class masses at about the same time that the four-instrument ensemble was emerging as a favorite dance group among urban working-class Mexicans. This ensemble came to be associated with cumbia music (música tropical) in Mexico and the American Southwest. At about the same time, however, a slow-dance genre, influenced by American rhythm and blues, surged in popularity in Mexico— the *balada* (from the American pop "ballad," a lyrical love song). Popularized by such groups as Los Angeles Negros (The Black Angels), Los Terrícolas (The Earthlings), and others, the Mexican balada came to be known generally as "música romántica" (or "moderna"—the two terms are interchangeable), and in time most grupos tropicales/modernos began to alternate between the cumbia and the balada to fill out their repertories.

Besides Los Angeles Negros (who seldom performed the cumbia), the best-known exponents in the relatively short span of música tropical/moderna in Mexico and the United States have been Rigo Tovar (who is of Afro-Caribbean ancestry), Los Bukis (The Bukis), Los Sonics (The Sonics), Los Yonics, (The

Ionics), and Los Temerarios (The Fearless). Besides their reliance on record sales for financial support, most of the commercially popular grupos tropicales/modernos also rely on personal appearances at large public dances. At these dances the cumbia reigns supreme, although, again, most groups depend to one extent or another on the balada, which, with its slow 4/4 or 6/8 meter, offers a contrastive alternative to the usually up-tempo, lighthearted spirit of the cumbia.

Almost nothing has been written about the Mexican grupo tropical/moderno, which for the past twenty-five years has been undisputed king among certain working-class segments of Mexican society. By musical standards, it is an unspectacular style, one that is dwarfed by both salsa and La Onda Chicana. But it exerts a powerful influence on the millions of Mexican proletarians who subscribe to it. In the United States, one has only to attend certain ballrooms in cities such as Los Angeles, San Jose, Phoenix, or El Paso to observe the enormous drawing power that groups such as Los Bukis, Los Yonics, and others command, especially among the undocumented and recently documented immigrants from Mexico.

Clearly, música tropical/moderna is more than a temporary escape for the Mexican working class from the drudgery of its daily existence as a poorly paid underclass. A thorough ethnographic study would reveal that, much like música norteña, it represents a working-class cultural alternative that tacitly resists the assimilative pressures of a dominant Anglo-European majority, while it reinforces a Mexican working-class identity.

The late twentieth century has witnessed some notable changes in the music of Latinos in the United States. A "meltdown" has occurred, resulting from styles that have crossed over and overlapped with others. The most important example of this crossover comes from Texas, where Norteño (more particularly the Texan-Mexican conjunto) and orquesta have witnessed a dramatic convergence. The traditional orquesta, as epitomized by Little Joe y la Familia, has virtually disappeared in the 1990s, replaced by such groups as Mazz, La Mafia, and others. These carry on the basic stylistic features that identify the music as "tejano," but the mainstay of the orquesta—the horns—have been replaced by electronic keyboards that imitate the sounds of trumpets and saxophones. At the same time, these ensembles often incorporate the accordion, thus lending them a hybrid character.

Also on the trend-setting Texas scene, the absorption of country western elements into tejano music has intensified since the 1980s. Borrowing from country western is not new to tejanos (it took place as early as the 1960s), but in the '80s and '90s this absorption has accelerated. Thus, conjunto performers such as Emilio Navaira and Roberto Pulido, and especially The Texas Tornados, a new group made up of veteran musicians (Freddie Fender, Flaco Jimenez, Doug Sahm), have fused conjunto with country western to produce a novel sound that adds a new dimension to tejano music.

Whether these musical developments signal a new, dynamic phase in at least one segment of Latino music, or they represent a new layer of commercial exploitation, remains uncertain. The cultural significance of these new musical developments also remains to be seen: Are they a response to cultural movements at the "organic" level or do they, like Latin rock, reflect the commercial stimulation of Latino music by the large recording labels, which have recently entered the field in earnest? Time will answer that question. In any case, there is no question that Latinos in the United States continue to leave an astonishing record of musical activity.

Hispanics are a widely diverse group of people; yet they share one common characteristic: all of them, due to their Afro-Indo-Hispanic background, have experienced varying degrees of conflict with the dominant Anglo-European majority. The various Hispanic music forms have served to mediate this conflict, despite their differences in style and cultural function. It is the legacy of conflict and accommodation, then, that channels Hispanic musical creation and the proliferation of culturally powerful traditions. Finally, as the various sectors of the Hispanic population continue to confront, accommodate, and otherwise amalgamate with the Euro-American majority, we may expect more musical experimentation and, perhaps, even new traditions to be forthcoming.

References

Acuña, Rudolfo. *Occupied America: A History of Chicanos.* New York: Harper and Row, 1981.

Baqueriro-Foster, Gerónimo. *La música en el periodo independete.* Mexico City: Fondo de Cultura Ecónomica, 1964.

Bascom, William. "The Yoruba in Cuba." *Nigeria* 37 (1951): 14-20

Davis, Martha Ellen. *Voces del purgatorio: Estudio de la selva dominicana.* Santo Dominican Republic: Museo del Hombre Dominicano, 1981.

Dinger, Adeline. *Folklife and Folklore of the Mexican Border.* Edinburg, Tex.: Hidalgo County Historical Museum, 1972.

Duany, Jorge. "Popular Music in Puerto Rico: Toward an Anthropology of *Salsa*." *Latin American Music Review* 5, no. 2 (1984): 186-216.

Ervin, Susan M. and Charles E. Osgood. "Second Language Learning and Bilingualism." In *Psycholinguistics: A Survey of Theory and Research Problems.* Charles

Osgood and Thomas A. Sebeok, eds. Bloomington: Indiana University Press, 1954.

García, Mario T. "Americans All: The Mexican American Generation and the Politics of Wartime Los Angeles, 1941-45." *Social Science Quarterly* 65, no. 2 (1984): 278-89.

Limón, José. "Folklore, Social Conflict, and the U.S.-Mexico Border." In *Handbook of American Folklore*, edited by Richard M. Dorson. Bloomington: Indiana University Press, 1983.

Loza, Steven. "Music and the Afro-Cuban Experience." Master's thesis, University of California, Los Angeles, 1979.

Manuel, Peter. "The Anticipated Bass in Cuban Popular Music." *Latin American Music Review* 6, no. 2 (1985): 249-61.

Marks, Morton. "Uncovering Ritual Structures in Afro-American Music." In *Religious Movements in Contemporary America*, edited by Irving Zaretzky and Mark Leone. Princeton N.J.: Princeton University Press, 1974.

Mayer-Serra, Otto. *Panorama de la música mexicana.* Mexico City: Fondo de Cultura Económica, 1941.

Ortner, Sherry. "On Key Symbols." *American Anthropologist* 75 (1973): 1338-1346.

Padilla, Felix M. "Salsa: Puerto Rican and Latin Music." *Journal of Popular Culture* 24, no. 1 (1990): 87-104.

Paredes, Américo. "The Mexican Corrido: Its Rise and Fall." In *Madstones and Twisters,* edited by Mody C. Boatright, Wilson M. Hudson, and Allen Maxwell, 91-105. Publications of the Texas Folklore Society, no. 28. Dallas, Tex.: Southern Metodist University Press, 1958a.

———. *"With His Pistol in his Hand:" A Border Ballad and its Hero."* Austin: University of Texas Press, 1958b.

———. "The Anglo-American in Mexican Folklore." In *New Voices in American Studies,* edited by Ray B. Browne and Donald H. Winkleman. Lafayette, Ind.: Purdue University Press, 1966.

———, *A Texas-Mexican Cancionero.* Urbana: University of Illinois Press, 1976.

Peña, Manuel. "Folksong and Social Change: Two *Corridos* as Interpretive Sources." *Aztlán Journal of Chicano Studies* 13, nos. 1 and 2 (1982): 13-42.

———. *The Texas-Mexican Conjunto: History of a Working-Class Music.* Austin: University of Texas Press, 1985a.

———. "From *Ranchero* to *Jaitón*: Ethnicity and Class in Texas-Mexican Music." *Ethnomusicology* 29, no. 1 (1985b): 29-55.

———. "Notes Toward an Interpretive History of California-Mexican Music." In *From the Inside Out: Perspectives on Mexican and Mexican-American Folk Art,* edited by Karana Hattersley-Drayton, et al., eds. San Francisco: The Mexican Museum, 1989b.

Peñalosa, Fernando. *Chicano Sociolinguistics.* Rowley, Mass.: Newbury House Publishers, 1980.

Roberts, John Storm. *The Latin Tinge.* New York: Oxford University Press, 1979.

Robinson, Alfred. *Life in California before the Conquest.* San francisco: Thomas C. Russell, 1925.

Rubel, Arthur J. *Across the Tracks: Mexican-Americans in Texas City.* Austin: University of Texas Press, 1966.

Simmons, Merle E. *The Mexican Corrido as a Source for the Interpretive Study of Modern Mexico.* Bloomington: Indiana University Press, 1957.

Singer, Roberta L. "Tradition and Innovation in Contemporary Latin Popular Music in New York City. *Latin American Music Review* 4, no. 2 (1983): 183-202.

———, and Friedman, Robert. "Puerto Rican and Cuban Musical Expression in New York." *Caliente = Hot: Recorded Anthology of American Music, Inc.* (LP). New York: New World Records, 1977.

Turner, Victor. *The Ritual Process.* Chicago: Aldine Publishing, 1969.

———. *Dramas, Fields, and Metaphors.* Ithaca, N.Y.: Cornell University Press, 1974.

Vaid, Jyotsna. *Language Processing in Bilinguals: Cycle Linguistic and Neopsychological Perspectives.* Hillside, NJ: Lawrence Erlbaum Associates, 1986.

Selected Discography

Afro-Caribbean and Latin Jazz/Rock

Aragón, Orquesta. *Original de Cienfuegos.* Cariño, DBLI-5011.

Arcano y sus Maravillas. *Danzón mambo.* Cariño DBMI-5806.

Barretto, Ray. *Charanga moderna.* Tico, SLP 1087.

Canario y su Grupo. *Plenas.* Ansonia ALP 1232.

Colón, Willie, and Ruben Blades. *Siembra.* Fania, JM 00-537.

Cortijo, Rafael, y su Combo. *Cortijo en New York.* Gema, LPG-1115.

Grupo folklórico de Alberto Zayas. *Guaguancó afro-cubano.* Panart, LP 2055.

Machito. *Afro-Cuban Jazz.* Verve, VE-2-2522.

Palmieri, Charlie. *Charanga Duboney: Echoes of an Era.* West Side Latino, WS-LA-240-1.

Palmieri, Eddie. *The Best of Eddie Palmieri.* Tico, CLP 1317.

Puente, Tito. *Dance Mania.* RCA LSP-1092.

Rodriguez, Arsenio. *El sentimiento de Arsenio.* Cariño, DBMI-5802.

Rodriguez, Tito. *Estoy como nunca.* West Side Latino, LT-LA 129-D.

Santamaria, Mongo. *Afro-Roots.* Prestige, PR-24018.

Santana. *Abraxas.* Columbia, KC 30130.

Orquesta, Norteña, and Múxica Tropical

Ayala, Ramón, y los Bravos del Norte. *Ramón Ayala y los Bravos del Norte.* Freddie, LP-1165.

Bernal, Conjunto. *Una noche en la villita.* Bego, BG-1015.

Bernal, Conjunto, et al. *Las más alegres polkas.* Ideal, ILP-127.

Bukis, Los. *Los Bukis.* Profono, PI-3050.

De la Rosa, Tony. *Las polkas de oro.* Freddie, LP-1194.

De la Rosa, Tony, et al. *Las más alegres polkas.* Ideal, ILP 127.

Hernandez, Little Joe y la Familia. *Para la gente.* Buena Suerte Records, BSR 1038.

———. *Sea la paz la fuerza.* Leona Records Corporation, LRC 019.

Jordan, Steve. *Soy de Tejas.* Hacienda Records, LP 7905.

Latin Breed, The. *Powerdrive*. GCP, GCPLP-124.

Relámpagos del Norte, Los. *El disco de oro*. Alto Records, Alto 1125.

Sunny and the Sunliners. *Los enamorados*. Key-loc, KL 3020.

———. *Grande, Grande, Grande*. Key-loc, KL 3028.

Temerarios, Los. *Te Queiro*. TH/Rodven, 2717. *Texas-Mexican Border Music*. Arhoolie/Folklyric, vol. 3-7; 11-13; 16-21; 23-24.

Tortilla Factory. *Mis favoritas*. Falcon Records, GLP-011. Tovar, Rigo, y su Costa Azul. *El nuevo contacto musical*. Melody Records, MEL-293.

[Treviño], Jimmy Edward. *My Special Album*. Texas Best Records, TXB-LP-1001.

Villa, Beto. *Beto Villa*. Falcon, FLP 108.

———. *Saludamos a Texas*, Ideal, ILP 104.

Yonics, Los. *Porqué volví contigo*. Fonovisa, 9012.

Manuel Peña

Media

✹ Treatment of Hispanics in Mainstream Media ✹ Newspapers ✹ Films ✹ Television ✹ Advertising ✹ Hispanic-Oriented Print Media

This chapter focuses primarily on mass communication as it pertains to newspapers, magazines, film, radio, television, and advertising. Excluded are discussions on books, the music recording industry, and theater, which are covered in other chapters.

✹TREATMENT OF HISPANICS IN MAINSTREAM MEDIA

The treatment of one ethnic group by another is quite often influenced by economic or political factors in their nation, state, or region. This is certainly true regarding the relations between Anglos and Latinos. The conflict and cooperation between these groups has been shaped by the political and economic relations between the United States and Hispanic American countries.

The mainstream mass media, which so often reflect the prevalent perspectives of the dominant groups in society, have historically replicated those views in their treatment of Hispanics. Therefore, an avenue for partially understanding contemporary Hispanic life in the United States is the assessment of messages that the media disseminate about them. There are two related reasons that media are the focus of analysis. First, at all levels of society they are the most *pervasive* sources of news and information. For many people they are also the most relied-upon source for entertainment. Second, the messages presented by the media may have significant effects on the audience, especially regarding events, topics, and issues about which the audience has no direct knowledge or experience. Thus, for millions of people in this country, a significant part of the information they receive and the notions they develop about Hispanics may often be products of mass media messages.

While a comprehensive treatment of the topic of "media effects" is beyond the scope of this work, it is imperative to realize that there are conditions under that media may have maximal influence on the audience—conditions that are germane to the critical discussion that follows about the mainstream media's treatment of Hispanics. One of those conditions occurs when viewers do not have other sources of information or experiences that provide a standard against which to assess the media messages. To the extent that non-Hispanics live segregated lives with limited opportunities to interact effectively with a variety of Hispanics in constructive or productive ways, the media images of Hispanics will be among the most important sources for non-Latinos to learn and interpret who Hispanics are and how they think. Another factor that increases the "symbolic" media's influence occurs when the values or views presented by them are recurrent. To date, the values and views presented about Latinos are predominantly negative and recurrent across media and time.

Furthermore, the treatment of Latinos in mainstream media has its impact on Hispanics, who suffer the consequences of the recurring negative imagery. For example, they face the psychological pain that emerges from the negative portrayals and lack of recognition of their own people and values. They also have to endure the social scorn that emerges when the treatment they receive from other people, and sometimes from those of their own ethnic background, is consciously or unconsciously based on stereotyped notions disseminated by the media.

✹NEWSPAPERS

Mainstream newspapers were probably the first major means of mass communication through which fragmented and distorted news, information, and images of Hispanics were created and promoted. While much has changed from the early depictions, the treatment and employment of Hispanics in newspapers is still far from adequate in this media institution.

Portrayals

Evans's (1967) study of the roots of three popular stereotypes (the "Indian savage," the "Mexican bandit," and the "Chinese heathen") reveals that "the Anglo image of the Mexican as a bandit is largely an outgrowth of the Manifest Destiny policy of the early 1800s." His review of nineteenth-century English-language American newspapers in California and Texas discusses how circumstantial events related to economic and political relations between the people who inhabited the expansive Mexican territories of the Southwest and the Anglo-European settlers and gold prospectors led the latter group to create stereotypes of the former to justify the conquest of that region. The political, religious, and economic beliefs of Anglo-European superiority were constantly revealed as they depicted the native-american and Mexican inhabitants as people destined to be conquered and unworthy of keeping their lands and resources.

After the conquests of the southwestern territories, the mainstream press of the early twentieth century continued a pattern of false depictions of Hispanic people. In other instances, the mainstream press simply ignored the mainstream experiences of Hispanics. The most blatant act of negative stereotyping occurred during the 1940s through exploitation of social and economic tensions between Hispanics and Anglos in Los Angeles. The press gave undue prominence to Mexican Americans in crime news. Alarmist headlines and stories blaming these Hispanics for many of the city's social ills were part of the 1943 "Zoot-suit" riots and their aftermath (see McWilliams 1949).

In subsequent decades, changing journalistic standards of increased professionalism, balance, and objectivity helped diminish such blatant anti-Mexican racism. Yet negative, limited, or inadequate portrayals of Hispanics in newspapers of the latter half of this century have been systematically documented. One of the first studies in this area was Fishman and Casiano's (1969) analysis of Puerto Ricans in *The New York Times* and *The* (New York) *Post*; they also studied the Spanish-language dailies *El Diario* and *El Tiempo*. The authors found that the English dailies showed little interest in Puerto Ricans, who were referred to with negative attributes and covered primarily in terms of their community needs or problems (for which solutions were infrequently offered). The same was not true in the Spanish dailies, where more positive and solution-oriented stories were observed.

Negative and biased coverage of Mexican, American was also evident in a handful of unpublished master's theses regarding pretrial criminal news reporting (Valdéz 1970) and general reporting (Lee 1973; Sánchez 1973). Also, Chavira (1975, 1977), comparing immigration and deportation news in the *Los Angeles Times* and the Spanish-language daily *La Opinión* during the 1930s, 1950s, and 1970s, found that the plight of Mexicans was covered much more sympathetically and humanistically in the latter paper (see also Arias 1985).

Yet some improvements have been made, at least according to the two most recent studies of the mainstream press. In the most systematic and quantitatively oriented study of the coverage of Hispanic Americans in the English-language dailies of Santa Fe (New Mexico), Tucson (Arizona), and Salinas, San Bernardino, Stockton, and Visalia (California), Greenberg and colleagues conclude (from their two-week sample) that "sports news and photo coverage get high marks for their inclusion of local Hispanics" and that "local news coverage exclusive of sports gets a passing grade—good, not excellent, but better than it is currently receiving credit for." They add, however, that "editorial coverage and bulletin listings of Hispanic people and activities are below average and in need of considerable attention" (1983, 223).

The most promising assessment is provided by VanSlyke Turk, Richstad, Bryson Jr., and Johnson (1989, 113). In their study of the Albuquerque *Journal* and the San Antonio *Express*, they found some examples of parity in the inclusion of Hispanics and conclude that "Hispanics and Hispanic issues are . . . present in the newspaper newshole in proportion to their presence in the population" (1989). They also found that in comparison to stories about Anglos, Hispanic stories were adequately treated in terms of length and placement. However, as was the case in previously cited studies, Hispanics were much too prominently reported as "problem people," for example, in judicial and crime news, news of riots, and accident and disaster news.

In spite of these studies, the prognosis of Hispanic treatment in mainstream newspapers has consistently remained culturally insensitive and nonsupportive. From his observations and personal experiences, Charles A. Erickson, founder and editor of *Hispanic Link, Inc.,* summarized that "the relationship between 20 million Americans crowded under the umbrella Hispanic and the nation's establishment print media sprawls across the spectrum from non-existent to quaint, to precarious, to outright antagonistic" (1981, 3). Erickson then identifies six dimensions of mainstream press irresponsibility: "the press will not allow Hispanics to be authorities on general issues"; "the press will not even allow

Hispanics to be authorities on issues where Hispanics have the obvious expertise"; "the press still views the Hispanic community in stereotype"; "the press fails to provide Hispanics with information of critical interest and importance to their welfare and progress"; "the press does not hire enough Hispanics or other reporters and editors with Hispanic cultural awareness and expertise"; and "the press tends to smother those Hispanics they do hire." For each dimension, Erickson provides various examples to support his case. For instance, regarding the press's viewing the Hispanic co mmunity in stereotype, he states, "Traditionally, non-Hispanic reporters have attached negative adjectives to the word "barrio." For example, Houston's barrios were described in a series one of its papers ran some months ago as places where shoppers haggle and Latin rhythms blare. A Chicago reporter described New York's Spanish Harlem as "grim, rat-infested." A *Christian Science Monitor* writer chose the words "[t]he often-steamy barriors [*sic*] of East Los Angeles" (Erickson 1981, 7).

A decade following Erickson's critique of the mainstream press, David Shaw's nine-article series in *The Los Angeles Times* assessing the status of reporting about and hiring minorities found many of the same situations and problems discussed by Erickson. The headline of the first story summarized the issue: "Negative News and Little Else." The story went on to say that "by focusing on crime, poverty and aberrant behavior newspapers fail to give a complete portrait of ethnic minorities" (Shaw, 1990a, A1). An example of continued stereotyping presented by Shaw (1990d) is the use of the word "aliens" (which can make Latinos seem "inhuman—strange outcasts from another world") instead of "illegal immigrants" or "undocumented workers."

In trying to understand some of the reasons that lead to the continued fragmentation and distortion of news about Hispanics and other minorities, Erickson, Shaw, Lewels, Gutiérrez, and others who have written on this subject would probably agree that the lack of Hispanics in the newsrooms and in their management is one of the major factors to be considered.

Employment

Wilson and Gutiérrez (1985) point out that when the first counts of minority participants in the mainstream press were conducted in the early 1970s, these groups constituted less than 2 percent of the total. About a decade later, in 1984, the total had only made it to 5.8 percent among the approximately 1,750 daily newspapers in the nation. As low as these figures are, one must realize that they are for all minorities, which means that the situation for Hispanics is more dismal. This is a problem that continues even today, according to the most recent surveys of the National Association of Hispanic Journalists (NAHJ) and the American Society of Newspaper Editors (ASNE).

According to the NAHJ's third annual survey (for which 125 newspapers with circulations over 100,000 were queried and almost half responded), Hispanics accounted for a mere 3.2 percent of this labor force in general; only 2 percent were managers. According to the ASNE survey (for which 1,545 newspapers were queried, 65 percent of which responded), approximately 1,349 Hispanics were employed in those newspapers and constituted a scant 2.4 percent of the work force of about 55,714.

In addition to the problem of low employment, Hispanics who have succeeded in gaining employment in journalism encounter various burdens often related to their ethnicity. As suggested by Erickson, Hispanic reporters face unwarranted challenges of their latitude and credibility as professional journalists (1981, 5-11). He points out that while too often Hispanics are considered to lack the intellect to write about issues other than ethnic problems or strife, they are also perceived as too partial for "objective" in-depth reporting about educational, economic, and other types of policy issues of importance to their community. Moreover, many Hispanic journalists are burdened with requests to be translators in situations beyond their reporting duties; for example, to assist in answering Spanish-language business calls or correspondence not related to their responsibilities. Yet, these tasks and Hispanics" bilingual abilities usually go without compensatory pay.

Given these current employment figures and practices, one can understand some of the factors related to the inadequate treatment of Hispanics in newspapers. Unfortunately, given the slow progress in newsroom integration and the limited sensitivity of many Anglo reporters and editors, it will be some time before Hispanics make sufficient inroads to professional positions, which is necessary to help improve the portrayal of their communities.

In spite of these difficulties, many newspapers have been hiring hiring more Latino and other ethnic minority journalists and improving their working environment, especially with respect to training, promotions, and distribution of assignments. These efforts have also included second-language courses (especially Spanish) and racial and ethnic awareness workshops for all employees of the newspaper. In the late 1980s, some newspapers, such as *The Los Angeles Times* and the *Fresno Bee,* began publishing weekly supplements in Spanish. This practice, which is quite recent in these papers, has been going on with mixed success since the 1840s in various locations, especially in border towns (see Wilson and Gutiérrez 1985).

The concerted efforts of organizations such as the National Association of Hispanic Journalists, the National Hispanic Media Coalition, the Hispanic Academy of Arts and Sciences, and the National Association of Hispanic Publications have been major factors in the push for positive changes and will undoubtedly contribute to improving both the portrayal and employment of Hispanics in the media.

✳ FILMS

While newspapers were the first mass medium to widely disseminate images of Hispanics, their circulation and influence were more limited than that of films. Since the inception of moving pictures, stereotypes of minority and ethnic groups have been a standard feature. (For a more extensive study of Hispanics in the motion picture industry, see Chapter 20.)

Portrayals

Hispanics have been regularly stereotyped in films dating back to the early days of silent cinema. Early Westerns, such as the so-called greaser films like *Bronco Billy and the Greaser* (1914), instituted in films the Mexican or half-breed bandit, one of several Mexican stereotypes that Pettit (1980) says derives from Western dime novels. By the early 1920s, the six major Hispanic stereotypes were well established in Hollywood movies. Following Pettit (1980), Woll (1980), and Wilson and Gutiérrez (1985), Berg (1990) has delineated them in six major categories: el bandido, the half-breed harlot, the male buffoon, the female clown, the Latin lover, and the dark lady.

While the overall thrust of Hollywood's portrayal of Hispanics has been quite uniform, political and economic forces have accounted for several well-differentiated stages in the history of that depiction. In the beginning, Hollywood stereotyped with impunity. Even before the appearance of the "greaser" films, Hollywood was portraying Mexicans as vengeful, cruel, and violent (Lamb 1975). For a time, with the beginning of World War I, there was a shift away from negative Mexican stereotypes. But afterward the same stereotypical patterns continued, and derogatory depictions of Mexicans and Mexico led the government of Mexico to threaten to boycott such films (Delpar 1984). Hollywood's response was to change the setting of many films from Mexico to some fictional Latin American country. For example, the setting of Harold Lloyd's comedy *Why Worry?* (1923), about an American hypochondriac who finds himself in the midst of revolutionary turmoil in what is obviously Mexico, is set in "Paradiso." Hollywood continued to adjust its productions to take Mexican objections into account, but the results were often just as stereotypical. The producers of *Viva Villa!* (1934) got the approval of the Mexican government for the film's shooting script, although the movie itself is full of mean-spirited, hateful, and moronic Mexicans (Delpar 1984).

The Second World War quickly reversed such imagery, however, as Hollywood hastened to solidify relations with Mexico and Latin America against the Axis powers. An era of "Good Neighborism" (1939-1945) followed, in which Latin America and Latin Americans were portrayed positively, if rather one-dimensionally. Typical of the change was *Juarez* (1939), a Hollywoodized biography of the Mexican revolutionary leader, and the Disney studios" animated travelogues, *Saludos Amigos* (1943) and *The Three Caballeros* (1945). It was this era that saw the rise of such Latin stars as María Montez, Ricardo Montalbán, Fernando Lamas, and Carmen Miranda.

In many ways, the period immediately following World War II was the most interesting in terms of how Hollywood dealt with Hispanics and Hispanic themes. Two major postwar genres predominantly featured Hispanic characters and issues: *film noir*, a group of dark, bleak films with betrayal as a central theme, and the social melodrama, movies that directly addressed social problems. Of the *film noirs*, those treating Hispanics included Billy Wilder's *Ace in the Hole* (also known as *The Big Carnival*; 1951), Orson Welles's *Touch of Evil* (1958), and Ralph Nelson's *Requiem for a Heavyweight* (1962), films that also critique the massive corruption within the Anglo world.

There were several social melodramas that dealt with Hispanic issues. Notable among them was *Salt of the Earth* (1954), a joint venture by blacklisted Hollywood filmmakers (screenwriter Michael Wilson, director Herbert Biberman, producer Paul Jerico) depicting in gritty terms a miners" strike in New Mexico. *The Lawless* (1954) was another Chicano-centered film made by a blacklisted filmmaker, Joseph Losey. Two boxing films were also produced in the postwar period, the formulaic *Right Cross* (1950, directed by John Sturges), with Ricardo Montalbán as a Chicano fighter with an anti-Anglo chip on his shoulder, and the much more intriguing *The Ring* (1952, directed by Kurt Neumann), starring Lalo Ríos as a young man trying to box his way out of East Los Angeles. Irving Pichel's *A Medal for Benny* (1945) and William Wellman's *My Man and I* (1952) both condemned the hypocrisy within the Anglo mainstream. Surprisingly, *Giant* (1957), a blockbuster directed by George Stevens, was one of the most progressive of all these films, indicting not only racism but also patriarchy, the imperialistic bent of America's westward expansion, the class system, and the social construction of "manhood."

From the 1960s to the present, Hollywood's stereotyping of Hispanics can be placed into two broad categories: repeated and countered. In the main, Hollywood continued its policy of stereotyping Hispanics. The bandido stereotype, for example, can be found in several film genres. Updated variations include the young Puerto Rican toughs in *West Side Story* (1961) and the well-meaning courtroom drama *The Young Savages* (1961) (for one of the few analyses of Puerto Ricans in Hollywood film, see Richie Pérez 1990), as well as the East L.A. Chicano gang members in *Colors* (1988). Perhaps the most widely seen example occurred in the opening of Steven Speilberg's *Raiders of the Lost Ark* (1981). In the film's first fifteen minutes, Indiana Jones, somewhere in South America in 1936, is menaced by all manner of Latino culprits. He is abandoned (an Indian carrier leaves the Jones expedition screaming hysterically), betrayed (one of his remaining native guides tries to shoot him in the back, the other leaves him for dead in the underground passageway), and threatened (a tribe of Latin American Indians chases and tries to kill him). Another example of a widely seen recent Hollywood bandido is seen in the Latin American bad guys in *Romancing the Stone* (1984), particularly in the corrupt villain (played by Mexican actor Manuel Ojeda).

The other five Hispanic stereotypes—the half-breed harlot, the male buffoon, the female clown, the Latin lover, and the dark lady—had similar Hollywood incarnations during the same period. But during this time there was a promising development, namely, the countering of such pervasive imagery. This stage was precipitated by the emergence of talented Hispanics who began working *behind* the camera. Because of them, the opportunity for opposing long-standing Hollywood stereotypes became a reality. The narrative strategy of these filmmakers was to revise standard Hollywood genres. Familiar story formulas were given an ethnic twist, which subverted standard Hollywood practice and promoted a more pluralistic view of the world. A good example of this sort of counterimagery is found in León Ichaso's *Crossover Dreams* (1985), a Hispanic rendition of the well-known show-biz success story. An ambitious New York salsa musician (Rubén Blades) turns his back on his friends, his barrio, and his roots to achieve mainstream success, but fails to make it in the big time. In the film's final scene, the character swallows his pride, returns to his old neighborhood, and asks his old partner to start another salsa band.

The film thus critiques dominant notions of the American dream as well as celebrates and reaffirms traditional Hispanic values.

A more problematic version of the same story was Luis Valdez's *La Bamba* (1987), whose compliant rock and roll hero Richie Valens (Lou Diamond Phillips) conforms to mainstream requisites for success (he even changes his name) to facilitate his rise to stardom. Much more powerful was Valdez's first feature, *Zoot Suit* (1981), a filmed version of his hit stage play of the same name. It was an assault on Hollywood in its form (a provocative combination of broad comedy, courtroom melodrama, social criticism, Brechtian distancing devices, and song and dance) and on the justice system in its content (a depiction of Los Angeles's notorious Sleepy Lagoon trial).

Director-turned-producer Moctezuma Esparza revised the Western genre in *The Ballad of Gregorio Cortez* (1982, directed by Robert M. Young), based in part on Américo Paredes's account of the real-life exploits of the man who eluded the Texas Rangers around the turn of the century. Victor Villaseñor's script tells the story from multiple perspectives and manages an even-handed account while at the same time revealing the prejudice prevalent in Texas at that time. It remains the most eloquent reversal of the bandido stereotype yet put on film. Esparza also produced Robert Redford's *The Milagro Beanfield War* (1988), an earnest though less-than-successful attempt to portray an entire New Mexico community—both Anglo and Chicano—during a municipal crisis.

Another notable film of this "counterimage" phase was Gregory Nava's *El Norte* (1984), a retelling of the familiar coming-to-America story from the point of view of a Central American brother and sister fleeing political oppression in their homeland. By impressively combining graphic realism with lyrical magic realism, the film deftly depicts both the danger and the hopefulness of their flight. Cheech Marin's *Born in East L.A.* (1987), about the deportation to Mexico of a Mexican American, is a comic inversion of the same story. In its own raucous way, it examines the contradictions inherent in America's definition of citizenship. Finally, there is the Chicano version of *Goodbye, Mr. Chips*, Ramón Menéndez's *Stand and Deliver* (1988). The film was based on the true-life story of Jaime Escalante, a courageous and visionary East Los Angeles high school math teacher (played by Edward James Olmos, who was nominated for a Best Actor Academy Award for the role). Using humor, threats, and shrewd psychology, Escalante inspires his students to master calculus and in so doing gives them a positive sense of self-worth and a key to self-actualization.

As remarkable as these counterimagery strides have been, however, it remains to be seen whether this trend will continue. After the advancements of the 1980s, production on Hispanic themes in movies initiated by Hispanics has slowed down considerably since the peak period of 1987-88. There is no comparison with Afro-American filmmaking, for example, which has witnessed an unprecedented explosion during the same time period. In 1991, for example, there were nineteen Afro-American-directed feature films released by Hollywood. In contrast, since 1988 there has been only one Latino-directed film made, Isaac Artenstein's independently produced *Break of Dawn*, and it never found a mainstream distributor.

✳ TELEVISION

Not surprisingly, the treatment of Hispanics on mainstream television has not been sharply different from that in the film industry. Although there have been occasional breaks with stereotypical imagery, in some respects the portrayal has been more critical of Hispanic culture and life. In addition, the situation is worse in the number of Hispanics employed in front or behind cameras. This conclusion is quite evident from even cursory watching of American television.

Portrayals

Since television's widespread appeal in the late 1950s, the masters of television images have been less than fair in their portrayals of Hispanics. Reyes's brief review (1983) of the Hispanic image on network television from 1951 through 1983 lends qualitative support to this judgment. For example, the first "prominent" Hispanic male buffoon (as Berg, 1990, would classify it) was seen for many years on the "I Love Lucy" show (CBS 1951-61), where Lucille Ball's husband, Ricky Ricardo, played "the good-looking, excitable, short tempered Cuban band leader who spoke with an accent and occasionally rattled off expletives in Spanish" (Reyes 1983, 11). Interestingly, in "Desi and Lucy: Before the Laughter," a two-hour special broadcast on February 20, 1991, on CBS, he is stereotyped prominently as an irresponsible Latin lover.

Other Hispanic male buffoons include Pancho, the sidekick to the Cisco Kid in the syndicated series (1951-56) "The Cisco Kid"; José Jiménez, the Puerto Rican bumbling doorman and elevator operator in "The Danny Thomas Show" (NBC 1953-71); and Sgt. García in the "Zorro" series (ABC, 1957-59). The last of the successful (in terms of ratings and continuity) Hispanic male buffoons on network television was probably Freddie Prinze, who in "Chico and the Man" (NBC, 1974-78) played Chico, a Hispanic "streetwise kid working in a garage with a bigoted old man."

With such exceptions as "Chico and the Man," which was terminated shortly after Prinze's suicide in early 1977, Hispanics as major comic characters in successful network programs have been few. CBS came up with an innovative strategy to market its "Latino Odd Couple" sitcom "Trial and Error" (1988). It was simulcast in Spanish on Spanish-language radio stations. The show centered around two unlikely roommates: Tony (Paul Rodríguez), a T-shirt salesman on Los Angeles's Olvera Street, and John (Eddie Vélez), a newly graduated Puerto Rican lawyer working in an established law firm. The comedy was strained and the series never gained acceptance; it only attracted 8 percent of the available audience (Valle 1988). Much more noteworthy was the short-lived "I Married Dora," which had a brief run on ABC during the fall 1987 season. An admirable attempt to center a situation comedy around a Salvadoran woman, it reversed cultural fields by making Dora (Elizabeth Peña) smart and self-assured and her uptight, "open-mind ed" Anglo husband the butt of many jokes because he held stereotypical ideas about Hispanics. The series dealt meaningfully with Latino immigration to the United States and the misconceptions the two cultures often have about one another. Sadly, it was canceled before establishing a consistent tone and finding an audience.

The Hispanic bandidos, (bandits, criminals, and lawbreakers) were also adapted promptly and prominently by television. The Hispanic "stock bandido, spitfire or peon" (Reyes 1983) was common in innumerable Western cowboy series. Also, the numerous urban counterparts have been constantly present, starting with "Dragnet" (NBC 1951-59; 1967-70) and "Naked City" (ABC 1958-59; 1960-63), as part of the detective and police dramas. Most recently, they were quite salient in the underworld activities (especially regarding drug traffic and dealings) in "Hill Street Blues" (NBC 1981-86) and "Miami Vice" (ABC 1984-89).

Mainstream television has allowed a few law-enforcer or lawmaker Hispanic stereotypes. From "The Cisco Kid" and "Zorro" in the 1950s to more recent shows such as "CHiPs," "Miami Vice," and "L.A. Law," there have been shown some relatively positive Hispanic male figures. One notable early example was Walt Disney's "The Nine Lives of Elfago Baca" (1958). Based on the exploits of the legendary Mexican-American lawman, the miniseries was an all-too-rare instance of television depicting a Chicano hero. More often, Hispanics have been cast in secondary or insignificant roles. For example, Beale points out how on "Hill Street Blues" the Hispanic officer who is second in command is "often given little to do and is generally dull or a buffoon" (1986, 136).

Most attempts at centering a law enforcement series around a Hispanic character have been disappointing. "Juarez" (1988) was conceived as a gritty portrayal of the life of a Mexican-American border detective (it was shot on location in El Paso). ABC lost confidence in the project, however, and suspended production shortly after only two episodes (of the six initially ordered) were completed. That episode was subsequently broadcast with little fanfare and soon forgotten. NBC's "Drug Wars: the Kiki Camarena Story" (1990) was replete with updated bandido stereotypes and so offensive to Mexico that it issued formal complaints about the mini-series (which went on to win an Emmy). Paul Rodríguez's private investigator in "Grand Slam" resulted in little more than yet another instance of the comic buffoon.

In contrast, Edward James Olmos's Lieutenant Martin Castillo in "Miami Vice" is one of the most positive Hispanic characters in television history. Because Olmos was initially reluctant to take the part (he turned down the role several times before finally accepting), the show's producers gave him complete control over the creation and realization of Castillo. He fashioned a dignified, honorable character of quiet strength and considerable power, thereby helping to offset the show's facile stereotyping of villainous Latin American drug smugglers. Finally there is the formidable presence of Victor Sifuentes (Jimmy Smits) on "L.A. Law," who provides the law firm (and the series) with a healthy dose of social consciousness.

Other stereotypes of Hispanics on television could be reviewed, as could the occasions when some Hispanic actors (for example, Ricardo Montalbán) and actresses (for instance, Rita Moreno) have been called upon to play a variety of roles beyond the usual stereotypes. What has been most neglected, however, is regular positive roles for Hispanic women and, equally important, the Hispanic family. This is one area in which Hispanics television have been worse off than in film. In this respect, they have also fared much worse than Afro-Americans.

According to Reyes, during the early 1950s, Elena Verdugo starred in the comedy series "Meet Millie," but not as a Hispanic woman. Instead, she played "an all-American girl." Reyes points out that "the image of the Hispanic woman has been usually relegated to the overweight *mamacita*, the spitfire or señorita, and the suffering mother or gang member's girlfriend" (1983, 12). He adds that images of "strong, self-reliant, attractive, all knowing" Hispanic females were notable in Linda Cristal's role as Victoria Cannon in "The

High Chaparral" (NBC 1967-71) and Elena Verdugo as nurse Consuelo in "Marcus Welby, M.D." (ABC 1969-76). More recently this shortage of strong Latina characters remains the predominant pattern. Two notable exceptions are the previously discussed character of Dora in "I Married Dora" (ABC 1987) and Pilar in "Falcon Crest" (CBS 1987-89)—the latter played a character who managed to be more than a simple one-dimensional love interest and was a forceful businesswoman.

Hispanic *families* have also been absent from the center stages of mainstream network television. In "The High Chaparral," a Mexican cattle-ranching family was "very prominently portrayed alongside the gringo family" (Reyes 1983, 12). After that series, consequential inclusions of Hispanic families have eluded long runs on the small screen. "Viva Valdez," a poorly conceived and received situation comedy about a Chicano family living in East Los Angeles, was aired on ABC only between May 31 and September 6, 1976.

It was not until the spring of 1983, when ABC aired "Condo," that a middle-class urban Hispanic family was first introduced to TV viewers in the United States. That situation comedy series featured "a textbook WASP and an upwardly mobile Hispanic who find themselves as condominium neighbors on opposite sides of almost every question, but are faced with impending family ties" (Subervi-Vélez 1990, 311). This modern-day Romeo and Juliet—in the very first episode the oldest Anglo son and a Hispanic daughter fall in love, elope, and begin a series of adventures that embroil the families in joy and sorrow—was also short-lived as its quality declined and ratings faltered against the competition of CBS's "Magnum, P.I." and NBC's "Fame." Yet during "Condo's" twelve episodes, another TV first was set as the featured Mexican-American family was shown interacting as *equals* with an Anglo family that sometimes acceptingly participated with them as Hispanics (Subervi-Vélez 1990).

On March 6 of the following year, ABC tried Norman Lear's "a.k.a. Pablo," another situation comedy which was centered on Hispanic comedian Paul Rodríguez but also featured his working-class family. Unfortunately, Pablo's pungent jokes, often about Mexicans and Hispanics in general, irked enough Hispanics and others whose strong protest to the network contributed to the show's cancellation after only six episodes. The wealthiest urban Hispanic family ever featured was in another sitcom, "Sánchez of Bel-Air" on the USA Cable Network. In this program, the nouveau riche Sánchez family faced numerous social class and cultural challenges after they moved up from the barrio to live in one of the most

Wanda de Jesús as "Santa Andrade" in NBC's "Santa Barbara."

upscale areas of Los Angeles. The program ran only thirteen episodes between 1986 and 1987. As of this writing, mainstream network television has no Hispanic "Huxtables," "Windslows," or even "Jeffersons."

Until very recently, the absence of notable Hispanic female figures and families was also evident in the soap opera genre, which neglected blacks, Latinos, and most other ethnic minorities. At the time of this writing, "Santa Barbara" is the only ongoing contemporary soap with recurring roles for

Hispanics, five of which are regularly included. Payne indicates that according to Jerry Dobson, one of the show's writers, a commitment was made to have a Hispanic family "because there are large numbers of Latinos in Santa Barbara" (1985, 27). Payne adds that "while originally the only Hispanic character with a major storyline was Santana (who was played by a non-Hispanic actress), Cruz (A. Martínez), the lead Hispanic male character, has been promised a major storyline, replete with romance" (1985, 27). The producers of the show have made good on their prom-

A. Martínez as "Cruz Castillo" in NBC's "Santa Barbara."

ise and viewers have since been introduced to Cruz's family circle and given him a major role, too.

One other contemporary program with a prominent Hispanic female is "Dangerous Women," where actress María Rangel is one of six main characters. She plays the role of an ex-convict Hispanic woman who, after being unjustly jailed for murdering her abusive husband, works seeking to reform the abuses of the penitentiary system. The show is a one-hour syndicated nighttime soap opera/drama aired in various major markets such as Los Angeles, New York, Chicago, Phoenix, Minneapolis, San Francisco, and Houston. Prior to this show, the only other prominent role for a Hispanic female was found in the daytime soap opera "Rituals" (1984-85), which unfortunately was also short-lived.

Studies originating from government, academic, and professional circles corroborate the previous findings and reveal additional shortcomings about the treatment of Hispanics on mainstream television. In 1977 and 1979, the U.S. Commission on Civil Rights published two reports on the portrayals and employ-

Henry Darrow as "Cruz Castillo's" father in NBC's "Santa Barbara."

ment of women and minorities in television. While many results were reported with aggregated data on all minorities, specific findings about "people of Spanish origin" [sic] were noted in the 1977 report. For example, from the content analysis of one sample week of programming during the fall of 1973 and 1974, only three Hispanics, all males, were found in "major" roles; twelve Hispanic males and one female were found playing minor roles. The highest-status occupation shown was a lawyer in a minor role.

The first academically based systematic analysis of this subject was conducted by Greenberg and Baptista-Fernández (1980), who examined sample weeks of commercial fictional programming during three television seasons (1975-76, 1976-77, and 1977-78). Among the 3,549 characters with speaking roles observed in the 255 episodes coded, they were able to find only "53 different individuals who could reliably be identified as Hispanic-Americans. . . . [these] constitute slightly less than 1.5 percent of the population of speaking TV characters" (1980, 6). Summarizing their findings, Greenberg and Baptista-Fernández stated that Hispanic characters on television are "hard to find," "mostly males of dark complexion,

with dark hair, most often with heavy accents," and that "women are absent and insignificant" (1980, 11). They also stated that the characters were "gregarious and pleasant, with strong family ties," that "half work hard, half are lazy, and very few show much concern for their futures," and that "most hav e had very little education, and their jobs reflect that fact" (1980, 11).

Mainstream television's neglect of Hispanics was similarly documented in a report commissioned by the League of United Latin American Citizens (LULAC) and prepared by Public Advocates, Inc. (1983). In the Public Advocates audit of all sixty-three prime-time shows during the first week of the fall 1983 television season (September 26-October 2), Hispanics played half of 1 percent (3 characters out of 496) of the significant speaking roles and only 1 percent (10 characters out of 866) of the those who spoke one or more lines. With the exception of Geraldo Rivera, there was "a total absence of positive Hispanic characters" (1983, 3). Comparing the networks, CBS was consistently the worst (1 Hispanic character out of 212); ABC and NBC "showed significant decreases in the percentage of Hispanics portrayed" (1983, 3). Also, on ABC, "Two-thirds of all speaking parts for Hispanics were criminals"; on CBS there were "no Hispanics in any significant speaking roles"; and on NBC "only one of its 189 (1/2 of 1%) *significant* roles included an Hispanic" (1983: 4).

The very low percentage of Hispanic participation in television was also found in a study by Lichter, Lichter, Rothman, and Amundson (1987). Analyzing 620 episodes of prime-time series randomly selected from the Library of Congress's holdings from 1955 to 1986, they observed that "since 1975, nearly one in ten characters have been black (from a low of under 1 percent in the 1950s), while Hispanics have hovered around the 2 percent mark for three decades" (1987, 16). Furthermore, in almost every comparison Lichter and colleagues made of the social background (for example, education, employment) and plot functions (starring role, positive/negative portrayal, having committed a crime, and so on) of the white, black, and Latino characters, the latter group was consistently worst off.

The previous findings are again reaffirmed in the most recent study of this topic. In the National Commission on Working Women's (NCWW's) examination of thirty network entertainment programs in which minority characters were featured, only nine Hispanics (five women, four men) were found; in the same shows there were sixty-five blacks, three Asians, and one native American. The NCWW's qualitative commentaries of some of the scenes that included Hispanics found occasional redeeming contributions by some the leading characters (1989, 33-36). A more optimistic view on redeeming participation of minorities and the fading away of their stereotypes on television was provided recently by Tyrer (1991).

Public television has fared just slightly better than the commercial networks. In his brief overview of Latinos on television, Beale (1986) summarizes some past offerings of the Public Broadcasting System (PBS). For example, he indicates that "Sesame Street," "3-2-1 Contact," and "The Electric Company," children's shows produced by Children's Television Workshop for PBS, regularly feature Hispanic role models, adults as well as children (Beale 1986, 137-138). Beale also points to the airing of Latino themes, dramas, and films such as Jesús Salvador Treviño's *Seguín,* Robert M. Young's *Alambrista,* Moctezuma Esparza and Robert M. Young's *The Ballad of Gregorio Cortéz,* and Gregory Nava's *El Norte,* adding that "PBS deals with a broader range of Hispanic issues than the commercial networks, which are obsessed with immigration and revolution in their documentary treatment of Latino themes" (1986, 138).

Happily, this trend has continued. More recently, PBS has broadcast Luis Valdez's *Corridos!* (1987), dramatizations of traditional Mexican narrative ballads, Jesús Salvador Treviño's *Birthright: Growing Up Hispanic* (1989), interviews with leading Hispanic writers, Isaac Artenstein's *Break of Dawn* (1990), a docudrama based on the life of singer and Los Angeles radio personality Pedro J. González, and Héctor Galán's hard-hitting documentaries *New Harvest, Old Shame* (1990) and *Los Mineros* (1991). However, exemplary series such as "Villa Alegre," "Carrascolendas," and "Qué Pasa, U.S.A." have been canceled due to lack of funds or low ratings. The lack of funding is certainly at the core of the problem as "only about 2% of funds for television production allocated by the Corporation for Public Broadcasting in the past fourteen years have gone to produce programs specifically geared to the Hispanic communities of the United States" (Treviño, 1983). Even in early 1991, no nationally broadcast shows for or about Hispanics are regularly scheduled on PBS.

The final area of interest regarding the images of Hispanics in mainstream television is news coverage. Ironically, researchers of media news content have themselves shown little concern for this population. Among the scores of articles published about the characteristics and biases of television news, *not even one* has given systematic attention to the portrayal of Hispanics in newscasts. For studies that have focused on the major network news, part of the problem may be the few stories broadcast about Hispanics. For example, a U.S. Commission on Civil Rights report mentions in passing that in the 230 stories examined from fifteen network news programs aired between March 1974 and February 1975 that "4 men of Spanish origin" were identified as newsmakers (1979, 51); but no further explanation is given about who or why they were in the news. The commission's 1979 update, for which fifteen newscasts from 1977 were coded, makes very brief mention about two stories related to Hispanics. The handful of studies published systematically analyzing Hispanics in the news have all focused on print media.

Given these findings, one can very easily agree with Greenberg and Baptista-Fernández's view that "in essence, it seems that television has yet to do much with, or for, the Hispanic-American either as a television character or as a viewer. It might be improper to characterize them as invisible, but the portrayal is blurred or certainly hard to follow" (1983, 11).

Employment

Behind the cameras and in the offices, the treatment of Hispanics is likewise inadequate. From the first reports of the U.S. Commission on Civil Rights (1977, 1979) to more recent configurations of minority employment in the broadcasting industry, Hispanic participation has been and continues to be extremely small, much below Hispanic population proportions, and it is inferior to that of Afro-Americans. For example, in the Civil Rights Commission's 1977 report, the average number of "Spanish origin" persons employed by forty stations surveyed in 1971 was 1.4 percent for males and .56 percent for females; in 1975 the respective figures were 2.2 percent and 1.14 percent. In the commission's 1979 update based on the 1977 data, these latter averages remained unchanged. These averages, based on aggregate data for various positions and localities, hide the more negative situation that existed with respect to Hispanics in decision-making versus non-decision-making positions.

Stone's findings based on a 1987 study of 375 television stations across the country showed, unfortunately but not surprisingly, similar figures with respect to the percentages of Hispanics on television news staffs (1988). In fact, the average for Hispanic females in these capacities was lower, .9 percent, while for males it remained at 2.2 percent. However, in his discussion of the placement of minorities on the "talent track," Stone observes, "On the talent track, minority women are as likely as non-minority men and women to be reporting or anchoring. But minority men are much less likely than minority women to have jobs that put them on the air as reporters or anchors. So although black, Hispanic and other minority women are winning on the talent track but tending to lose on the managerial track, minority men [including Hispanics] are double losers. They are underrepresented in both pipelines to advancement in broadcast news" (1988, 18).

Finally, Bielby and Bielby's (1987 and 1989) reports suggest that when it comes to writing the scripts for television, Hispanics have been given minimal opportunities. Their studies, which aggregate data for all minorities, show participation at rates of at best 3 percent for minority writers for prime-time series.

In spite of the bleak picture summarized in this synopsis of Hispanic portrayals and employment in mainstream television, there is evidence that some changes have taken place throughout the years. One of the forces contributing to the gradual changes has been the complaints and protests of concerned individuals and organizations. In her study of how various advocacy groups have affected prime-time television, Montgomery discusses the efforts and struggles of Latino groups (1989, see especially pages 55-65). For example, she states that Justicia was a national Mexican-American organization "active in media reform campaigns during the early sixties and seventies"; other organizations, such as the National Latino Media Coalition, La Raza, the League of United Latino Citizens (LULAC), and the Mexican-American Anti-Defamation Committee "focused on grassroot efforts for reforming local television, although they [also] made some moves to change entertainment television" (1989, 55).

As in the mainstream film industry of the United States, Hispanics have been neglected and poorly depicted in a television industry oriented to the dominant society. The future treatment of Latinos in this medium may be contingent on some inroads that individual actors and actresses make. It may also depend on the continued process of organized activities being carried out by advocacy and Latino community groups.

✳ADVERTISING

Wilson and Gutiérrez state that "advertisers have reflected the place of racial minorities in the social fabric of the nation by either ignoring them or, when they have been included in advertisements for the mass audience, by processing and presenting them so as to make them palatable salespersons for the products being advertised" (1985, 113). While no systematic studies have yet been conducted on Hispanic advertising images across time, there is some evidence to support these authors" proposition. For years Hispanics have been practically invisible in mainstream advertising and by extension in employ-

ment in this industry (there are no accurate figures of Hispanic employment in this field). When Hispanics have been included in ways palatable to the Anglo majority society, their images have often been quite offensive to fellow Hispanics. Martínez's (1969) work, which discusses various examples of the derisive commercials at the time, pointed out the "Granny Goose chips featuring fat gun-toting Mexicans; an d advertisement for Arrid underarm deodorant showing a dusty Mexican bandito spraying his underarms after a hard ride as the announcer intoned, 'If it works for him it will work for you'; a magazine advertisement featuring a stereotypical Mexican sleeping under his sombrero as he leans against a Philco television set; . . . a Liggett & Meyers commercial for L&M cigarettes that featured Paco, a lazy Latino who never "feenishes" anything, not even the revolution he is supposed to be fighting" (as cited in Wilson and Gutiérrez 1985, 115-116).

In 1967, the most controversial advertisement with a "Hispanic character" was the Frito Bandito—the Mexican bandit cartoon figure utilized repeatedly by the Frito-Lay Corporation in its television and print promotions of corn chips. In discussions about advertising racism and mistreatment of Hispanics, this example is often cited because of the complaints it generated among Hispanics, especially among Chicano activist and civic groups. Thanks in part to the public protests against Frito-Lay and activists threatening boycotts of television stations airing the commercials, the Frito Bandito figure was discontinued in 1971. The public objections by Hispanics during the 1970s, including the position paper by Latino media activist's Reyes and Rendón (1971), led to some positive changes in the media during the 1970s, just at the dawn of the so-called Hispanic decade. Then, as advertising and marketing companies began to recognize the profitability of this growing sector of society, Hispanic-oriented strategies be gan to emerge in these industries.

✳HISPANIC-ORIENTED PRINT MEDIA

Unlike any other ethnic group in the history of the United States, Latinos have had a broad range of mass media directed at them. Beginning with the border newspapers of the 1800s up to present-day inroads in telecommunications, Hispanics have worked hard at establishing and maintaining print and electronic channels through which they can be informed and entertained in ways more relevant to their particular populations and cultures. While most of the Hispanic-oriented media have been in the Spanish language, many have been bilingual and in more recent times, fully English-language products specifically directed at Latinos. Likewise, Hispanics have been owners and producers of a number of mass media institutions oriented to them. However, a significant part of such media have been wholly or partially owned and operated by Anglo individuals or corporations. Whatever the language or ownership, one of the common aspects of all these media is that in their portrayals via images or words, and in their general emp loyment practices, Latinos have been treated much more adequately. In these media, Hispanic life in the United States has been and continues to be presented and reflected more thoroughly, appropriately, and positively.

Newspapers

The Early Years. The Spanish-language press within the national boundaries of the United States had its beginnings in 1808 in New Orleans, Louisiana, with *El Misisipí,* a four-page commercial- and trade-oriented publication "printed primarily in Spanish, but with English translations of many of the articles and almost all of the advertising" (Wilson and Gutiérrez 1985, 175). According to these authors, the paper, which was started by the Anglo firm of William H. Johnson & Company, appeared to be a business venture, its content was heavily influenced by events outside the United States, and it was directed toward Spanish-speaking immigrants—characteristics that were similar to those of other Hispanic-oriented publications that followed.

After the inauguration of *El Misisipí,* dozens of Spanish-language newspapers and periodicals, founded by Mexican pioneers of the times, were published in the southwestern territories, which belonged to Mexico until the 1850s. In fact, the very first printing press in the Americas was brought to Mexico from Spain in 1535. Thus, for over four centuries, "Hispanic" publications have circulated in this part of the world; some have lasted various decades while others only issued an edition or two. Among the U.S. Hispanic-oriented newspapers, the majority have been published in Spanish but many have been bilingual and a few have been in English but specifically directed at the regional or national Hispanic populations.

Current Status of Newspapers

At present, five Spanish-language newspapers are published daily—two in New York, two in Miami, and one in Los Angeles. Basic information about the history, ownership, editorial policy, and circulation of these is presented in the following pages.

La Opinión (Los Angeles) began publishing on September 16, 1926. It was founded by Ignacio E. Lozano, Sr., a Mexican national who wanted to provide news of the native homeland as well as of the new country for the growing Mexican population in southern California. Lozano went to Los Angeles after working during four years for two Texas newspapers and owning and editing his own paper—*La Prensa* of San Antonio—from 1913 to 1926 (see special edition of *The Americas Review*, 1989). The move to California was the result of Lozano's view that there were greater Mexican readership needs and opportunities on the West Coast.

From its beginning, *La Opinión* was owned and operated by Lozano and his family, which in 1926 formed Lozano Enterprises, Inc. This company also publishes *El Eco del Valle*, a weekly tabloid distributed in the San Fernando Valley since 1985. On September 28, 1990, 50 percent interest in Lozano Enterprises was purchased by the Times Mirror Company. This major media conglomerate has interests in broadcasting and cable television, and book and magazine publishing; it publishes *The Los Angeles Times*,

Ignacio E. Lozano, Jr., Editor-in-Chief of *La Opinión*.

Mónica Lozano-Centanino, Associate Publisher of *La Opinión*.

Program. With this program, *La Opinión* is now being used for instructional purposes in over forty-eight classes in twenty-five schools.

La Opinión is a broadsheet paper of approximately forty-eight pages daily; the Sunday edition consists of about eighty-eight pages, including a thirty-two-page, tabloid-style TV guide. Apart from the daily news, opinions, sports, entertainment, and advertising sections, *La Opinión* has special supplements on various weekdays. For example, on Thursdays there is "Comida," a food supplement, and on Fridays, "Deportes locales," with expanded news about local sports, such as the soccer clubs; "Panorama," a tabloid entertainment section; and "De viernes a viernes," a calendar section with special events of the week. On Sundays, there are also various special sections such as "Encuentro," dealing with arts and literature; "Comentarios," with editorials and op-ed columns and opinions; "Viajes," regarding travel and leisure; "Acceso," a life-style section; "TV guía," a television listing guide; and "Tiempo extra," a sports pull-out section.

As of mid-1991, approximately 500 people worked at *La Opinión,* forty of them (including 8 translators) in the editorial department. In addition to its 15

Newsday (New York), and five other newspapers nationwide. With this association, *La Opinión* has acquired financial resources to enable it to continue improving its product. In spite of this new financial affiliation, the Lozano family maintains a majority on the board of directors and continues its full editorial policy and operational control.

As of March 31, 1991, *La Opinión's* circulation was assessed by the Audit Bureau of Circulations (ABC) at 109,558 Monday through Saturday, and 81,773 on Sundays. The vast majority of *La Opinión* newspapers are sold in street stands and a variety of neighborhood stores. Only about 1,300 copies are delivered to home subscribers and approximately 1,000 are sent by mail. According to a 1990 profile of the newspaper's readers, the majority are Mexican and Mexican American (66 percent), but increasingly Central American (15 percent) and South American (5 percent), reflective of the immigration influx of the last two decades. In an effort to better serve the Hispanic community, as well as increase its visibility and number of subscribers, in January 1991, Marti Buscaglia, marketing director of *La Opinión*, initiated the paper's participation in the Newspapers in Education

José I. Lozano, Publisher of *La Opinión*.

versified Media, merged *El Diario* and *La Prensa* ; he directed the paper from 1963. In 1981, he sold it to the Gannett Company, a major media conglomerate, which at the time owned a chain of ninety English-language papers. In 1989, El Diario Associates, Inc., was formed by Peter Davidson, a former Morgan Stanley specialist in newspaper industry mergers and acquisitions. This new company then bought *El Diario-La Prensa* from Gannett in August of that year for an estimated twenty million dollars. Carlos D. Ramírez, a Puerto Rican from New York who had been publisher of this newspaper since 1984, stayed on board to participate as a partner of El Diario Associates.

Approximately 139 persons work at the newspaper about 44 of these in the editorial department (writing and editing the news, sports, editorials, and opinions). The newspaper's reporters regularly cover city hall, Manhattan, the Bronx, Brooklyn, and Queens, but *El Diario* also relies on the Associated Press (AP) news wire services for some state and local news. The other major news wire sources it receives are EFE (Spain), Notimex (Mexico), AFP (France), and Deutsche Press Agenteur (Germany). Also, two corre-

Marti Buscaglia, Director of Marketing, *La Opinión*.

reporters, the major news wire services subscribed to are United Press International (UPI, United States), EFE (Spain), Notimex (Mexico), and Agence France Press (AFP, France). While reporters regularly cover the greater Los Angeles area, no foreign correspondents are permanently located in Latin America or elsewhere.

El Diario-La Prensa   (New York) started in the summer of 1963 from the merger of two newspapers, *La Prensa* and *El Diario de Nueva York.* The former had been operating since 1913 under the ownership of José Campubrí, a Spaniard who kept the paper until 1957, when it was purchased by Fortune Pope. Pope, whose brother was the owner of *The National Enquirer,* was also the owner of the New York Italian paper *Il Progreso* and of WHOM-AM which later became WJIT-AM, one of the most popular Spanish-language radio stations in New York. In 1963, Pope sold *La Prensa* to O. Roy Chalk, who had been owner of *El Diario de Nueva York* since he purchased it in 1961 from Porfirio Domenicci, a Dominican who had started *El Diario* in 1948.

With both papers under his control, Chalk, a Jewish American businessman and president of Di-

Peter W. Davidson, President, *El Diario-La Prensa*.

Carlos D. Ramírez, Publisher, *El Diario-La Prensa*.

spondents cover events in Puerto Rico and the Dominican Republic.

Within its daily average of fifty-six tabloid-size pages, *El Diario-La Prensa* publishes, in addition to the daily news, opinions, sports, entertainment and advertising sections, a pull-out supplement each day of the week: Mondays, "Deportes," details of weekend sporting events; Tuesdays, "Artes y Ciencias," arts and sciences; Wednesdays, "Buen Vivir," food and supermarket specials; Thursdays, "Comunidad," community developments and events; Fridays, "Espectáculos," entertainment; and for the Saturday-Sunday edition, "Siete Días," a summary of the week, and reviews and opinions on diverse topics such as literature, poetry, movies, and politics. During the calendar year, a bridal supplement and another ten to twelve special supplements are published related to events such as the Puerto Rican Parade, the Dominican Republic Parade, Thanksgiving Day, Christmas, New Year's Day, and so forth.

According to ABC's assessment of March 31, 1991, the circulation of *El Diario-La Prensa* was 54,481 from Monday through Friday, and 36,786 for the combined Saturday-Sunday (weekend) edition. Given the difficulty of home delivery in the city of New York,

and the transient characteristic of many residents, the newspaper depends almost entirely on "point sales," that is, street sales. Since their beginnings, *La Prensa* and *El Diario de Nueva York* had been primarily directed at the Puerto Rican, Spaniard, and Dominican communities in New York. Presently, *El Diario-La Prensa* caters to a more diverse Hispanic population that, although still principally Puerto Rican, is increasingly more Dominican and Central and South American. Veciana-Suárez, writing about the editorial policy of *El Diario-La Prensa,* stated that "the primary focus of the editorial, without a doubt, is on Hispanic issues, whether local, national, or international" (1987, 28). She also indicated that the newspaper has a five-member editorial board that, according to publisher Ramirez, spans a broad range of the political spectrum and gives the paper "a definite independent editorial policy," according to Veciana-Suárez's citation of publisher Ramírez (1987: 28).

Noticias del Mundo (New York) began publishing on April 22, 1980, under the ownership of News World Communications, Inc., an organization founded in 1976 by the anti-Communist crusader the Reverend Sun Myung Moon and his Unification Church International. News World Communications also publishes the *Washington Times,* the *New York City Tribune, Advista* (a monthly newsletter for the Hispanic marketing community), and various other publications, including *Ultimas Noticias*, a daily newspaper in Uruguay. Although now *Noticias del Mundo* functions more independently from its staunch conservative founder, author Veciana-Suárez cites editor in chief José Cardinali as stating "we are against dictatorships . . . . we cannot abide Marxism"; she adds that the editorial stands are "decidedly conservative in international affairs and pro-Hispanic on domestic issues (1987, 21).

Noticias del Mundo is a broadsheet newspaper with an average of twenty pages published from Monday through Friday. Difficulty in home delivery also makes this newspaper depend primarily on "point sales." In one of their promotional fliers "More Than Just News," it is indicated that *Noticias* "publishes four editions which serve the primary market areas of New York City, New Jersey, Los Angeles, and San Francisco" and that "each edition reaches into secondary areas such as Philadelphia and Connecticut on the East Coast and San Jose, Las Vegas, Palm Springs/Indio and San Bernardino on the West Coast" for total distribution in twenty-two cities. Yet its circulation as of mid-1991 was reported at 32,000 in the New York metro area and for their new routes in New Jersey and Boston (started in fall 1990), the

Phillip V. Sánchez, Publisher, *Noticias del Mundo* and *New York City Tribune*.

figures were 7,300 and 2,450, respectively. Currently, the circulation is not audited by the industry's standard for these matters—the ABC.

In addition to the typical news, opinions, sports, entertainment and advertising pages, *Noticias del Mundo* has regular weekly sections on legal orientation (Mondays); community, focusing on Puerto Rico and Cuba (Tuesdays); women (Wednesdays); religion and community, focusing on Peru and the Dominican Republic (Thursdays); and entertainment and restaurants (Fridays). On Tuesdays, two thousand copies of *Noticias* are distributed to five high schools that participate in the Newspaper in Education Program. According to a *Noticias del Mundo* fact sheet, when the paper began to participate in that program in 1986, it became the first Spanish-language newspaper in the United States to do so.

Approximately 150 persons work at this newspaper, about 55 of them in the editorial department. Major Hispanic population centers in New York and surrounding cities are regularly covered by the newspaper's staff. Its principal sources of news wire services include the UPI, AP, Reuter, and EFE. The newspaper has regular free-lance contributors and

commentators throughout Latin America and Spain who act as their foreign "correspondents."

El Nuevo Herald (Miami) was started on November 21, 1987, as a new and improved version of *El Miami Herald,* which had been continuously published since March 29, 1976, as an insert to *The Miami Herald*. Both the Spanish-language and the English-language newspapers are owned by The Miami Herald Publishing Company, a subsidiary of the Knight-Ridder newspaper chain, which has holdings in twenty-nine newspapers across the United States.

In 1987, The Miami Herald Publishing Company recognized the geometric growth of the Hispanic populations in south Florida and, with the support and approval of the Knight-Ridder Corporation, began assessing what Hispanic readers wanted in their Spanish-language daily. The outcome of the study was *El Nuevo Herald*, which moved to a separate building from that of its English-language counterpart to begin publishing from a location closer to the Hispanic community. Other improvements included a 150 percent increase of the daily news space (which now runs approximately thirty-four pages daily and fifty on Sundays), more better coverage of the Cuban and Latin American events and communities, and the use of color in the more modern format, graphics, and layout. Also expanded was the news staff, which increased from 23 to more than 65 in mid-1991. An additional 2,500 persons work for the two Herald newspapers, which share the advertising, marketing, and circulation departments.

As might be expected, given the demographics of Miami and southern Florida, since its beginnings the principal readers of *El Nuevo Herald* have been immigrant Cuban and Latin American populations residing in that area. This paper, in contrast to its New York counterparts, reaches the majority of its readers via home delivery. The June 1990 circulation, as verified by the ABC, was 102,856 Monday through Saturdays and 118,756 on Sundays; This broadsheet newspaper also has special weekly sections in addition to the standard sections. Among others these include: a travel section (Sundays); "Vida Social," about social life (Tuesdays); "Gusto," a food section (Thursdays); "A la carte," restaurant listings (Fridays); "Diseñado para vivir," a real estate section; and an automotive section (Saturdays). During the year, an additional fifty special topic sections are also published.

Aside from the news gathering by its own staff, *El Nuevo Herald* can benefit from the work of its English-language partner, including the use of translated stories from the international correspondents. For major stories, *El Nuevo Herald* may send its own reporters to Latin America. Thus, *The Miami Herald* may use stories gathered by *El Nuevo Herald's* foreign or local reporters. The major news wire services for *El Nuevo Herald* are the Spanish-language version of the AP, AFP, Reuter, and EFE. Syndicated information services from various major newspapers are also subscribed to.

Since the 1987 reorganization, *El Nuevo Herald* does not publish editorials. Instead it has its own policy regarding the op-ed page, where various prominent Cuban and Latin American columnists write about politics and other topics. The majority are about Hispanic issues or Cuban interpretations of national or international events. Veciana-Suárez wrote about the Herald's op-ed policy prior to the change: "When dealing with politics, [the columns] tend to be anti-communist and conservative, a reflection of the overwhelming feeling of Miami's Cuban community" (Veciana-Suárez 1987, 41). This general policy holds today. Prior to the 1987 reorganization, *El Nuevo Herald* only published translations of editorials that appeared on the same day in *The Miami Herald*. At the time, the editor of *El Nuevo Herald* was a member of the English-language paper's editorial board and participated in the discussions about the subjects and points of view. Political candidates were also endorsed in unison by *The Herald's* board.

El Diario de las Américas (Miami) was founded on July 4, 1953, by Horacio Aguirre, a Nicaraguan lawyer who had been an editorial writer for a Panamanian newspaper, *El Panamá-América,* directed by Harmodio Arias, a former president of that country. Part of the financial support needed for starting *El Diario de las Américas* was made possible thanks to a Venezuelan builder-investor and two Pensacola, Florida, road builders who also believed in the founder's mission. The paper is published by The Americas Publishing Company, which is owned by the Aguirre family. *El Diario de las Américas* remains the only Spanish-language daily owned and operated by Hispanics without full or partial partnership by Anglo corporations.

This broadsheet newspaper publishes twenty-eight pages Tuesday through Friday and approximately forty-five on Sundays (it is not published Mondays). In mid-1991, the respective circulation for these days was 66,770 and 70,737, as indicated in a sworn statement filed with the Standard Rate and Data Service (SRDS). While a few papers are sold at newsstands, practically all of the circulation is based on home delivery, including 13,367 mail subscriptions to major United States cities and various locations outside the Florida area. Since its beginnings, the principal readers of *El Diario de las Américas* were the Latin American residents of the Miami and southern Florida area. After the massive migration of Cubans from their island in the 1960s, these became the major clients of the paper. A reader profile conducted in 1990 for the paper by Strategy Research Corporation shows that 79.2 percent of the *Diario's* readers were born in Cuba; Nicaragua, with 8.5 percent of the readers born there, was the distant second (*El Diario de las Américas* 1990, 3).

The Cuban and Latin American interests of that readership are evidently reflected in the strong international—particularly Latin American—news coverage of the paper. Those interests are even more notable in the editorial policy of *Diario*. Veciana-Suárez quotes publisher and editor Horacio Aguirre as saying, "Since the fall of Cuba, we consider that one of the biggest problems we face is the Russian-Soviet border ninety miles from here. . . . And we now have Central America in a precarious situation" (1987, 34). She goes on to point out that "Aguirre's political leanings are reflected clearly and eloquently in *Diario's* editorials," which he writes and which are, according to Aguirre, "moderately conservative with a strong defense of individual rights" (1987, 34). These perspectives are typically expressed in the many opinion columns from various Spanish-speaking writers and the translated columns of well-known Anglos.

To provide the international news of interest to its readers, *El Diario de las Américas* relies more on the news wire services of UPI, AP, AFP, EFE, Agencia Latinoamericana (ALA), Editors Press, and a few other syndicated services. In addition to its news, opinions, sports, and advertising pages, it has various special weekly sections, such as "Vida Sana," about health (Wednesdays); "De la cocina al comedor," regarding food and cooking (Thursdays); "Sábado Residencial," a home section (Saturdays); "Viajes y turismo," the travel and tourism pages (Sundays); and a restaurant feature, "Buen Provecho," and automotive section, "Automovilismo" (Fridays). *El Diario de las Américas* has a staff of 20 reporters and editorial department employees, and an additional 100 people work in other parts of production at this paper.

The preceding discussion has only provided some of the basic information about the history, ownership, editorial policy, and circulation of the *major* Spanish-language daily newspapers currently published in the United States for Hispanic populations. At least these five enterprises seem to be reaching and serving their respective Hispanic communities while maintaining a stable circulation and advertising base.

Other Daily Publications In addition to these five major dailies, there are five more daily publications that serve U.S. Hispanic communities. The oldest is the Spanish-language page of *The Laredo Morning Times*. This seven-day-a-week news page has been published continuously since 1926. Also produced in the U.S. is *El Heraldo de Brownsville* (Texas), published seven days a week by *The Brownsville Herald*. This is a six-page broadsheet edition inaugurated on November 11, 1934, by Oscar del Castillo, who was the founder and editor from its beginning until his death on January 19, 1991. Marcelino González is the current director of this paper serving the Texas Rio Grande Valley region. As of March 31, 1991, this newspaper had an ABC-audited paid circulation of 3,701 weekdays and 4,436 Sundays.

The three other daily publications are *El Fronterizo, El Mexicano,* and *El Continental*—respectively the morning, afternoon, and evening editions published by the Compañia Periodística del Sol de Ciudad Juárez. *El Fronterizo,* published since 1943, is the largest of the three, with six daily sections each of approximately eight pages. As of mid-1991, its circulation was approximately 36,000 Monday through Sundays. *El Mexicano,* published since 1950, is more condensed and contains about ten pages; its circulation figures are 29,000 Monday through Saturdays. *El Continental*, founded in 1933, has only eight pages and a Monday through Saturday circulation of 8,000. While all three newspapers have as major clients the Mexicans and U.S. Hispanics in El Paso and surrounding communities, they are published in Ciudad Juárez by the Organización Editorial Mexicana, representing seventy-eight newspapers in that country.

One final newspaper that during the late 1980s and early 1990s has occasionally published on a daily schedule is *El Mañana* (Chicago). It was founded in May 1971 by Gorki Tellez, who at the time was a community activist and owner of a small truck catering business. Financial difficulties have restricted the continuity and success of this newspaper's daily publication effort.

Aside from the aforementioned dailies, it is estimated that across the nation over 250 newspaper-type publications directed especially to the diverse Hispanic populations in the United States are produced from as frequently as twice a week to once or twice a month. Many of these publications have been and still are the product of extraordinary efforts of individuals in their local communities. The irregular and transitory nature of their products, which often have very limited circulation, has made it very difficult to develop any comprehensive and updated directory of all such newspapers.

Nevertheless, the most recent edition of the *Hispanic Media and Markets* guide, produced by the SRDS (1991) lists 101 of what could be classified as the most enduring of these publications. Our analysis of the information in the "Community Newspaper" section of this directory yields the following data. Spanish is the main language of the publications, with seventy-four titles; twenty-four are bilingual; and three are printed in English with a Spanish-language page. Of the first group, fifty-eight are published at least once a week and of these weeklies nineteen are produced in California. Forty-five of the Spanish-language weeklies are distributed for free and only six report selling most of their papers; this data was not indicated for seven titles. Thirty-two of these Spanish-language weeklies indicate circulations of over 20,000 copies; twelve circulate between 10,000 and 20,000 copies; the remainder print 5,000 or less. Two of the bilingual periodicals are published by major English-language newspapers, both in California. *Nuestro Tiempo*, with a paid circulation of about 100,000 and free delivery of over 354,000, is published fifteen times per year by *The Los Angeles Times*. *Vida en el Valle*, which circulates 30,000 free copies in the San Joaquín Valley, is produced by the *Fresno Bee*.

Finally, dozens of Spanish-language newspapers from Spain, Mexico, Puerto Rico, Venezuela, Colombia, Chile, and numerous other Latin American countries also reach the newsstands in U.S. cities with large Hispanic populations. While few, if any, of these are published primarily for the Latin American immigrant or U.S. Hispanic, they are important sources of information widely sought and read, especially by the most recent of the immigrants.

Magazines and Other Periodicals

Long before the turn of the century, a variety of publications that can be classified as "U.S. Hispanic-oriented magazines" have been produced. The rich history of these publications can be observed in the holdings of major libraries such as the Benson Mexican American collection at the University of Texas at Austin and the Chicano Studies Collections of the University of California, Berkeley, Los Angeles, and Santa Barbara. Alejandra Salinas (1990) recently compiled a partial listing of 137 titles of past and present Hispanic magazines, journals, and newsletters. While a comprehensive anthology of all such publications is still lacking, even a cursory review of the titles shows that culturally- riented magazines have abounded, as have many with political, social, education, business, and entertainment topics. Cortés (1991, 11-12) briefly mentions the following among those that have ceased to publish but were prominent during the last thirty years: Los Angeles' iconoclastic *La Raza* (1967-75), Denver's establishmentarian *La Luz* (1971-1981), the National Council of La Raza's policy-oriented *Agenda* (1970-1981), and New York's (later Washington's) feature-oriented *Nuestro* (1974-1984)." Although copies of these now can only be found in some libraries, dozens of others magazines, especially consumer-oriented publications, are attempting to fill the demands of Hispanic readers.

The 1991 edition of the *Hispanic Media and Markets* guide of the Standard Rate & Data Service provides descriptions of advertising-related information of sixty-five titles under its section "Consumer Magazines." While this catalog contains indispensable data for marketing and advertising interests, it is neither comprehensive nor the most accurate listing of U.S. Hispanic-oriented magazines. For example, the list includes many specialty magazines (such as in-flight publications for Latin American airlines), magazines published in Puerto Rico primarily for Puerto Ricans, and various other titles for which U.S. Hispanics are not the primary targets. On the other hand, it excludes smaller magazines and various academic journals with limited state or regional circulation.

Nevertheless, from data in the SRDS publication

Cover of *Réplica* magazine.

Cover of *Temas* magazine.

and other information about this field, highlights can be provided about nine Hispanic-oriented magazines with national circulation produced and published in the United States. Four are published in Spanish, three in English, and two in both. The distribution figures in this section are divided into paid, free, and "controlled" circulation. The difference between the second and the third terms is that under "controlled" circulation the magazine knows who it gratuitously sends the publication to, thus it has some knowledge and control of the demographics of its audience. This is usually not the case under "free" circulation of magazines in which they are placed in public places for readers to pick up at will. Some publications also have their circulation verified; for magazines this is usually done by the Business Publications Audit (BPA).

Of the Spanish-language magazines, the oldest is *Temas,* which has been published on a monthly basis continuously since November 1950 in New York City by Temas Corporation, whose main partners are Spaniards and U.S. Hispanics. It circulates over 110,000 copies per month, of which 106,000 are paid purchases. *Temas* averages sixty-two pages and measures 8 1/2 by 11 inches and features articles on culture, current events, beauty, fashion, home decoration, and interviews with personalities of various artistic and academic backgrounds of interest to the Spanish-speaking populations in the United States. This general interest, family-oriented magazine was founded by publisher and editor José de la Vega, a Spaniard, who has indicated that *Temas* is the only national magazine published in Castilian Spanish without trendy "idioms." Given this editorial style, many of its articles are widely reprinted in high school and university reading packages across the country.

The second Spanish-language magazine is *Réplica,* which was founded in 1963 by Alex Lesnik, a Cuban immigrant who still owns the publication. From its base in Miami, this monthly magazine had as of March 1991 a circulation (BPA-verified) of 110,745 nationwide, of which approximately 96 percent was controlled—targeted to reach bilingual, bicultural, affluent opinion makers and other influential Hispanics in the United States. In its fifty pages, which measure 8 1/2 by 11 inches, there are a variety of articles on topics such as travel, fashion, sports, entertainment, and news events related to Latin America and the Caribbean Basin.

Cover of *La Familia de Hoy* magazine.

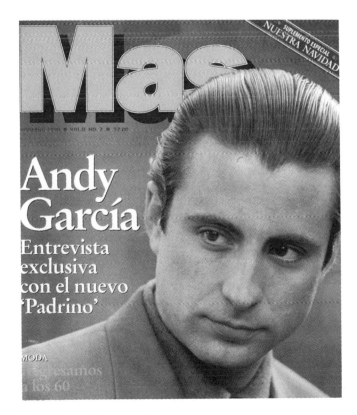

Cover of *Más* magazine.

Another publication in this category is *Más (More).* Its first issue was published in September 1989, when it started on a quarterly basis; that year there was also a winter edition. In 1991, it became bimonthly starting with the January-February issue. According to BPA figures, as of November 1990, approximately 562,000 subscribers received the magazine free of charge. One reason for this gratuitous service is that the magazine is produced in New York by Univisión Publications, part of Univision Holdings, which is owned by Hallmark Cards, Inc. This greetings card company is also owner of the Spanish-language television network *Univisión. Más* is this company's first magazine and provides significant promotion for its television programs and personalities. Its average eighty-eight pages, measuring 8 1/2 by 11 inches, feature stories about television programs and personalities and a variety of topics, such as music, fashion, beauty, sports, cuisine, travel, and occasionally politics.

A recent Spanish-language magazine is *La Familia de Hoy.* This larger-size magazine, measuring 10 by 13 inches and averaging fifty-six pages, was founded with an issue dated March/April 1990. It continues to be published six times a year in Knoxville, Tennessee, by Whittle Communications, which is half owned by Time-Warner Corporation, a major U.S. media conglomerate. The circulation, approximately 50,000 and BPA-verified, also relies on complimentary controlled subscriptions, which are provided mainly to beauty salons, doctors, dentists, and similar qualified offices in the top thirty-three markets with high Hispanic populations and clientele. Its home circulation is about 3,000.

Three English-language magazines of particular note are *Hispanic, Hispanic Business*, and *Hispanic Link*. *Hispanic* published its premier issue in April 1988. According to one of its promotional pages, the major focus of this "magazine for and about Hispanics" is on contemporary Hispanics and their achievements and contributions to American society. Thus, the stories cover a broad range of topics, such as entertainment, education, business, sports, the arts, government, politics, literature, and national and international personalities and events that may be of importance and interest to Hispanics in the United States. *Hispanic* is owned by Hispanic Publishing Corporation, based in Washington, D.C. This is a family company of chairman and founder Fred Estrada, a native of Cuba. His son, Alfredo, is the current publisher. The first publisher was Jerry Apodaca, a Mexican American and former governor of New Mexico. A total of 150,000 copies of *Hispanic,* which measures 8 1/2 by 11 inches and averages sixty-six pages, are printed for each of the eleven monthly issues (the December-January magazine is a combined number). The BPA audits indicate that approximately 40,000 copies are for paid subscriptions and the majority of the remainder are for controlled distribution directed to, among others, the U.S. Hispanic Chamber of Commerce and the Hispanic National Bar Association. Also, 1,500 copies are distributed to three hundred schools that participate in a special academic-oriented program known as America's Hispanic Education Achievement Drive (AHEAD).

Hispanic Business, according to its own promotional material, is "the oldest established business magazine oriented toward the US Hispanic market." It is published in Santa Barbara, California, by Hispanic Business, Inc., under the directorship of editor and publisher, Jesús Chavarría, a Mexican American who started the magazine in 1979 as a newsletter; it was turned into a regular monthly publication in 1982. The magazine, averaging fifty-six pages and measuring 8 1/2 by 11 inches, has a circulation recently certified at 150,000. Over 90 percent of the distribution is controlled. One of its regular departments covers news related to "Media/Marketing." Special monthly topics include, among others, statis-

tics and trends in the Hispanic media markets (December); the Hispanic "Business 500"—the annual directories of the leading Hispanic-owned corporations in the United States (June); and Hispanics in the mainstream television, film, music, and related entertainment businesses (July).

The third English-language Hispanic-oriented publication is *Hispanic Link*. Although it is a newsletter and not a "magazine" per se, it is a very important and influential publication that provides a succinct summary of the major issues and events related to education, immigration, business, legislative, political, policy, and economic concerns of the Hispanic populations in the United States. Weekly summary columns include "Arts and Entertainment" and a "Media Report." It averages six pages, measuring 8 1/2 by 11 inches and is published weekly (fifty weeks per year) in Washington, D.C., by Hispanic Link News Service, Inc. *Hispanic Link* was founded by Mexican American Charles A. Erickson in February 1980 as a column service for newspapers. In September 1983 it became a regular newsletter. Although it only claims approximately 1,200 subscribers, its circulation and readership is much higher as it reaches many libraries, Hispanic organization leaders, peo-

Cover of *Hispanic* magazine.

AUGUST 1991 $2.00

Hispanic BUSINESS

Fast Moves in a Slow Season

The 100 Fastest Growing Companies

Cover of *Hispanic Business* magazine.

ple in corporations with major responsibilities toward Hispanics, journalists, Hispanic advocacy groups, and influential government officials working with or interested in legislation and policy issues related to Hispanics. *Hispanic Link* solicits columns from various journalists and experts on subjects concerning Hispanics and provides those articles as a syndicated service of three columns per week to more than eighty-five newspapers across the country via the *Los Angeles Times* syndicated news service.

The two most notable bilingual magazines are *Vista* and *Saludos Hispanos* (*Regards, Hispanics*). *Vista*, with its headquarters in Miami, Florida, started in September 1985 as a monthly supplement insert to selected Sunday newspapers in locations with large Hispanic populations. Although *Vista* was published in English on a weekly basis from late 1989 through June 1991, financial problems resulting from the general national economic situation, particularly insufficient advertising support, made it return to its monthly schedule. Since June 1991, in addition to its English-language articles, it has incorporated "mosaico"—a Spanish-language supplement with three stories. It has also increased to twenty-four pages on average (when it was a weekly,

it averaged twelve pages). *Vista*, measuring 10 1/2 by 11 inches, is aimed at informing, educating, and entertaining Hispanic American readers with stories that focus on Hispanic role models, positive portrayals of Hispanics, and their cultural identity. As of September 1991, *Vista* was inserted in thirty-one different newspapers in eight states—Arizona, California, Colorado, Florida, Illinois, New Mexico, New York, and Texas. Given its form of distribution, its total circulation, which is BPA-verified, was estimated at approximately 924,000. *Vista* was originally published by Horizon Communications, a Hispanic company owned by Arturo Villar, the first publisher, and Harry Caicedo, editor at the time; the former is a Spanish Cuban and the latter of Colombian ancestry. In February 1991, these initial founders were dismissed from *Vista* after a series of disagreements with other members of the magazine's management. At the time, *Vista's* two largest shareholders were Hycliff Partners, a New York investment group, which owned 28 percent, and Time-Warner Inc., which held 25 percent (*The Wall Street Journal* 1991). In April 1991, Hycliff Partners and Times-Warner reduced their share of *Vista* to 12 percent each as

Charlie Erikson, founding editor of Hispanic Link News Service.

majority ownership (approximately 65 percent) of the magazine was purchased by Fred Estrada and his Hispanic Publishing Corporation, which, as indicated earlier, is also the owner of *Hispanic* magazine.

Saludos Hispanos, "the official publication of the United Council of Spanish Speaking People," is owned by Rosemarie García-Solomon, a Mexican American. When it began publishing in September 1985, it was a quarterly magazine, but as of January 1991 it turned to six publications per year with a national circulation of approximately 300,000. Since this date, it has also been changing its distribution from a free insert in selected newspapers to direct paid subscription to individuals and sales at magazine stands. Nevertheless, a significant part of its circulation still goes to about three thousand schools, universities, and various institutions in California, Florida, Illinois, New York, and Texas, which use the magazine for educational purposes. One reason for *Saludos Hispanos's* educational value is that within its average nintey-two pages, which measure 9 by 12 inches, it publishes side-by-side Spanish and English versions of most of its stories. Furthermore, it stresses positive role models for and about Hispanics. In addition to articles on the feature topic, the regular departments include, among others, role models, music, careers, earth watch, university profile, fashion, law and order, museums, and food. Another educational distinction of this publication company is its *Saludos Hispanos Video Magazín*—a three-part video program that has been used by over four thousand schools and organizations for recruitment and retention of Hispanic youth in the educational system. According to its promotional page, the video, available in English and a Spanish-language dubbed version, is designed to motivate Hispanic youth to stay in school, to improve relationships, and to stress the importance of cultural pride and self-esteem as keys to success.

In addition these publications, there are dozens of Spanish-language consumer magazines with specialized topics related to parenthood, fashion, hobbies, and social, cultural, and political interests. All are readily available in the United States via subscriptions or magazine racks in Hispanic communities in major cities. Examples of these are *Buenhogar, Cosmopolitan, Geomundo, Hombre del Mundo, Harper's Bazaar en Español, Mecánica Popular, Selecciones del Reader's Digest, Tu Internacional,* and *Vanidades Continental,* just to name a few of the most popular. As can be observed by the titles, some are Spanish-language editions of English-language publications. Regardless of where these are produced, be it Spain, the United States, or Latin America, they have as primary clients any and all Spanish-

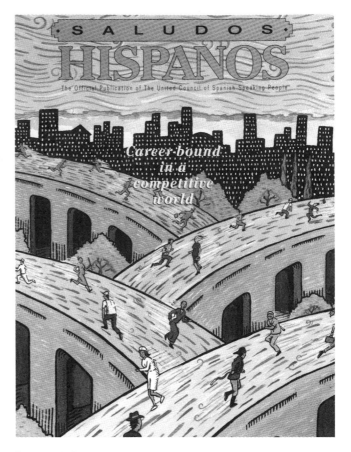

Cover of *Saludos Hispanos* magazine.

speaking populations. Other specialized magazines in Spanish and/or English are produced with the U.S. Hispanic as the primary client, for example, *Automundo, Buena Salud, Career Focus* (also targeted to Afro-Americans), *Embarazo, Hispanic American Family, Hispanic Youth-USA, Mi Bebé, Ser Padre, Teleguía, TV y Novelas USA, Una Nueva Vida,* the northeastern U.S. edition of *Imagen,* and the Hispanic youth-oriented automobile publication *Lowrider.*

Furthermore, there are journals with specialized topics related to academia, professions, and organizations. Among the current academic journals are *Aztlán, The Americas Review,* the *Bulletin of the Centro de Estudios Puertorriqueños,* the *Hispanic Journal of Behavioral Sciences, Journal of Hispanic Policy,* and the *Latino Studies Journal.*

And finally, there are state and regional publications aimed at the respective Hispanic or Spanish-speaking populations. Examples of these are *Adelante* (Washington, D.C.), *Avance Hispano* (San Francisco), *Cambio!* (Phoenix), *La Voz de Houston* (Houston), *La Voz* (Seattle), *Miami Mensual,* and *Bienvenidos a Miami, Tele Guía de Chicago* and *Lea* (directed at Colombians residing in the United

States). In these cities and dozens of others with large Hispanic concentrations, one can even find Spanish and/or Hispanic yellow pages—the telephone-type directories.

As can be discerned from this section, the number of magazines and other periodicals available to Hispanics in the United States is very extensive and diverse. No other ethnic minority population in this country has such an array of printed materials.

✳ HISPANIC-ORIENTED ELECTRONIC MEDIA

"Hispanic broadcasting comes of age," proclaimed *Broadcasting* magazine in a 1989 special report reviewing the growth, financial status, and related developments of Spanish-language radio and television. Why such assessment? One reason is that the number of stations, companies, and organizations related to Spanish-language radio and television in this country has grown, as has the content they offer. Radio, for example, not only offers *rancheras* and *salsa*, but also Top 40, mariachi, *norteña*, Tex-Mex, Mexican hits, adult contemporary, contemporary Latin hits, international hits, Spanish adult contemporary, romantic, ballads, traditional hits and oldies, folkloric, regional, *boleros*, progressive *tejano*, *merengue*, and even bilingual contemporary hits. Television is no longer song-and-dance shows with some novellas and old movies. It is also drama, talk shows, comedy, news, investigative journalism, sports, contemporary movies, entertainment magazines, dance videos, and many specials from all over the world. All of these options have been brought by the search for new markets by both Hispanic and Anglo entrepreneurs, and the combined growth of the Hispanic population and its purchasing power.

In fact, in some markets the Hispanic audience for selected Spanish-language radio and television stations is larger than that of many well-known English-language stations; for example, in Los Angeles, KLVE-FM and KWKW-AM have more listeners than KNX-AM and KROQ-FM (Puig 1991). The "coming of age" that was evident in 1989 is even more evident today. Radio directed especially to the U.S. Hispanic market has grown from an occasional voice heard on isolated stations in the Southwest and on big city multilingual stations to a multimillion-dollar segment of the broadcast industry" (Gutiérrez and Schement 1979, 3). Today there are hundreds of Spanish-language radio stations, a couple of Hispanic commercial and public radio owners" associations, various specialized news services, and at least five major advertising representatives for this expanding market.

Radio

The Early Years. Spanish-language radio programs transmitted from within the boundaries of the United States began as early as the mid-1920s—almost immediately after the inauguration of commercial broadcasting in this country. While Hispanic-oriented radio is now quite diversified and can be found in almost every community with an established Hispanic population, its development has been and difficult. In their accounts of the history of this ethnic medium, Schement and Flores (1977) and Gutiérrez and Schement (1979) indicate that Spanish-language radio started in the mid-1920s when English-language radio stations began selling time slots to Latino brokers. These brokers, some of whom had previous radio experience in Mexico, "paid the stations a flat rate for the airtime, sold advertisements to local business and programmed the broadcasts themselves. The difference between what they took in from advertising and paid to the station for the airtime was their profit" (Gutiérrez and Schement 1979, 5). During the early days of radio, the stations that sold these slots and the time frames that were made available to brokers depended on the local market competition

Pedro J. González, pioneer of Spanish-language radio in California.

Pedro J. González's singing group, "Los Madrugadores."

González's show and his progressive political stands made him a threat to the establishment, resulting in trumped-up rape charges against him in 1934. He was convicted and condemned to six years in San Quentin prison, released in 1940, and immediately deported to Mexico. In Tijuana he reestablished and continued his radio career until the 1970s, when he returned and retired in the United States. Many others across the Southwest followed Pedro's footsteps in the new medium.

In San Antonio, Lalo Astol was an early voice heard on Spanish-language radio as emcee for the program "La Hora Comercial Mexicana" on English-language station KMAC. Astol was a well-known theater personality and appeared on stage at the Nacional and other theaters. As gathered during interviews by Kanellos (1990), in 1952 Astol also began doing soap operas in Spanish on Cortez's KCOR, acted in a radio drama series, "Los Abuelitos," and emceed a quiz show, "El Marko." In 1956, Astol moved on to Spanish-language television, where he participated in various writing, directing, and acting roles. He currently works for San Antonio radio

among stations and the profitability of the various airtimes. Invariably, space for foreign-language programming was provided primarily during the least profitable time (early mornings or weekends) and by stations seeking alternative avenues for revenue.

One of the most well known pioneers of Spanish-language radio in California was Pedro J. González, about whom two films have been made: the documentary *Ballad of an Unsung Hero* (1984, Paul Espinosa, writer and producer) and the full-length feature *Break of Dawn* (1988, Isaac Artenstein, director). According to the interviews and documents gathered by Espinosa, between 1924 and 1934 González was responsible for shows such as "Los Madrugadores" ("The Early Birds").

This program was broadcast from 4:00 to 6:00 A.M., primarily on Los Angeles station KMPC, which thanks to its 100,000-watt power could be heard at that time all over the Southwest—even as far as Texas—thus reaching thousands of Mexican workers as they started their day. The dynamics of

Banner headlines in *La Opinión* newspaper announcing the guilty verdict in the Pedro J. González case.

KUKA doing "El Mercado del Aire" (Kanellos 1990, 93).

Even through the early brokerage system, Spanish-language radio thrived. By the late 1930s, numerous stations carried Spanish-language programs either full-time or part-time. In response to the market demands, in 1939 the International Broadcasting Company (IBC) was established in El Paso, Texas, to produce and sell Spanish-language programming to various stations and brokers across the country. As a result of the efforts of services like the IBC and the work by dozens of independent brokers, by 1941 it was estimated that 264 hours of Spanish were being broadcast each week by U.S. broadcasters (Arheim and Bayne 1941).

Gutiérrez and Schement (1979), citing sources who have written of the early days of radio, indicate that ethnic-language programming, especially in Spanish, proved economically successful, as the emotional impact of an advertising message wrapped in the music and drama of the listener's native language was more appealing than the same message in English. Therefore, from the beginning, the goal behind foreign-language programming was the same as with English-language broadcasting: to make profits via advertising.

In Texas, Raúl Cortez was one of the earliest Chicano brokers and eventually was successful enough to establish and operate his own full-time Spanish-language station—KCOR-AM, a 1,000-kilowatt "daytime only" station in San Antonio—which went on the air in 1946. Nine years later, Cortez ventured into the Spanish-language television industry (discussed later). Gutiérrez and Schement indicate that after World War II, Anglo station owners and Hispanic brokers saw increasing opportunities in the Hispanic market via Spanish-language radio. This allowed some brokers to follow Cortez's lead and become owners of full-time stations. Most, however, were made employees of the stations they had been buying time from. Such were the initial stages of Spanish-language radio programming and stations.

From the 1950s to the 1970s, Spanish-language radio was in transition. During those decades, this radio format continued to grow but began moving away from the brokerage system in favor of the more independent, full-time stations in AM and subsequently in FM—many transmitting up to twenty-four hours per day. In terms of the content, the early "broker" years were characterized by poetry, live drama, news, and live music programming. Most of the live music was "Mexican" and the majority of the news was from foreign countries, predominantly Mexico. As musical recordings became more common, this less expensive form of programming replaced the live music, allowing brokers and the stations to keep more of their profits for themselves. During the transition years, "personality radio" was at its best; brokers and announcers who had control over their programs and commercials became popular themselves. By the late 1960s, the format became more tightly packaged and was less in the hands of individual radio stars. Music was selected by the station management to give a consistent sound throughout the programs. These broadcasts had less talk than before and were very much like other music-oriented English-language programs. In the 1970s, the stations" growth also brought increased attention to format programming on the air and to sophisticated marketing techniques on the business side. One interesting note about Spanish-language broadcast stations is that almost all the announcers came from Latin America, in spite of the growth of the U.S. Hispanic audiences. While no research has been done to explain this employment practice, it is perhaps because station managers perceived that the Spanish of U.S. Hispanics was of poorer quality.

The phenomenal expansion of Spanish-language radio in the United States, especially during the late 1980s, is illustrated by the following figures. In 1974, there were 55 stations that broadcast in Spanish at least half of their airtime and there were an additional 425 that broadcast in this format less than half of their airtime (Gutiérrez and Schement 1979). By 1980, the respective numbers were 64 and 436 (Schement and Singleton 1981). In 1986, 73 stations broadcast over half their time in Spanish (no comparable figures were provided for part-time Spanish-language stations).

Current Status of Radio. According to the 1991 Standard Rate and Data Service's (SRDS's) *Hispanic Media and Markets* guide, as of June 1991 there were 35 AM and 112 FM full-time Spanish-language radio stations and an additional 77 AM and 16 FM stations that dedicated a significant part (but not the majority) of their broadcast time to Spanish programming. This SRDS data, however, is less comprehensive than the 1991 *Broadcasting Yearbook,* which lists 185 AM and 68 FM stations transmitting full-time in Spanish. Under this publication's "Special Programming" section, an additional 197 AM and 203 FM stations are listed as airing Spanish programs at least a few hours per week. Regardless of which source one chooses to view, the statistics provide indisputable evidence that Spanish-language radio is a powerful and growing ethnic medium in the United States.

While these numbers attest to a remarkable growth of the Hispanic-oriented radio industry, Hispanic *ownership* of these radio stations has not followed similar patterns. According to Schement and Singleton (1981), in 1980, of the 64 primary Spanish-language radio stations identified in their study, only 25 percent were owned by Latinos. In the top ten markets (for example, New York, Los Angeles, Chicago, Miami, San Antonio), Latinos owned only about 10 percent of these types of stations. Primary Spanish-language radio (PSLR) stations are those that transmit in Spanish 50 percent or more of their broadcast day. After discussing figures on ownership of assets and employment statistics at the various levels of a station's hierarchy, Schement and Singleton conclude that "PSLR stations can be described as owned and operated predominantly by Anglos" (1981, 81).

More recent statistics gathered by the National Association of Broadcasters and the Minority Telecommunications Development Program (MTDP) of the National Telecommunications and Information Administration on minority-owned and -controlled broadcast stations shed some additional light on the issue of Hispanic control over radio stations.

Apparently these two agencies used different criteria for identifying or classifying Hispanic-owned and -controlled radio. Otherwise, it seems that the number of Hispanic-owned radio stations more than doubled between 1986 and 1990. However, the Minority telecommunications Development Program (MTDP) data suggest that there has been a decline between 1990 and 1991. It will be important to observe future statistics from this same source to assess which way the market is going. One other fact to keep in mind when considering these statistics is that they are not indicators of the programming language the Hispanic-owned stations; it is unclear whether Spanish or English is used full- or part-time. It is only coincidental that all the Hispanic-owned stations listed in the radio directory in the 1990-91 MTDP report are primarily Spanish-language stations. This fact allows for an approximate calculation of the current percentage of Hispanic-owned PSLR stations. In 1991, the 58 AM and the 21 FM stations listed in Table 22.1 respectively constitute 32 percent and 31 percent of the Spanish-language AM and FM stations listed in the *Broadcasting Yearbook* that same year. Altogether, this represents a slight increase from the 25 percent assessed by Schement and Singleton (1981) ten years ago.

Another important issue about the ownership of Hispanic-oriented radio is the trend toward concentration of various stations, particularly the most profitable ones, under major corporate groups. The

TABLE 22.1
RADIO STATIONS OWNED AND CONTROLLED BY HISPANICS

	1982	1983	1984	1985	1986	1990	1991
AM	33	31	31	29	35	64	58
FM	13	9	8	8	9	24	21

Sources: 1982-86 data: National Association of Broadcasters, Department of Minority and Special Services (1986); 1990-91 data: Minority Telecommunications Development Program of the National Telecommunications and Information Administration, U.S. Department of Commerce (October 1991).

McHenry Tichnor, founder of the Tichnor Media Systems.

oldest and largest of these is Tichenor Media System, Inc., a family-owned private company based in Dallas, Texas, which presently owns eleven full-time Spanish-language radio stations in the following locations: New York (WADO-AM), Miami (WQBA-AM and FM), Chicago (WIND-AM and WOJO-FM), San Antonio (KCOR-AM), Houston (KLAT-AM), Brownsville-Harlingen-McAllen (KGBT-AM and KIWW-FM), and El Paso (KBNA-AM and FM). Tichenor also has partial ownership of another Spanish-language station in Corpus Christi (KUNO-AM). This company was started in 1940 by McHenry Tichenor, a successful Anglo newspaperman who in 1941 bought his second radio station in south Texas, which at the time broadcast half a day in English and half a day in Spanish. This was the family's first venture into the Hispanic market. According to a Tichenor Media System summary sheet, the expansion into the Spanish radio field began in 1984 when, "under the directions of the second and third generations of the Tichenor family, the Company restructured its Corporate goal and formed Tichenor Spanish Radio." At that time, the non-Spanish-language broadcast properties, including television, were

divested to allow for the new ventures into the Hispanic market. In 1990, Spanish Radio Network was formed in partnership with SRN Texas, Inc. (a wholly owned subsidiary of Tichenor Media System) and Radio WADO, Inc., in order to purchase the Miami and the New York stations. As of this writing, the Tichenor company, with McHenry Taylor Tichenor, Jr., as president, continues to seek new stations in major Hispanic markets, particularly in Los Angeles. This corporate goal can be understood, because in 1991, five of the company's stations were among the nation's top ten in billings for this market and accounted for as much as $21.4 million in revenues (Lopes 1991).

The second-largest group owner of Spanish-language radio stations is Spanish Broadcasting System (SBS), which was started in 1983 by Raúl Alarcón, Jr. This company, the only radio group company whose proprietors are Hispanics, now owns six stations in the top three Latino markets: New York (WSKQ-AM and FM), Los Angeles (KSKQ-AM and FM), and Miami (WCMQ-AM and FM), plus a station in Key Largo, Florida (WZMQ-FM), that retransmits the Miami station's signals. According to Lopes (1991), the combined AM/FM stations were also among the top ten in billings in 1991, accounting for $23.1 million in revenues for SBS. Mendosa states that Alarcón has been successful in acquiring so many stations because he is extremely "persistent in taking advantage of several options that the FCC makes available to minority broadcasters" (1990b, 58). In addition to its own stations, SBS is the national sales representative for six stations in Texas, six in California, and three in Illinois. The company also develops revenues from its SBS Promotions (for example, of concerts, sporting events, supermarket tie-ins, and on-air contests) and from Alarcón holdings in real estate. In 1990, SBS's combined capital of $32.3 million made it, according to Mendosa (1990a), the fifty-second-largest Hispanic company in the United States.

Lotus Communications Corporation owns a third group of Spanish-language radio stations. The flagstaff operation is KWKW-AM, a station that has been serving the Hispanic community in Los Angeles and vicinities since 1942. It was purchased by Lotus in 1962 for approximately one million dollars. The price was a reflection of the large audience it attracts, especially among the Mexican and Mexican-American populations of that region. A recent audience estimate placed the number of listeners at over one million (at least during one "day-part," that is, time segment), making it among the largest in the United States and a few Latin American cities. Other Spanish-language stations owned by Lotus are KOXR-AM in Oxnard, California (bought in 1968), WTAQ-AM in Chicago (since 1985), and KGST-AM in Fresno (since 1986). All four of these stations are identified as La Mexicana in their respective markets because the music, programming, and the disc jockeys follow a Mexican format in idioms and accents. Another distinctiv e programming feature of these stations is that they broadcast Los Angeles Dodger baseball games and retransmit these to 148 stations in Mexico. Lotus owns ten other radio outlets in the United States, all of which are English-language stations. In addition, under Lotus Hispanic Reps, this company is sales representative to approximately one hundred Spanish-language radio stations in the United States. The president of Lotus Communications is Howard Kalmenson; the vice president is Jim Kalmenson. Both are Anglos, as are the other owners of the company. The executive vice president is Joe Cabrera; he is Hispanic, as are the respective station managers. In 1991, billings for KWKW on its own totaled $10.3 million, making it the single most profitable Spanish-language station in the country. According to Kalmenson, the success of this station has helped fund the growth of the entire company, which continues its operations with no capital debt.

A fourth Spanish-language radio group is *Radio América*, founded in 1986 when brothers Daniel and James Villanueva, of Mexican heritage, bought stations KBRG-FM in the San Francisco Bay Area. In 1988, they acquired station KLOK-AM in the San Jose/San Francisco area. Lopes (1991) estimates that these two stations had net billings of $3.4 million in 1991. According to a fact sheet provided by the corporate management, KLOK was bought "using a separate shell company—Bahia Radio." The fact sheet adds that at the end of 1991, the Villanuevas, under a separate company called Orange County Broadcasting, purchased station KPLS-AM in Los Angeles. A distinctive characteristic of this station, with 20 percent ownership by Fernando Niebla, also of Mexican descent, is that it is the first "all talk" Spanish-language station in the Los Angeles and southern California area (there are four "talk" stations in the Miami market). Daniel Villanueva also has minority (20 percent) interests in Washington, D.C.'s Los Cerezos Broadcasting Company, which owns WMDO-AM and WMDO-TV Channel 48—a Univisión affiliate.

Yet another Spanish-language radio group is the *Viva América* company, which was started in 1989 with 49 percent owned by Heftel Broadcasting and 51 percent owned by Mambisa Broadcasting Corporation. Heftel owns stations in Los Angeles (KLVE-FM and KTNQ-AM). Mambisa is divided among Amancio V. Suárez, his son Amancio J. Suárez, and cousin

Charles Fernández, all of whom are of Cuban descent. In Miami, the Viva America Media Group owns two stations (WAQI-AM and WXDJ-FM). In addition, under the corporate heading of the Southern Media Holding Group, presided over by Amancio V. Suárez, it is also linked to *Mi Casa*—a monthly Spanish-language newspaper. In spite of its recent entry into the market, Viva América earned $10.1 million in billings in 1991, almost doubling the figure of the previous year; the two Heftel stations were the top in the Spanish-language radio market, totaling $16.3 million for the same year (Lopes, 1991).

A final group of stations that are especially distinct from the aforementioned ones are administered by the nonprofit Radio Bilingüe (Bilingual Radio) network in California. Efforts to establish this network date to 1976, when Hugo Morales, a Harvard Law School graduate of Mexican Mixtec Indian heritage, and Lupe Ortiz y Roberto Páramo, in collaboration with a group of Mexican peasants, artists, and activists sought to use radio to improve life and sustain the cultural identity of farm workers of the San Joaquin Valley (see Corwin 1989; Downing 1990). With the significant backing of a grant from a Catholic charity, KSJV-FM was launched in Fresno, Cali-

Amancio V. Suárez of the Viva America Media Group.

fornia, on July 4, 1980. It transmits a variety of music programs, plus a diversity of information related to health, education, immigration, civic action, and the arts. Supported primarily by donations from community members, businesses, and some foundations, the Radio Bilingüe network now reaches across central California via KSJV and two retransmitting stati ons in Bakersfield and Modesto. In southern California, some of the network's programs are also aired by affiliate KUBO-FM, which started in El Centro on April, 1989, producing some of its own independent programming. Radio Bilingüe also sponsors the "Viva El Mariachi" ("Long Live the Mariachi"), a music festival that serves as an important fund-raiser for the network. One of the distinctive features of this network is the operational and programming support it receives from innumerable volunteers who produce diverse music and public service programs in English, Spanish, and bilingual format. Radio Bilingüe is currently the largest noncommercial producer of Spanish-language and bilingual programs. Another feature of Radio Bilingüe is its news service, "Noticiero Latino" ("Latin Newscast"), which is described later.

Due to increased pressures in the commercial and public radio markets, two organizations serving the interests of this sector were established in 1991. The first was the American Hispanic-Owned Radio Association (AHORA), which started with fifty-five Hispanic station owners concerned with competition for the Hispanic market and with the rapid pace at which Spanish-language radio stations are being bought by non-Hispanics. According to *Broadcasting* magazine, AHORA, under the direction of Mary Helen Barro (majority owner of KAFY-AM in Bakersfield, California), seeks to "increase the number of business opportunities for Hispanic broadcasters and to attract more Hispanic talent to broadcasting"; its agenda also includes encouraging the government to include Spanish-language radio stations in government media buys (1991b, 40).

With June 1991 as its organization date, another professional radio group is Hispanics in Public Radio (HPR). A press release provided by Florence Hernández-Ramos, general manager of KUVO-FM in Denver, Colorado, indicates that this "nonprofit professional organization designed to provide a forum for the expression of the needs and interests of Hispanic Americans involved with public radio" proposes to "represent the interests of Hispanic-controlled public radio stations with the goal of improving the financial resources of the stations." The inaugural press release also indicates that HPR's main activities will be "information sharing, joint fundraising, training, and program development."

The Radio News and Other Program Providers. Although some stations produce everything they broadcast, including news and commercials, many stations depend on various companies dedicated to packaging programs for the Spanish-language radio market. Two types of providers merit special attention: those that provide news services and the ones that provide "full service."

Among the major news service providers, the oldest is *Spanish Information Systems* (SIS), inaugurated in 1976. From its headquarters in Dallas, Texas, it distributes via satellite to forty-six stations five-minute Spanish-language news programs from 6:00 A.M. to 9:00 P.M. Monday through Friday and 8:00 A.M. to 3:00 P.M. (Central Time) on weekends. Monday through Friday at noon, they also transmits "SIS al Día" ("SIS to Date"), a fifteen-minute radio magazine that includes segments on current affairs, cooking, health, and sports. Additional sportscasts are also distributed at 7:45 A.M., 3:45 P.M., and 5:45 P.M. on weekdays and 2:45 P.M. on weekends. CBS Hispanic Radio Network (discussed later), represents SIS in nationwide sales. SIS is a division of Command Communications, Inc., an Anglo-controlled company that also owns Texas State Network—a nationwide English-language information service and sports news network.

Another radio news provider is Radio Noticias (News Radio), which began in 1983 as a division in Spanish of United Press International (UPI), once one of the major wire services in the world. From its base in Washington, D.C., Radio Noticias distributes to forty-two affiliated stations its seven-minute news program on an hourly basis from 6:00 A.M. to 9:00 P.M. Monday through Friday. There is no service on weekends.

A third news provider is Noticiero Latino, produced by Radio Bilingüe in Fresno, California. This news service, which began in 1985, is unique in that it is the only Spanish news service produced by a nonprofit network in the United States whose proprietaries and coordinators are Latino residents of this country. It is also unique because it is exclusively dedicated to informing and helping to interpret events in the United States, Latin America, and the Caribbean that are related to Hispanics in the United States, for example, immigration, civil rights, health, education, culture, and successes of Hispanics. Using information gathered by its local reporters and network of correspondents in the United States, Mexico, and Puerto Rico, Noticiero Latino offers a daily eight-to-ten-minute news program that is transmitted by telephone line Monday through Friday and by satellite two times a week. Noticiero Latino's news services are used by more than forty stations in the

United States, one in Puerto Rico, and an other thirty in Mexico. The Mexico links are facilitated through the Instituto Mexicano de la Radio's Programa Cultural de las Fronteras and through Radio Educación.

Among the "full service" providers of Spanish-language programming, the largest is Cadena Radio Centro (CRC)—a network founded in 1985 in Dallas, Texas. CRC is a subsidiary of Organización Radio Centro, a Mexican company controlled by the Aguirre family, which also owns nine radio stations and has more than one hundred affiliates. In the United States the president of Cadena Radio Centro is Barrett Alley, and the vice chairman is Carlos Aguirre—a controlling family heir. This U.S. radio network offers its news services every hour on the hour twenty-four hours a day to sixty affiliated Spanish-language stations linked via satellite. CRC programming service operates seven days a week with two information lines. One transmits its five-minute news reports every hour; three of these daily transmissions originate directly from Mexico City, and another three focus on Latin American news. The other line transmits a variety of programs, including "En Concierto" (prominent Hispanic artists introducing their music), "Cristina Opina" (opinions by Cristina Saralegui on a wide range of subjects), "Tribuna Deportiva" (a live sports call-in talk show), and news of special events. All or some of these programs are purchased by affiliated stations, depending on local or regional interests.

With its starting date in March 1991, a recent Spanish-language radio program provider is Hispano U.S.A., which claims to be the first Hispanic-owned and -operated Spanish network service. According to a company informational brochure, Hispano U.S.A. sells twenty-four daily hours of "Spanish radio programming for the 90's, designed for cost-efficient station operations which benefits resident as well as absentee ownership." The programming, which is transmitted via satellite, features "top 40 Hispanic dance tunes," and national and international news, including sports and weekend special reports. Nine months after its start-up, Hispano U.S.A. had contracted with eighteen stations covering the southern United States from California to Florida.

One other major provider of Spanish-language radio programs is CBS Hispanic Radio Network (CBSHRN). This special-events network was founded in 1990 by Columbia Broadcasting System. According to a company fact sheet, CBSHRN was created "to sell, affiliate and produce Spanish-language broadcasts of the Crown Jewels [i.e., the play-off games and World Series] of Major League Baseball to the United States and Latin America." It also transmits National Football League postseason and Super Bowl games, world soccer championship games, and, more recently, entertainment specials such as "Navidad Mágica en Disneyland" ("Magical Christians in Disneyland"). The programs are provided via syndication free of charge to affiliates in exchange for carrying the network's commercials; local commercials are allowed between selected breaks. For 1992, the network plans to offer more entertainment programs. CBS Hispanic Radio Network started its Spanish-language programming in Latin America in the mid-1970s with baseball specials . When it began in the United States, it was affiliated with Caballero Hispanic media representatives to provide such programs to the stations represented by Caballero, but in 1990 it established its own syndication network.

In sum, as of 1991, Spanish-language radio stations, whether owned by Hispanics or Anglos, could be heard in practically every region of the United States. In some major metropolitan cities with large concentrations of Hispanics (New York, Los Angeles, Miami, Chicago, San Antonio, and Houston), Hispanics have a variety of such stations to choose from, each with a distinct format and music to please almost any of the major Latin American and United States Hispanic musical traditions. Through the news and other programming services, Spanish-speakers in the United States also have many opportunities to keep ties to their countries of origin, enjoy the diversity of entertainment shows, and be part of the news and cultural events in this country as well as around the Hispanic world.

Television

The Early Years. As was the case for radio, Spanish-language television transmissions started almost as soon as they began in the English-language medium. Since the 1940s, entrepreneurs have found a significant market and profits transmitting to the Hispanic populations in the United States. Spanish-language television has grown enormously from the early days of a few brokered hours on some English-language stations in San Antonio and New York. In 1991, over $332 million in advertising was spent on the three broadcasting networks and various cable companies that make up Spanish-language television. These businesses differ considerably—some operate independently, while others have corporate ties to both U.S. and Mexican media.

The first Spanish-language television station in the United States was San Antonio's KCOR-TV Channel 41, which began some evening programs in 1955. But a few years before KCOR and similar stations started, several Spanish-language radio entrepreneurs recognized the potential of the Spanish-speaking television audiences and pioneered the way by producing special TV programs. Following the pattern used in the early stages of Spanish-language radio, time was brokered for these programs in the nascent English-language stations in selected cities.

One of the earliest of such Spanish-language television programs was "Buscando Estrellas" ("Looking for Stars"), which began in 1951 and was produced and hosted by José Pérez (Pepe) del Río, a Mexican national of Spanish heritage. With Pioneer Flour Mills of San Antonio, Texas, as the primary commercial sponsor, this weekly entertainment and variety talent-search show lasted approximately three years. It was broadcast live on Sunday afternoons initially from the studios of KERN Channel 5—an English-language station in San Antonio. "Buscando Estrellas" brought to Texas a variety of talent from Mexico and provided opportunities for local amateurs to present their artistic aspirations to the public at the recording studios and to television viewing audiences. Another characteristic of this precursor of U.S.-Hispanic television was that its production and broadcasting location rotated every thirteen weeks to three other Texas cities: Corpus Christi, Harlingen, and Laredo. In each city, the concept of the show was sold and time was brokered for it from English-language stations that found it profitable to sell those slots. Between 1956 and 1961, Pepe del Río hosted another popular Spanish-language program in San Antonio: "Cine en Español," which featured old movies brought from Mexico, Spain, and Argentina. Broadcast from the studios of KERN, those movies were also quite popular among the Spanish-speaking audiences of the time.

In New York, the precursors of Spanish-language television were the well-known radio personalities Don Pessante and Don Mendez. Some anecdotal evidence indicates that during the late 1940s they might have hosted the very first U.S. Hispanic-oriented television entertainment programs by brokering time on one of the English-language channels (9, 11, or 13).

More anecdotal evidence was obtained about another Hispanic-oriented program in New York during the early 1950s: "El Show Hispano," which aired on the once-commercial WATV Channel 13 between 11:00 A.M. and 12:00 A.M. on weekends (this station later became WNJU Channel 47). This program began in early 1952 and lasted for approximately two years; it was brokered by an Anglo who also saw the potential audience and profit among the growing Hispanic populations in New York. One of the distinctive features of this show, which was cohosted by Don Mendez and Aníbal González-Irizarry, was that in addition to its musical and comic segments, it also had a fifteen-minute news section. González-Irizarry was responsible for this part of the program, making

him probably the first Hispanic television newscaster in the early stages of this medium in the United States. In addition to working on the weekend television scene, González-Irizarry was a well- known disc jockey and newscaster on two of the early Spanish-language radio stations in New York (WWRL and WBNX). When he returned to Puerto Rico in 1955, Aníbal González-Irizarry eventually became the most prominent and respected anchorman on Puerto Rican television for over twenty years, on WKAQ Channel 2.

During the 1960s, part-time Spanish-language programs on English-language stations also emerged in various other cities with large concentrations of Hispanics, such as Los Angeles, Houston, Miami, Phoenix, Tucson, and Chicago (Valenzuela 1985a, 129). Most often such programs sponsored primarily by a local company—would be the outcome of personal efforts of Hispanic entrepreneurs, many of whom had experience with radio. Some stations provided time for these in order to seek alternative sources of profits or to comply with Federal Communications Commission (FCC) requirements of public service programs to serve community needs and interests.

The Spanish International Network.   The experiences of Hispanic entrepreneurs and their part-time Spanish-language television programs eventually led the way to establish separate stations especially directed at Hispanic viewers. As mentioned, the first primarily Spanish-language television station in the United States was San Antonio's KCOR, which transmitted on Channel 41 using the newly created ultra high frequency (UHF) band. The principal pioneer behind this effort was Raúl Cortez, the same owner of KCOR-AM, which was itself the first Hispanic-owned and operated Spanish-language radio station in the United States. KCOR-TV began in 1955 broadcasting from 5:00 P.M. to midnight. Emilio Nicolás, one of the first general managers of the station, recalls that approximately 50 percent of the programs were live variety and entertainment shows that featured a host of the best available talent from Mexico (pers. com., 1992). Many of these shows took place in the studios of Cortez's radio station, which aired these programs simultaneously. Movies and other prerecorded programs imported primarily from Mexico accounted for the rest of the early offerings of Channel 41.

Although the station was very popular among the Mexican and other Spanish-speaking residents of San Antonio and vicinities, Nicolás recalls that advertisers did not acknowledge this market and failed to use it extensively for commercial promotions. During those early years of the medium, Hispanic viewers were not accounted for in the standard ratings services. One reason for this, according to Nicolás, was that in the 1940s and 1950s Mexicans were cautious in either acknowledging their heritage or exposure to Spanish-language media for fear of blatant discriminatory practices. Thus, Cortez, after spending heavily on the live talent imported from Mexico and receiving limited financial support from the advertising agencies, was forced to sell the television station to an Anglo. He kept the KCOR call letters for his radio station, but the television station's were changed to KUAL. The station continued some Spanish-language programs, and in 1961 these call letters changed again to KWEX when Channel 41 was sold to Don Emilio Azcárraga Vidaurreta and his financial partners, who then went on to establish the first Spanish-language television network.

Until his death in 1972, Don Emilio Azcárraga Vidaurreta was the most prominent media magnate in Mexico. With his family, he owned and operated a significant part of the country's commercial radio system and the emerging Telesistema Mexicano, S.A. (Sociedad Anónima), broadcasting empire. In the United States, Don Emilio, his son Emilio Azcárraga Milmo, and Reynold (René) Anselmo became central figures in not only the purchase of San Antonio's Channel 41 but also in the establishment of the largest and most influential businesses related to Spanish-language television broadcasting.

From the works of these authors it can be summarized that the most significant development of Spanish-language television in the United States began when Spanish International Communications Corporation (SICC) was initiated and organized by René Anselmo and bankrolled by Azcárraga Vidaurreta along with minority investors having U.S. citizenship. Since SICC (which at one point was called Spanish International Broadcasting Corporation, SIBC) was to hold the licenses of the stations, the corporation was structured so that Azcárraga Vidaurreta, a Mexican citizen, would own only 20 percent of the company. Most of the other partners were U.S. citizens so as to conform with Federal Communication Act Section 310, which "prohibits the issuing of broadcast licenses to aliens, to the representatives of aliens, or to corporations in which aliens control more than one-fifth of the stock" (Gutiérrez 1979, 141). Anselmo, a Boston-born Italian and associate of Azcárraga's Mexican media, was the main U.S. partner in the ens uing enterprises. Among other principal U.S. citizens of SICC at the time were Frank Fouce, owner of Los Angeles Spanish-language movie houses, including the famous Million Dollar Theater, and Edward Noble, an advertising executive in Mexico City. After obtaining KWEX, the SICC with the assistance of a few other partners bought Los Angeles station KMEX Channel 34 in 1962.

Gutiérrez points out that "although there is a limitation in the amount of stock a foreign national can hold in a broadcast license, there apparently is no such restriction on U.S. television networks" (1979, 144). Thus, in 1961 Don Emilio and Anselmo established the sister company Spanish International Network (SIN) to purchase and provide programming, virtually all of which originated from Azcárraga's production studios at Telesistema (later known as Televisa) in Mexico. The other function of SIN was to provide advertising sales for the SICC stations. Over the next ten years the licensee corporation went through a series of expansions, mergers, and reorganizations as it added three other stations: WXTV Channel 41 in New York (1968); WLTV Channel 23, Miami (1971); and KFTV Channel 21, Fresno/Hanford (1972). The network was also extended with stations owned by some principals of SICC/SIN: under the Bahía de San Francisco company it was KDTV Channel 14, San Francisco (1974), and under Legend of Cibola (later known as Seven Hills Corporation) it was KTVW Channel 33, Phoenix (1976). In addition, SIN had the affiliation of five stations owned and operated by corporations not related to SIN/SICC; these were located in Albuquerque, Chicago, Corpus Christi, Houston, and Sacramento. Furthermore, SIN had four stations owned and operated by this company's parent corporation, Televisa, S.A. From their locations on the Mexican border at Juárez, Mexicali, Nuevo Laredo, and Tijuana, these stations served U.S. cities at, respectively, El Paso, El Centro, Laredo, and San Diego.

Until the mid-1970s, most of these stations shared the programming, which primarily came from Mexico's Productora de Teleprogramas (ProTele, S.A.), a company created and controlled by Televisa as its export subsidiary. SIN imported and licensed taped shows, movies, and other programs that were transported to the Los Angeles station, sent to San Antonio, and then passed along in a "bicycle type network" to the other owned and affiliated stations. In September 1976, SIN became the first major broadcasting company, preceding CBS, ABC, and NBC, to distribute programming directly to its affiliates via domestic satellite. SIN signals reached the San Antonio station from Mexico City by terrestrial microwave and from there it was distributed by the Westar satellite (Gutiérrez and Schement 1981; see also Valenzuela 1985a,b). That same year another related service had been started by Televisa to provide live, direct Spanish-language programming to Spanish-speaking audiences worldwide, but particularly to the United States. A major incentive for this new company was to sell advertising in Mexico for SIN programs, which would be aired in both countries. Between 1978 and 1979, live interconnections were established via satellite among eleven of SIN's stations. In 1979, as cable connections became more readily available, another precedent was established as SIN began paying cable franchise operators to carry its satellite signals. Then in early 1980, SIN's outlets expanded further as the network was granted permission to establish low-power television (LPTV) stations (those whose signals only reach a radius of approximately twelve to fifteen miles), beginning with Denver affiliate K49TE Channel 49, which at the time served just as a retransmitter with no local programs. Another LPTV was licensed to Los Cerezos Television Company, Washington, D.C. Additional LPTVs were licensed in Austin, Bakersfield, Hartford, Philadelphia, and Tucson. Altogether, by 1983 the Spanish-language television stations represented by SIN/SICC were reaching over 3.3 million Hispanic households across the United States. Advertising for the stations was sold in the United States, Mexico, and other Latin American countries.

Although KMEX had turned a profit in 1964, most of the SICC stations did not operate in the black until a decade or more after they began operations. Nevertheless, the Azcárragas and their fellow investors recognized the growth potential of the Spanish-speaking television audience and market in the United States, and were willing to subsidize the station group. When SICC did eventually generate profits, many of them found their way back to Mexico through the SIN pipeline. A falling-out between Frank Fouce, one of SICC's principal investors, and René Anselmo, one of the creators and president of both SICC and SIN, led to a long, bitter stockholder derivative lawsuit that took over ten years to settle. A second legal action against SICC was initiated at the FCC in 1980 when a group of radio broadcasters (the now-defunct Spanish Radio Broadcasters Association) charged that the company was under illegal foreign control. In January 1986, a judge appointed by the FCC ruled not to renew the licenses of the thirteen SICC stations and ordered their transfer to U.S.-based entities. This decision was followed by numerous legal appeals and challenges (these have been summarized by Seijo-Maldonado, 1989, and Wilkinson, 1991).

An intense and controversial bidding war in the same court that had heard the stockholder suit culminated in July 1986. Hallmark Cards, Inc., and its 25 percent partner, First Capital Corporation of Chicago, won with a $301.5 million bid for the SICC licenses and properties. The losing bidder was TVL Corporation, directed by a group of Hispanic investors who submitted a higher bid ($320 million) but whose financing was less secure. TVL's principal investors were Raúl R. Tapia, a partner in the Washington, D.C., law firm of Tapia & Buffington and former deputy special assistant of Hispanic affairs during President Jimmy Carter's administration; Alfred R. Villalobos, vice chairman and president of a management company; David C. Lizárraga, chairman, president and chief executive officer of TELACU; and Diego C. Ascencio, former ambassador to Brazil and assistant secretary of state for consular affairs. Other Hispanic notables who at some time expressed an interest in acquiring SICC were Miami politician Raúl Ma svidal, investor Enrique (Hank) Hernández, and Los Angeles surgeon and Republican party leader Tirso del Junco. Among the unsuccessful Anglo bidders, there were producers Norman Lear, A. Jerrold Perenchio, and the former U.S. ambassador to Mexico John Gavin. Legal challenges of the sale process brought by losing bidders were not resolved until April 1991.

As various appeals were being deliberated in federal court and at the FCC, SIN and SICC were renamed Univisión on January 1, 1987. In February, the cable service Galavisión, which was not included in the deal, split from Univisión and remained under the control of Televisa and Univisa. Univisa was Ascárraga's new enterprise established to house Galavisión and his remaining U.S. companies. In July of that year, Hallmark and First Capital paid $286 million for the five original SICC stations and in August obtained actual control of the channels. Later, San Francisco station KDTV was purchased for an additional $23.6 million and the Phoenix station was bought for $23 million. In February 1988, the SIN network was also acquired by Hallmark for an additional $274.5 million. With the transition, both the station group and the network continue operations under the name Univision Holdings, Inc., of which Hallmark became sole owner by February 15, 1988.

In terms of programming content, Gutiérrez and Schement (1981) state that "by 1979 SIN was feeding over 64 hours of programming to eight affiliates by Westar II satellite, 50 hours of which came from Televisa. The remainder was originated in the United States or imported from Venezuela, Spain, Argentina, or Brazil. The network feed consisted primarily of *novelas* (soap operas), variety shows, and the news [the program *24 Horas*] from Mexico City" (1980, 196). From the 1960s to the 1970s, Hispanic programs made within the United States usually consisted of public affairs programming and local newscasts, some of which were acclaimed for their excellent coverage of issues of concern to the local Hispanic communities.

In addition, some of the special programs at the time included, as summarized by Gutiérrez, "salutes to Latin American countries produced on location by Radio Televisión Española, New Jersey's Puerto Rican Day parade, a Fourth of July special from Miami and New York, and live coverage of the OTI (Organización de la Televisión Iberoamericana) Latin song festival"; there were also sporting events such as boxing matches, soccer, and World Cup competitions (1979, 153-54). In fact, SIN began carrying selected games of the World Cup Soccer Championship as early as 1970. At first these were shown on closed-circuit television and in rented theaters; regular broadcasts began in 1978.

Among the network's various programs, "Noticiero SIN" ("SIN Newscast"), the national news program, merits a special historical review because of its development and impact in the United States and Latin America. One of the pacesetters in this area is Gustavo Godoy, a native of Cuba who in Miami worked with CBS's affiliate television station as a producer and with ABC's affiliate in the news department. From there he went on to WLTV Channel 23 and later with the SIN network news. In sharing some of his recollections (pers. com., 1992) of the early years of the "Noticiero SIN," he indicated that from the start, the network established that there would be a standard of local newscasts from 6:00 to 6:30 P.M. followed by the national program from 6:30 to 7:00 P.M. in order to provide viewers with one solid hour of news focusing on events and people related to U.S. Hispanics and Latin American communities. During its beginnings the national news program was produced at the television studios of the School of Communication at Howard University in Washington, D.C. On June 14, 1982, the national news department was transferred to Miami, where it continued productions until January 1987, when it was moved to Laguna Niguel in southern California. It returned to Miami in January 1991, along with other Univisión operations. While regional newscasts were done from San Antonio and some of the larger stations, for the international news-gathering activities, news bureaus were established, beginning in 1982, in Washington, D.C., New York, El Salvador, Argentina, Mexico, Puerto Rico, Israel, and London. The satellite uplink operations, which had been in San Antonio since 1976, were also moved to Laguna Niguel in January 1987, where they remained for four years.

There are several special programs produced by the SIN news department, including "Temas y Debates" ("Themes and Debates"), a talk show that started in 1982 in Washington, D.C., and continues to this day. "Temas y Debates" airs interviews with government and public personalities who are impor-

Gustavo Godoy, Hispanic American Broadcasting Corporation, founder.

tant newsmakers and interpreters for the week. Another notable accomplishment of SIN news was its coverage of U.S. and Latin American political developments. The first U.S. national election night coverage in Spanish was in 1968; similar reports followed in subsequent years. Starting with the 1981 elections in Miami, in which two Hispanic candidates were finalists for mayor of that city, "Noticias 23" ("News 23") and "Noticiero SIN" at the national level began giving ample time to present and analyze in Spanish the campaigns, issues, and personalities of the time. Pre- and postexit polls were also conducted by the stations and the network to share their projections and predictions of the electoral outcomes, especially a mong the Hispanic populations. At each station and at the network level, there was also a very strong campaign for voter registration.

In 1984, SIN launched "Destino "84" ("Destiny "84"), which further promoted voter registration and, through a series of special programs and reports, gave ample coverage to the presidential elections in the United States. Cameras and reporters followed the candidates and events of the primaries, the conventions, and the final campaign up to election night.

That year, the NBC network sent a camera and reporter to SIN news to follow up the trends in Hispanic voting at the national level. Godoy and his staff proceeded with similar coverage in Latin America, including polling activities beginning with the 1984 congressional and presidential elections in El Salvador, where their surveys were quite accurate in predicting the voting results. In subsequent years ample coverage was given to and more exit polls were conducted of elections in Guatemala, Peru, Honduras, Colombia, Costa Rica, and many other locations.

In 1985, the first summit meeting between U.S. President Reagan and the former USSR's President Gorbachev was covered live from Geneva, Switzerland. According to Godoy (pers. com., 1992) thanks to SIN's live satellite transmissions from Latin America, these crucial electoral processes were placed in an international spotlight, thus creating a public attention that may have contributed to an increased sense of honesty and balance in such events. The amplitude and time of "Noticiero SIN's" live coverage of these Latin American developments have not been matched by any English-language network in the United States. The same can be said about the telethons in benefit of victims of the earthquakes and other natural disasters in Chile, Colombia, Puerto Rico, and Mexico.

One of the most significant internal turmoils in the history of "Noticiero SIN" began to take place in 1986, when the Mexican parent company, seeking to exert stronger control of the U.S. news activities, considered absorbing the "Noticiero" under Televisa's new international news enterprise, ECO (Empresas de Comunicaciones Orbitales). This takeover was prompted when Azcárraga established ECO to optimize the gathering and production of television news for his Univisión and for additional subscribers in the United States and Latin America. In August 1986, Godoy, who was then executive vice president for news at SIN, was informed that there would be limited funds for the coverage and conducting of polls of the elections in the Mexican state of Chihuahua. This was interpreted as an attempt to suppress uncloaking of electoral corruption and mismanagement by the main Mexican political party—the Partido de la Revolución Institucional (PRI).

In November 1986, Televisa's Jacobo Zabludovsky, who for sixteen years had been anchorman for that company's "24 Horas" ("24 Hours") news program, was appointed to take charge of the SIN news operations in the United States. Shortly after, Godoy and approximately thirty-five others at SIN resigned to protest Televisa's and, indirectly, the Mexican government's interventions. Without ever having established an operational office in the United States,

Zabludovsky was eventually "prevented from working as president of ECO due to charges by Latino journalists and politicians about the Televisa news division's constant praise of the Mexican government" (Lozano, 1988: 5). By then, Godoy had formed his own news production company, Hispanic American Broadcasting Corporation, which from 1987 to 1988 provided news for a competing network, Telemundo (discussed later). Lozano indicates that "in the end, former UPI chief, Luis G. Nogales, replaced Zabludovsky as president of ECO and started a radical restructuring of Noticiero Univisión" along with editor Sylvana Foa, who stressed that the intention was to follow "the American TV networks" style at the start of Noticiero Univisión" (1988, 5). When Hallmark took control of the network, Guillermo Martínez was appointed news director and vice president of Univisión news. Martínez, a native of Cuba, had been a journalist and editorial writer for *The Miami Herald*, and for a few months news director at WLTV in Miami.

Telemundo. While SIN and SICC were developing their powerful and far-reaching dominion, the growth and market potential of the Hispanic audi-

Henry R. Silverman, Telemundo founder.

Saul P. Steinberg, Telemundo founder.

English-language subscription television station. The station in Puerto Rico had been a major component of the Fundación Angel Ramos media enterprises and had its own islandwide retransmitter and affiliation network under the name adopted for the U.S. group—Cadena Telemundo. The WKAQ facilities consist of 250,000 square feet of operations space, including three master control rooms and nine fully equipped modern studios. In December 24, 1986, Reliance completed its acquisition of 100 percent of the outstanding common stock of Blair. Altogether, Reliance paid $325 million ($215 million of it for Blair's debt retirement) and immediately began selling off properties not connected to Spanish-language broadcasting. The change of name to Telemundo Group, Inc., was officially established on April 10, 1987. The company went public with offerings of common stock and bonds during the summers of 1987 and 1988.

Prior to forming the Telemundo Group, Reliance had entered the Hispanic media market in April 1985 with its ownership interests in Estrella Communications, Inc., which had been formed in January of that year for the purpose of buying Channel 52 in Los Angeles. Under the call letters KBSC and the corporate name SFN Communications, Inc., this station was owned by Columbia Pictures and A. Jerrold Perenchio, who had launched it in the late 1970s to compete with KMEX for Los Angeles's Hispanic audience. At the time, KBSC split its broadcast schedule, offering approximately ninety-five hours a week in Spanish. The remaining hours were sold to other programmers. According to Valenzuela, "in 1980 KBSC offered a pay-television service (ON-TV) in English at night and switched to full-time Spanish-language programs during the day" (1985a, 131). He adds that much of that station's Spanish-language programming was supplied by government station Channel 13, of Mexico. When KBSC was put on the market in 1985, Reliance Cap ital, a large shareholder of Estrella Communications, purchased a greater proportion of the stock for $38 million and began operating the station with the new call letters KVEA. By December 1986, Reliance had spent $13.5 million to buy out the remaining minority holders of Estrella Communications, including some shares held by Hallmark Cards.

The third major component of the Telemundo Group was WNJU Channel 47, licensed in Linden, New Jersey, and serving the metropolitan New York area. This station was founded by Ed Cooperstein, who had been the general manager of its predecessor—the English-language WATV Channel 13, which had started in the early 1960s in New York. That station soon underwent a series of ownership and programming changes. While in 1965 WNJU was

ence was being recognized by other interested parties, such as Saul Steinberg, chairman of the board and chief executive officer (CEO) of Reliance Capital Group, L.P., and Henry Silverman, the eventual president, CEO, and director of Telemundo. Together with their investment partners, they founded the Telemundo Group, Inc., which is currently the second-largest Spanish-language television network in the United States. Some discussions of this network and its financial underpinnings have been published by several authors from which we draw for this section (see Beale 1986, 1988; Valenzuela 1985a). The most detailed financial accounts stem from the Telemundo Group's own corporate prospectus (Drexel Burnham Lambert 1987).

The organization of the Telemundo Group began in May, 1986, when Reliance Capital Group acquired John Blair & Company, a diversified communications business. Blair had fallen prey to corporate raiders after an attempt at expansion left it overburdened with debt. Telemundo, as the successor to Blair, thus obtained stations WSCV Channel 51 in Miami and WKAQ Channel 2 in San Juan, Puerto Rico, which had been purchased by Blair in 1985 and 1983, respectively. Prior to its acquisition by Blair, WSCV was an

primarily an Anglo station transmitting in the evenings, it also broadcast some Spanish-language variety shows. According to some historical internal files of the station, by early 1966 "slightly half of WNJU-TV's programming catered to the Hispanic market." In 1971, the station was bought by Columbia Pictures via its subsidiary Screen Gems, which also owned WAPA Channel 4 in Puerto Rico. With the new structure, WNJU had access not only to Columbia's repertoire of films regularly marketed to Latin America but also to a great variety of Spanish-language programs from Puerto Rico's WAPA. From these and other sources, WNJU broadcast 60 percent Spanish-language programs, such as *novelas* (soap operas), live musical variety shows, sports, news, and community public affairs. Despite the new options for programs, Channel 47 faced numerous financial difficulties during its early years, leading to the firing of founder and general manager Ed Cooperstein in 1972, who was eventually replaced by Carlos Barba (Valenzuela 1985a). The challenge was even greater after SIN's WXTV Channel 41 was inaugurated in 1968 and began competing for the New York-New Jersey Hispanic audience, which at the time had limited access to the UHF receivers. In 1980, Columbia relinquished its holdings to the station and it was purchased jointly by A. Jerrold Perenchio, Norman Lear, and other investors under Spanish-American Communications Corporation (SACC). These new owners planned to feature primarily sports and entertainment on prime time, but owing to commitment problems they continued to run the Spanish-language programming—WNJU's strongest time block totaling seventy-four hours per week. It was because of the strength of the Spanish-language programs and Hispanic audience that WNJU was bought for approximately $75 million in December 1986 from Perenchio, Lear, and SACC by Steinberg and his Reliance Capital Group.

The growth of Steinberg's television network continued in August 1987, when Telemundo bought out (for $15.5 million) National Group Television, Inc., the license holder of station KSTS Channel 48, serving the San Jose and San Francisco area. For the Houston/Galveston market, Telemundo invested $6.428 million to obtain the outstanding stock of Bluebonnet, which operated KTMD Channel 48 in that area in 1988. Another significant Hispanic market penetration came that year when Telemundo won over the affiliation, of Chicago's WSNS Channel 26, which had been associated with Univisión. Until then, Telemundo's link to Chicago had been WCIU Channel 26. A year later, entry was made into San Antonio with the affiliation, of KVDA Channel 60. In August, 1990, Telemundo paid $2.975 million to purchase 85 percent of the stock of Nueva Vista, which operated KVDA. With these stations, its affiliations and cable linkages, the Telemundo network was firmly established and potentially available to over 80 percent of Hispanic households in the United States.

During the early years, the Telemundo stations shared some novelas and entertainment programs made available from WKAQ Channel 2 in Puerto Rico. It also imported other novelas from Brazil, Mexico, Venezuela, Argentina, and Spain. In 1987, of the thirty hours of weekly network programming, twenty hours consisted of novelas. A variety of movies and entertainment shows were also imported from these countries. From mid-1987 through 1989 "Super Sábados" ("Super Saturdays") was among the programs broadcast via satellite from the studios in Puerto Rico. This five-hour variety and game show had large audience following on the island since 1984. Telemundo also broadcast international sports competitions, particularly soccer matches. One of the distinct characteristics of this network's programming was the prompt venture to make local productions a large percentage of the offerings. A notable first was the start-up in July 1988 of "MTV Internacional"—a one-hour Spanish-language version of the MTV network's programming. Aimed at the bilingual Hispanic-American youth market, this new show is hosted in Spanish by Daisy Fuentes, a native of Cuba. It features rock music videos by groups performing in both Spanish and English, music news, artist interviews, and concert footage. (This show, syndicated by Viacom Latino Americano, a division of Viacom International, Inc., can also be seen in many Latin American countries.) Another first for Telemundo was the novela "Angélica, Mi Vida" ("Angelica, My Life"), produced in Puerto Rico. This soap opera, launched in August 1988, was specially directed to and based on the local audiences, as "the plot appealed to regional Hispanic differences by webbing Mexican, Puerto Rican and Cuban immigrant families into [the traditional] *novela* elements: passion, power struggles, love and desire" (Seijo-Maldonado, 1989: 26). Another notable program, no longer on the air, was "Feria de la Alegría" ("The Happiness Fair"), a contest and game show with audience participation. It was the first live Spanish-language television show of its kind broadcast by a network on *weekdays* in the continental United States.

From 1987 to mid-1988, the "Noticiero Telemundo" ("Telemundo Newscast"), the national news segment for this group's stations, was produced in Hialeah, Florida, by the Hispanic American Broadcasting Corporation (HBC). This company was founded by

TABLE 22.2

STATIONS OWNED AND OPERATED BY THE UNIVISIÓN SPANISH-LANGUAGE TELEVISION GROUP (LATE 1991)

FULL-POWER STATIONS		CITY
KLUZ	41	Albuquerque, NM
KCFP	30	Austin, TX
KUVN	23	Dallas/Ft. Worth, TX
KFTV	21	Fresno, CA
KMEX	34	Los Angeles, CA
WLTV	23	Miami, FL
WXTV	41	New York, NY
KTVW	33	Phoenix, AZ
KWEX	41	San Antonio, TX
KDTV	14	San Francisco, CA
LOW-POWER STATIONS		**CITY**
K39AB	39	Bakersfield, CA
W47AD	47	Hartford, CT
W42BI	42	Philadelphia, PA
K52AO	52	Tucson, AZ

TABLE 22.3

UHF AFFILIATES OF THE UNIVISIÓN SPANISH-LANGUAGE TELEVISION GROUP (LATE 1991)

FULL-POWER STATIONS		CITY
WCIU	26	Chicago, IL
KORO	28	Corpus Christi, TX
KCEC	50	Denver, CO
KINT	26	El Paso, TX
KXLN	45	Houston, TX
KNVO	48	McAllen, TX
KREN	27	Reno, NV
KCSO	19	Sacramento, CA
KSMS	67	Salinas, CA
WMDO	48	Washington, DC
LOW-POWER STATIONS		**CITY**
K27AF	27	Las Vegas, NV
K51BX	51	Lubbock, TX
W46AR	46	Milwaukee, WI
K04NT	4	Palm Springs, CA
W33AR	33	Rockford, IL
K19BN	19	San Diego, CA
K07TA	7	Santa Maria, CA
W69BT	69	South Bend, IN
K52AY	52	St. Louis, MO
W61BL	61	Tampa, FL
W48AW	48	Washington, DC

Gustavo Godoy (formerly at SIN news) with the financial assistance of Amancio V. Suárez (of the Viva América radio group). Godoy's newscasts for Telemundo began on January 12, 1987, and marked the first national transmission for the emergent Telemundo. However, HBC's telecasts were short-lived, and in January 1988 Telemundo acquired this production company and facilities as part of its network-building strategy. In May, Telemundo entered a co-production venture with Ted Turner's Cable News Network. "Noticiero Telemundo-CNN" combines news videos with Spanish-speaking journalists, camera crews, and news anchors who use as their headquarters the CNN facilities in Atlanta, Georgia. From 1988 through 1990, Godoy was general manager of KTVW, a Univisión station in Phoenix, from which he returned to Telemundo, where he is president and director of news operations.

Galavisión. A third major player in Spanish-language television in the United States is Galavisión. This television company was launched in 1979 under parent company Univisa, Inc., a subsidiary of Mexico's Televisa. At that time, Galavisión was a premium cable service, offering recently produced Spanish-language movies along with coverage of select sporting events and special entertainment shows. In early 1988, it had only 160,000 subscribers. But in September of that year, after the entry of the Telemundo network and the consolidation of Hallmark's Univisión network, Univisa started to convert Galavisión's cable operations to an advertising-based basic cable service. This change expanded Galavisión's audience substantially as potentially two million cable subscribers were able to receive Galavisión's programs.

The new format offers twenty-four-hour-a-day programming via a network feed provided by the Galaxy I and Spacenet 2 satellites. In addition, Galavisión expanded to over-the-air offerings when it affiliated stations KWHY Channel 22 in Los Angeles, KTFH Channel 49 in Houston, KSTV Channel 57 in Santa Barbara, and low-power retransmitters in seven other cities. KWHY and KTFH were converted from English-language stations; KSTV was licensed for the first time for Galavisión. Some stations broadcast

Rosita Perú, senior vice president and director of programming, Univisión.

Galavisión part-time (typically from 3:00 P.M. to 2:00 A.M.), while others have twenty-four-hour coverage.

Galavisión, operating under the separate entity of SIN, Inc., was not included in the sales of SICC and SIN to Hallmark. Univisa operates from Los Angeles, where it is parent to other companies. Among these are Video Visa (a videocassette distributor), and in Mexicali, Mexico, Plasticus, a videocassette manufacturing operation that produces more cassettes than Sony, Kodak, or 3M and also operates the world's largest video dubbing facility, Central de Video, S.A. de C.V.

Current Status of U.S. Hispanic Television. At present, the Spanish-language television industry in the United States is still dominated by the three major networks: Univisión, Telemundo, and Galavisión. However, special niches of the Hispanic television market are being targeted by two new companies, International TeleMúsica, Inc., and Viva Television Network, Inc.; by English-language cable operators such as MTV and HBO and by primarily English-language broadcasting companies that offer second audio programs in Spanish. Yet, even in this me-

Joaquín F. Blaya, president of Univisión.

Univisión news studio.

dium's fifth decade in the United States, it continues to have a substantial foreign connection in its corporate structures, on-camera and off-camera personnel, and in programming (Mydans 1989; *The Foreign Connection* 1989).

Univisión. As of January 1992, under the parent company Hallmark Cards, Inc., the Univisión-owned and operated Spanish-language television group consists of ten full-power stations and four low-power stations (see Table 22.2). In addition, Univisión counts on the affiliation of ten full-power and eleven low-power stations (see Table 22.3), plus 566 cable carriers that operate in forty of the fifty states and the District of Columbia. Some of the full-power stations on these lists were formerly low-power stations under different call letters. The satellite used for program transmissions and station connections is the SATCOM 1R. Two stations in Guadalajara and Sonora, Mexico, purchase some Univisión programs but are not owned by the network.

Since 1988, the president of the Univisión television station group has been Joaquín Blaya, a native of Chile, where he worked as a journalist, radio newscaster, disc jockey, and production manager.

Prior to this position, he was an account representative at WXTV in New York, and eventually president and general manager of station WLTV in Miami. As of mid-1991, he was also acting president of Univisíon Holdings, which includes Univisíon Publications, Univisíon News, and the Univisíon Network and its various components.

Three other key directors of Univisíon are Raúl Torano, senior vice president for sales and marketing executive of the network, the stations, and *Más* magazine; Rosita Perú, senior vice president for programming; and Ray Rodríguez, responsible for international coproductions and talent management functions. Peru is a Buenos Aires-educated native of Lima, Peru. The family roots of the other two are from Cuba. Guillermo Martínez remains vice president for Univisíon News.

In its continued expansion in this country, Univisíon, on March 9, 1991, inaugurated its state-of-the-art-technology network television center in west Dade County, Florida. The 139,000- square-foot facility now houses many of the network's departments, including news, special events, merchandising, programming, talent relations, sports, programming development and its regional sales office. The opera-

Jorge Ramos and María Elena Salinas of "Noticiero Univisión," the Monday through Friday evening news broadcast

tions, news, and promotions departments formerly based in Laguna Niguel in southern California moved to the Miami facilities during the summer of 1991 amid protests from Mexican Americans who feared a greater Cuban influence in Univisión's news, programming, and personnel (Bergsman, 1989b).

For the expansion of its national and international news coverage, Univisión's news department, under the direction of Guillermo Martínez, hired sixteen additional correspondents to work in the United States and Latin America. To improve the network's knowledge of Hispanic public opinion, Univisión enlisted the services of Sergio Bendixen and his survey research company, Bendixen and Associates. Bendixen started doing research for SIN in 1985 and has continued for Univisión, conducting surveys related to political opinions and orientations of the general public and particularly of Hispanics.

In terms of the other programs, a recent fact sheet about Univisión stated that these are "obtained from various Latin American sources, but an increasing amount . . . is produced by Univisión, as well as by independent producers in the United States," and that approximately 44 percent of the programs are U.S.-based. A typical Univisión week, which runs twenty-four hours a day, seven days a week, consists of the program types and hours shown in Table 22.4. (Domestic productions are found primarily among the news programs and the talk, variety, and comedy-type shows.)

In an interview with *Hispanic Business*, Blaya stated that the "main thrust of the program development in the United States is to address . . . "the born-again Hispanic'—the young Hispanics who were not watching Spanish-language television; he added that Univisión is "not a Latin American television network in the United States; [it is] an American television network that speaks Spanish" (Mendosa 1991, 18). In addition to the "Noticiero Univisión," and "Temas y Debates," there are several other programs that exemplify this mold. For debates and presentations related to public issues, there is "Cristina," a talkshow hosted by Cuban-born Cristina Saralegui—Univisión's version of Oprah Winfrey—in which issues and subjects formerly taboo in the Hispanic community are discussed. Other programs include "Portada" ("Cover Story"), a news magazine hosted by Puerto Rican Ana Azcuy and called "a Spanish-language version of an investigative report program

TABLE 22.4
UNIVISIÓN PROGRAMMING (MID–1991)

TYPE OF PROGRAM	WEEKDAY		SATURDAY		SUNDAY	
	ORIGINAL	REPEAT	ORIGINAL	REPEAT	ORIGINAL	REPEAT
Novelas (serials)	7.5	3.5	2.0	–	0.5	–
Talk/variety/comedy	2.5	3.0	6.5	5.0	3.5	3.5
Movies	2.0	2.0	2.0	2.0	4.0	2.0
News	1.0	0.5	–	–	0.5	–
Cartoons/children shows	1.5	–	2.5	–	1.5	–
Sports	–	–	2.0	–	5.0	–
Educational/religious	0.5	–	1.0	1.0	2.0	1.5

similar to the general market's 20/20, and, "Noticias y Más," a live daily show with human interest stories.

For comedy, games, and variety there is "Corte Tropical" ("Tropical Cut"), a zany situation comedy portraying a Latin-style pursuit of the elusive American dream and produced by Cuban Mimi Belt-Mendoza. On Saturdays there is "Sábado Gigante" ("Gigantic Saturday"), a variety game show, which is top-rated in the United States and many Latin American countries; it features games, contests, talent searches, celebrity guest appearances, and musical entertainment. It is hosted by Chilean Mario Kreutzberger, familiarly known as Don Francisco.

There is a daily afternoon show called "Hola America" ("Hello America") in which viewers can call in to play and compete for prizes, also featuring news briefs and interviews with celebrities, some of whom sing or perform in brief comedy sketches. It is hosted by José Rondstadt (a cousin of the famous Mexican-American singer Linda Rondstadt), María Olga Fernández, a native of Chile, and Cuban-born Maty Monfort-Novia.

For the younger Hispanic-American viewers, Univisión produces "Cita con el Amor" ("Date with Love"), a Spanish-language version of "The Dating Game" hosted by Venezuelan Henry Zakka. There are also the prime-time talk entertainment shows "Desde Hollywood" ("From Hollywood") and "El Show de Paul Rodríguez" ("The Raul Rodríguez Show"). The former, hosted by Luca Bentivoglio, a Venezuelan born of Italian parents, features interviews with celebrities, show business news, and gossip. The latter, a late-night show, carries the name of its host, a Los Angeles Mexican-born comedian who does occasional comedy sketches and conducts interviews with guests from the world of entertainment. Another late-night show is "Charitín" which carries the name of a popular Puerto Rican singer and host. In her weekly show, Charitín also hosts artists for interviews, singing, or participating in comedy sketches. The success of Univisión's efforts to offer these and other programs for U.S. Hispanics will be gauged when the results of the Nielsen Ratings research, jointly funded by Univisión and Telemundo, are published in 1992.

Aside from these regularly scheduled programs, Univisión also produces musical and variety specials. The most popular of these are the national (United States) and international OTI song festivals, which have been telecast since 1972, and "Premio Lo

Nuestro a la Música Latina" ("Our Prize for Latin Music"), the annual Spanish-language version of the "Grammy awards. This latter special, produced in conjunction with *Billboard* magazine, started in May 1989. Other specials celebrate Mother's and Father's Day, beauty pageants, Hispanic achievements and heritage days in the United States, and national independence days in the Americas. For 1992, this included programs related to the quincentennial commemoration of Columbus's exploration of the Americas. Under the theme "Encuentro con lo Nuestro" ("Encounter with What's Ours"), Univisión scheduled two hundred historical vignettes that explored key elements of the commemoration, forty-one capsules on past and present Hispanic achievements, and another half dozen special shows. Given the success of Univisión's productions, future goals include global programming to reach the five hundred million Spanish-speakers worldwide.

Telemundo.   As of January 1992, the Telemundo Group, Inc. consisted of six full-power stations and

Don Francisco, host of the most popular variety show on Hispanic television, Univisión's "Sábado Gigante" (Giant Saturday).

Cristina Saralegui, host of the most popular talk show in Spanish-language television, Univisión's "El Show de Cristina."

four low-power stations (Table 22.5). It also continues to own the station in San Juan, Puerto Rico, which is the network's only VHF station. Furthermore, Telemundo counts on the affiliation of six full-power and sixteen low-power stations (Table 22.6), plus seven cable carriers that operate in fourteen of the fifty states and the District of Columbia. Some of the full-power stations on these lists were formerly low-power stations under different call letters. Three

TABLE 22.5
STATIONS OWNED AND OPERATED BY THE TELEMUNDO
SPANISH-LANGUAGE TELEVISION GROUP (LATE 1991)

FULL-POWER STATIONS		CITY	LOW-POWER STATIONS		CITY
KTMD	48	Houston, TX	K60EE	60	Odessa, TX
KVEA	52	Los Angeles, CA	K61FI	61	Modesto, CA
WSCV	51	Miami, FL	K15CU	15	Salinas, CA
WNJU	47	New York, NY	K52CK	52	Stockton, CA
KVDA	60	San Antonio, TX			
KSTS	48	San Jose, CA			
WKAQ	2	San Juan, PR			

other stations affiliated with Telemundo transmit from Tijuana, Juárez, and Matamoros to serve the U.S. Hispanic communities in, respectively, San Diego, El Paso, and McAllen/Brownsville. Altogether, the Telemundo television network currently has the potential of reaching over 84 percent of U.S. Hispanic households. The satellite used for program transmissions and station connections is the Spacenet II.

For Telemundo, Steinberg continued as chairman of the board of Reliance Holdings Group, L.P. But in February 1990, with Silverman's departure from Telemundo, Steinberg assumed his responsibilities until 1991. That year, upon the resignation of the network's vice president, Carlos Barba (now president of Venevisión International), Telemundo created a three-member office of the president. The directors are W. Gary McBride, president of the network and responsible for all network activities, including programming, promotion, market research, marketing, and network sales; Donald M. Travis, president of the station group, who oversees Telemundo's seven stations and local and national spot sales; and Peter J. Housmann II, president of business and corporate affairs, who is responsible for finance, legal affairs, human resources, affiliate relations, and engineering. At this time, no person of Hispanic heritage is either a member of the board of directors or in the highest echelons of the network. The main facilit ies, measuring fifty thousand square feet and containing five productions studios, are located in Hialeah, Florida, in the former building of the Hispanic American Broadcasting Corporation.

Luca Bentivoglio, host of Univisión's "Desde Hollywood," with Julio Iglesias.

The "Noticiero Telemundo-CNN" arrangement as discussed previously continues to date. However, Te-

TABLE 22.6
STATIONS AFFILIATED WITH THE TELEMUNDO SPANISH-LANGUAGE TELEVISION GROUP (LATE 1991)

FULL-POWER STATIONS		CITY	LOW-POWER STATIONS		CITY
WSNS	44	Chicago, IL	K59DB	59	Albuquerque, NM
KFWD	52	Dallas/Ft. Worth, TX	K11SF	11	Austin, TX
KUDB	59	Denver, CO	W19AH	19	Boston, MA
KMSG	59	Fresno, CA	K49AY	49	Cheyenne, WY
KLDO	27	Laredo, TX	K49CJ	49	Colorado Springs, CO
WTGI	61	Philadelphia, PA	K66EB	66	Corpus Christi, TX
			W13BF	13	Hartford, CT
			K46CS	46	Lubbock, TX
			K61FI	61	Modesto, CA
			W07BZ	7	Orlando, FL
			K64DR	64	Phoenix, AZ
			K52CK	52	Stockton, CA
			K14HR	14	Tucson, AZ
			K51BG	51	Victoria, TX
			W42AJ	42	Washington, DC
			K17CJ	17	Yakima, WA

lemundo also has its own news bureaus in Mexico, New York, Washington, and another in Miami for coverage of the Caribbean and Central America. To supplement its knowledge of the Hispanic community, various studies have been commissioned by Telemundo. The most recent study, conducted by the Research Network Co. in Tallahassee, Florida, was the "Telemundo Hispanic Opinion Poll: A National Survey of the U.S. Hispanic Viewpoint." Released in April 1991, this study inquired about Hispanics" opinions on numerous issues, including quality of life, economic concerns, discrimination, bilingual education, the political status of Puerto Rico, the free trade agreement with Mexico, and relations with Cuba.

A typical Telemundo week, which broadcasts approximately 126 hours between 7:00 A.M. and 1:00 A.M., consists of the program types and hours shown in Table 22.7.

The majority of domestically produced programs are news programs and talk, variety, and comedy-type shows. A recent fact sheet about Telemundo stated that "more than 50% of all programming aired on the network is produced in the United States at the company's production center in Hialeah, Florida, as well as at its stations in Los Angeles and Puerto Rico." It adds that "these programs are directly targeted to the needs and lifestyles of Hispanic Americans." When the network was launched, it was pointed out that U.S.-based programming especially for U.S. Hispanics was a key to Telemundo's long-term strategy as it sought to differentiate itself from Univisión and win the viewership of the more acculturated Hispanics. Currently, in addition to the national and local news programs and the "MTV Internacional," there are various programs that seek to meet these standards. The most prominent is "Cara a Cara" ("Face to Face") a talk show hosted by Cuban-born María Laria.

This program, Telemundo's own version of the "Oprah Winfrey Show," also covers controversial topics, such as abortion, drugs, sex, religion, politics, crime, and AIDS. Another domestic program is "Occurió Así" ("It Happened That Way"), a daily news-magazine show hosted by Enrique Gratas, a native of Argentina. It is an investigative news reporting program that utilizes the network's news bureaus in New York, Los Angeles, and Latin America to probe "the news behind the news that shapes our world." For late-night comic relief there is Argen-

TABLE 22.7
TELEMUNDO PROGRAMMING (MID-1991)

TYPE OF PROGRAM	WEEKDAY ORIGINAL	WEEKDAY REPEAT	SATURDAY ORIGINAL	SATURDAY REPEAT	SUNDAY ORIGINAL	SUNDAY REPEAT
Novelas (serials)	6.0	–	2.0	–	–	–
Talk/variety/comedy	3.0	1.0	2.0	–	6.0	1.0
Movies	6.0	–	9.5	–	6.0	–
News	1.5	0.5	1.0	–	–	–
Cartoons/children shows	–	–	–	–	1.0	–
Sports	–	–	2.5	–	1.0	–
Educational/religious	–	–	1.0	–	4.0	–

tine comedian Jorge Porcel's "A la Cama con Porcel" ("To Bed with Porcel"), a zany variety, interview, music, and humor show.

In mid-1991, Telemundo was also broadcasting "El Magnate" ("The Magnate"), another locally produced *soap opera,* this one in the form of a dramatic series with the backdrop of modern Miami. Except for "Cara a Cara" and the national news, the other programs originate in Florida.

Telemundo has also embarked on the production of specials. One of their more popular offerings is "Esta Noche con Usted" ("Tonight with You"), a four-times-a-year series of "in-depth, one-on-one interviews with noted Latino personalities in film, music, television, the performing arts, science and business." This one-hour program is currently hosted by a former Miss Universe, Chilean Cecilia Bolocco, who had also been coanchor of the "Noticiero Telemundo-CNN." "Columbus Day," another special for 1992, focused on the theme of the quicentennial anniversary of the navigator's voyage to the Americas. That voyage and related activities taking place in Spain during 1992 were also featured in the weekly cultural magazine "Línea América" ("America on the Line"). In addition, Telemundo produces or distributes spe-

cials such as "Carnaval Internacional de Miami" ("Miami International Carnival"), featuring musical and artistic highlights of the carnival; and the "Miss Hispanidad" ("Miss Hispania") beauty pageant, which draws contestants to the Miss Universe pageant. Other musical and variety specials are regularly imported from Venezuela, Mexico, Argentina, and Spain. Future plans for Telemundo include increased local productions, some of which may be exported to Latin America.

In November 1991, the Telemundo Group also became involved in a different type of venture—the collaborative promotion of the first Spanish-English bilingual credit card. The bank issuing the Visa and Master Cards is the People's Bank of Connecticut. Through the Telemundo stations, the public is informed that the network is part of this financial service targeted primarily to Hispanic Americans. The service is distinct in that it provides bilingual applications, customer information and assistance, as well as lower-than-average interest rates (13.9-16.9 percent).

Galavisión. The structure of Galavisión continues as described previously in terms of the principal directors, the Univisa, Inc., subsidiary companies, the owned and operated stations, as well as the affiliate linkages. The principal executives of Galavisión are the president, Jaime Dávila, a native of Mexico; vice president of broadcasting operations, Stuart Livingston, a native of the United States; and Vera González, a native of Guatemala, who is national director of cable operations. As of late 1991, the Galavisión network's affiliates in the United States consisted of three full-power UHF stations and seven low-power stations (Table 22.8). In addition, programming is provided via cable affiliations with 228 systems across the United States. Through its Mexican network, Galavisión's programs can also be seen most everywhere in that country as well as in Latin American, western Europe, and northern Africa.

In terms of programming, Galavisión executives have stated the network intends to tailor its offerings primarily to Hispanics of Mexican and Central American origin. They feel that Univisión and Telemundo attempt to reach too diverse an audience by broadcasting coast to coast. Galavisión is concentrating its efforts west of the Mississippi River, where its target audience typically resides. Thus, Galavisión provides

Andrés García and Rudy Rodríguez, Stars of Telemundo's Soap Opera, "El Magnate."

"unfiltered" Mexican television to the United States twenty-four hours a day, seven days a week. The major block of daily programs, thirteen hours, consists of news from the ECO system (Empresas de Comunicaciones Orbitales). Via satellite, ECO links a news production center in Mexico City to the rest of Latin America, Europe, and the United States. Movies are transmitted two hours per weekday and eighteen hours on weekends. Novelas (soap operas) take about four hours from Monday to Friday, but none of these or the other shows are made in the United States with Hispanic Americans. A typical Galavisión week consists of the types of programs and hours shown in table 22.9.

Galavisión's parent company, Televisa, sees the U.S. Hispanic market as one of the top growth areas for the next decade. Continued inroads into this market, especially the Mexican component, are to be expected.

Other Hispanic-Oriented Television Companies and Program Ventures. It can be expected that the aforementioned networks will capture the majority of the U.S. Hispanic audience in terms of general program-

Enrique Gratas, host of Telemundo's "Ocurrió Así."

TABLE 22.8
AFFILIATES OF THE GALAVISIÓN SPANISH-LANGUAGE TELEVISION GROUP (LATE 1991)

FULL-POWER STATIONS		CITY	LOW-POWER STATIONS		CITY
KTFH	49	Houston, TX	K58DJ	15	Bakersfield, CA
KWHY	22	Los Angeles, CA	K22BH	22	Corpus Cristi, TX
KSTV	57	Santa Barbara, CA	K06MB	6	Palm Springs, CA
			K67FE	67	Phoenix, AZ
			K17BY	17	San Antonio, TX
			K22DD	22	San Jose, CA
			K43CW	43	Tuscon, AZ

ming. However, several companies are seeking their own niche in this market. One of them is International TeleMúsica, Inc., which produces a show featuring international music videos, entertainment news, promotions and life-style segments. The programs, hosted by Alex Sellar, a Spaniard, and Pilar Isla, a native of Mexico, are produced in Hollywood using various California landscapes for settings. The target audience is Hispanic and Latin American youth. In 1990, Jesus Garza Rapport, executive vice president of Telemusica, started the company with full financial backing from Radio Programas de México (RPM). A Mexican company, RPM owns thirty and operates fifty radio stations in that country, and also owns one television station in Guadalajara, Mexico. The owners of RPM, Clemente Serna and family, are am ong the principal contenders for acquiring the Red 7, a group of Mexican government stations that are to be sold to the private sector. After experimenting during 1990, in RPM's Channel 6 in Guadalajara, TeleMúsica's first two-hour show in the United States was telecast from Miami on the Univisión network on September, 1991. That same month, distribution began for five separate one-hour shows, to air Monday through Friday, aimed at the Mexican market via the Red 7 network.

In October the weekday shows reached the five South American affiliates—Ecuador, El Salvador, Nicaragua, Guatemala, and Costa Rica—via the Pan American International Network Satellite launched by René Anselmo. Puerto Rican John Figueroa, vice president of affiliate relations, indicates that the shows are reaching their targeted youth audience, even beyond the locations where TeleMúsica is licensed, as evidenced by fan-club correspondence from all over Latin America.

Viva Television Network, Inc., "the first US Latino owned national cable television network," as proclaimed in an informational brochure of the company, is also seeking its niche in the U.S. Hispanic market. With a launch date set for June 1992, Viva's goal was to provide sixteen-hour daily Spanish-language (and some English-language) programs, such as documentaries, public affairs, music, sports, comedy, news, children's shows, art films, and movies catering to the eighteen- to forty-nine-year- old Hispanic audience. The chief executive officer and one of the founders is Mark Carreño, a native of Cuba who has served as executive director of the Latino Consortium, a nationally syndicated network based at KCET-TV, Los Angeles's Public Broadcasting Sta-

TABLE 22.9
GALAVISIÓN PROGRAMMING

TYPE OF PROGRAM	WEEKDAY	SATURDAY	SUNDAY
Novelas (serials)	4.0	–	–
Talk/variety/comedy	2.5	0.5	9.0
Movies	2.0	14.0	4.0
ECO news	13.5	9.5	5.0
"24 Horas" news	2.0	–	–
Sports	–	–	6.0

tion. Other founders and executive staff include chief operating officer Guillermo Rodríguez, a native of Puerto Rico who has worked with KMEX-TV and Lorimar Telepictures, and the vice president of international operations, Esteban de Icaza, of Mexican heritage, who was president of Azteca films, the foreign distribution company of the Mexican government. De Icaza's connections with that company and Imevisión, the Mexican government's educational television company, helped Viva obtain exclusive rights for telecasting selections from these companies" movie and video libraries, as well as Imevisión's newscasts. For program delivery, Viva subleased a transponder from the General Electric cable satellite and has agreements with multisystem cable operators in major Hispanic markets. The expected potential audience numbers from 300,000 to 1.5 million cable subscribers in the United States and Puerto Rico.

Home Box Office's Selecciones en Español (Selections in Spanish) is another significant venture to capture a niche in the U.S.-Hispanic television audience. In January 1989, this service was inaugurated to provide to HBO and Cinemax cable subscribers the option of Spanish-language audio for the telecast of motion pictures and even some sporting events, such as boxing matches. This service is the brainchild of Lara Concepción, a native of Mexico, who after eight years of trying was able to persuade HBO's executives that there was a viable Hispanic market for such a service. The turning point for Concepción came shortly after the box office success of the Hispanic-theme movie La Bamba. Following a market study that further convinced HBO that it could expand its business with the Spanish-speaking audience, HBO scheduled about ten Spanish-dubbed movies per month in 1989. At first, Selecciones en Español was provided to twenty HBO and Cinemax cable operators in five cities: El Paso, Miami, New York, San Antonio, and San Diego. Shortly thereafter, the service was requested by an additional thirty-five cable firms and later by another fifteen. By the end of 1989, HBO expanded its dubbed activities and was offering an average of twenty movies per month in Spanish. In 1991, Selecciones en Español was carried by 182 cable systems within the United States. HBO and Cinemax cable operators have three methods for delivering this service: a channel dedicated to Selecciones, a Second Audio Program (SAP) channel available for stereo television sets or videocassette recorders with multiple channel television sound (MTS), and an FM tuner in which the affiliates can transmit the second audio feed via an FM modulator (that is, cable subscribers listen to the Spanish soundtrack on their FM radio).

Following up on its formidable success with the U.S. Spanish-speaking audience, HBO in October 1991 launched HBO-Olé Pay-TV service in Latin America and the Caribbean Basin. This allows cable subscribers in over twenty Latin American countries prompt access in Spanish to HBO's movies and other shows, which are supplied by Warner Brothers, 20th Century Fox, and Columbia TriStar International Television, which provides feature films from Columbia Pictures and TriStar Pictures. (The sports cable network ESPN also began providing Spanish-language telecasts for the Latin American market in January 1991, but has yet to provide this service for U.S. Hispanic audiences.)

Long before HBO started applying the Sanish-language audio and related technologies to establish their particular niches in the Hispanic market, other Anglo television businesses had successfully used SAP to provide selected programs to their audiences.

María Laria, host of Telemundo's "Cara a Cara."

Laura Fabián, Star of Telemundo's Soap Opera "El Magnate."

In Los Angeles, one of the most successful ventures with Second Audio Program was Fox affiliate KTLA Channel 5. This station, now owned by the Tribune Broadcasting Company, was the pioneer in taking advantage of the Federal Communication Commission's 1984 rule authorizing broadcasters and cable providers to split up the single soundtrack into four audio channels. Henceforth, the first track was for the English audio, the second for stereo, the third for any alternate language, and the fourth for data transmission. In October 1984 KTLA broadcast the movie *2001: A Space Odyssey* and began offering the "The Love Boat," "McMillan & Wife," "Columbo," and "McCloud" in Spanish via the third audio channel. Dubbed editions of these programs were readily available because some Hollywood producers had a long-standing policy of dubbing many of their programs for their Latin American markets. Then, in February 1985, KTLA hired Analía Sarno-Riggle to be the Spanish interpreter of the "News at Ten," which airs Monday through Friday from 10:00 to 11:00 P.M. While in 1984 the pilot program with three other interpreters had not succeeded, the public response to Sarno-Riggle was formidable, as she developed an accurate technique to provide the Spanish-speaking viewers an adequate representation of what they were getting on the screen. She also strived to establish her own "audio personality," not just mimic the people she was interpreting.

Given her success, especially as evidenced by ratings among Hispanic viewers, by July 1985, KTLA had made Sarno-Riggle a regular staff employee and committed to continue the service. Sarno-Riggle, a native of Argentina, considers her own simulcast interpretations an alternative to Univisión's and Telemundo's news. She believes it offers access to a larger and more diverse amount of local news, which may be preferred by some assimilated Hispanics, or by those who simply wish to be informed on the same issues their neighbors are tuned into. Subsequently, KTLA assigned her to the Hollywood Christmas parade and various other specials. The station also expanded its offerings of Spanish-language audio for more of its prime-time programs, such as "Airwolf," "Magnum P.I.," and "Knight Rider." These programs were also among those dubbed for foreign distribution by their producers. Currently, KTLA schedules approximately twenty hours per week of Spanish-language audio.

Milagros Mendoza, Host of Telemundo's "Esta Noche con Usted."

The Hispanic audience ratings of KTLA did not go unnoticed by other stations and networks in Los Angeles and elsewhere. Second Audio Program has already been adopted by various other Anglo broadcasters in large Hispanic markets, including the Tribune Broadcasting Company's Chicago and New York stations WGN Channel 9 and WPIX Channel 11. Even some nonprofit stations began this language option. For example, KCET Channel 28 hired Sarno-Riggle for ten months to do the Spanish-language audio for "By the Year 2000," a weekly half-hour public affairs program for southern California. Also, under Sarno-Riggle's guidance, on January 14, 1991, New York station WNET Channel 13 began the second audio for "The MacNeil/Lehrer News-Hour." Presently, Bolivian native Oscar Ordenes is the Spanish-language voice for this show, which in the United States is carried by thirty-three Public Broadcasting System stations either via Second Audio Program or as a separate show repeated later in the evening. In addition, thirty-two cities in twenty-six Latin American countries receive videos of this version of the "MacNeil/Lehrer News Hour" by way of the United States Information Agency's Worldnet information program.

Finally, English-language musical programs specifically oriented toward U.S. Hispanics are also making their debut. In June 1991, MTV launched "Second Generation," a half-hour mix of videos, comedy, and entertainment news aimed primarily at second-generation Hispanics in the United States. Hosted by New York Puerto Rican Andy Panda and Colombian Tony Moran, this program is being broadcast by thirty-one primarily English-language stations from the east to the west coast.

References

Bielby, William and Denise Bielby. *The 1987 Hollywood Writers' Report: A Survey of Ethnic, Gender, and Age Employment Practices.* Commissioned by the Writers Guild of America, West, Los Angeles, Calif., 1987.

——, and Denise Bielby. *The 1989 Hollywood Writers' Report: Unequal Access, Unequal Pay.* Commissioned by the Writers Guild of America, West. Los Angeles, Calif., 1989.

"The Coming of Age of Hispanic Broadcasting: Special Report." *Broadcasting,* April 3, 1989.

Chacón, Ramón. "The Chicano Immigrant Press in Los Angeles: The Case of *El Heraldo de México,* 1916-1920." *Journalism History,* 4(2), 48-49.

Cortés, Carlos. "The Mexican American Press" in *The Ethnic Press in the United States: A Historical Analysis and Handbook,* edited by S. M. Miller. New York: Greenwood Press, 1987.

Downing, John D. H. "Ethnic Minority Radio in the United States. *The Howard Journal of Communications.* 2 (Spring 1990), 135-148.

González, Juan. "Forgotten Pages: Spanish-language Newspapers in the Southwest. *Journalism History*, 4 (February 1977), 50-51.

Greenberg, Bradley S., Michael Burgoon, Judee Burgoon, and Felipe Korzenny. *Mexican Americans and the Mass Media.* Norwood, N.J.: Ablex, 1983.

Griswold del Castillo, Richard. "The Mexican Revolution and the Spanish-language Press in the Borderlands." *Journalism History*, 4 (February 1977), 42-47.

Gutiérrez, Felix F. "Spanish-language Media in America: Background, Resources, History." *Journalism History*, 4 (February, 1977), 34-41.

———, and Jorge R. Schement. *Spanish-language Radio in the Southwestern United States.* Austin: Center for Mexican American Studies, Monograph No. 5, University of Texas, 1979.

"Hispanic Owners Band Together." *Broadcasting*, May 20, 1991.

Lamb, Blaine P. "The Convenient Villain: The Early Cinema Views of the Mexican American." *Journal of the West*, 14 (April 1975), 75-81.

"Mac Tichenor: Banking on Hispanic Radio." *Broadcasting*, May 13, 1991.

Pettit, Arthur G. *Images of the Mexican American in Fiction and Film.* College Station: Texas A&M University Press, 1980.

Schement Jorge R. and Ricardo Flores. "The Origins of Spanish-language Radio: The Case of San Antonio, Texas." *Journalism History*, 4 (February 1977), 56-58.

Straton, Porter A. *The Territorial Press of New Mexico, 1834-1912.* Albuquerque: University of New Mexico Press, 1969.

Subervi-Vélez, Federico A., "Spanish-language Daily Newspapers and the 1984 Elections." *Journalism Quarterly*, 65 (March 1988), 678-685.

———. "Interactions between Latinos and Anglos on Prime-time Television: A Case Study of 'Condo.'" In *Income and Status Differences between White and Minority americans: A Persistent Inequality.* Lewiston, N.Y.:Edwin Mellen Press, 1990.

Veciana-Suárez, Ana. *Hispanic Media, USA .* Washington, D.C.: The Media Institute, 1987.

———. *Hispanic Media: Impact and Influence .* Washington, D.C.: The Media Institute, 1990.

Wilson, Clint, Jr. and Félix Gutiérrez, Felix F. *Minorities and the Media: Diversity and the End of Mass Communication.* Beverly Hills, Calif.: Sage, 1985.

Federico Subervi

Science

The story of Hispanics in the sciences is really a bittersweet tale of outstanding achievement, on the one hand, and underrepresentation of U.S. Hispanics in math and science careers, on the other. Hispanics have contributed to world scientific and classical learning since the Middle Ages in Spain, developed excellent medical schools in Spain and Spanish America, and founded the first universities in the New World. The American Indian tradition, which enriched the culture of the Spanish and Europeans that settled in the New World, was also one of achievement in such sciences as astronomy and horticulture. However, today the record of Hispanics born or raised in the United States shows high dropout rates, and low college admission and retention rates, with dismally few Hispanic students going into math and science. While there are many Hispanic scientists, engineers, and mathematicians, many of these were born and educated in Spain and Spanish America and have come to the United States to benefit from our excellent graduate schools or the excellent research institutions and industries here that can provide the intellectual communities, resources, and salaries that their own countries cannot. Many of these scientists remain in the United States, contribute greatly to world knowledge, become citizens here, and enrich all of our lives in and out of the Hispanic communities.

Deeply ingrained in Spanish and Hispanic cultures are the attitudes about the natural world and the sciences that the Arabs brought to the Iberian Peninsula during their eight hundred years of living there, from the beginning of the eighth century until 1492. Arab civilization was a crucial link with the classical learning of the Greeks, whose work they translated, advanced, and began to introduce to medieval Europe. Furthermore, the Arabs established universities, academies, and seats of learning long before such institutions were established in Europe.

In extending their commerce to the far reaches of Asia and Africa, they learned many things from the cultures that they encountered. The expansion and domination by Islam of lands and peoples far and wide during the Middle Ages was built on the bedrock of solid technological and scientific knowledge. In Spain, the Arab cities of Córdoba, Sevilla and Toledo became centers of learning that drew students from the rest of western Europe. Arabs were the inventors of algebra, and they were able to apply the principles of mathematics to everything that they did, including architecture, design, and landscaping. Originating in arid climates, they became superb horticulturists and agronomers, and developed systems of water management and irrigation that still survive in many parts of the Americas today. Their advances in the medical sciences even extended to mastering delicate corneal operations. All of this and much more is part of the Arab contribution to Hispanic culture everywhere.

The native peoples of the Americas had also advanced scientific knowledge and its application long before the arrival of the Europeans. In particular, the native Americans were outstanding horticulturists and agronomists. Over thousands of years, they took the wild plants of the Americas and developed them into foodstuffs that eventually would revolutionize the diet of the whole planet. The native Americans took a wild grass and a variety of tubers and developed them into foods that would become staples for millions upon millions of people around the world: corn and potatoes. In addition, they developed myriad varieties of other foods that are common parts of our diets today, including beans, tomatoes, squash, and many fruits. The native Americans were ecologists and land and game managers who respected the wildlife and all of the natural world in everything that they did. Only recently has modern man really begun to learn from them in this regard, now that we are suffering so much from the degradation of the natural environment that has come with wasteful industrial overdevelopment and pollution.

Native Americans throughout the hemisphere were attentive astronomers who arrived at complex calculations that even modern scientists cannot achieve by using the types of instruments that were available to these native peoples. Achievements by such cultures as the Mayan even included the construction of modern-looking observatories. The Mayan mathematicians even invented the concept of zero. Little is known of the medical advances and the medicines developed from plants of the Americas by these peoples, except what little has come down to us in the techniques and folk medicines of such healers as *curanderos* (folk healers). We cannot be sure today how many scientific and medical advances were achieved by the peoples of the Americas before the arrival of the Spaniards, for these Europeans burned the Mayan books and destroyed temples with hieroglyphs throughout Mesoamerica and the Andes, the seats of highest learning, in their fervor to convert the "Indians" to Christianity.

Today there are many outstanding universities and research institutions in the Hispanic world, especially in Argentina, Chile, Cuba, Mexico, Puerto Rico, and Spain. But many of the countries in Spanish America suffer from economic and industrial underdevelopment as a result of at least four centuries of European and U.S. colonialism and exploitation of their natural resources, including the export and exploitation of their human resources, be they laborers or intellectuals. Many foreign students are drawn to the excellent graduate schools of the United States, quite often with scholarships and support from their home countries. After becoming scientists or doctors here, it is often quite difficult for them to return to their homelands because of the superior research facilities and resources here, and the greater opportunities for teaching and making a comfortable living within the relatively prosperous economy of the United States.

Also, the scientific and scholarly community of the United States is very rich, drawing on scientists and teachers from throughout the world and boasting the most advanced communications, publications, and conferences. Many other doctors and scientists from Spanish America and Spain, without having been trained in the United States, are drawn to these benefits and come to make their homes here. Then, too, political disruptions have also precipitated the immigration to the United States of many intellectuals and scientists from Spanish America and Spain: the Spanish Civil War, the Mexican and Cuban Revolutions, and periodic violent dictatorships in Argentina, Chile, Nicaragua, El Salvador, and elsewhere.

What is certain is that the United States has benefited greatly from this "brain drain," often at the expense of the home countries that, as Third World nations, direly need physicians, scientists, and teachers. The Hispanic communities within the United States have always benefited as well from this continued source of renewal of creative and intellectual membership. The Hispanic medical and scientific community has always actively contributed to community life in the large urban areas of Hispanic concentration. In fact, it is precisely Hispanic community life that quite often draws these doctors and scientists to settle in such communities as Houston, Los Angeles, Miami, New York, or San Antonio. The Houston Medical Center, for example, is not only replete with doctors and researchers from throughout the Hispanic world, but it has also become one of the principal medical centers for all of Latin America.

While there are many doctors and researchers that have moved to the United States from Spain and Spanish America—thus proving that Hispanics can indeed become successful doctors and scientists—Hispanics raised and educated in the United States have had a dismal record of entering the medical and scientific professions. In various chapters of *The Hispanic Almanac* many statistics and reasons are provided to explain the high dropout rates and low college admission and graduation rates of Hispanics. The rate of their going on to and graduating from graduate and medical schools is far worse. All of the effects of poverty, discrimination, and culture clash, poor schools and educational tracking, as well as many other barriers have resulted in a serious lack of doctors and scientists coming out of the Hispanic communities of the United States.

There are programs and organizations today that aim to provide greater opportunities for Hispanics in these fields. And there are outstanding teachers, such as Jaime Escalante, who are proving that students even from the poorest and most crime-ridden neighborhoods can be outstanding achievers in math and science. Even the College Board has taken on as its number one priority equity in admissions and graduation rates for minorities by the year 2000.

Despite these problems, the scientists and doctors that Hispanic communities have produced, and the ones that have come from their homelands to make their careers in the United States, have achieved a record of outstanding success, working within the most respected hospitals, universities, laboratories, and research institutes we have to offer. Below are just a few of these outstanding researchers.

✳ PROMINENT HISPANIC SCIENTISTS

Carlos Alberto Abel (1930-)
Medicine

Born in Argentina on May 7, 1930, Abel graduated from the medical school of the University of Buenos Aires in 1957. He began his career at the Children's Hospital in Buenos Aires, but by 1959 had moved to Providence, Rhode Island, as an intern at St. Joseph's Hospital. Through years of residencies and further scientific study in Maryland, California, and England, Abel became a specialist in biophysics and genetics and became a noted immunologist. From 1970 to 1984, he taught at the University of Colorado Medical Center, rising to the rank of full professor. Since 1984, he has been a senior scientist in immunology at the Institute for Cancer Research of the Medical Research Institute of San Francisco. His research has centered on lymphocytes and the relationships of their components with various immunological functions. In particular, he has been researching the AIDS virus and how to combat it. He is a member of the University of California Task Force on AIDS.

Daniel Acosta, Jr. (1945-)
Pharmacology

Born on March 25, 1945, in El Paso, Texas, Acosta received his B.S. degree from the University of Texas in 1968 and his Ph.D. degree in pharmacology from the University of Kansas in 1974. He began as an assistant professor at the University of Kansas, and is currently a full professor at the University of Texas. He has been an Eli Lilly Centennial Fellow and a Ford Fellow. Acosta's research is in cell toxicology, particularly studying the effects of drugs and toxicants at the cellular and subcellular levels; he is particularly interested in heart cells and injury to them.

José Ramón Alcalá (1940-)
Anatomy, Biochemistry

Born in Ponce, Puerto Rico, on May 1, 1940, Alcalá began his high school education in Santurce, Puerto Rico, and finished it in Waynesville, Missouri, where he graduated in 1957. His stepfather, a career army man had been transferred to Fort Leonard Wood in 1956. Alcalá went on to receive his B.A. and M.A. degrees in zoology from the University of Missouri in 1964 and 1966, respectively. He received his Ph.D. degree in anatomy from the University of Illinois Medical Center in 1972. Since 1972, he has taught and conducted research at the School of Medicine at Wayne State University, where he has been a full professor since 1987. Since 1990, he has been the director of the gross anatomy programs of the School of Medicine. Alcalá specializes in the anatomy of the eye, studying the biochemistry and immuno-chemistry of lens plasma membranes. This research has had great methodological and conceptual impact in the field of lens research for its first clear delineation of the protein composition of lens fiber plasma membranes. His continued work in this area has had impact on research on cataracts.

Kenneth B. Alonso (1942-)
Pathology, Nuclear Medicine

Born in Tampa, Florida, on November 26, 1942, Alonso received his A.B. degree from Princeton University in 1964 and his M.D. degree from the University of Florida in 1968. He has worked as an intern, resident, and pathologist at various hospitals around the country from 1968 to 1976. In 1976, he became the director of laboratory procedures for Upjohn South Company in Georgia, and from 1978 to 1984, he worked as chief of staff and pathology for two hospitals. Since 1984, he has been the director of Lab Atlanta in Riverdale, Georgia. His research interests include immunological disorders, especially receptors, membrane transport, human tumor stem cell assay, and monoclonal antibodies.

Anne Maino Alvarez (1941-)
Plant Pathology

Born on April 14, 1941, in Rochester, Minnesota, Alvarez received her B.S. degree from Stanford University in 1963 and her M.S. and Ph.D. degrees from the University of California, Berkeley, in 1966 and 1972, respectively. Since that time she has worked at the University of Argentina in Nequen, from 1969 to 1970, and at the University of Hawaii, where she is currently a researcher and educator in plant pathology. Alvarez has done field research in Argentina, Costa Rica, and Mexico on bacterial diseases in fruits and crops and on epidemiology and disease control. She has particularly studied the orchard and postharvest diseases of the papaya.

Luis Walter Alvarez (1911-)
Experimental Physics

Born in San Francisco, California, on June 13, 1911, Luis Alvarez has become one of this country's most distinguished and respected physicists. With B.S. (1932) and Ph.D. (1936) degrees from the University of Chicago, Alvarez has also received a number of honorary degrees from universities in the United States and abroad. He developed most of his work at the University of California, Berkeley, from 1936 to the present; he is now professor emeritus. From 1954 to 1959 and from 1976 to 1978, he served as associate director of the prestigious Lawrence Berkeley Lab. In 1986, Alvarez was awarded the Nobel Prize in physics; he has also received the Collier Trophy (1946), the Scott Medal (1953), the Einstein Medal (1961), the National Medal of Science (1964), and many other awards. Alvarez has been a pioneer in particle physics, astrophysics, ophthalmic and television optics, geophysics, and air navigation.

Angeles Alvariño de Leira (1916-)
Marine Biology

Born on October 3, 1916, in El Ferrol, Spain, Alvarino received her master's (1941) and doctorate degrees in chemistry and sciences in 1951 and 1967, respectively, from the University of Madrid. From 1941 to 1957, she worked at universities and institutes in Spain as a biological oceanographer; in 1957, she began her career in the United States as a biologist at the Scripps Institute of Oceanography of the University of California, La Jolla. In 1970, she assumed her current position of fishery research biologist at the National Marine Fisheries Service in La Jolla. Alvarino has held concurrent positions at universities in England, Mexico, and Venezuela, and she has been a Fulbright and a National Science Foundation fellow a number of times. Alvarino has been the discoverer of eleven new species of chaetognatha and three new species of syphonophorae, which are her specialty, along with zooplankton and medusae.

Dr. Angeles Alvariño de Leira.

Ralph Amado (1932-)
Theoretical Physics

Born in Los Angeles on November 13, 1932, Amado received his B.S. degree from Stanford University in 1954 and his Ph.D. degree from Oxford University, England, in 1957. After graduating, he began his career as a research associate at the University of Pennsylvania and has remained at that institution; his current title is professor of physics. Besides research and teaching duties at Penn, Amado has worked as a consultant to the Arms Control and Disarmament Agency. His specialties are theoretical nuclear physics, many-body problems, particle physics and scattering theory.

Elías Amador (1932-)
Medicine, Pathology

Born in Mexico City on June 8, 1932, and educated at the Central Mexico University (B.S. degree, 1959) and the National University of Mexico (M.D. degree, 1956), immediately after becoming a doctor Amador relocated to the United States and developed his career here at various hospitals and universities. Since 1972, he has served as professor and chairman

of the Department of pathology of the Charles R. Drew Postgraduate Medical School, professor at the University of Southern California, and chief of pathology of the Martin Luther King, Jr., General Hospital, all three positions held concurrently. He has been a teaching fellow at Harvard Medical School (1957-58) and at the Boston University School of Medicine (1959-60). His research concerns the development of accurate and sensitive methods for diagnosis and detection of disease.

Francisco José Aisle (1934-)
Genetics

Born on March 12, 1934, in Madrid, Spain, Aisle received his B.S. degree from the University of Madrid in 1955 and his M.S. and Ph.D. degrees from Columbia University in 1963 and 1964, respectively. Since 1964, he has worked as a researcher and professor at various universities and institutes. Since 1974, he has been a professor of genetics at the University of California, Davis. He is the associate editor of *Molecular Evolution and Paleobiology*, a research journal. He also serves as the chairman of boards at the National Academy of Sciences and the National

Research Council. His research concentrates on evolution, population genetics, and fitness of natural and experimental populations, among other subjects.

Alberto Vinicio Baez (1912-)
Physics

Born in Puebla, Mexico, on November 15, 1912, Baez received his B.S. degree from Drew University in 1933, his M.A. degree from Syracuse University in 1935, and his Ph.D. degree from Stanford University in 1950. Over his long career he has taught and conducted research at various universities, including Cornell, Drew, Stanford, Wagner (New York), and Redlands and Harvey Mudd (both in California). Between 1961 and 1974, he worked for UNESCO in New York and Paris in science education. He has also held various international board and committee positions, and from 1974 to 1978, served as the chairman of the Committee on Teaching Sciences of the International Council of Science Unions. Since 1984, he has been chairman emeritus of Community Education, International Union for the Conservation of Nature and Natural Resources, Glantz, Switzerland. In 1991, the S.P.I.E. conferred the Dennis Gabor Award on Baez and his coresearcher, Paul Kirkpatrick, "in recognition of their important role in the development of x-ray imaging optics. Their early discoveries that grazing incidence optical systems could be used to focus x-rays gave birth to the field of x-ray imaging optics. . . . Their pioneering contributions to this field include the Kirkpatrick-Baez x-ray double reflecting imaging system. The Kirkpatrick-Baez Lamar x-ray telescope has been approved for flight on the Freedom Space Station." In his research, Baez specialized in x-ray radiation, optics, and microscopy, as well as in science and environmental education.

Teresa Bernárdez (1931-)
Medicine, Psychiatry

See Chapter 13

Caridad Borras (1942-)
Radiological Physics

Born in Spain on February 18, 1942, Borras received her M.S. and Ph.D. degrees from the University of Barcelona in 1964 and 1974, respectively. Until 1966, she worked in Barcelona in hospitals; in 1967, she relocated to Thomas Jefferson University in Philadelphia as an assistant physicist. Since 1974, she has served as a radiological physicist at the West Coast Cancer Foundation. Since 1982, she has also been a clinical assistant professor at the University of California. Borras studies the radioembryopathological effects of high LET nuclides, as well as the physics of diagnostic radiology and radiation therapy.

César A. Cáceres (1927-)
Medicine, Computer Science

Born on April 9, 1927, in Puerto Cortés, Honduras, Cáceres received his B.S. and M.D. degrees from Georgetown University in 1949 and 1953, respectively. He then served as an intern and resident in Boston hospitals, but returned as a fellow in cardiology to George Washington University from 1956 to 1960, and from 1960 to 1971 he moved up the ranks there from assistant professor of medicine to full professor and department chairman. From 1960 to 1969, he was also chief of the Medical Systems Development Lab for the United States Public Health Service. In 1971, he founded his own company, Clinical Systems Associates, for which he still serves as president to date; he also worked concurrently as a professor of electrical engineering at the University of Maryland from 1971 to 1976. Cáceres specializes in electrocardiography, cardiology, medical diagnosis, and computers in medicine.

Alberto V. Baez.

Marta Cancio (1928-)
Biochemistry

Born in San Sebastián, Puerto Rico, on December 8, 1928, Cancio received her B.S. degree from the University of Puerto Rico in 1949 and her M.S. and Ph.D. degrees from the University of Missouri in 1952 and 1954, respectively. In 1954, she began as an associate biochemist at the University of Puerto Rico School of Medicine and moved up the ranks. Since 1966, she has served as the supervisory research chemist for the Veterans Administration Hospital, and since 1971, as associate professor of biochemistry and nutrition at the University of Puerto Rico Medical School. Her research concerns lipid and protein chemistry, malabsorption, and immunochemistry.

Graciela Candelas (1922-)
Molecular Biology

Born in Puerto Rico in 1922, Candelas received her B.S. degree from the University of Puerto Rico in 1944, her M.S. degree from Duke University in 1959, and her Ph.D. degree from the University of Miami in 1966. Since 1966, she has moved up the ranks at the University of Puerto Rico; since 1971, she has been a full professor of cell and molecular biology there. She has also held visiting and concurrent positions at the University of Syracuse, Rockefeller University, City University of New York, and the Medical College of Georgia. She was given the Special Science Award by the Puerto Rican Institute in New York in 1985 and the Distinguished Alumnus Award by the Alumni Organization of the University of Puerto Rico in 1988. One of her research interests is fibroin synthesis and its regulation using a pair of glands from the spider *Nephila clavipes*.

Oscar A. Candia (1935-)
Physiology, Biophysics

Born in Buenos Aires, Argentina, on April 30, 1935, Candia received his M.D. degree from the University of Buenos Aires in 1959. After working as a researcher in Buenos Aires, he relocated to the University of Louisville in 1964 as a research associate and moved up the ranks there to full professorship. Since 1984, he has been professor of opthalmology and physiology at Mt. Sinai School of Medicine in New York. He received career development awards from 1966 to 1971 from the National Institutes of Health. He is an associate editor of *Investigations in Opthalmology and Visual Science*, a research journal. In 1985, he won the Alcon award. His principal research concern is ion transport in biological membranes.

Graciela Candelas.

Fernando Caracena (1936-)
Atmospheric Physics, Physics

Born on March 13, 1936, in El Paso, Texas, Caracena received his B.S. degree from the University of Texas at El Paso in 1958 and his M.S. and Ph.D. degrees from Case Western Reserve in 1966 and 1968, respectively. From 1958 to 1961, he worked as an atmospheric physicist for the Department of Defense at White Sands Missile Range, and from 1969 to 1976, he worked as an assistant professor at Metropolitan State College, Denver, Colorado. Since 1976, he has been working as an atmospheric physicist at the Environmental Research Labs of the National Oceanic and Atmospheric Administration. His research concerns air safety, especially clear air turbulence, low altitude wind shear, and the meteorology of wind-shear-related aircraft accidents.

Mary Janet M. Cárdenas (1942-)
Biochemistry

Born in Miami, Oklahoma, on January 31, 1942, Cárdenas received her B.A. degree from Oklahoma State University in 1963 and her M.S. and Ph.D. degrees from the University of Illinois in 1965 and

1967, respectively. From 1967 through 1981, she taught at various universities, achieving the rank of associate professor of chemistry at the University of North Carolina. Since 1981, she has been health science administrator at the National Eye Institute of the National Institutes of Health. Her research concerns the sensorimotor aspects of vision, especially culomotor disorders.

Manuel Cardona (1934-)
Physics

Born in Barcelona, Spain, on September 7, 1934, Cardona received his B.S. degree in physics from the University of Barcelona in 1955 and his Ph.D. degree in applied physics from Harvard University in 1959. After graduation, he worked until 1964 at RCA Laboratories in Switzerland and in Princeton, New Jersey. Since then he has been a researcher associated with various universities and institutes, most notably as professor of physics at Brown from 1964 to 1971, and, since 1971, as the director of the Max-Planck-Institut for Solid State Research in Stuttgart, Germany. In 1967, Cardona became a naturalized citizen of the United States. He is the author of some seven hundred scientific publications in journals and nine

monographs on solid-state physics. Among his many awards are the Grand Cross of Alfonso el Sabio from Spain (1987), the Príncipe de Asturias Prize from Spain (1988), and the Kronland Medal from Czechoslovakia (1988). He is a member of both the American and European Academies of Science.

David Cardús (1922-)
Cardiology, Biomathematics

Born on August 6, 1922, in Barcelona, Spain, Cardús received his M.D. degree from the University of Barcelona in 1949. He did his internship and residency in Barcelona and postgraduate work in cardiology and physiology there. In 1960, Cardús relocated to Texas and embarked on a career at the Baylor University College of Medicine as a professor and researcher in cardiology and rehabilitation. He moved up the ranks to his present positions: professor of physiology, professor of rehabilitation, head of the cardiopulmonary lab, and director of biomath. Among his many awards are a Gold Medal from the Sixth International Congress on Physical Medicine in 1972, a Licht Award for Excellence in Science Writing in 1980, and the Narcis Monturiol Medal from Catalunya, Spain, in 1984. He has researched

Manuel Cardona.

David Cardús.

experimental exercise and respiratory physiology, mathematical and computer applications to the study of physiological systems, and rehabilitation medicine.

Alberto Castro (1933-)
Biochemistry, Endocrinology

Born on November 15, 1933, in San Salvador, El Salvador, Castro received his B.S. degree from the University of Houston in 1958 and his Ph.D. degree in biological chemistry from the University of El Salvador in 1962. He moved up the ranks from assistant to full professor at the University of El Salvador from 1958 to 1966. From 1966 to 1970, he was an NIH fellow at the University of Oregon, and from 1970 to 1973, he was a lab director at the United Medical Lab. From 1973 to 1977, he once again moved up the ranks to full professor of medicine, pathology and microbiology at the University of Miami Medical School. Since 1973, he has been the director of the Hormone Research Lab there. His primary work is in carbohydrate biochemistry, metabolism, and modes of action, and hormone mechanisms and their interrelationship to hypertension.

George Castro (1939-)
Physical Chemistry

Born on March 23, 1939, in Los Angeles, California, Castro received his B.S. degree in chemistry from the University of California, Los Angeles, in 1960 and his Ph.D. degree in physical chemistry from the University of California, Riverside, in 1965. He has been a postdoctoral fellow at the University of Pennsylvania, Cal Tech, and Dartmouth, but has worked as a researcher for IBM since 1968. Since 1986, he has been the manager of Synchrotron Studies for IBM at the Almaden Research Center. In 1978, he received the Outstanding Innovation Award from IBM, and in 1990, he was elected a fellow of the American Physical Society. Castro is the discoverer of the mechanism of the intrinsic charge carrier of organic photoconductors. Years later, such materials in the form of organic polymeric films became the basis for flexible photoconductors that are used in photocopying machines and high-speed printers. Castro assumed the leadership of the physical sciences of the IBM San Jose Research Lab in 1975, three years after its formation. He has built the organization into one that is world-famous for its scientific discoveries. These include the discovery of the first superconducting polymer, novel organic metals and superconductors, high-resolution laser techniques, and new methods of investigating magnetic materials.

Peter Castro (1943-)
Zoology, Parasitology

Born on July 20, 1943, in Mayaguez, Puerto Rico, Castro received his B.S. degree from the University of Puerto Rico at Mayaguez in 1964, and his M.S. and Ph.D. degrees in zoology from the University of Hawaii in 1966 and 1969, respectively. From 1970 to 1975, he worked as a teacher and researcher in the biology department of the University of Puerto Rico at Mayaguez. Since 1975, he has been an associate professor of Biological Sciences at California State Polytechnical Institute in Pomona. Castro has been a fellow and visiting researcher at Stanford, the Smithsonian Institute, and Moss Landing Marine Labs. Castro's research concerns ecological, physiological, and behavioral aspects of marine symbiosis.

Asunción Elena Charola (1942-)
Analytical Chemistry, Physical Chemistry

Born in Argentina on February 23, 1942, Charola received her Ph.D. degree in analytical chemistry from the National University of La Plata in 1974. After receiving a fellowship to New York University from 1974 to 1976, Charola remained in the United States as an assistant professor of chemistry at Manhattan College from 1978 to 1981 and at the Metropolitan Museum of Art from 1981 to 1985. Since 1985, she has been an associate scientist at the ICCROM in Rome, Italy. Her research concerns solid-state chemistry, polymorphism, and x-ray crystallography, among other subjects.

Guillermo B. Cintrón (1942-)
Medicine

Born on March 28, 1942, in San Juan, Puerto Rico, Cintrón received his B.S. degree from the University of Puerto Rico in 1963 and his M.D. degree from Loyola-Stritch School of Medicine in Chicago in 1967. After residencies in Washington, D.C., Cintrón returned to Puerto Rico, where from 1975 to 1983, he taught and conducted cardiac research at the University of Puerto Rico Medical School. Since 1983, he has

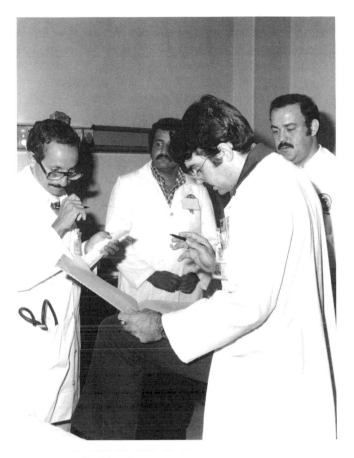

Guillermo B. Cintrón.

been an associate professor at the University of Southern Florida School of Medicine. Since 1987, he has been the associate director of cardiology there. His principal research concerns heart disease and its causes and prevention.

Antonio E. Colás (1928-)
Biochemistry

Born on June 22, 1928, in Muel, Spain, Colás received his B.S. degree from the University of Zaragoza in 1951 and his M.D. degree from the University of Madrid in 1953. In 1955, he received his Ph.D. degree in biochemistry from the University of Edinburgh in Scotland. Following his studies at Edinburgh, Colás took various teaching and research positions in Spain, Colombia, and finally, in 1960, in the United States at the University of Oregon Medical School, where he served as professor of obstetrics and gynecology until 1968. Since then, he has been professor of obstetrics and gynecology and physiological chemistry at the University of Wisconsin Medical School. His research interests include the biochemistry and metabolism of steroid hormones; he has published more than eighty research articles.

Antonio E. Colás.

Julio Cordero (1923-)
Fluid Engineering

Born on January 10, 1923, in San José, Costa Rica, Cordero received his B.S. degree from Wayne State University in 1948 and his M.S. degree from the University of Minnesota in 1951. From 1951 to 1976, he worked as a research scientist at a number of universities and industries. Since 1976, he has been chief engineer at the Magnetohydrodynamics Research Facility of the Massachusetts Institute of Technology. His principal research concerns shock wave phenomena and supersonic and hypersonic aerodynamics.

Francisco Dallmeier (1953-)
Wildlife Biology

Born on February 15, 1953, in Caracas, Venezuela, Francisco Dallmeier received his licentiate in biology from the Central University of Venezuela in 1979 and his M.S. and Ph.D. degrees in wildlife biology from the University of Colorado in 1984 and 1986, respectively. From 1973 to 1977, he was the director of the La Salle Museum of Natural History and a member of the ecology team of the Institute of Tropical

Zoology of the Central University of Venezuela. From 1977 to 1986, he worked as a biologist and researcher in various positions in Venezuela and the United States. Since 1986, he has worked for the Smithsonian Institute in Washington, D.C., for which he has served as director of the Man and the Biosphere Biological Diversity Program since 1989. In that capacity, he coordinates field biodiversity research and training in Bolivia, Brazil, Peru, Ecuador, Guatemala, Panama, Puerto Rico, the Virgin Islands, Tennessee, and Washington, D.C. His major research focuses on the integration of biological diversity and natural resources and conservation and management programs. His latest studies concern neotropical waterfowl and wetlands ecology and management.

Henry Frank Díaz (1948-)
Atmospheric Sciences

Born in Cuba on July 15, 1948, Díaz received his B.S. degree from Florida State University in 1971, his M.S. degree from the University of Miami in 1974, and his Ph.D. degree in geology and climatology from the University of Colorado in 1985. From 1974 through 1985, Díaz worked as a meteorologist at the Environmental Data Service, the National Climate Center,

Francisco Dallmeier.

disorders, including testing for new treatments. He is also a specialist in cross-cultural psychiatry as it concerns somatization traits across different cultures.

George Castro.

José Alberto Fernández-Pol (1943-)
Medicine

Born on March 17, 1943, in Buenos Aires, Fernández received his M.D. degree from the University of Buenos Aires in 1969. From then until 1971, he was affiliated with various hospitals in Buenos Aires; in 1971, he became a resident physician at the State University of New York, Buffalo. After that he worked at various microbiology and cancer research labs in the United States, notably at the National Cancer Institute of the National Institutes of Health from 1975 to 1977. In 1977, he began as an assistant professor of medicine at St. Louis University; since 1985, he has been a full professor there. Fernández's research concerns growth control mechanisms in normal and cancerous cells, oncogenies.

and the Environmental Research Lab. Since 1985, he has been acting director of the Climate Research Program of the National Oceanic and Atmospheric Administration. In 1977 and 1983, he received awards for outstanding achievement at the Environmental Research Lab. Díaz researches climatology and climatic variation, developing long-term historical climatic data bases.

Javier I. Escobar (1943-)
Psychiatry, Psychopharmacology

Born on July 26, 1943, in Medellín, Colombia, Escobar received his M.D. degree from the University of Antioquia in Colombia in 1967; in 1969, he became a resident at the University of Minnesota Hospitals, and by 1976, had attained the rank of associate professor of psychiatry there. From 1976 to 1979, he worked at the University of Tennessee, and in 1979, he became an associate professor of psychiatry at the University of California, Los Angeles. Today he is a full professor at that institution. Escobar has worked with many hospitals and numerous research projects on a regional and national level. His research concerns clinical projects in schizophrenia and affective

José Alberto Fernández-Pol.

Jorge Fischbarg.

Jorge Fischbarg (1935-)
Opthalmology

Born on August 14, 1935, in Buenos Aires, Argentina, Fischbarg received his early education there and graduated with a B.S. degree from the Colegio Nacional de Buenos Aires in 1953. He received his M.D. degree from the University of Buenos Aires in 1962 and his Ph.D. degree in physiology from the University of Chicago in 1971. From 1961 to 1969, he held various postdoctoral fellowships and traineeships in Buenos Aires, Louisville, Kentucky, and Chicago. From 1970 to the present, he has pursued a career in physiology (ophthalmology) research and teaching at Columbia University. Since 1984, he has been head of the Membrane Biology Laboratory (Eye Research Division) at Columbia. He has received research awards from and worked closely with the National Institutes of Health, and has been a visiting scientist in France (1974 and 1978) and England (1976-1977). In 1986, he was awarded the Alcon Recognition Award from the Alcon Research Institute. Fischbarg has been a member of the editorial board of *Experimental Eye Research* since 1986. His research interests include the transport of fluid and electrolytes across epithelial membranes, corneal physiology, and molecular biophysics of water channels in cell membranes.

Alfredo Mariano García (1927-)
Biology, Anatomy

Born on September 12, 1927, in Itati-Corrientes, Argentina, García received his M.D. degree from the University of Buenos Aires in 1953 and a Ph.D. degree in zoology from Columbia University in 1962. Since 1957, he has worked in the United States at various hospitals and research institutes. Since 1964, he has been a professor of anatomy at the State University of New York Upstate Medical Center in Syracuse; he achieved full professorship status in 1974. His research concerns quantitative cytochemistry and fine structure and nucleic acid metabolism of mammalian blood cells.

Carlos Ernesto García (1936-)
Mechanical Engineering

Born on May 14, 1936, in Las Vegas, New Mexico, García received his three degrees from New Mexico State University: B.S. (1958), M.S. (1962), and D.Sc.

(1966). He has worked as a research engineer at a variety of government institutions and private industries, including the Atomic Energy Commission, from 1971 to 1973, as a weapons development engineer. Since 1984, he has been the director of the environmental safety and health division of the U.S. Department of Energy. His specialty is hydromechanical missile control systems and shock wave phenomena, including the study of underground nuclear explosions.

Celso Ramón García (1921-)
Obstetrics and Gynecology

Born on October 31, 1921, in New York City, García received his B.S. degree from Queens College in 1942 and his M.D. degree from the State University of New York in 1945. He has worked as a professor and researcher at various hospitals and universities, including Harvard and the University of Puerto Rico. Since 1970, he has held the William Shippen Jr. Chair in Human Reproduction at the School of Medicine at the University of Pennsylvania. From 1973 to 1978, he was the vice chairman of the Department of Obstetrics and Gynecology and the director of the Division of Human Reproduction. Since 1978, he has been the director of reproductive surgery. Included among his many awards are the Carl Harman Award from the Human Fertility Society (1961), Extraordinary Professor, University of San Luis Potosí, Mexico (1974), and the Pincus Lecturer, School of Medicine, Wayne State University (1974). His specialty is reproductive physiology and infertility.

José D. García (1936-)
Physics

Born in Santa Fe, New Mexico, on January 3, 1936, García received his B.S. degree from New Mexico State University in 1957, his M.A. degree from the University of California, Berkeley, in 1959, and his Ph.D. degree from the University of Wisconsin, Madison, in 1966. In 1967, he joined the faculty of the University of Arizona; since 1975, he has been a full professor of physics at Arizona. He has a been a Fulbright fellow (1957), a NASA postdoctoral fellow (1963), a NORDITA visiting fellow in Stockholm (1972), and an elected fellow of the American Physical Society since 1979. His principal research concerns quantum theory and ion-atom and ion-surface interactions.

Elma González (1942-)
Cell Biology

Born in the United States on June 6, 1942, González received her B.S. degree from Texas Woman's Univer-

Celso Ramón García.

sity in 1965 and her Ph.D. degree in cell biology from Rutgers University in 1972. After working with a fellowship in plant physiology at the University of California, Santa Cruz, from 1972 to 1974, González became an assistant professor of cell biology at the University of California, Los Angeles in 1974. Since 1981, she has been an associate professor there. Her research concerns the mechanisms and regulation of the formation of microbodies and other metabolic compartments.

Paula González (1932-)
Environmental Science, Bioethics

Born on October 25, 1932, in Albuquerque, New Mexico, González received her A.B. degree from the College of Mt. St. Joseph in 1952, her M.S. degree from the Catholic University of America in 1962, and her Ph.D. degree in cell physiology from there in 1966. González has taught at high schools, schools of nursing, and at the university level. From 1965 to 1982, she moved up the ranks from assistant professor to full professor at the College of Mt. St. Joseph; from 1968 to 1973, she served as the chairman of the Department of Biology. Her research concerns nucleolar

José D. García.

changes during the cell cycle, energy and environment, and biomedical advances and their human implications.

Richard Rafael González (1942-)
Physiology

Born on September 15, 1942, in El Paso, Texas, González received his B.S. degree from the University of Texas in 1962, his M.S. degree from the University of San Francisco in 1966, and his Ph.D. degree in Physiology and Biophysics from the University of California-Davis in 1970. After spending two years as a U.S. Public Health Service fellow at Yale University, during the next four years he went from assistant professor to associate professor of environmental physiology at Yale University. Since 1976, he has worked in ergonomics and environmental medicine at the U.S. Army Research Institute. His research concerns thermal physiology, peripheral circulation, and environmental physiology.

Enrique Hernández (1951-)
Medicine

Born on October 25, 1951, in Vega Baja, Puerto Rico, Hernández received his B.S. and M.D. degrees from the University of Puerto Rico in 1973 and 1977, respectively. From then until 1981, he was a fellow, intern, and resident at the Johns Hopkins Hospital. After academic appointments at the Johns Hopkins University School of Medicine and the College of Osteopathic Medicine of the Pacific, he joined the faculty of the Medical College of Philadelphia, where he has been a full professor since 1989. He has had a number of hospital appointments in Philadelphia and Hawaii, as well as numerous consulting positions. In 1985, he became a fellow of the American College of Obstetricians and gynecologists, and in 1986, a fellow of the American College of Surgeons. One of his main research interests is cancer of the female reproductive tract; he is the coauthor of the *Manual of Gynecological Oncology*, as well as of many other studies published in medical journals.

Gonzalo J. Hernández (?-)
Optics, Atmospheric Physics

Born in San José, Costa Rica, Hernández received his B.S. degree from the University of Notre Dame in 1958 and his Ph.D. in physical chemistry from the University of Rochester in 1962. From 1961 to 1969, he worked as a physicist at the Cambridge Research Lab of the air force, and from 1970 to 1985, he was the director of the Fritz Peak Observatory. Since 1985, he has been a research scientist at the Space Physics Research Lab of the University of Michigan. Also, since 1969, has been a physicist for the Environmental Research Labs of the National Oceanic and Atmospheric Administration. He is a specialist in upper atmosphere physics and high-resolution spectroscopy.

Michael Louis Ibáñez (1916-)
Pathology

Born on November 9, 1916, in Havana, Cuba, Ibáñez received his M.D. degree from the University of Havana in 1948. He became an intern at Hermann Hospital in Houston in 1949-50 and developed a career in pathology there and at other hospitals. Since 1975, he has been professor of pathology, and since 1974, pathologist for the Cancer Center of the M. D. Anderson Hospital and Tumor Institute in Houston. Ibáñez has researched the pathologic anatomy of cancer and the pathology of the thyroid gland.

Vicente José Llamas (1944-)
Solid-State Physics

Born on February 15, 1944, in Los Angeles, California, Llamas received his B.S. degree from Loyola University of Los Angeles in 1966 and his M.S. and Ph.D. degrees from the University of Missouri, Rolla, in 1968 and 1970, respectively. From 1970 to 1984, he went from assistant to full professor of physics at New Mexico Highlands University. Since 1984, he has been chairman of the Department of Physics and Math. His research concerns surface studies of alkali halides in the infrared, as well as the atmospheric study of air pollutants.

Joseph Llauradó (1927-)
Nuclear Medicine, Biomedical Engineering

Born on February 6, 1927, in Barcelona, Spain, Llauradó received both M.D. (1950) and Ph.D. (1960) degrees from the University of Barcelona. After teaching and researching in countries around the world, including England, Italy, Holland, New Zealand, and Venezuela, he became a senior endocrinologist for Pfizer & Co. in Connecticut from 1959 to 1961. From 1963 to the present, he has been a researcher and professor at universities in the United States. Since 1983, he has been professor of radiation science at the Loma Linda School of Medicine and chief of nuclear medical services of the Veterans Administration Hospital in Loma Linda. Llauradó researches radionuclides in cardiology and radionuclide treatment of pulmonary cancer.

Rodolfo Llinas (1934-)
Neurobiology, Electrophysiology

Born on December 16, 1934, in Bogotá, Colombia, Llinas received his M.D. degree from the Pontificial Universidad Javierana in Bogotá in 1959 and a Ph.D. degree in neurophysiology from the Australian National University in 1965. He has worked at the National University of Colombia, the University of Minnesota, the American Medical Association, and the University of Iowa. Since 1976, he has been professor and chairman of physiology and biophysiology at New York University Medical Center. Since 1975, he has been the editor-in-chief of *Neuroscience Journal*. He conducts structural and functional studies of neuronal systems and also studies the evolution and development of the central nervous system.

Diana Montes de Oca López (1937-)
Microbiology, Immunology

Born on August 26, 1937, in Havana, Cuba, López received her B.S. degree from the University of Havana in 1960 and her M.S. and Ph.D. degrees in microbiology from the University of Miami in 1968 and 1970, respectively. From 1970 to 1983, she went from research associate to full professor of microbiology at the University of Miami School of Medicine, where she continues to pursue her career. Since 1980, she has been the section leader in tumor virology and immunology for the state of Florida Comprehensive Cancer Center. Her research concerns tumor immunology, viral oncogenesis, and cell kinetics.

Cynthia Luz Marcelo (1945-)
Cell Physiology

Born on August 13, 1945, in New York City, Marcelo received her B.S. degree from Mt. St. Vincent College in 1967 and her M.S. and Ph.D. degrees in cell physiology from the State University of New York at Buffalo in 1969 and 1973, respectively. From 1975 to 1983, she went from assistant to associate professor of physiology in dermatology at the University of Michigan; since 1983, she has been the director of the research division of dermatology there. Her research concerns the control of epidermal cell function and the use of tissue culture technology to study growth factors and the effects of hormones and vitamin A on growth and function.

Michael Allen Mares (1945-)
Mammalian Biogeography

Born on March 11, 1945, in Albuquerque, New Mexico, Mares received his B.S. degree from the University of New Mexico in 1968, his M.S. degree from Kansas State University in 1969, and his Ph.D. degree in zoology from the University of Texas in 1973. He went from assistant to associate professor of ecology at the University of Pittsburgh from 1973 to 1981. In 1981, he went to the University of Oklahoma; he is currently a professor of zoology there and director of the Stovall Museum. Mares has been a fellow and fieldworker in Argentina as well as in the Southwest of the United States. In his research, he examines convergent evolution, adaptation and community organization of desert rodents of the world, as well as ecology, conservation, evolution, and systematics of South American mammals.

Richard Isaac Martínez (1944-)
Physical Chemistry

Born on August 16, 1944, in Havana, Cuba, Martínez received his B.S. degree from McGill University in 1964 and his Ph.D. degree in chemistry from the University of California, Los Angeles, in 1976. Martínez has worked as a research chemist at San Diego State University, Shell Oil, and UCLA. Since 1976, he has been a research chemist for the National Bureau of Standards of the U.S. Department of Commerce. In 1981, he was the recipient of the Bronze Medal Award from the Department of Commerce, and in 1983, he received the Independent Research 100 Award. He has worked on the development and application of tandem mass spectrometry MS/MS to the study of kinetics of complex organic reaction systems relevant to oxidation and atmospheric chemistry.

José Méndez (1921-)
Physiology, Nutrition

Born on August 17, 1921, in Tapachula, Mexico, Méndez received his B.S. degree from the Universidad de San Carlos in Guatemala City in 1947, his M.S. degree from the University of Illinois in 1948 and his Ph.D. degree in physiology from the University of Minnesota in 1957. From 1965 to 1966, he was associate professor of nutrition at the Massachusetts Institute of Technology; since 1966, he has been professor of health and applied physiology at Penn State University. He is a specialist in nutrition studies and nutrition training in developing countries and the adaptation of man to different environmental stresses.

Manuel Gaspar Meléndez (1935-)
Atomic Physics, Molecular Physics

Born in New York City on June 15, 1935, Meléndez received his B.Ch.E. and his Ph.D. degrees in chemical physics from the University of Florida in 1958 and 1963, respectively. From 1965 to 1966, he worked as an atomic physicist at the National Bureau of Standards and as a staff scientist at Martin Marietta from 1966 to 1969, when he relocated to the University of Georgia. He is currently professor of physics at Georgia. His research concerns ionization mechanisms at intermediate and low energies.

Teresa Mercado (1921-)
Histochemistry, Cytochemical Pathology

Born on October 15, 1921, in Ponce, Puerto Rico, Mercado received her B.S. degree from the College of Mt. St. Vincent in 1947 and her M.S. and Ph.D. degrees in biological physiology from the Catholic University of America in 1947 and 1950, respectively. Since 1949, she has been a research physiologist at

Teresa Mercado.

the National Institute for Allergy and Infectious Diseases of the National Institutes of Health. Her research is in pathologic physiology, histochemistry, biochemistry, and cytochemistry of parasitic diseases, especially experimental malaria and trypanosomiases.

Héctor Rolando Nava-Villarreal (1943-)
Medicine, Oncology

Born in Nuevo Laredo, Tamaulipas, Mexico, on May 23, 1943, Nava received all of his education in Mexico, including his M.D. degree from the Universidad de Nuevo León in 1967. He did his internship in Corpus Christi and his residency at the Roswell Park Cancer Institute in Buffalo, New York, where he also served as a fellow in surgical oncology from 1974 to 1976. From 1968 to 1970, he served in active duty in the U.S. Army, spending time from 1969 to 1970 as a battalion surgeon in Vietnam. From 1976 to the present, he has been a cancer researcher at the Roswell Park Cancer Institute. From 1991 to the present, he has been the vice chairman of the surgical oncology program there. Nava has been a pioneer in the use of lasers to treat cancer.

Isabel Cristina Pérez-Farfante (1916-)
Zoology

Born on July 24, 1916, in Havana, Cuba, Pérez received her B.S. degree from the University of Havana in 1938 and her M.S. and Ph.D. degrees in biology from Radcliffe College in 1944 and 1948, respectively. From 1948 to 1960, she was a professor of invertebrate biology at the University of Havana. Since 1966, she has worked as a systematics zoologist at the National Marine Fisheries Service. Her research interests include systematics, morphology, and distribution of decapod crustacea, with special reference to western Atlantic and eastern Pacific regions.

Víctor Pérez-Méndez (1923-)
Physics

Born on August 8, 1923, in Guatemala City, Guatemala, Pérez received his B.S. degree in 1947 from the Hebrew University in Jerusalem and his Ph.D. degree in physics from Columbia University in 1951. He became a research scientist at the Lawrence Berkeley Lab in 1953 and has remained there until this date. Since 1969, he has been a professor of physics (radiology) at the University of California, San Francisco; from 1969 to 1977, he was the head of that department. Pérez has published more than three hundred papers on his research in the fields of nuclear and high-

Isabel Pérez-Farfante.

energy physics, radiation detectors, and medical imaging.

David Pimentel (1925-)
Ecology, Entomology

Born on May 24, 1925, in Fresno, California, Pimentel received his B.S. degree from the University of Massachusetts in 1948 and his Ph.D. degree in entomology from Cornell University in 1951. From 1951 to 1953, he was chief of the Tropical Research Lab at the U.S. Public Health Service in San Juan, Puerto Rico. From 1955 to 1976, he moved up the ranks from assistant to full professor of insect ecology at Cornell University, which is his current position. He has had a number of prestigious fellowships in the United States and Europe, and from 1964 to 1966, he was a member of the President's Science Advisory Council; he has also worked extensively with the United Nations, UNESCO, the National Academies of Science, HEW, USAID, the Environmental Protection Agency, and the Department of Energy. He has also been a lecturer and keynote speaker at the principal biological and entomological societies in Africa, Europe, Canada, and the

United states. His research concerns ecology and genetics of insect-plant, parasite-host, and predator-prey population systems.

Fausto Ramírez (1923-)
Organic Chemistry

Born on June 15, 1923, in Zulueta, Cuba, Ramírez received his B.S., M.S., and Ph.D. degrees from the University of Michigan in 1946, 1947, and 1949, respectively. He made his career at the University of Virginia, Columbia University, the Illinois Institute of Technology, and the State University of New York at Stoney Brook, where he was professor from 1959 to 1985; today he is professor emeritus there. Ramírez developed a record of lectures, fellowships, and honors around the world. In 1969, he was awarded the Silver Medal of the City of Paris, and in 1968, the Cresy-Morrison Award from the New York Academy of Sciences. His research concerns the theoretical and practical aspects of the chemistry of phosphorus and sulfur compounds, organic synthesis, and molecular biology.

Marian Lucy Rivas (1943-)
Medical Genetics, Computer Systems

Born on May 6, 1943, in New York City, Rivas received her B.S. degree from Marian College in 1964 and her M.S. and Ph.D. degrees in medical genetics from Indiana University in 1967 and 1969, respectively. After serving with a fellowship at Johns Hopkins University from 1969 to 1971, Rivas worked as an assistant professor of biology at Douglas College of Rutgers University from 1971 to 1975; thereafter, she was an associate professor from 1975 to 1982 at the Hemophilia Center of the Oregon Health Science University. Since 1982, she has been a full professor there, and since 1978, an associate scientist at the Neurological Science Institute of Good Samaritan Hospital. She has served in genetics committees at the National Institutes of Health and in adjunct positions at universities in the United States and in Venezuela. Her research concerns human gene mapping, genetic aspects of epilepsy, computer applications in clinical genetics, and genetic counseling.

Evelyn Margaret Rivera (1929-)
Endocrinology, Cancer

Born on November 10, 1929, in Holister, California, Rivera received her A.B., M.A., and Ph.D. degrees in zoology from the University of California, Berkeley, in 1952, 1960, and 1963, respectively. She was a fellow of the American Cancer Society in England from 1963 to 1965. From 1965 to 1972, she went from assistant to associate professor of zoology at Michigan State University; from 1972 on, she has been a full professor. In her research she has worked for the National Cancer Institute and held fellowships for her work on cancer and endocrinology from a number of institutions. In 1965, Rivera was given the UNESCO Award from the International Cell Research Organization. Rivera's research interests include cell transformation and the biology of tumors.

Juan Guadalupe Rodríguez (1920-)
Entomology

Born on December 23, 1920, in Española, New Mexico, Rodríguez received a B.S. degree from New Mexico State University in 1943 and M.S. and Ph.D degrees from the University of Ohio in 1946 and 1949, respectively. From 1949 to 1961, he went from associate entomologist to full professor of Entomology at the University of Kentucky, where he still does research and teaches in the College of Agriculture. He has been awarded the Thomas Poe Cooper Award for Distinguished Research by the University of Kentucky. Rodríguez's research concerns axenic culture of arthropods, insect and mite nutrition, and insect pest management.

Juan Carlos Romero (1937-)
Animal Physiology, Computer Science

Born on September 15, 1937, in Mendoza, Argentina, Romero received his B.S degree from San José College in Argentina in 1955 and his M.D. degree from the University of Mendoza in 1964. From 1968 to 1973, Romero worked as a research associate physiologist at the University of Michigan. From 1973 to 1980, he ascended the ranks to become a professor of physiology at the Mayo School of Medicine of the Mayo Foundation, a position he still holds today. Since 1982, he has also served as the director of the Hypertension Research Lab. He has been associated with and served on numerous committees that deal with heart disease and hypertension, including the Pan American Council on High Blood Pressure, the National Heart, Lung and Blood Institute of the NIH, the American Heart Association, and NASA. In his research, Romero studies mechanisms by which the kidney can produce high blood pressure; he identifies hormones that control renal circulation and excretion of salt.

Albert William Saenz (1923-)
Theoretical Physics

Born in Medellín, Colombia, on August 27, 1923, Saenz received his B.S., M.S., and Ph.D. degrees in physics from the University of Michigan in 1944, 1945, and 1949, respectively. He has made almost his entire career at the Naval Research Laboratory, where he serves today as the head of the theory consulting staff of the condensed matter and radiation science division. He has been a visiting scientist at the Oak Ridge National Lab, the Massachusetts Institute of Technology, Johns Hopkins University, Princeton University, and elsewhere. In 1969, he was the recipient of the Pure Science Award at the Naval Research Lab. His research interests include special and general relativity, symmetry and degeneracy in quantum mechanics, and quantum scattering theory.

Pedro Antonio Sánchez (1940-)
Agronomy, Soil Fertility

Born on October 7, 1940, in Havana, Cuba, Sánchez received his B.S., M.S., and Ph.D. degrees in soil science from Cornell University in 1962, 1964, and 1968, respectively. From 1968 to the present, he has been associated with North Carolina State University, where he has been a professor of soil science and leader of the Tropical Soils Program since 1979. His research and consultancies have taken him abroad, most frequently to Latin America. For his outstanding service, the government of Peru awarded him the

Pedro A. Sánchez.

Orden de Mérito Agrícola Medal. Currently, Sánchez is professor emeritus from North Carolina State and director of the International Centre for Research in Agroforestry (ICRAF), Nairobi, Kenya. ICRAF is devoted to alleviating poverty, tropical deforestation, and land degradation, through improved agroforestry systems. He also serves as chairman of the board of the worldwide Tropical Soil Biology and Fertility Program and as chairman of the National Academy of Sciences panel on sustainable agriculture and the environment in the humid tropics. Sánchez's research concerns the fertility and management of tropical soils, especially rice soils and tropical pastures.

Margarita Silva-Hunter (1915-)
Mycology, Microbiology

Born on November 28, 1915, in Río Piedras, Puerto Rico, Silva received her B.A. degree from the University of Puerto Rico in 1936 and her M.S. and Ph.D. degrees from Harvard University in 1945 and 1952, respectively. From 1945 to the present, she has worked in the College of Physicians and Surgeons of Columbia University, where she has been an associate professor of dermatology since 1963. She has worked as a consulting mycologist and researcher at a number of hospitals and institutes, including the U.S. Public Health Service, the Squibb Institute for Medical Research, and the American Board of Medical Microbiology. Her research concerns the morphology, taxonomy, and biology of pathogenic fungi.

Aída R. Soto (1931-)
Organic Chemistry, Biochemistry

Born on December 3, 1931, in Havana, Cuba, Soto received her B.S. degree from the University of Havana in 1953 and her M.S. and Ph.D. degrees in chemistry from the University of Miami in 1962 and 1966, respectively. After serving as an instructor in the Department of Pharmacology and the School of Medicine of the University of Miami, in 1969 Soto became a researcher for the Dade division of the American Hospital Supply Company, where she has been a section head since 1984. Among her research interests are clinical enzymology, radioimmunoassays, and the use of immunologic techniques in clinical chemistry.

John Taboada (1943-)
Physical Optics, Applied Physics

Born on September 8, 1943, in Tampico, Mexico, Taboada received his B.A. degree from Trinity Uni-

James J. Valdés.

versity (San Antonio) in 1966 and his M.S. and Ph.D. degrees in physics from Texas A&M University in 1968 and 1973, respectively. Since 1966, he has worked for the U.S. Air Force, first in the radiation science division, and since 1968 in the data Science division. In 1915, he received the Outstanding Technical Achievement Award, and in 1975, the Outstanding Science Achievement Award from the air force. Taboada's research concerns the biophysics of ultrashort pulsed lasers, laser spectroscopy, nonlinear optics, and applied optics.

Gladys Torres-Blasini (19?-)
Microbiology

Born in Ponce, Puerto Rico, Torres received a B.S. degree from the University of (San Antonio) Puerto Rico in 1948 and M.S. and Ph.D. degrees in bacteriology from the University of Michigan in 1952 and 1953, respectively. From 1952 on, she made her career at the Medical School of the University of Puerto Rico, where she has been head of the Department of Microbiology and Medical Zoology since 1977. She has held grants from the U.S. Public Health Service, Hoffman-LaRoche, the National Institutes of Health, and Veterans Administration hospitals. Her research in bacteriology includes the comparison of the phagocytosis of various candid species.

Pedro Ramón Urquilla (1939-)
Clinical Pharmacology

Born on July 18, 1939, in San Miguel, El Salvador, Urquilla was educated in El Salvador and received his M.D. degree from the University of El Salvador in 1965. From 1966 to 1969, he held fellowships from the Pan American Health Organization and from the National Institutes of Health. From 1969 to 1979, he developed a career as a professor of pharmacology at the University of Madrid. Since 1979, he has worked in private industry in the United States; since 1981, he has been the associate director of clinical research for Pfizer, Inc. His research concerns the analysis of the pharmacological receptors of the cerebral arteries.

James J. Valdés (19?-)
Biotechnology

Valdés received his B.S. degree in psychology and biological sciences from Loyola University in Chicago in 1973. He received an M.S. degree in physiological psychology from Trinity University in San Antonio in 1976 and a Ph.D. degree in neuroscience from Texas Christian University in 1979. From 1979 to 1982, he did postgraduate work in toxicology and environmental health sciences at Johns Hopkins University. From 1982 to the present, he has worked as a researcher for the Department of the army at its Aberdeen Proving Ground in Maryland. Valdés has won many awards from the army for his achievements as a researcher. His research interests include biosensors, receptor and ion channel response to toxic commands, and mechanisms of neurotransmission.

Gaspar Rodolfo Valenzuela (1933-)
Electronic Engineering

Born on January 6, 1933, in Coelemu, Chile, Valenzuela received his B.S. and M.S. degrees in electrical engineering from the University of Florida in 1954 and 1955, respectively; he received his Dr. Eng. degree from Johns Hopkins University in 1965. Between 1957 and 1968, he worked as a research engineer at Johns Hopkins. Since 1968, he has been a research electronic engineer for the Naval Research Lab in Washington, D.C. His research concerns electromagnetic theory, rough surface scattering theory, and the interaction of electromagnetic waves with the ocean.

Carlos Vallbona (1927-)
Community Medicine

Born on July 29, 1927, in Granollers, Barcelona, Spain, Vallbona received all of his primary education there, and his B.S. and M.D. degrees from the University of Barcelona in 1944 and 1955, respectively. He did postgraduate work in Barcelona, Paris, and Louisville, Kentucky. Vallbona began at the Baylor College of Medicine in Houston, Texas, as a pediatric resident in 1955 and has remained with that institution throughout his career. He is currently distinguished service professor and chairman of the Department of Community Medicine at Baylor and chief of staff of the Community Health Program of the Harris County Hospital District. He has received numerous awards for his contributions to academic medicine and to community health. Vallbona has done extensive research on the applications of computers in medicine, cardiorespiratory problems of disabled persons, community medicine, and the control of hypertension and diabetes in the community.

References

Jaques Catell Press, eds. *American Men & Women of Science.* 16th ed. New York: R. R. Bowker, 1986.

Amy L. Unterburger, ed. *Who's Who among Hispanic Americans.* Detroit, Mich.: Gale Research, 1991.

Nicolás Kanellos

Sports

✳ Baseball ✳ Rodeo ✳ Other Sports ✳ Prominent Hispanic Athletes

Hispanic participation and achievements in sports have been determined by Hispanic traditions of work, play, and ritual, both in the United States and in the greater Spanish-speaking world. As Hispanic customs in the United States and throughout Latin America have derived from the blending of various bloodlines and cultures—European, Amerindian, and African—so too the types of sports practiced by Hispanics has evolved out of the rituals and traditions that can quite often be traced back to the peoples that encountered each other in the early sixteenth century when the Spaniards evangelized the Mesoamerican Indians and began importing slaves from Africa. In the United States, the descendants of this encounter also adopted Anglo-American traditions in sport and shared their own with the Anglo-Americans. The prime examples of this exchange are rodeo and baseball. Ranching and sport with horses and cattle were introduced to the Americas by the Spaniards. The Spanish customs mixed with some American Indian traditions and then were learned by Anglo-Americans and European immigrants.

The American cowboy was born when the United States expanded westward and encountered the Mexican cattle culture. Today's rodeo owes a great deal to the *charrerías* (contests) of the Mexican vaqueros, or cowboys. The "national pastime" of baseball developed in the United States in the nineteenth century and was introduced then to Cuba and other nearby Hispanic countries by the last part of that century. As American teams needed warm wintering grounds and off-season play, the climates and facilities in Mexico and the Spanish-speaking Caribbean attracted American baseball players, thus exposing more and more Hispanics to the "all-American" sport.

But Hispanic participation, especially in professional sports in the United States, has also depended on of factors, other than customs and traditions.

Ramón Ahumada (rt.), known as "El Charro Plateado" (the Silver Plated Cowboy), was elected to the Cowboy Hall of Fame. (Photo, circa 1890. Courtesy of the Arizona Historical Society.)

Various sports demand certain body types that seem to present relative advantages for success. The prime example, of course, is basketball, where tall players have proven to be more successful. Most Hispanics have descended from American Indians and Spaniards, both of whom are relatively short peoples com-

697

pared to northern Europeans and many African peoples. As would be expected, there are very few Hispanics represented in professional basketball. The same is true of football, which also demands very large and strong bodies. Notwithstanding the general disadvantage of Hispanics as a whole, there have been great achievers, even in such contact sports as football, as the careers of Manny Fernández, Anthony Muñoz, and Tom Flores attest.

Another factor is education. College sports are quite often training grounds for the professional leagues. Hispanic dropout rates in high school are the highest in the country, and their admission to and graduation from college is the lowest compared with Anglos and Afro-Americans. Hispanics thus have fewer opportunities to get involved in college sports, especially football and basketball, not to mention other more elite sports, such as tennis and golf. But, there are also "back doors" of entry to these sports, such as working as caddies and greens keepers, as the careers of Chi Chi Rodríguez and Lee Treviño exemplify.

Furthermore various sports have traditionally been associated with certain social classes and have been restricted to members of these classes principally because of economic barriers, such as membership fees in private country clubs, the payment of fees for private lessons, the lack of public facilities, the high expense of specialized equipment, such as golf clubs and gear, and the high tuition of private schools where these sports are cultivated. Prime examples of these sports are polo, golf, lacrosse, and, before the construction of numerous tennis courts in public parks, tennis. On the other hand, boxing classes and sports faciltes have traditionally been accessible to poor inner-city youths through boys clubs, police athletic leagues, and the military services. In addition, boxing has been a traditional avenue to economic success and fame for one immigrant and minority group after another and for poor inner-city youths in the United States. Hispanics have developed a long tradition of achievement in boxing, especially in the lighter-weight classes.

There are relative advantages to being short, lightweight, and quick in the wide world of sports. Hispanics not only have excelled as bantamweights and lightweights in boxing, but also have earned an outstanding record as jockeys, quick-handed infielders in baseball, and star players in such sports as soccer, where speed and endurance are important. And soccer has also provided an opportunity for Hispanics to participate in professional football, which has recruited various Hispanic placekickers for the accuracy they have developed with their angled and powerful kicking. But all of the above conditions are changing rapidly. American society is becoming more and more democratic and open. In the late 1940s, American baseball ceased to be segregated, then football also opened up. In modern life today, sports facilities are accessible to people from all social classes in public parks and schools, and universities are making more of an effort to recruit minorities. Universities are even recruiting and training from such countries as the Dominican Republic, Panama, and Puerto Rico players of Afro-Hispanic background for their basketball, football, and track teams.

❊ BASEBALL

Although many sportswriters in the United States have considered the presence of ballplayers from Latin America to be an "influx," as if baseball were a uniquely American sport being invaded by outsiders, the truth of the matter is that baseball in Spanish-speaking countries has not only had a parallel development to baseball in the United States, but it has been intertwined with American baseball almost from the beginning of the game itself. The professional Cuban Baseball League (Liga de Béisbol Profesional Cubana) was founded in 1878, just seven years after the National Baseball Association was founded in the United States. But, reportedly, Cuban baseball goes back to 1866, when sailors from an American ship in Matanzas harbor invited Cubans to play the game; they built a baseball diamond together at Palmar del Junco and began playing while the ship remained in harbor. By 1874, Cuban teams had devloped and were playing each other regularly.

By 1891, there were seventy-five teams active on the island. From that time on, Cuban baseball—and later, Mexican and Puerto Rican baseball—has served baseball in the United States in various ways: as a training ground for the majors, formalized when the Cuban Sugar Kings were made a Triple A minor league team; as wintering and spring training grounds for the majors; and as permanent homes for players from the U.S. Negro leagues, also providing a baseball team, the Havana Cubans, to the Negro leagues. Since the early days of the National Baseball Association until Jackie Robinson broke the color line in 1947, about fifty Hispanic-American ballplayers played in the major leagues, some even becoming Hall of Famers and one achieving the position of manager. However, for the most part, these were Cuban players who were white or could pass for white. In fact, the acceptance of progressively darker-skinned Hispanics was used as a barometer by the Negro leagues for the eventual acceptance of Afro-Americans into the majors. The Hispanics that could

A baseball team of Mexicans and Anglos in Los Angeles in the 1870s (Courtesy of the Huntington Library, San Marino, California).

not "pass" either played in the Negro leagues or in Cuba, Mexico, or Venezuela. What is clear is that Cuba served as a free ground exempt from the segregation that dominated U.S. sports and provided playing fields where major-leaguers and players from the Negro leagues and Latin America could play openly together.

As baseball continued its development in Mexico, pressure from fans and investors increased for expanding the U.S. major leagues to Mexico and for the creation of Mexico's own professional leagues. In 1946, the wealthy Pasquel family in Mexico founded a professional league and set about enticing major league and Negro league stars from the United States with salaries quite higher than were being offered in the United States. The whole Pasquel venture, which was seen by the U.S. media as "robbery" and a threat to the national pastime, even led to an official complaint by the U.S. State Department. Some twenty-three players jumped to Pasquel's league, but after continued financial problems the league ceased to exist in 1953. The northern teams of the league merged with the Arizona-Texas and Arizona-Mexico leagues from 1953 to 1957. The Mexican League began

functioning again in 1955 and has continued to do so. The Mexican Central League has served since 1960—a year after the Cuban Revolution curtailed Triple A ball on the island—as a Class A minor league and was later joined by other Mexican leagues based on the earlier Pasquel circuit. Today the league has fourteen teams playing in two divisions, and both supply young ballplayers to the majors and receive former major-leaguers on their way out of baseball.

The Majors

The first Hispanic ballplayers in the United States played in the National Association and in the Negro League. Before 1947, the major league clubs that employed the most Hispanics were in Washington, Cincinnati, Chicago, Cleveland, and Detroit. The New York Yankees did not employ Hispanics after 1918 and Pittsburgh did not employ any until 1943, when it hired one. According to Brown, the first Hispanic to join the majors was third baseman Esteban Bellán, a black Cuban who was recruited from Fordham College by the Troy Haymakers in 1869 and actually took to the field in 1871—the year of the founding of the

National Baseball Association—to spend three years in the majors. By the turn of the century, no black Cubans were allowed in the majors, despite major leaguers observing their talents firsthand and suffering defeats from them. One such powerhouse was pitcher José Méndez, Méndez played with the Cuban Stars against the best of the Negro teams and won forty-four victories, with only two defeats on a tour of the United States in 1909. In Cuba, Méndez beat the Phillies and split two games against future Hall of Famers Christy Mathewson and John McGraw of the New York Giants. But light-skinned Cuban and Hispanic ballplayers soon began appearing more and more in American baseball, despite complaints that the racial puirity of the American sport was being contaminated. In 1911, the Cincinnati Reds had affidavits prepared to prove that their new Cuban players, Armando Marsans and Rafael Almeida, had only the purest Castilian blood flowing through their veins. Marsans and Almeida had been brought up to the majors from the Negro leagues" Cuban Stars team; this was seen by the Negro press as an indication that the majors would soon be opening up:

Now that the first shock is over it would not be surprising to see a Cuban a few shades darker than Almeida and Marsans breaking into the professional ranks, with a coal-black Cuban on the order of the crack pitcher, Méndez, making his debut later on. . . . With the admission of Cubans of a darker hue in the two big leagues it would then be easy for colored players who are citizens of this country to get into fast company. The Negro in this country has more varied hues than even the Cubans, and the only way to distinguish him would be to hear him talk. Until the public got accustomed to seeing native Negroes on big league (teams), the colored players could keep their mouths shut and pass for Cubans. (Quoted by Robert Peterson in *Only the Ball Was White* from an unidentifiable newspaper clipping, p. 62.)

In 1912, Cuban Miguel González began playing for Boston as a catcher. González played for seventeen years on various teams and served fourteen seasons as a Cardinals coach, the first Hispanic to do so. But the greatest longevity by any Hispanic in major league baseball was attained by Adolfo Luque. A dark-skinned Cuban pitcher, Luque was jeered at and continuously faced racial epithets from fans from the time he took to the field for the Braves in 1914 until his retirement in 1935. Having played for the Braves, Cincinnati, Brooklyn, and the New York Giants, Luque pitched in two World Series, was credited with

the decisive win in one of them and during his best year, 1923, led the league for Cincinnati in wins (27), earned run average (1.93), and shutouts (6).

The greatest number of Hispanic ballplayers by far was employed by the Washington Senators, beginning in 1911 but reaching its peak from 1939 to 1947 with a total of nineteen players of Hispanic background. At Washington, as at other major league clubs, the Hispanics suffered not only racial attacks from fans and sportswriters, but also segregation in housing, uniforms, equipment, and travel conditions. Many of these conditions improved noticeably during the 1940s with the competition for ballplayers that was exerted by the Mexican league.

After the the color barrier was broken in 1947, things became much easier for Hispanic ballplayers of all colors and nationalities, and their representation in the major leagues quickly climbed. By the 1970s, a full 9 percent of the players were Hispanics. Due to the restrictions that came about after the Cuban Revolution—even baseball equipment was not to be had in Cuba due to the U.S. economic embargo—the flow of players from Cuba into the major leagues was curtailed. During the 1970s and 1980s Cubans no longer were the Hispanic nationality most represented. The lead passed to the Dominican Republic and Puerto Rico, with Venezuela and Mexico also making a strong showing. But by 1963, the Cuban National Team had begun to dominate amateur baseball and to cement its perennial championship of the Pan American Games. And the caliber of play is equivalent to that of major league teams, but the broken political relations between the United States and Cuba has made international professional play between the two countries impossible.

Major league baseball in the United States is and will continue to be a strong draw for Hispanic ballplayers, not only as an economic springboard with its lucrative salaries, but also because of the excellence and competitive nature of the game played here, made even more competitive by the quality Hispanic ballplayers have always contributed to the majors.

The Negro Leagues

The Negro leagues were a haven for Hispanic ballplayers whose skin color was a barrier to their admission to the major leagues in the United States. In Robert Peterson's book *Only the Ball Was White*, the contribution of Hispanic, mainly Cuban, ballplayers to the sport in the United States is amply documented. The Negro leagues and the leagues in Cuba, Mexico, Puerto Rico, and Venezuela were completely open to each other. Both black and white players from the Hispanic world and from the United

States played on the same teams and against each other freely in Cuba. In Latin America there were no color lines. By the 1920s, not only were many Hispanics playing in the Negro leagues, but many American blacks had incorporated into their routine playing the winter season in Cuba, then later Puerto Rico, Mexico, and Venezuela. Among the Hispanic greats to play in the Negro leagues were Cristóbal Torriente, Martín Dihigo, José Méndez, Orestes "Minnie" Miñoso, Alejandro Oms, Luis Tiant, Sr., and scores of others.

As early as 1900, two of the five black professional teams bore the name of Cuba: the Cuban Giants (with its home city shifting from year to year from New York to Hoboken, New Jersey, to Johnstown, Pennsylvania, and so) on and the Cuban X Giants of New York. (These teams should not be confused with one of the first black professional ball teams of the 1880s, which called itself the Cuban Giants, thinking that fans would be more attracted to the exotic Cubans than to ordinary American blacks). In the 1920s, both the Eastern Colored League (NNL) and the Negro National League (NNL) had a Cuban Stars baseball team, one owned by Alex Pómpez, who at one point was vice president of the NNL, and the other by Agustín Molina. Cuban teams continued to be prominent during the heyday of the Negro leagues from the 1920s through the 1940s. There were also Hispanic players on teams throughout the Negro leagues, from the Indianapolis Clowns and Cleveland Buckeyes to the Memphis Red Sox and the New York Black Yankees. And, aside from the teams that identified themselves as Cuban, such as the New York Cubans and the Cuban Stars, there were others that had their rosters filled with Hispanics, such as the Indianapolis Clowns, which at one point was even managed by a Hispanic, Ramiro Ramírez. (In his long career from 1916 to 1948, Ramírez managed or played with most of the Cuban teams, plus the Baltimore Black Sox, the Bacharach Giants, and the Clowns.)

✷ RODEO

The Spaniards introduced cattle ranching to the New World, and with this industry the early settlers and soldiers also introduced the horse and its use for work and sport. Much of contemporary sports culture that depends upon horsemanship and cattle, such as equestrian contests, horse racing, bullfighting, and rodeo, is heavily indebted to the Spanish and Hispanic-American legacy. The evolution of rodeo as a sport goes back to the blending of Spanish and American Indian customs of animal handling and sport. A class of mestizo (mixed Indian and Spanish) vaqueros, or cowboys, developed in Mexico during the seven-

teenth, eighteenth, and nineteenth centuries on the large haciendas. These mestizo cowboys, called *charros,* eventually evolved their own subculture of unique customs, dress, music, and horsemanship, which in turn owed much to the Arab horsemen that had influenced Spanish culture during the seven hundred years of Moslem occupation of the peninsula. The charros, in fact, were the models for the development of the American cowboy, just as was Mexican ranching culture was essential in the development of that industry in the United States. During the late eighteenth and early nineteenth centuries, Anglo-American cowboys began working alongside Mexican cowboys on the same ranches in Texas and California.

The style of dress and horsemanship of the charro became more popularized even in the cities during the nineteenth century and was eventually adopted as the national costume. Their contests and games, *charrería,* became the Mexican national sport. The skillful games of the charros became games and shows on the large haciendas during the festive roundups in the nineteenth century, which drew guests from hundreds of miles around. The charros dressed in their finest outfits and displayed their skills in such contests as correr el gallo (running the rooster), horse racing, wild horse and bull riding, and roping horses or steers by their horns or back or front feet, bulldogging, and throwing bulls by their tails. Correr el gallo involved picking up something as small as a coin from the ground while riding a horse at full gallop. These fiestas were perhaps the most important forerunners of the modern American rodeo, and their events included almost all of those associated with today's rodeos. More important, these equestrian sports became part of the standard celebrations at fiestas and fairs among Mexicans and Anglos all along both sides of the border. And charrería, as a separate institution from rodeo, has continued to this day to be practiced by Mexicans in Mexico and throughout the American Southwest.

According to Mary Lou LeCompte, in her article "The Hispanic Influence on the History of Rodeo," after much of today's American Southwest was expropriated from Mexico as a result of the Mexican-American War, Mexican charrería continued to flourish quite often in the heart of Anglo society for some sixty years before Anglo-sponsored cowboy events existed. It was Colonel W. F. "Buffalo Bill" Cody who played a key role in the development of the American rodeo by bringing together many of the traditional events of charrería in his Wild West Show. Between 1883 and 1916, Cody's show and a host of imitators toured the major cities of the United States and Europe. Integrated in Cody's and the other shows were numerous

Mexican vaqueros, many of whom had been recruited in San Antonio, Texas. Among these were superstar Antonio Esquivel and roper Señor Francisco. But the most famous and influential Mexican charro of all was Vicente Oropeza. A Mexican native, Oropeza made his American debut in July 1891 in San Antonio and went on to become a headliner in shows touring throughout the United States. Oropeza was the greatest trick, and fancy roper of all time, and he became a star of Cody's show for some sixteen years, even influencing one of America's greatest rodeo stars, Will Rogers.

During the early years of the twentieth century, local and state fairs and celebrations among Anglos in the West featured cowboy events in what they called "stampedes," "roundups" and "frontier days." These proliferated to the extent that professional contestants began to make a living traveling the circuit of these fairs. The events that became the heart of these contests were the traditional charro events of bronc riding, steer roping, and trick fancy roping. The first cowboy to win the World Chamionship of Trick and Fancy Roping in 1900 was Vicente Oropeza. Oropeza and many other charros and American cowboys continued to compete in both the United States and Mexico throughout the 1930s. By 1922, with the production by Tex Austin of the first World Championship Cowboy Contest in New York's Madison Square Garden, rodeo had officially become a sport, not just a show. Eight of the ten events featured in this new sport had long been a part of charrería. More important, the five standard events of contemporary professional rodeo all owe their roots to charrería: bareback bronc riding, saddle bronc riding, bull riding, steer wrestling, and calf roping.

✳OTHER SPORTS

While baseball and rodeo are two sports that have been highly influenced by Hispanics in their evolution, there are other sports that have benefited from the participation of outstanding Hispanic atheletes. First and foremost is boxing, which has a long history of Hispanic champions, especially in the lighter-weight classifications, where the speed and lighter body weight of many Cuban, Mexican, and Puerto Rican boxers has been used to advantage.

From the days of Sixto Escobar and Kid Chocolate to the present, boxing has also served for Hispanics, as it has for other immigrants and minorities, as a tempting avenue out of poverty. With more colleges and universities recruiting and graduating Hispanics, some of the other "money" sports, such as football and basketball, will also begin to incorpo-

rate more Hispanics in their ranks. Already, such football stars as Manny Fernández, Tom Flores, Anthony Muñoz, and Jim Plunkett have appeared on the scene, and there are many more to follow, especially from the universities of the Southwestern Conference.

Finally, the mere fact that an island such as Puerto Rico, which extends only thirty-five by one hundred miles, has as many as ten professional-quality golf clubs has had its impact on that sport. Such golfers as Juan "Chi Chi" Rodríguez have become world-class competitors after beginning as humble caddies for tourists. And as more and more facilties, such as golf courses and tennis courts, become accessible in the United States through public parks or public schools, greater Hispanic participation and achievement will be recorded.

✳PROMINENT HISPANIC ATHLETES

Luis Aparicio (1934-)
Baseball

Venezuelan Luis Aparicio was one of the greatest shortstops of all time. He still holds the records for games, double plays, and assists and the American League record for putouts. His 506 stolen bases also rank among the highest. Playing from 1956 to 1973, mostly with the White Sox, Aparicio began his career as Rookie of the Year and proceeded to maintain outstanding and inspired performance throughout his life as a ballplayer. Aparicio played on All-Star teams from 1958 to 1964 and then again from 1970 to 1972. He was the winner of the Gold Glove eleven times. In 1984, Luis Aparicio was inducted into the Hall of Fame.

Rod Carew (1945-)
Baseball

Born in the Panama Canal Zone, Carew moved with his mother to New York at age 17. He signed his first professional contract while he was still in high school in 1964, and when he made it into the majors in 1967 with the Minnesota Twins, he was named Rookie of the Year. From 1969 on, he had fifteen consecutive seasons batting over .300. Carew won seven American League batting championships, In his Most Valuable Player year he batted .388, fifty points better than the next-best average and the largest margin in major league history. His career batting average was .328, with 1,015 runs batted in and 92 home runs. In 1979, Carew forced a trade, in part because of racist comments regarding black fans by Twins owner Calvin Griffith; he was traded to the Angels for four players. In 1977, Carew received over four million All-Star votes, more than any other player ever. He would

Rod Carew.

have played in eighteen consecutive All-Star games, but missed 1970 and 1979 because of injuries, and for the same reason was not chosen in 1982. Carew was one of the best base stealers, with 348 career stolen bases. In 1969, Carew tied the record with seven steals to home. He led the league three times in base hits and once in runs scored.

Rosemary Casals (1948-)
Tennis

Born on September 16, 1948, in San Francisco, the daughter of Salvadoran immigrants, Rosemary Casals was brought up by her great-aunt and great-uncle. Casals began playing tennis at Golden Gate Park under the guidance of her adoptive father, Manuel Casals Y. Bordas, who has been her only coach to this date. Casals won her first championship at age 13 and by age 17 she was ranked eleventh by the United States Ladies Tennis Association (USLTA). At eighteen, her ranking was third in the nation. Casals and Billie Jean King were doubles champions five times from 1967 to 1973 at the All-England Championships at Wimbledon and twice at the USLTA championships at Forest Hills. The Casals-King team is the

only doubles team to have won U.S. titles on grass, clay, indoor, and hard surfaces. Nine times, Casals was rated as number one in doubles by the USLTA, with teammates that included King, Chris Evert Lloyd, and Jo Anne Russell. Casals has also won mixed doubles championships, playing with Richard Stockton and Ilie Nastase.

Hugo M. Castelló (1914-)
Fencing

Born in La Plata, Argentina, on April 22, 1914, Hugo Castelló moved to the United States with his family at age 8 and received his public education in New York City. He earned his B.A. degree at Washington Square College in 1937 and his law degree from Georgetown University in 1941. Castelló became one of the nation's most outstanding fencers and fencing instructors and coaches. He was nationally ranked among the top four senior fencers from 1935 to 1936, the years that he was National Intercollegiate Foil Champion, and he was a member of the U.S. Olympic team in 1936. Castelló served as adjunct associate professor and head fencing coach at New York University from 1946 to 1975. Castelló is among a select group of coaches who have won at least ten National Collegiate team championships. Only five other NCAA coaches in all sports have won ten national team titles. Castelló was also director and head coach of the United States" first Olympic fencing training camp in 1962. He has also served as chief of mission and coach at the Pan American Games (1963)in Sao Paulo and at World Championships in Cuba (1969), Minsk (1970), and Madrid (1972). Castelló is a member of the Helms Sports Hall of Fame, the New York University Sports Hall of Fame, and the PSAL Hall of Fame.

Orlando Cepeda (1937-)
Baseball

Orlando Cepeda was born in Ponce, Puerto Rico, on September 17, 1937. After growing up playing sandlot baseball and later organized team play in New York City, Cepeda was discovered by talent scout Alex Pómpez and began as a major league outfielder with the San Francisco Giants in 1958, when he was named Rookie of the Year. Hitting his stride in 1961, Cepeda led the league in home runs. Cepeda remained on the team until May 1966, when he was transferred to the St. Louis Cardinals after having missed almost a whole season because of a leg injury. He stayed with the Cardinals until 1968. Before his retirement, he also played for the Braves, the A's, the Red Sox, and the Royals. He made a remarkable comeback with the Cardinals, winning the National League's Most Valuable Player award, leading the league in runs batted in 1967 and making the All-Star team in that year, as well. Orlando Cepeda played on World Series teams in 1962 and 1967. In all, Cepeda played 2,124 games, with a lifetime batting average of .279. He hit 379 home runs and had 1,364 runs batted in. Cepeda had nine .300 seasons and eight seasons with twenty-five or more home runs. Cepeda has never been named to the Hall of Fame, possibly because of his serving time in prison for marijuana smuggling after his baseball career had ended.

Roberto Clemente (1934-1972)
Baseball

Roberto Walker Clemente is celebrated for being a heroic figure both on and off the baseball diamond. One of the all-time greats of baseball, he died in a tragic plane crash in an effort to deliver relief supplies to the victims of an earthquake in Nicaragua. Born on August 18, 1934, Clemente rose from an impoverished background in Carolina, Puerto Rico, to become the star outfielder for the Pittsburgh Pirates from the years 1955 to 1972. He assisted the Pirates in winning two World Series in 1960 and 1971. Among Clemente's achievements as a player, he was four times the National League batting champion—1961, 1964, 1965, and 1967—and he was voted the league's most valuable player in 1966. He was awarded twelve Gold Gloves and set a major league record in leading the National League in assists five times. He served on fourteen all-star teams, and he was one of only sixteen players to have 3,000 or more hits during their career. Clemente was promising a great deal more before his untimely death. Clemente had accumulated 240 home runs and a lifetime batting average of .317. Upon his death the Baseball Hall of Fame waived its five-year waiting period after a player's retirement and immediately elected him to membership. For his generosity, leadership, outstanding athletic achievements, and heroism, Roberto Clemente is considered by Puerto Ricans to be a national hero to this day.

Dave Concepción (1948-)
Baseball

Venezuelan David Concepción was one of baseball's greatest shortstops, playing for the Cincinnati Reds from 1970 to 1988. In 1973, Concepción was named captain of the Reds, and in 1978 he became the first Cincinnati shortstop to bat .300 since 1913. In

Roberto Clemente.

Dave Concepción.

World Series play, Concepción hit better than .300 three times and better than .400 in the 1975 and 1979 league championships. His lifetime batting average is .267 for 2,488 games played. He made All-Star teams in 1973 and from 1975 to 1982. He was also winner of the Gold Glove each year from 1974 to 1977 and in 1979. In 1977, he was the winner of the Roberto Clemente Award as the top Latin American ballplayer in the major leagues.

Angel Cordero (1942-)
Horse Racing

Angel Tomás Cordero, born in San Juan, Puerto Rico, on November 8, 1942, is one of the most winning jockeys of all time. By December 1986, he was fourth in the total number of races won and third in the amount of money won in purses: $109,958,510. Included among Cordero's important wins were the Kentucky Derby in 1974, 1976, and 1985; the Preakness Stakes in 1980 and 1984; and the Belmont Stakes in 1976. He was the leading rider at Saratoga for eleven years in a row. In 1982, he was named jockey of the year.

Martín Dihigo
Baseball

Born in Matanzas, Cuba, Martín Dihigo is one of the few baseball players named to the American Hall of Fame based on his career in the Negro leagues. In addition, he was named to the Halls of Fame of Cuba, Mexico, and Venezuela. He was perhaps the best all-around baseball player that ever existed, yet there are few statistics and records to document his outstanding achievements. Called the "Black Babe Ruth," he played as an outstanding pitcher and outfielder, but he also played *every* other position. He was an outstanding hitter, as well. Dihigo began his career in the Negro leagues in 1923 with Alex Pómpez's Cuban Stars when he was only fifteen years old. By 1926, he was considered one of the top pitchers in black baseball. During his career he played ball in all of the countries that have named him to their Hall of Fame. In each of these countries he led the leagues in home runs, batting average, number of victories, and lowest earned run average (ERA). In 1929, he is reported as having batted .386 in the American Negro League; in 1938, he batted .387 in the Mexican League and pitched 18-2 with an ERA of 0.90.

After the failure of the Negro National League—when baseball was desegregated—Dihigo played in Mexico during the 1950s. He was then too old for the U.S. major leagues. After the Cuban Revolution, Dihigo—who had spent much of dictator Fulgencio Batista's rule in exile—returned to Cuba to assist in organizing amateur baseball leagues and to teach the game.

Roberto Durán (1951-)
Boxing

While not truly a Hispanic of the United States, Roberto Durán deserves mention because of the many fights he has had here and because he is one of the most colorful figures in boxing. Born on June 16, 1951, in Chorillo, Panama, he began boxing in 1967; in 1972, he won the lightweight championship from Ken Buchanan. In 1980, he won the World Boxing Council welterweight title but lost it that following November.

Sixto Escobar (1913-)
Boxing

Sixto Escobar, known as *El Gallito de Barceloneta* (The Barceloneta Fighting Cock), was the first Puerto Rican boxer to win a world championship when he knocked out Tony Marino on August 31, 1936, in the thirteenth round. Escobar was born in Barceloneta, Puerto Rico, on March 23, 1913, and only grew to fight at 118 pounds and five feet, four

Roberto Durán.

Sixto Escobar.

inches. Although born in Puerto Rico, Escobar spent most of his professional career in New York; he also fought in Canada, Cuba, Mexico, and Venezuela. Escobar fought as a professional boxer from 1931 to 1941, after which he joined the U.S. Army. He is one of the few boxers ever to have regained his lost throne, accomplishing this feat twice: in 1935 and 1938. Escobar fought sixty-four times and was never knocked out. He ended his hold on the championship in 1939, when he could no longer make the required weight of 118 pounds.

Manuel José Fernández (1946-)
Football

Born on July 3, 1946, in Oakland, California, "Manny" was educated at Chabot University and the University of Utah, and went on to become an outstanding defensive tackle on one of professional football's winningest teams, the Miami Dolphins under Don Shula. Fernández has achieved the highest distinction of any Hispanic in football: he was named to the All Time Greatest Super Bowl All-Star Team. During his career with the Miami Dolphin's, from 1968 to 1977, Fernández was voted the Dolphin's Most Valuable Defensive Lineman six consecutive years, 1968-73. He helped the Dolphins win two Super Bowls, 1972-1973 and become the only undefeated team in NFL history, in 1973.

Tony Fernández (1962-)
Baseball

Born on June 30, 1962, in San Pedro de Macoris, Dominican Republic, Tony Fernández has been a Toronto Blue Jays shortstop since 1983. He made the American League All-Star Team in 1986, 1987, and 1989. He holds the major league baseball record for highest fielding percentage in 1989, and the American League record for the most games played at shortstop, 1986.

Thomas Raymond Flores (1937-)
Football

Born on March 21, 1937, in Fresno, California, Thomas Flores, the son of Mexican-American farm workers, has risen to become an outstanding professional coach and manager. In fact, he is ranked as one of the most successful coaches in the National Football League, named to head the Oakland Raiders in 1979. Flores worked in the fields through elementary and junior high school, managed to get his high school and college education (University of the Pacific, 1958), and was drafted by the Calgary Stampeders (Canada) in 1958. After that he played with the Redskins and in 1960 joined the Raiders. As a quarterback for the Raiders for six seasons, he completed 48.9 percent of his passes for 11,635 yards and 92 touchdowns. Flores finished his ten years as a professional player with the Kansas City Chiefs in 1969. From then on he worked as a coach and was named assistant to Coach John Madden of the Raiders in 1972. When Madden resigned after the 1978 season, Flores took his place. In his second year as coach, the Raiders won Super Bowl XV. After two more years, Flores led the Raiders to another Super Bowl victory. Flores is only one of two people in NFL history to have a Super Bowl ring as a player, assistant coach, and head coach. After eight seasons, Flores's record with the Raiders was 78-43 in the regular season and 8-3 in playoffs and Super Bowls. In 1989, Flores became the president and general manager of the Seattle Seahawks, the highest rank ever achieved by a Hispanic in professional sports in the United States.

Lefty Gómez (1908-1988)
Baseball

Born on November 26, 1908, in Rodeo, California, Vernon Louis Gómez, also known as "Lefty" and "The Gay Castilian," probably referring to his Span-

Tom Flores.

ish ancestry (he was half Irish, half-Spanish), was one of baseball's most successful pitchers, ranking third in regular season wins, with 189 for the New York Yankees. He also holds the record for the most wins without a loss in World Series play (6-0) and three wins against one loss in all-star play. Gómez was active from 1930 to 1943, pitching 2,503 innings, winning 189 games to 102 losses, and earning an ERA of 3.34. He scored twenty wins or more in 1931, 1932, 1934, and 1937. Gómez is number thirteen on the all-time winning percentage list. In all, Gómez made all-star teams every year from 1933 to 1939, and he is a member of the Hall of Fame. During winter seasons, he played ball in Cuba, where he served for a while as manager of the Cienfuegos team, and once he taught a class on pitching at the University of Havana. Gómez died on February 2, 1989, in San Rafael, California.

Richard Alonzo González (1928-)
Tennis

"Pancho" González was born on May 9, 1928 in Los Angeles to Mexican immigrant parents. His father, Manuel, fitted furniture and painted movie sets, and his mother, Carmen, was an occasional seamstress. González was a self-taught tennis player, having begun at age 12 on the public courts of Los Angeles. He won his first tournament as an Edison Junior High School student; because of excessive absenteeism, González was not allowed to compete in tennis while in high school. González served in the U.S.

Pancho González winning the U.S. Men's Singles Lawn Tennis Championship in 1948 (Courtesy of the National Archives).

Navy and competed in the U.S. singles championship upon his return in 1947. That same year he placed seventeenth in the nation. In 1948, González became U.S. singles champion at Forest Hills and played on the U.S. Davis Cup team. He won Forest Hills again in 1949. After having won the U.S. grass, clay, and indoor championships, González turned pro. From 1954 to 1962, he was world professional singles champion. In 1968, he coached the U.S. Davis Cup team, and he was named to the International Tennis Hall of Fame.

Keith Hernández (1953-)
Baseball

Born on October 20, 1953, in San Francisco, Keith Hernández attended San Mateo College. He played with the St. Louis Cardinals from 1974 to 1983, and then with the New York Mets until 1989; since 1990 he has been with the Cleveland Indians. Hernández has been considered the best fielding first baseman of his time, having won eleven Gold Gloves and leading the league in double plays and lifetime assists. He played on National League All-Star teams in 1979, 1980, 1984, 1986, and 1987. Hernández assisted the Cardinals in achieving pennant and World Series victories, and, was Most Valuable Player in 1979 and an all-star in 1979, 1980, 1984, 1986, and 1987. In 1983, he was released under suspicion of using drugs; which later was proved to be true. A reformed and repentant Hernández was active with the Mets until 1989. In 1987, he was named team captain.

Al López (1908-)
Baseball

Al López has been rated as the seventh-best catcher and the seventh-best manager of all time, and he was elected to the Hall of Fame in 1977. For many years he held the record for the most games caught in the major leagues (1918) and for the most years (twelve) spent in the National League, catching in one hundred games or more. He tied the record for the most games caught in the National League without a passed ball in 1941, with 114 games. López played for the Dodgers from 1930 to 1947, and later with the Braves, the Pirates, and the Indians. He was an outstanding manager for the Indians from 1951 to 1956 and for the White Sox from 1957 to 1965 and 1968 to 1969. His record as a manager was 1,422-1,026 for a winning percentage of .581, the ninth all-time highest.

Keith Hernández.

Nancy López (1957-)
Golf

Nancy Marie López was born to Mexican-American parents in Torrance, California, on January 6, 1957, was raised in Roswell, New Mexico, and rose to become one of the youngest women golfers to experience professional success. She learned golf from her father, and by age 11 was already beating him. She won the New Mexico Women's Open when she was only twelve. In high school, López was the only female member of the golf team, and as an eighteen-year-old senior, she placed second in the U.S. Women's Open. After high school, she attended Tulsa University on a golf scholarship, but dropped out to become a professional golfer. In 1978, during López's first full season as a pro, she won nine tournaments, including the Ladies Professional Golf Association. She was named Rookie of the Year, Player of the Year, Golfer of the Year, and Female Athlete of the Year; she also won the Vare Trophy. Also in 1978, she set a new record for earnings by a rookie: $189,813. In 1983, she had a break from her career when she became the mother of Ashley Marie, the product of her marriage to baseball star Ray Knight. Two months after having Ashley, López began touring again, and by 1987, she had won thirty-five tournaments and qualified to become the eleventh member of the Ladies Professional Golf Association Hall of Fame. López's most outstanding year was 1985, when she won five tournaments and finished in the top ten of twenty-one others; that year she also won the LPGA again. Through 1987, she had earned over $2 million.

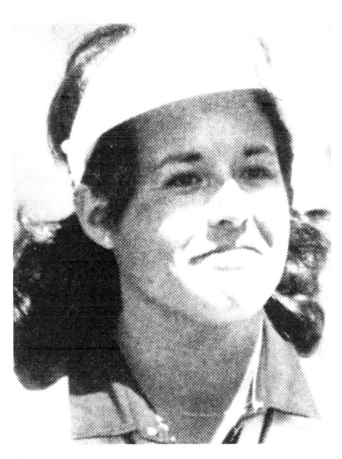

Nancy López.

Juan Marichal (1937-)
Baseball

Juan "Naito" Marichal is the right-handed Dominican pitcher who was signed to the minor leagues at age 19 and whose wide variety of pitches and motions took him to the Hall of Fame. Marichal started with the San Francisco Giants in 1962, and from 1962 to 1971 he averaged twenty wins per year. He led the National League in wins in 1963 with a record of 25-8 and in 1968 with 26-9, in shutouts in 1965 with ten and 1969 with and in ERA in 1969 (2.10). He pitched in eight all-star games for a 2-0 record and an 0.50 ERA for eighteen innings. Marichal's total innings pitched were 3,509, for a record of 243-142 and an ERA of 2.89. He was an all-star from 1962 to 1969 and again in 1971, and was inducted into the Hall of Fame in 1983.

Rachel Elizondo McLish (1958-)
Body Building

Born in Harlingen, Texas, McLish studied health and physical education at Pan American University. McLish has been a national champion bodybuilder, a successful model and actress, and spokesperson for health and physical fitness. McLish was the U.S. Women's Bodybuilding Champion in 1980, Ms. Olympia in 1980 and 1982, and world champion in 1982.

José Méndez (1888 or 1889-1928)
Baseball

Cuban José Méndez was an outstanding pitcher and infielder who, because of his African ancestry and dark skin, was never allowed to play in the majors. Instead, he played in the Negro National League and in Cuba, and thus many of his statistics are missing. Such witnesses as Hall of Famer John Henry Lloyd said that he never saw a pitcher superior to Méndez, and Giants Manager John McGraw said that Méndez would have been worth $50,000 in the majors, an unusually high figure back in those days. Méndez came to the United States in 1908 with the Cuban Stars. In 1909, he went 44-2 as a pitcher for the Stars. During the winters he played in Cuba, where he compiled a record of 62-17 by 1914. From 1912 to 1916, Méndez played for the All-Nations of Kansas City, a racially mixed barnstorming club. From 1920 to 1926, he served as a player manager for the Kansas City Monarchs and led them to three straight Negro National League pennants from 1923 to 1925. During his long career, he also played for the Los Angeles White Sox, the Chicago American Giants and the Detroit Stars.

Orestes Miñoso (1922-)
Baseball

Born in Perico, Cuba, on November 29, 1922, Saturnino Orestes Arrieta Armas Miñoso, nicknamed "Minnie," had one of the most outstanding careers of any Hispanic ballplayer in the major leagues. He began his career in Cuba on the semiprofessional Club Ambrosia team in 1942, and played semiprofessional ball on the island until he took to the field as a third baseman with the New York Cubans of the Negro leagues from 1946 to 1948. In 1949, he made his major league debut with the Cleveland Indians, but was soon traded to San Diego, returned to the Indians in 1951, and that same year went to the Chicago White Sox. He spent the greater part of his career playing on one or the other of these two teams, and with St. Louis and Washington until 1964. In 1976, Miñoso made a return as a designated hitter for the Chicago White Sox; he thus became one of only six players to be active in four separate decades, and only two other players in major league history have played at an older age: Satchel Paige and Nick Altrock. After that he remained active as a player-manager in Mexico. He ended his career as a third-base coach for Chicago. Miñoso's lifetime batting average was 299, with 1023 runs batted in, 186 home runs, and 205 bases stolen.

Amleto Andrés Monacelli (1961-)
Bowling

Born on August 27, 1961, in Barquisimeto, Venezuela, Amleto Andrés Monacelli is a college graduate who has become one of the most popular and successful members of the Professional Bowling Association tour. After becoming a professional in 1982, his earnings continually grew until, by 1991, he was winning $81,000 in prizes, and in 1989 even achieved a record $213,815. The list of tournaments he has won includes the Japan Cup (1987), the Showboat Invitational (1988), the Miller Challenge (1989), the Wichita Open (1989 and 1990), the Budweiser Touring Players Championship (1989), the Cambridge Mixed Doubles (1989 and 1990), the Columbus Professional Bowling Classic (1990), the Quaker State Open (1991), and the True Value Open (1991). Among his many awards are the Professional Bowlers Association Player of the Year in 1989 and 1990, and the Harry Smith Point Leader Award in 1989. In 1990, he won the Budweiser Kingpin Competition for the highest average for the year. In 1990, the sportswriters named him Bowler of the Year. Monacelli is still a Venezuelan citizen; this is the first time that a foreigner has ever been named Bowler of the Year. In his professional career, Monacelli has rolled sixteen perfect games, seven of them during the 1989 season, which established a new

Amleto Monacelli.

record for perfect games in a year. Three of these were accomplished during one week, thus tying the record.

Anthony Muñoz (1958-)
Football

Born on August 19, 1958, in Ontario, California, Muñoz is a graduate of the University of Southern California. He has played football with the Cincinnati Bengals since 1980, distinguishing himself as All-Pro offensive tackle eight times. He was selected for the Pro Bowl in 1982, 1983, and 1984. In 1988, he was chosen as the Miller Lite/NFL Lineman of the Year.

Tony Oliva (1940-)
Baseball

Pedro "Tony" Oliva, a native Cuban, has been the only player to win batting championships during his first two major league seasons. Throughout his career, Oliva was an outstanding hitter and outfielder; however, an injured knee shortened his career. He was active from 1962 to 1976 with the Minnesota Twins, winning Rookie of the Year in 1964 and the league batting title in 1964, 1965 and 1971. Oliva led the league in hits five times in his career. He made all-star teams from 1964 to 1971, tying Joe DiMaggio's record of having been named an all-star in each of his six first seasons, and won the Golden Glove in 1966 as the league's best defensive right fielder. Oliva's career batting average was .304, with 220 home runs and 947 runs batted in, for 1,676 games played. Because of his knee, which had been operated on seven times, Oliva served the last years of his career mostly as a designated hitter and pinch hitter. Since 1977, he has been coaching for the Minnesota Twins.

Alejandro Oms (1895-1946)
Baseball

Martín Dihigo considered Alejandro Oms to have been the best batter in Cuban baseball. Born to a poor family in Santa Clara, Cuba, in 1895, he had to work as a child in an iron foundry. He started playing organized baseball in 1910 as a center fielder. He played in the Negro National League on the Cuban Stars and the New York Cubans from 1921 to 1935, while still managing to put in outstanding seasons during the winter in Cuban professional ball. On the most famous Cuban team of all times, Santa Clara, Oms batted .436 in the 1922-23 season. In Cuba, Oms achieved a lifetime batting average of .352; his aver-

Anthony Muñoz.

age in the United States is not known. He was batting champion on the island three times: in 1924-25 with .393, in 1928-29 with .432 and in 1929-30 with .380. In 1928, he established a Cuban record for most consecutive games with hits: 30. In his last years, he was penniless and his vision was failing; he died at the age of 51 in 1946.

Vicente Oropeza (?-?)
Rodeo

The most famous and influential Hispanic rodeo performer of all time, the Mexican native Vicente Oropeza called himself the "premier charro Mexicano of the world," and on his first appearance in the United States in July, 1891. As a headliner and champion in both Mexico and the United States, he is credited with having introduced trick and fancy roping in the United States. In 1893, Oropeza became the star of "Buffalo Bill" Cody's "Mexicans from Old Mexico" feature in his Wild West Show. In 1900, Oropeza won the first World's Championship of Trick and Fancy Roping, which was a major contest up through the 1930s. One of the most famous American ropers of all time, Will Rogers, credited Oropeza for inspiring his career. Oropeza was selected as a member of the National Rodeo Hall of Fame for his contributions to what may be considered both a sport and an art.

Carlos Ortiz (1936-)
Boxing

Carlos Ortiz was the second Puerto Rican boxer—the first being Sixto Escobar—to win a world title. Born in Ponce, Puerto Rico, on September 9, 1936, Ortiz made his professional debut in 1955. He was undefeated that year and in 1956, 1957, and almost all of 1958, suffering his first defeat on December 31 in a fight with Kenny Lane in Miami Beach. He later beat Lane in a rematch to win the junior welterweight championship. After losing the junior welterweight championship to Duilio Loi, he turned lightweight in 1962, and on April 21 won the world championship in that division from Joe Brown. He successfully defended his crown various times until April 10, 1965, when he lost in Panama to Ismael Laguna. But he recovered the title on November 13 of the same year in San Juan, Puerto Rico. Again he successfully defended his crown until losing in the Dominican Republic to Carlos "Teo" Cruz on June 29, 1968.

Manuel Ortiz (1916-1970)
Boxing

A native of El Centro, California, Mexican-American boxer Manuel Ortiz became the bantamweight champion on August 7, 1942, when he beat Lou Salica. Ortiz totaled 41 knock-outs in his career and never once suffered one himself in 117 bouts. Ortiz tied Henry Armstrong in defending his title twenty times (only two other fighters had defended more often), and even successfully defended it three times in 1946 after a tour of duty in the army. Ortiz finally lost the crown on January 8, 1947, to Harold Dade in San Francisco, but he took it back on March 11 that same year. He lost it again on May 31, 1950, to Vic Toweel in Johannesburg, South Africa.

James Plunkett (1947-)
Football

James William "Jim" Plunkett was born in Santa Clara, California, the son of William and Carmen Blea Plunkett, who had met at a school for the blind in Albuquerque, New Mexico. His father managed a newsstand in San Jose, where Plunkett became an outstanding year-round athlete in high school. Later, at Stanford University he became starting quarterback as a sophomore. During his junior year he threw passes for 2,671 yards and twenty touchdowns. He was named to the Associated press's all-American second team, won the Voit Memorial Trophy as the PAC's outstanding player and was eighth in the Heisman Trophy selection. It was as a senior that he finally was awarded the Heisman Trophy, as well as many other awards. He became the first major college football player to surpass 7,000 yards on offense. In 1971, Plunkett was the first pick for the New England Patriots, and passed for 2,158 yards and 19 touchdowns; he was chosen as NFL Rookie of the Year. Plunkett was injured during the next few years and was traded to the San Francisco 49ers who later released him. In 1978, he was signed by the Oakland Raiders, and in 1980 he led the Raiders to the Super Bowl. He became Super Bowl MVP and was named the NFL 1980 Comeback Player of the Year. In 1983,

Jim Plunkett.

Plunkett again led the Raiders to a Super Bowl victory. That year he recorded his best seasons, with 230 completions for 1,935 yards and 20 touchdowns. Now retired, Plunkett passed for a total of 25,882 yards , with 164 touchdowns during his career.

Armando Ramos (1948-)
Boxing

In nine years as a professional boxer, Armando "Mando" Ramos only fought forty bouts, but that was enough for him two win two world titles as a lightweight. Born on November 15, 1948, in Los Angeles, the Mexican-American boxer won his first seventeen bouts, eleven by knockouts. On February 18, 1969, he won the lightweight championship from Carlos Cruz in Los Angeles. On February 19, 1972, Ramos won the World Boxing Congress lightweight championship over Pedro Carrasco. In 1973, he retired after suffering a knockout by Arturo Piñeda.

Juan (Chi Chi) Rodriguez (1935-)
Golf

Born on October 23, 1935, in Río Piedras, Puerto Rico, Rodríguez came from an extremely impoverished family and found his way into golf as a caddy on the links that served Puerto Rico's booming tourism. His is one of the most famous Hispanic "rags to riches through sports" tales, his career earnings having passed the $3 million mark, and because he contributes financially to charities, including the Chi Chi Rodríguez Youth Foundation in Clearwater, Florida. Included among the important tournaments that he has won are the Denver Open (1963), Lucky Strike International Open (1964), Western Open (1964), Dorado Pro-Am (1965), Texas Open (1967), and Tallahassee Open (1979). As a member of the Senior PGA Tour, he has won numerous tournaments, including the Silver Pages Classic (1987), GTE Northwest Classic (1987), and Sunwest Senior Classic (1990).

Lauro Salas (1927-)
Boxing

Lauro Salas's boyhood dream was to become a bullfighter, but he started boxing as a teenager in his native Monterrey, Mexico, for the money. He left home and moved to Los Angeles at age 19 to become a professional boxer. There he won fourteen of his first seventeen pro bouts as a featherweight. In 1952, he won the lightweight championship over Jimmy Carter, but lost it back to him that same year at Chicago Stadium. Salas retired in 1961 after being knocked out by Sebastiao Nascimento and Bunny Grant.

American twice as a two- and three-mile racer. In 1976, he entered the University of Oregon, where he was coached by Olympian Bill Dellinger. In 1978, he won the NCAA individual championship. He went on to become a three-time cross-country all-American and helped Oregon win the 1977 NCAA team title and finish second in 1978 and 1979. In 1979, he set a U.S. road record of 22:13 for five miles. In 1980, Salazar made the Olympic team, but that was the year that the United States boycotted the games in Moscow. That same year, however, Salazar won the New York Mar-

Juan "Chi Chi" Rodríguez.

Alberto Bauduy Salazar.

Alberto Bauduy Salazar (1958-)
Field and Track

Born in Havana, Cuba, one year before the triumph of the Cuban Revolution, future track marathoner Alberto Salazar moved to Manchester, Connecticut, with his refugee parents when he was only two years old. The family moved to Wayland, Massachusetts, where Salazar was named high school all-

athon with the record for the fastest first marathon in history, and the second-fastest time ever run by an American. The next year he won more championships, often by establishing new records, and once again he was victorious in the New York Marathon, setting a new world record of 2:08:13. In 1982, Salazar won the Boston and New York Marathons and various other events around the world; that year and in 1981 and 1983 he was selected the top U.S. road racer. Despite some setbacks and injuries, Salazar made the U.S. Olympic team for the second time in 1984, but finished only fifteenth in the games at Los Angeles. Salazar has set one world record and six U.S. records, the most of any U.S. runner since Steve Prefontaine.

Vicente Saldívar (1943-)
Boxing

Vicente Saldívar became the first undisputed Mexican featherweight world champion and the twelfth left-handed title holder in history with his win over Sugar Ramos on September 26, 1964. Born the son of a businessman in Mexico City on May 3, 1943, Saldívar turned professional in 1961. On his way to the world crown he knocked out twenty-five opponents, and he won thirty-six of his first thirty-nine pro bouts. Saldívar defended his title in eight straight bouts, winning five by knockout. He retired in October 1967, but made a comeback and regained the championship on May 9, 1970, from Johnny Famechon in a fifteen-round decision. Saldívar lost the title to Kuniaki Shibata by knockout in the thirteenth round on December 11, 1970.

Eligio "Kid Chocolate" Sardiñas (1910-)
Boxing

"Kid Chocolate" was one of the most celebrated Hispanic boxers of all time. Born in Havana, Cuba, on October 28, 1910, his career became an example of the fate that befalls boxers who battle their way out of poverty into fame and temporary riches. After winning eighty-six amateur and twenty-one professional fights in Cuba, he made his New York debut in 1928 and fought over one hundred bouts in the United States over the next ten years. He became a true champion, supported his community, and was memorized on stage and screen. However, he was severely exploited by his managers and owners and ultimately was done in by poverty and alcoholism.

Luis Tiant (1940-)
Baseball

Luis Clemente Tiant Vega, the Cuban pitcher, broke into professional baseball in the Mexican League in 1959. Although best known for his play with the Boston Red Sox, Tiant's major league career in the United States—from 1964 to 1982—included seasons with the Indians, the Twins, the Yankees, the Pirates, and the Angels. After making an outstanding start as a rookie for Cleveland with a 10-4 record and a 2.83 ERA, Tiant hit his stride in 1968 with a 1.60 ERA, nine shutouts, 5.3 hits per nine innings, striking out more than one batter per inning and finishing the season with a 21-9 record. On July 3 of that year, he struck out nineteen Twins in a ten-inning game, setting an American League record. In his previous start he had struck out thirteen Red Sox for a major league record. While suffering a series of problems, including a hairline fracture, Tiant was traded and released various times during the next few years, finally joining Boston in 1971 after a stint with the Red Sox's Louisville farm team. In 1972, he was named Comeback Player of the Year and he won the ERA title with a 1.91 and a season record of 15-6. The next two years he won twenty and twenty-two games and in 1974 led the league with seven shutouts. Tiant helped the Sox to a pennant and the World Series championship that year. In 1976, Tiant won twenty games for the last time and went 21-12 for the season. Tiant was known for his masterful changes of speed and a wide variety of release points and deceptive pitching motions.

José Luis Torres (1936-)
Boxing

The third Puerto Rican boxer to ever win a world championship was José Luis "Chegui" Torres, who won the medium heavyweight championship from Willie Pastrano on March 30, 1965, with a technical knockout in the ninth round at Madison Square Garden in New York. Without a rival in the middle heavyweight division, Torres took on Tom McNeely in the heavyweight class, winning in a ten-round decision. Torres defended his medium heavyweight crown and fought as a heavyweight successfully on a number occasions until December 16, 1966 when, weakened from an old pancreatic injury, he lost on points to the Nigerian Dick Tiger, whom he had beaten earlier in his career. Born into a large, poor family, in Ponce, Puerto Rico, Torres dropped out of high school and joined the army. There he learned to box well enough to win the Antilles, Caribbean, Second Army, All-Army and Interservice championships as a light middleweight. In 1956, he won the U.S. Olympic title, but lost on points at the games in Melbourne to the Hungarian Laszlo Papp. After the army, Torres moved to New York, where he fought as an amateur to win the National A.A.U. championship and then turned pro. During and after his professional boxing career, Torres also developed a career

event under par. In 1970, he was the leading money winner on the Professional Golf Association tour. In 1971, Treviño won the U.S. Open for a second time, won five tournaments between April and July, and also won the British Open in that year and again in 1972. For his achievements in 1971, Treviño was named PGA Player of the Year, Associated Press Athlete of the Year, and *Sports Illustrated* Sportsman of the Year. After that, he won the 1974 PGA again, among many other tournaments. In 1975, Treviño and two other golfers were struck by lightning during a tournament near Chicago. To this day he still suffers from back problems due to the accident; it seriously affected his game, even causing him to go winless in 1976 and 1978. In 1980, he made a comeback by winning the Texas Open and the Memphis Classic and earned $385,814 for the year. He was also awarded the Vardon Trophy for the fewest strokes per round (69.73 for 82 rounds), the lowest since Sam Snead in 1958. Treviño retired from the PGA tour in October 1985, with his thirty tour victories and total career earnings of over $3 million (third highest). Treviño has been elected to the Texas Sports, American Golf, and World Golf, Halls of Fame.

José "Chegüi" Torres. (José A. Martí Collection. Courtesy of the Center for Puerto Rican Studies Library, Hunter College, CUNY.)

as a singer and musician and worked in public relations, real estate, and as a New York newspaper columnist—all without a high school education!

Lee Treviño (1939-)
Golf

Lee Buck Treviño was born in Dallas, Texas, on December 1, 1939, into a Mexican-American family. Fatherless, he was raised by his mother, a cleaning woman, and his maternal grandfather, a gravedigger. Their four-room farmhouse was located at the back of the Glen Lakes Country Club fairways. As a boy Treviño studied the form of the golfers on the course from his own back yard. He dropped out of school in the seventh grade and made his way into what was then an exclusively Anglo rich man's sport by working as a greens keeper and as a caddy. He later joined the marines and played a great deal of golf while he was stationed in Okinawa. In 1966, Treviño became a professional golfer and achieved his first major victory in 1968 at the U.S. Open, where he became the first player in history to shoot all four rounds of the

Lee Treviño.

Fernando Valenzuela (1960-)
Baseball

Fernando Valenzuela has been one of the youngest and most celebrated baseball players because of his sensational introduction to the major leagues as an outstanding pitcher during his first seasons with the Los Angeles Dodgers. During his rookie year in 1981, Valenzuela won not only Rookie of the Year but also *The Sporting News* Player of the Year, and he was the first rookie ever to win the Cy Young Award. He won his first ten major league outings and his eight shutouts tied the rookie record in a season that was shortened because of a players'' strike. Valenzuela is considered to have the best screwball in baseball today. He led the league in strikeouts in 1981 and in wins in 1986. He was selected for the all-star team five times; in 1986 he tied Carl Hubbell's record of five straight strikeouts in an all-star game. That was also the year that he won the Gold Glove.

References

Brown, Bruce. "Cuban Baseball." *The Atlantic*, 253, no. 6 (June 1984): 109-14.

LeCompte, Mary Lou. "The Hispanic Influence on the History of Rodeo, 1823-1922," *Journal of Sports History* 12, no. 1 (Spring, 1985): 21-38.

Peterson, Robert. *Only the Ball Was White*. New York: McGraw-Hill, 1970.

Nicolás Kanellos

Prominent Hispanics

The following are short biographies of U.S. Hispanics who have excelled in their areas of endeavor. Virtually every field has been influenced by Hispanics or counts Hispanics among its outstanding practitioners. There are many other biographies in the other chapters of this book, which are dedicated to specific disciplines.

Michael J. Aguirre (1949-)
Law

Born in San Diego, California, on September 12, 1949, Aguirre was educated in California, attained a bachelor of science degree at Arizona State University in 1971, a law degree from the University of California, Berkeley, in 1974 and a master of public administration degree from Harvard University in 1989. He has worked as deputy legislative counsel for the California legislature, 1974-1975; as assistant U.S. attorney, 1975-76; assistant counsel for the U.S. Senate Subcommittee on Investigations, 1976-77; and as special reports legal counsel for the CBS network, 1977. Since that time he has worked in private practice. Since 1980, he has been the president of his own law firm, Aguirre & Meyer, A.P.C., which specializes in civil litigation. He has also been an adjunct professor and lectured in law at the University of California, San Diego, and at the University of Southern California. Aguirre is active in the community and has also been the author of various laws passed by the California legislature. His awards include the Wille Velásquez Community Service Award, given by the Chicano Federation in San Diego in 1989. In 1987, he was voted the most distinguished name in the San Diego legal community by the readership of the *San Diego Daily Transcript*.

Tomás A. Arciniega (1937-)
Higher Education

Born August 5, 1937, in El Paso,Texas, Arciniega received all of his higher education in New Mexico,

Michael Jules Aguirre.

graduating from the University of New Mexico in 1970 with a Ph.D. in educational administration. Arciniega went on to become an outstanding educator, administrator, lecturer, and creator of educational policy. He has served as assistant dean of the Graduate School of Educational Administration, University of Texas at El Paso, 1972-73; dean of education at San Diego Sate University, 1973-80; vice president of academic affairs, California State Uni-

Tomás A. Arciniega.

National Academy (1977) and has been a fellow of criminal justice at Harvard University School of Law (1970-71). Arreola's honors include a Detroit police department medal of valor in 1986, eleven merit citations, twenty commendations and two chief's merit awards.

Mary Helen Barro (1938-)
Radio Broadcasting

Born on June 17, 1938, in Culver City, California, Barro was educated in California, received a degree in management systems and procedures from the University of California at Los Angeles in 1967, and began a career in radio broadcasting. After working at various on-air and management positions in radio and television, from 1985 to 1986 she served as the general manager of the King Videocable Corporation. In 1986, she became a founder and partner of MC Gavren-Barro Broadcasting Corporation, serving as vice president and general manager. She has been an outstanding figure in broadcasting and a pioneer in creating emergency broadcasting procedures for the Spanish-speaking in the Los Angeles area. He honors include the Mexican American Opportunity Foundation's Woman of the Year Award in 1972 and resolu-

versity, Fresno, 1980-83; and President California State University, Bakersfield, 1983 to the present. He has won many awards for distinguished leadership in education, including being selected one of the top 100 leaders in American education by *Change* magazine in 1987. He received two commendations from the California legislature for contributions to California higher education, in 1975 and 1978.

Philip Arreola (1940-)
Law Enforcement

Born on February 4, 1940, in Acambaro, Guanajuato, Mexico, Arreola immigrated to the United States with his family and began his career as a policeman in the city of Detroit in 1960. Since that time he rose through the ranks of the Detroit and the Port Huron police departments, until becoming chief of the Port Huron police department in 1987. In 1989, he was appointed chief of police in Milwaukee and thus became one of the very few Hispanics to lead a major urban police force. Arreola's education includes a bachelor of science (with distinction) from Wayne State University in 1974 and a law degree from Wayne State in 1985. He is also a graduate of the FBI

Philip Arreola.

tions honoring her achievements from the city of Los Angeles (1972) and the California state legislature (1976).

Roy Benavides (1935-)
Military

Born on May 8, 1935, in Cuero, Texas, Benavides was educated in southeastern Texas and received his B.A. degree in 1981 from Wharton County Junior College many years after his secondary education and his life in the U.S. Army. Benavides served as a Green Beret in the U.S. Army from 1952 to 1976, when he retired as a master sergeant. He was one of the country's most decorated soldiers of the Vietnam War. His medals include the Congressional Medal of Honor, the Purple Heart with an Oak Leaf Cluster, the Defense Meritorious Service Medal, the Army Commendation Medal and many, many others. His valor and life story have been celebrated in books and in the founding of the Roy P. Benavides Airborne Museum. Benavides, with coauthor Oscar Griffin, published his autobiography, *The Three Wars of Roy Benavides,* in 1986.

Rubén Blades (1948-)
Popular Music and Film

Born on July 16, 1948, in Panama City, Panama, Blades received all of his early education and his bachelor's degree there. In 1985 he was awarded a law degree from Harvard University. Despite beginning life in both Panama and the United States as a lawyer, Blades has become an outstanding singer and composer of salsa music and a respected Hollywood actor. He has received four Grammy Awards and numerous gold records. His films include *The Last Fight* (1982), *Crossover Dreams* (1984), *Critical Condition* (1986), *The Milagro Beanfield War* (1986), *Fatal Beauty* (1987), and various made-for-television movies.

Tony Bonilla (1936-)
Civil Rights

Born in Calvert, Texas, on March 2, 1936, Bonilla received his higher education at Del Mar College and Baylor University (B.A. in 1958); he received a law degree from the University of Houston in 1960. Since that time he has worked as a partner with his brother, Rubén, and others in the law firm of Bonilla, Reed, Bonilla and Berlanga and served in the Texas legislature from 1964 to 1967. He has had a number of important political appointments, including the Governing Board for Texas Colleges and Universities. But his most important contributions have been made as president of the League of United Latin American Citizens, from 1972 to 1975, during which

Tony Bonilla.

time he was a national spokesperson on various Hispanic civil rights, economic, and educational affairs. He has also served as the chairman of the National Hispanic Leadership Conference, a position he holds at present. Among his awards are a gold medal from the president of Mexico in 1982 for his work on behalf of the Hispanic community of the United States.

Rubén Bonilla, Jr. (19?-)
Civil Rights

Born in Calvert, Texas, Bonilla received a B.A. degree from the University of Texas in 1968 and a law degree from there in 1971. Since that time he has worked as an attorney, as vice president of a law firm in partnership with his brother, Tony Bonilla, and has also served as the national president of the League of United Latin American Citizens from 1979 to 1981. He has been active in Democratic party politics in the state of Texas and has had a number of political appointments; in addition, he has served as the chairman of the Mexican American Democrats of Texas. His achievements have been recognized by *Esquire* magazine (1985) and *Texas Business* magazine. In 1980, he represented President Jimmy Carter at the inauguration of the president of Bolivia.

Harry Caicedo (1928-)
Journalism

Born on April 1, 1928, in New York City to Colombian parents, Caicedo was educated in the United States, received his bachelor of journalism from the University of Missouri in 1954, and has developed an outstanding career in journalism as an editor and director in various media. From 1955 to 1958, he served as associate editor of *Latin American Report* magazine; from 1958 to 1959, he was the chief of the *Miami Herald* news bureau, and from 1961 to 1978, he served the U.S. Information Agency and the Voice of America in various positions in the United States and in Latin America. In 1984, he became president of Inter American Editorial Services. From 1984 to 1991, he served as the founding editor of the nation's first Hispanic mass circulation magazine, *Vista*. Since 1991, he has been a media consultant.

Vikki Carr.

Harry Caicedo.

Vikki Carr (1940-)
Popular Music

Born on July 19, 1940, in El Paso, Texas, and baptized Florencia Bisenta de Casillas Martínez Cardona, under her stage name Vikki Carr has become one of the most successful Hispanic recording artists and international performers of popular music in history. Carr began her singing career in the Los Angeles area while still in high school. After touring with a band for a while, she signed her first recording

Lynda Carter.

contract with Liberty Records in 1961. Her first recording successes, however, were in Australia and England, and later in the United States. By 1967 Carr's international popularity was so great that she was invited to perform for Queen Elizabeth II at a command performance in London. The following year, she set a precedent for sold-out concerts in Germany, Spain, France, England, Australia, Japan, and Holland. In the United States, she became a favorite of the White House, performing repeatedly for each of the last four presidents. To date, Carr has recorded forty-nine best-selling records, including fifteen gold albums. In 1985, she won a Grammy for her Spanish-language album *Simplemente Mujer*. For her Spanish-language records, she has won gold, platinum and diamond records. Her 1989 album *Esos Hombres* won gold records in Mexico, Chile, Puerto Rico, and the United States. Among her other awards are the *Los Angeles Times* 1970 Woman of the Year Award, the 1972 American Guild of Variety Artists' Entertainer of the Year Award, the 1984 Hispanic Woman of the Year Award, and the 1991 Girl Scouts of America Award. In 1971, Carr founded the Vikki Carr Scholarship Foundation to provide higher education scholarships to Mexican-American youths. Carr is active in a number of other charities as well.

Lynda Córdoba Carter (19?-)
Television, Film

Born in Phoenix, Arizona, Lynda Carter began her show business career as a nightclub singer and dancer after finishing high school; she later attended Arizona State University. In 1970, she was crowned Miss World USA, which led her to Hollywood. She has since become a successful television actress. Her most famous role was Wonder Woman, from 1976 to 1979; she has also starred in various made-for-television movies, including *Stillwatch* and *Born to Be Sold* in 1981, *Rita Hayworth* and *The Love Godess* in 1983. During the 1980s, Carter also starred in her own variety shows, which highlight her singing and dancing: "Lynda Carter Celebration," "Lynda Carter: Body and Soul" and "Lynda Carter: Street Life." She is the founder of Lynda Carter Productions, which continues to launch new television programs. Included among her honors are the Golden Eagle Award for Consistent Performance in Television and

César Chávez.

Film and Mexico's Ariel Award as International Entertainer of the Year.

Lauro F. Cavazos (1927-)
Higher Education

Born on January 4, 1927, on the King Ranch in Texas, Cavazos was an outstanding student who eventually earned a bachelor's (1949) and master's degree (1952) in zoology at Texas Tech University and a Ph.D. in physiology (1954) from Iowa State University. Cavazos became an outstanding professor of anatomy and an educational administrator and rose through the ranks of academic administration at the Medical College of Virginia, Tufts, and Texas Tech, until finally becoming the first Hispanic president of a major research university, Texas Tech. But Cavazos only held that position for a short while before being chosen to become the first Hispanic U.S. secretary of education in 1988, a position that he resigned in 1990, because of political differences with the Bush administration. Cavazos's honors include the Medal of Honor from UCLA and the President's Medal from the City College of New York in 1989, election to the Hispanic Hall of Fame in 1987, the Outstanding Leadership Award in Education from President Reagan in 1984, and eleven honorary degrees.

César Chávez (1927-)
Labor Organizer

Born near Yuma, Arizona, in 1927, to a family of migrant farm workers, Chávez attended nearly thirty schools, eventually achieving a seventh grade education. During World War II he served in the navy, after which he returned to migrant farm labor. He eventually settled down in 1948 in the barrio of Sal Si Puedes (Get Out If You Can) in San Jose, California. It was in San Jose that he began working for the Community Service Organization (CSO) as a community organizer. By 1958, he had become general director of the CSO in California and Arizona. In 1962, wishing to organize farm workers, he resigned the CSO directorship and moved to Delano, California, where he became head of the United Farmworkers Organizing Committee, which has become today the United Farm Workers, AFL-CIO. From 1965 on, Chávez and his fledgling union embarked on a number of history-making strikes and national boycotts of agricultural products that have become the most successful in the history of farm labor in the United States. Principally because of Chávez and his organization's efforts, the California legislature passed the California Labor Relations Act in 1975, which provides secret ballot union elections for farm workers. Owing to his efforts, as well, there have been many improvements in wage, health, and housing conditions for farm workers in California and Arizona. Today, Chávez continues as a selfless and spiritual leader of farm workers everywhere, bringing to national attention their plight through media appearances and interviews, hunger strikes, and well-organized boycotts.

Bert Corona (1918-)
Labor Organizer

Born on May 29, 1918, in El Paso, Texas, Corona attended public schools in El Paso and college in California, where he graduated with a degree in law from the University of California, Los Angeles. Between 1936 and 1942, he was active in developing unions in the Southwest. He worked with the CIO in organizing cannery and warehouse workers. His union work eventually led to politics, where he became a pioneer in developing Mexican-American political organizations. In 1959, he was one of the principal founders of the Mexican American Political Organization (MAPA); he was also a founder of the National Congress of Spanish-Speaking People. Corona also was a pioneer in education for Mexican Americans, contributing to the development of the Mexican American Youth Conference and even serving as president of the Association of California School Administrators.

José R. Coronado (1932-)
Health Care

Born on April 3, 1932, in Benavides, Texas, Coronado has dedicated his life to health care. He received a B.S. degree in zoology and chemistry (1957) and an M.S. degree in education administration (1959) from Texas A&I and an M.S. degree in hospital administration (1973) from Baylor University. He has since become one of the very few Hispanics in the country to be the director of a major hospital: the Audie L. Murphy Memorial Veterans Hospital, a 704-bed tertiary health care facility and 120-bed nursing home affiliated with the University of Texas Health Sciences Center in San Antonio. Before becoming the director in 1975, Coronado had previously been assistant director there, and earlier in his career at two other veterans hospitals, in Kerrville and in Houston. In his present capacity, Coronado also holds

José R. Coronado.

Jaime Escalante.

various academic appointments in health care at Baylor University, Trinity University, the University of New Hampshire, Smith College, the University of Houston, and the University of Texas. In June 1991, Coronado was the first recipient of the Senior-Level Healthcare Executive Award for South Texas, presented by the American College of Healthcare Executives. His many other honors include a Presidential Rank Award for Meritoriuos Service from President Ronald Reagan in 1987 and the same award in 1989 from President George Bush.

Edward A. Corral (1931-)
Fire Chief

Born in Houston, Texas, on July 4, 1931, Corral received his primary education in Houston, attended the University of Houston in 1955, attended National Fire Academy seminars and short courses from 1956 to 1982, Houston Community College from 1975 to 1982, and Texas A&M University System Engineering Extension Service in 1968. From 1950 to 1951, Corral served in the air force, obtaining the rank of sergeant. From 1956 to 1969, he served as a Houston Fire Department senior inspector; from 1969 to 1973,

as an administrative aide in the mayor's office; from 1973 to 1981, as the fire department's chief inspector; and from 1981 to 1992, as the Houston fire marshall. He was appointed to the position of Houston fire chief in March 1992 by Mayor Bob Lanier. Included in Corral's innovative approaches to fire prevention was a program he initiated in 1982, the Juvenile Firesetters Prevention Program, which helped reduce fire damage by $11 million in its first year. Under the program, private companies pay the city to counsel some 2,000 area youths who have started fires.

Gilda Cruz-Romo (19?-)
Classical Music

Born in Guadalajara, Mexico, and educated there, Gilda Cruz-Romo graduated from the National Conservatory of Music in Mexico City in 1964 and embarked on her lifelong opera career as a soprano. From 1962 to 1967 she sang with the National Opera and the International Opera of Mexico, from 1966 to 1968 with the Dallas Civic Opera, and from 1969 to 1972 with the New York City Opera. Since 1970, she has been the leading soprano for the prestigious Metropolitan Opera Company of New York. As a professional opera singer, Cruz-Romo has sung in many countries and has won many awards, including first place in the Metropolitan Opera national auditions in 1970.

Jaime Escalante (1930-)
Education

Born on December 31, 1930, in La Paz, Bolivia, Escalante received his early education in Bolivia and a B.S. degree in mathematics from California State University in Los Angeles. Already a physics and mathematics teacher when he immigrated to the United States, he was not allowed to teach because he did not have a degree from an American institution; he therefore worked as a busboy, a cook, and then an electronics factory technician. After receiving his B.S. degree in mathematics from California State, he was hired at the impoverished barrio school of Garfield High School in East Los Angeles in 1974. He has subsequently become known as one of the nation's top teachers, because he has managed to teach and inspire his students to achieve at the nation's highest levels in mathematics and calculus, often sending them on with full scholarships to the nation's most prestigious colleges. Escalante taught at Garfield High School from 1974 to 1990. He currently works as an educational consultant and writes and stars in an educational program, "Futures," for television's Corporation for Public Broadcasting. In September 1991, Escalante began teaching math at Sacramento's Hiram High School, where he intends to replicate his success at East Los Angeles. Escalante's work has been the subject of a hit feature film and has inspired the creation of various scholarship funds in his name. His many awards include the 1989 White House Hispanic Heritage Award and the 1990 American Institute for Public Service Jefferson Award.

Joseph A. Fernández (1936-)
Education

Born and raised in New York City, Fernández has been awarded B.A. (1963), M.A. (1970), and Ph.D. (1985) degrees from the University of Miami. He has dedicated his entire career to education, beginning as a public high school teacher and rising to the post of superintendent of the Dade County Public Schools in Miami. He returned to his native New York in 1990 to become chancellor of the nation's largest school district. He has been known as a no-nonsense leader who has instituted many innovative programs in public education. In New York, he introduced the School-Based Management/Shared Decision-Making (SBM/SDM) model of school reform that he had pioneered in Miami. This program allows parents, teachers, and administrators to share decision-making authority

Joseph A. Fernández.

on everything from curriculum to budgets. Fernández has also been a pioneer in a number of other school reform areas. In 1991, he served as chairman of the Council to the National Urban Education Summit.

Ricardo R. Fernández (1940-)
Higher Education

Born in Santurce, Puerto Rico, on December 11, 1940, Fernández received his early education there and his higher education at Marquette University in Milwaukee (B.A. degree in philosophy, 1962, M.A. degree in Spanish Literature, 1965 and Princeton University (M.A. degree in Romance languages, 1967, and Ph.D. degree in Latin American Literature and Linguistics, 1970). However, his major work as a scholar and administrator has been accomplished in bilingual education and the education of Hispanic and minority students in a variety of positions for the state of Wisconsin and the University of Wisconsin, Milwaukee. From 1973 to 1978, he served as an assistant professor of cultural foundations at the university, and continued to develop his career after that in the field of education, rising to full professor and assistant vice chancellor for academic affairs by 1990. That same year he was named president of Lehman College of the City University of New York, and thus became one of a small handful of Hispanic college presidents in the United States. Among his leadership positions have been the following: president of the board of directors, Multicultural Training and Advocacy, Inc. (1986 to the present); member, board of directors, Puerto Rican Legal Defense and Education Fund (1981 to the present); and president, National Association for Bilingual Education (1980-81). His published books and research reports are pioneering studies on the causes of Hispanic school dropout, the desegration of Hispanic students, and bilingual education. Fernández's awards include the Lifetime Achievement Award in Education, National Puerto Rican Coalition (1990), a citation from the Wisconsin State Senate for his contributions in the field of education (1984), and the Hispanic Leadership Award from the Federal Regional Council-HEW Region V (1976).

Patrick F. Flores (1929-)
Religion

Born Patricio Fernández Flores on July 26, 1929, in Ganado, Texas, the seventh of nine children, Flores received his early education in Ganado and Pearland, Texas and graduated from Kirwin High School in Galveston. He then attended St. Mary's Seminary in La Porte, Texas, and St. Mary's Seminary in Houston. He was ordained a Catholic priest on May 26, 1956,

Archbishop Patrick F. Flores.

Ernesto Galarza (1905-)
Education, Labor

Born in Tepic, Nayarit, Mexico, Galarza immigrated to the United States as a refugee with his family during the Mexican Revolution. Galarza attended schools in Sacramento, California, where he was orphaned while in high school and thus had to support himself. Galarza went on to Occidental College and then received an M.A. degree from Stanford University in 1929. He later received a Ph.D. degree in education from Columbia University. Galarza then worked as a research assistant in education for the Pan American Union from 1936 to 1940, when he was promoted to chief of the Division of Labor and Social Information. In 1947, he became research director for the National Farm Labor Union, AFL, and moved to San Jose, California. During the next twelve years he dedicated his life to agricultural workers, serving as secretary-treasurer and vice president of the union. During the 1960s, Galarza worked as a professor, researcher and writer, writing various books on farm labor topics, and during the 1970s he developed

and served in a variety of functions in the diocese of Galveston-Houston, including as director of the Bishop's Committee for the Spanish-Speaking, until March 18, 1970, when Pope Paul VI appointed him to serve as auxiliary to the Archbishop of San Antonio. On May 5, 1970, he was consecrated as bishop. Bishop Flores was the first Mexican American elevated to the hierarchy of the Catholic church in the United States. On May 29, 1978, Bishop Flores was installed as the bishop of the diocese of El Paso, where he served until he was installed as the archbishop of San Antonio on October 13, 1979. Bishop Flores has received many honors and has pioneered programs in the church and in government on behalf of the civil rights of Hispanics and immigrants. In 1983, he was one of four bishops elected to represent the United States at the synod of bishops in Rome. In 1986, he was awarded the Medal of Freedom (Ellis Island Medal of Honor) in honor of the Statue of Liberty's one hundredth birthday.

Ernesto Galarza.

materials for bilingual education, including original books for children.

Héctor Pérez García (1914-)
Civil Rights

Born on January 17, 1914, in Llera, Tamaulipas, Mexico, he moved to south Texas with his family and was educated there; in 1936 he earned a B.A. degree from the University of Texas, and in 1940 his M.D. degree. But it was not as a doctor that García won national distinction, but as a civil rights activist. He is the founder and past president of the American G.I. Forum, an organization of U.S. Hispanic service veterans that has been a pioneer in securing the civil and educational rights of Hispanics. Besides working with the forum, García became a member of the Texas State Democratic Committee and in 1954 was appointed to the Democratic National Committee. He was also active in LULAC and in 1960 was a founder and first national president of the Political Association of Spanish-Speaking Organizations (PASO). During the 1960 election, García was the National Coordinator of the Viva Kennedy clubs. García has served as an alternative ambassador to the United Nations (1964), on the U.S. Commission on Civil Rights (1968), and as the vice president of the Catholic Council for the Spanish-Speaking of the Southwest. He is the recipient of the United States of America Medal of Freedom (1984), the Outstanding Democracy Forward Award, the U.S. Marine Corps Award, and many others. For his service in the U.S. Army Medical Corps during World War II, he was awarded the Bronze Star with six battle stars.

Elsa Gómez (1938-)
Higher Education

Born on January 16, 1938, in New York City, Elsa Gómez is the first Hispanic woman president of a four-year liberal arts college in the nation. Gómez received her B.A. degree in Spanish, magna cum laude, from the College of St. Elizabeth in 1960, her M.A. degree in Italian from Middlebury College in 1961, and her Ph.D. degree in Italian from the University of Texas in 1971. She taught and came up through the ranks at the University of Puerto Rico, Mayaguez, Indiana University of Pennsylvania, and Boston University. Before serving as president of Kean College, she was dean of the College of Arts and Sciences and director of the graduate program of Lock Haven University from 1987 to 1989 and director of academic programs for the Massachusetts Board of Regents of Higher Education from 1983 to 1987. Gómez has been named to various national and international honor societies as a scholar and administrator.

Elsa Gómez.

Raymond Emmanuel González (1924-)
Diplomacy

Born in Pasadena, California, on December 24, 1924, González received his B.A. and M.A. degrees from the University of Southern California in 1949 and 1950, respectively, and became a career diplomat for the United States. He served in various diplomatic capacities throughout Latin America and Washington, D.C., Belgium, and Italy, until finally serving as American ambassador to Ecuador from 1978 to 1982, at which time he retired. Since 1983, he has served as senior inspector, Office of the Inspector General in Washington, D.C. In 1970, he was the recipient of the Department of State Meritoriuos Award, and, in 1988, the Department of State Wilbur J. Carr Award.

Suzanna Guzmán (1955-)
Classical Music

Born in Los Angeles, California, On May 29, 1955, Guzmán is a 1980 graduate of California State University, Los Angeles, and the American Institute Music Theater in 1984. Although only at the beginning of her career, she has already sung as a soloist with the Los Angeles Philharmonic, the San Diego Opera, the

Washington Opera, the Metropolitan Opera, and at Carnegie Hall and the Kennedy Center for the Performing Arts. Her awards include First Place, Metropolitan Opera National Council in 1985; First Place, International Competition, Center for Contemporary Opera in 1988; Western Region First Place, San Francisco Opera Center, 1985, and others. Guzmán has been an active performer for Hispanic schoolchildren in southern California and for the handicapped.

Diego Edyl Hernández (1934-)
Military

Born on March 25, 1934, in San Juan, Puerto Rico, Diego Hernández received his B.S. degree from the Illinois Institute of Technology in 1955 and his M.S. degree from George Washington University in 1969; he attended the U.S. Naval War College in 1969. Hernández has pursued a career in the navy and has come up through the ranks to his present position of vice admiral. Since 1978, he served in a number of commanding officer positions in naval aviation, including on the aircraft carrier USS *John F. Kennedy*. In 1981, he became the chief of staff, Naval Air Forces, Atlantic Fleet, and was commander of the U.S. Third Fleet from 1986 to 1989. Since 1989, he has served as the deputy commander-in-chief of the U.S. Space Command. Among his many medals and awards are the Distinguished Service Medal with the Gold Star, The Distinguished Flying Cross, the Purple Heart, and many others.

Carolina Herrera (19?-)
Fashion

Carolina Herrera is one of the most respected fashion designers of the United States. Born in Caracas, Venezuela, Herrera became a fashion designer only after years of insistence by friends and retailers who marveled at the opulent creations she designed and wore to social functions internationally. She has headed her own design firm, House of Herrera, in New York City since 1981. Her clients have included Caroline Kennedy, Jacqueline Onassis, and Nancy Reagan. Herrera's design repertoire today includes the CH Collection, the Couture Bridal Collection, Carolina Herrera Costume Jewelry, Carolina Herrera Perfumes, and "Herrera for Men." Among her many honors are election to "The Best Dressed Hall of Fame" and *Elle* magazine's "Ten Most Elegant Women in the World." She has also received the MODA Award for Top Hispanic Designer in 1987.

Dolores Fernández Huerta (1930-)
Union Organizer, Lobbyist

Born in Dawson, New Mexico, Huerta received her early education in Stockton, California. In 1955, she became associated with Fred Ross and César Chávez, pioneer organizers of Mexican-American chapters of the Community Service Organization. Since that time, she has worked with Chávez in organizing and administering the United Farm Workers Union. With

Carolina Herrera.

Dolores Fernández Huerta.

years of experience in organizing migrant workers, striking, and negotiating contracts, Huerta eventually became the lobbyist for the UFW in Sacramento, California. She has gained an international reputation as an effective speaker and politician.

Tania J. León (1943-)
Classical Music

Born on May 14, 1943, in Havana, Cuba, Tania León received degrees from the National Conservatory of Music in Havana, a B.S. in music education from New York University in 1973, and an M.A. degree in music composition from New York University in 1975. One year after arriving in the United States in 1968, she became the first music director of the Dance Theater of Harlem, and she has continued to be an important composer for the Dance Theater. From then on, León studied conducting under such teachers and coaches as Laszlo Halasz, Leonard Bernstein, and Seiji Ozawa. She has maintained a busy schedule as a composer, recording artist, and as a guest conductor at most of the important symphonies throughout the United States and Puerto Rico, as well as in Paris, London, Spoleto, Berlin, and

Munich. From 1977 to 1988, she was the director of the Family Concert Series for the Brooklyn Philharmonic Community. In 1985, León joined the faculty of Brooklyn College as an associate professor, teaching both composition and conducting. She has also served as music director for Broadway musicals, such as *The Wiz*. León is just one of a handful of women to have made a successful career as a conductor. Her honors include the Dean Dixon Achievement Award in 1985, the ASCAP Composer's Award from 1987 to 1989, the National Council of Women Achievement Award in 1980, the 1991 Academy-Institute Award in Music of the American Academy and Institute of Arts and Letters, and many others.

Modesto A. Maidique (1940-)
Higher Education, Business

Born in Havana, Cuba, on March 20, 1940, Maidique was educated in Cuba and in the United States. He earned three degrees from the Massachusetts Institute of Technology: a bachelor of science degree (1962), a master of science degree (1964), and a Ph.D. degree in engineering (1970). Maidique is also the graduate of the Harvard Business School's Program for Management Development. Maidique has led an outstanding career as a scholar and educator, and as a business entrepreneur as well. He is the founder of Analog Devices Semiconductor, now a $300 million manufacturer of integrated circuits. He has been an advisor and consultant to major American firms in diverse fields and a general partner of Hambrecht & Quist, a leading venture capital firm. But it is in his academic career that Maidique has gained the most distinction; he is one of a very small handful of Hispanic college presidents. In 1986, he was appointed president of Florida International University in Miami. This followed upon a teaching career at MIT, Harvard, and Stanford, and his writing numerous articles and cowriting such books as *Energy Future*, which made the *New York Times* bestseller list. Under Maidique's leadership, Florida International University has been consistently named by *U.S. News & World Report* as one of America's best colleges. In 1991, Florida International University was ranked as one of the top ten comprehensive universities in the South.

Eduardo Mata (1942-)
Classical Music

Born in Mexico City on September 5, 1942, Eduardo Mata has dedicated his life to music and has become one of Mexico's most outstanding symphonic directors. Educated at the National Conservatory of Music from 1954 to 1963, and through private instruction, he began his conducting career in 1964 with the

Tania León.

Guadalajara Symphony Orchestra. From 1966 to 1975, he was music director and conductor of the Orquesta Filarmónica of the National University in Mexico City. In 1975, he became the director of the National Symphony in Mexico City and also directed a number of international music festivals, including the 1976 Casals Festival in Mexico. Mata has been a guest conductor around the world and throughout the United States. Since 1977, Mata has led the Dallas Symphony as music director, while also touring extensively and even continuing to serve as the princi-

pal conductor and musical advisor of the Phoenix Symphony (1974 to 1978) and the principal guest conductor of the Pittsburgh Symphony (since 1989). Mata was named conductor emeritus of the Dallas Symphony beginning with the 1993-94 season. Mata has also maintained a busy recording schedule that has resulted in top-quality albums of some of the world's leading orchestras under his direction. In Mexico he has been honored with the Golden Lyre Award (1974), the Elías Sourasky Prize in the Arts (1975), and the Mozart Medal conferred by the president of Mexico (1991). In the United States, he is the recipient of the White House Hispanic Heritage Award (1991).

Julián Nava (1927-)
Educator, Ambassador

Born on June 19, 1927, in Los Angeles, California, to a family that had fled Mexico during the Mexican Revolution, Nava grew up in East Los Angeles. He served in the Navy Air Corps during World War II and, upon return, obtained an education through the G.I. Bill. Nava graduated from Pomona College with an A.B. degree in 1951 and from Harvard University with a Ph.D. degree in 1955. Since graduation he has served as a lecturer and professor at various universities in Colombia, Venezuela, Puerto Rico, Spain, and California, where he is still a tenured professor of history at California State University at Northridge. In 1967, Nava was elected to the Los Angeles school board and later served as president of the board. Nava served as ambassador to Mexico from 1979 to 1981; he is the first Mexican American to ever hold that post.

Modesto A. Maidique.

Miguel A. Nevárez (1937-)
Higher Education

Born in McAllen, Texas, on June 20, 1936, Nevárez has devoted his life to education, first becoming an elementary teacher and then rising to become one of a small handful of Hispanic college presidents. After receiving his primary education in McAllen, Nevárez received a B.S. degree in agriculture from Texas A&I University in 1960; thereafter, he received a master's degree in elementary education from Michigan State University in 1968 and a Ph.D. degree in science education from New York University in 1972. Before becoming a university educator, Nevárez worked as an elementary science and math teacher from 1963 to 1967 and as an assistant principal from 1968 to 1969. In 1971, he became associate dean of men at Pan American University and by 1973 had risen to the rank of vice president. From 1981 to the present, he has served as president of that institution, which holds the highest enrollment of Hispanic students of any university in the United States. In 1985, President Ronald Reagan named Nevárez outstanding educator, and in 1987 he received Michigan State University's Distinguished Alumni Award.

Antonia Coello Novello (1944-)
Health Care

Born on August 24, 1944, in Fajardo, Puerto Rico, Novello was educated in Puerto Rico, where she became a physician, graduating from the University of Puerto Rico School of Medicine in 1970; she also received a Ph.D. degree from Johns Hopkins University School of Medicine in 1982. After attaining her M.D. degree in Puerto Rico, Novello did most of her residency work and received fellowships in the states from the University of Michigan (1971-74) and Georgetown University (1974-75). She pursued a career specializing in pediatrics and children's medicine at the National Institutes of Health (1975-86) and at the National Institute of Child Health and Human Development (1986-89). In her career, Novello became an international leader and a respected researcher in the field of children's health and nephrology. In 1989, she was named the surgeon general of the United States. She is the first Hispanic to ever hold that post.

Ellen Ochoa (1958-)
Astronaut

Born in 1958 in Los Angeles, California, Ochoa received her early education in Southern California and was awarded a B.S. degree in physics in 1980 from San Diego State University; she received M.S. and Ph.D. degrees in electrical engineering from Stanford University in 1981 and 1985, respectively. Following

Eduardo Mata.

her graduate studies, Ochoa became a research engineer at Sandia National Laboratories and later at NASA/Ames Research Center, where she rose to become the chief of the information sciences division. After that she became an astronaut, the first Hispanic female to do so. As a researcher, Ochoa holds to patents for work that she has developed. In 1989, she received the Hispanic Engineer National Achievement Award for the Most Promising Engineer in Government, and in 1990, she received the Pride Award from the National Hispanic Quincentennial Commission.

Raymond E. Orozco (1933-)
Fire Fighting

Born on December 7, 1933, in Chicago, Illinois, Orozco is a career fireman who has risen through the ranks to head the Chicago Fire Department after thirty years of service. After joining the department in 1959, he was promoted consistently until reaching battalion chief in 1979, deputy district chief in 1980, executive assistant to the fire commissioner in 1981, and a number of top deputy positions until being named fire commissioner on April 24, 1989. Through-

out his career Commissioner Orozco has undergone special training offered by the City of Chicago for fire fighters and for city administrators. In 1976, Orozco received his associate of arts degree in fire science from Daley College in Chicago.

Katherine D. Ortega (19?-)
Banking

Katherine D. Ortega was the first Hispanic to serve as treasurer of the United States. She was also the first woman to serve as the president of a California commercial bank (Santa Ana State Bank). Serving from September 1983 to June 1989, Ortega had both management and policy responsibilities over three of the Treasury's major bureaus: the U.S. Mint, the Bureau of Engraving and Printing, and the U.S. Savings Bonds Division. Prior to her appointment by President Ronald Reagan as treasurer, Ortega served as a commissioner of the Copyright Royalty Tribunal (1982-83) and as a member of the President's Advisory Commission on Small and Minority Business. Before entering government, Ortega was tax supervisor for Peat, Marwick, Mitchell & Co. (1969-72), served as vice president of the Pan American National Bank of

Julián Nava.

Los Angeles (1972-75), and as president and director of the Santa Ana State Bank (1975-78). Ortega graduated with honors from Eastern New Mexico University with a B.A. degree in business and economics. She holds three honorary doctor of law degrees and one in social sciences. In 1989, the secretary of the treasury presented her with the department's highest award, the Alexander Hamilton Award for outstanding service. Currently, Ortega serves on the board of directors of the Diamond Shamrock Corporation.

Francis V. Ortiz, Jr. (1926-)
Diplomacy

Born in Santa Fe, New Mexico, on March 14, 1926, Francis Ortiz received his B.S. degree from the School of Foreign Service at Georgetown University in 1950 and went on to pursue a career in diplomacy. He later attained an M.S. degree in 1967 from George Washington University and also studied at the National War College. His career in the foreign service took him to posts in Ethiopia, Mexico, Peru, Uruguay, Argentina, Barbados, and Grenada from 1953 to 1979. In 1979, he became the ambassador to Guatemala; from 1981 to 1983, the ambassador to Peru; and

from 1983 to 1986, the ambassador to Argentina. His honors include the 1952 Honor Award from the State Department, the 1964 and 1973 Superior Award, the 1980 Gran Cruz de Mérito Civil from Spain, and the 1964 U.S./Mexican Presidential Chamizal Commemorative Medal. From 1944 to 1946, Ortiz served in the U.S. Air Force; he received the Air Medal for his service.

Manuel Trinidad Pacheco (1941-)
Higher Education

Born on May 30, 1941, in Rocky Ford, Colorado, Pacheco has dedicated his life to education; having obtained a B.A. degree from New Mexico Highlands University (1962) and M.A. and Ph.D. degrees from Ohio State University (1966 and 1969), he pursued a career as a professor of Spanish and education and as an administrator at various universities. It is in educational administration that Pacheco made his mark, first becoming associate dean at the University of Texas at El Paso in 1982 and executive director for planning in 1984, then pesident of Laredo State University in 1984, president of the University of Houston-Downtown in 1988 and president of the University of Arizona in 1991. Upon assuming this last position, Pacheco became the first Hispanic president of a major research university in the United States. Among his many honors is that of being named a distinguished alumnus of Ohio State University in 1984 and named among the "100 Most Influential Hispanics" by *Hispanic Business* magazine in 1988.

Minerva Pérez (1955-)
Television Journalism

Born on October 25, 1955, in San Juan, Texas, Pérez was educated in south Texas, receiving her B.A. degree from the University of Texas-Pan American in 1980. Since 1979, she has embarked on a career in television journalism, working at KGBT-TV in Harlingen, Texas, as a reporter, then as producer and anchor. In 1982, she became a morning anchor and reporter for KMOL-TV in San Antonio, and in 1984, she held a similar position at an Austin station. From there she worked as a reporter in stations in Dallas and Phoenix. From 1987 to 1992, she worked as a reporter and anchor for KTLA-TV in Los Angeles. In 1992, she joined KTRK Channel 13 in Houston, Texas, as a weekend anchor and reporter. Pérez's outstanding work has been acknowledged through various awards: the Spot News Coverage Associated Press Media Award in 1987; an Emmy nomination for Best Host of a Community Affairs Program; and a Golden Mike Media Award, both in 1990; and others.

Miguel A. Nevárez.

Guadalupe C. Quintanilla (1937-)
Higher Education

Born on October 25, 1937, in Ojinaga, Chihuahua, Mexico, Quintanilla received her B.S. degree in biology from Pan American University in 1969 and her M.A. and Ed.D. degrees in education in 1969 and 1971, respectively, from the University of Houston. Quintanilla's career in education has spanned the gap from teacher aide (1964) to upper university administration, beginning in 1978 with her position as assistant provost for undergraduate affairs at the University of Houston. Since that time, she has also served as assistant vice chancellor (1981-85) and assistant vice president (1986 to the present). Throughout her career, Quintanilla has been in the vanguard of Hispanic studies, founding and directing one of the first Mexican-American studies programs (1972-78) and one of the first bilingual teacher education programs (1972-78), both at the University of Houston. She is a widely known writer and lecturer on Hispanic education and overcoming the barriers of poverty, prejudice, and not speaking English. She is the author of numerous books and articles on teaching Spanish to native speakers, bilingual education, and the teaching of Spanish to public servants, such as police and firemen. Her honors include a presidential appointment as a U.S. representative to the World Conference on International Issues and Women's Affairs (1991), induction into the National Hispanic Hall of Fame (1987), a National Heroine Award from *The Ladies' Home Journal* (1984), a presidential appointment as alternate delegate to the United Nations (1984), and many others.

Mario E. Ramírez (1926-)
Medicine

Mario Ramírez was born in Roma, Texas, on April 3, 1926. He received his early education there and went on to graduate from the University of Texas with a B.A. in 1945; after that he received his M.D. degree from the University of Tennessee College of Medicine in 1948. Since that time he has led a distinguished career in family practice and in medical education, rising to the governing boards of medical institutions in the state of Texas and to membership on the Coordinating Board of Texas Colleges and Universities (1979-85) and the Board of Regents of the University of Texas System (1988-95). Throughout his career he has won numerous awards, including the American Academy of Family Physicians and the *Good Housekeeping* magazine Family Doctor of the Year Award (1978) and the Bicentennial Dr. Benjamin Rush Award of the American Medical Association (1985).

Geraldo Rivera (1943-)
Journalism, Television

Born on July 4, 1943, in New York City, Rivera studied at the University of Arizona and Brooklyn Law School and received his law degree from the University of Pennsylvania and a degree in journalism from Columbia University. Rivera went on to become one of the nation's most celebrated and respected investigative television journalists, writing and producing various award-winning documentaries. He has won a Peabody Award and ten Emmys for distinguished broadcast journalism. After beginning his career as a reporter for WABC-TV in New York in 1970, he went on to become a reporter, producer, and host for various television news and entertainment shows. Since 1987, he has hosted and produced his own "Geraldo" talk show, which is nationally syndicated. Rivera is also the author of books, including

Manuel Pacheco (Photo by Julieta González).

his very controversial autobiography, which was published in 1991. Today, Rivera is one of the most visible and successful Hispanics in media and entertainment.

Katherine D. Ortega.

Guadalupe C. Quintanilla.

Austin. After initiating her career in education as a first- and second-grade bilingual teacher from 1970 to 1973, Rodríguez worked in a number of experimental programs and served as curriculum writer, project director, and principal investigator. In 1973, she founded the program for which she continues to this date as executive director: Advance Family Support and Education Programs, which provides support and education services to low-income families for their educational, personal, and economic success. The program has become a national model for community-based intervention, and Rodríguez is in high demand nationally as a consultant, speaker, board member, project director and as an expert witness before Congress. Rodríguez's honors include the *San Antonio Light* newspaper Woman of the Year Award in 1981, the Women in Communication Professional Achievement Award in 1987, and two Citations of Recognition from the San Antonio City Council in 1981 and 1986.

Paul Rodríguez (19?-)
Entertainment

Paul Rodríguez is the most recognized and popular Hispanic comedian in the United States. Born in 1977

Mario E. Ramírez (Photo by Gittings).

Gloria G. Rodríguez (1948-)
Education

Born on July 9, 1948, in San Antonio, Texas, Gloria Rodríguez has dedicated her life to education. She received a B.A. degree in elementary education and bilingual education from Our Lady of the Lake University (1970), two M.Ed. degrees (1973 and 1979) from Our Lady of the Lake and the University of Texas at San Antonio, and a Ph.D. degree in early childhood education (1991) from the University of Texas at

Paul Rodríguez.

Luis Santeiro.

in Mazatlán, Mexico, Rodríguez came to the United States as the son of immigrant farm workers. "My family never thought that being a comedian or an actor was an obtainable goal. Being farmworkers, all they wanted for their children was a steady job. But I knew I had to give it a chance." In 1977, after a stint in the air force, Rodríguez entered Long Beach City College on the G.I. Bill, where he received and associate arts degree, and then he enrolled in California State University, Long Beach, with the objective of becoming an attorney. During theater classes at the university, Rodriguez's comic talent became obvious to his professor, who led him to become associated with the Comedy Store in Los Angeles, and thus his standup comic career was launched. Currently, Paul Rodríguez has worked in three television major network sitcom series and various movies. He is the host and star of immensely popular "El Show de Paul Rodríguez" on the Univision

Spanish-language network. Rodríguez is the head of his own company, Paul Rodríguez Productions, which produced the one-hour special "Paul

Cristina Saralegui.

cials." Santeiro is among the most recognized Hispanics on television; he has won six Emmy Awards for his writing on "Sesame Street." Santiero is also a recognized dramatist with plays successfully produced in New York and Miami.

Cristina Saralegui (1948-)
Television, Journalism

Born on January 29, 1948, in Havana, Cuba, into a distinguished family of journalists, Cristina Saralegui's grandfather, Francisco Saralegui, was known throughout Latin America as the "paper czar"; he initiated his granddaughter into the world of publishing through such popular magazines as *Bohemia, Carteles,* and *Vanidades.* In 1960, she immigrated to Miami's Cuban exile community, but continued to develop the family profession by majoring in mass communications and creative writing at the University of Miami. In her last year at the university, she began working for *Vanidades*, the leading ladies' service magazine in Latin America. By 1979, she was named editor-in-chief of the internationally distributed *Cosmopolitan-en-Español.* In 1989, she resigned that position to become the talk show host for "The Cristina Show," which has become the number

Rodríguez behind Bars," which aired nationally on the Fox Network in 1991. His earlier special "I Need a Couch" had one of the highest ratings in the history of HBO comedy specials. In addition to his film and television work, Rodríguez is a comedy headliner at Las Vegas and Atlantic City, and in 1986 released his first comedy album, "You're in America Now, Speak Spanish."

Luis Santeiro (1947-)
Television Writer, Playwright

Born on October 9, 1947, in Havana, Cuba, Santeiro immigrated to Miami with his parents in 1960. He received a B.A. degree in sociology from Villanova University in 1969 and an M.A. degree in communications from Syracuse University in 1970. He became a free-lance writer and, since 1978 has served as a writer for the award-winning Children's Television Workshop and as the producer of "Sesame Street." Among the many shows he has written for television are thirty episodes of the bilingual comedy "Qué Pasa, USA?" (1977-80), and numerous episodes of the PBS series "3-2-1Contact!", "Oye, Willie!", "Carrascolendas," and the ABC "After School Spe-

Alberto Serrano.

Roberto Suárez.

one rated daytime show on Spanish-language television in the United States. Since 1991, Saralegui has also been the host for a daily nationally syndicated radio show, "Cristina Opina" (Cristina's Opinions) and the editor-in-chief of a new monthly magazine, *Cristina-La Revista* (*Cristina-The Magazine*), published by Editorial América in Miami. Through radio and television, Cristina reaches 6.5 million Hispanics daily throughout the United States and in twelve Latin American countries.

Alberto Serrano (1931-)
Psychiatry

Born on April 7, 1931, in Buenos Aires, Argentina, Serrano was raised and educated in Argentina, where he became a medical doctor after graduating from the Buenos Aires School of Medicine in 1956. He did his internship at the Clínica Córdoba and at the National Institute of Mental Health, both in Buenos Aires. In 1957, he immigrated to the United States and began developing his career in is psychiatry as a resident in the Department of Neurology and Psychiatry at the University of Texas Medical Branch in Galveston, Texas. Since that time he has grown to become one of the finest psychiatrists and professors of psychiatry, specializing in child psychiatry in the United States. He rose the ranks at the University of Texas, first in Galveston, then in San Antonio, where he became the director of child and adolescent psychiatry. From 1986 to the present, he has served as professor of psychiatry and pediatrics and director of the Division of Child and Adolescent Psychiatry at the University of Pennsylvania School of Medicine. In the communities that he has lived, Serrano has been a director of various mental health clinics; since 1986, he has been the medical director of the Philadelphia Child Guidance Clinic and the psychiatrist-in-chief and director of the psychiatry division of the Children's Hospital of Philadelphia. In 1991, he became associate chairman of the Department of Psychiatry of he University of Pennsylvania School of Medicine. Among his various international recognitions, the American Family Therapy Association recognized him in 1986 for his "Pioneering Contribution to Family Therapy."

Robert Suárez (1928-)
Journalism

Born in Havana, Cuba, on May 5, 1928, Suárez received his primary and secondary education there. He obtained a bachelor's degree in economics and finance from Villanova University in 1949. After returning to Havana, from 1959 to 1960 he was active in real estate, construction and finance. In 1962, he went to work for *The Miami Herald* as a part-time mailer. He advanced to controller of the Knight-Ridder subsidiary operations. In 1972, he joined Knight Publishing Company in Charlotte, North Carolina, as controller and was named vice president and general manager in 1978. He was named president in 1986. In 1990, he assumed his present position as president of *The Miami Herald* and Publisher of *El Nuevo Heraldo*, the Spanish-language newspaper published by *The Miami Herald* since 1987. His awards include the 1989 Gold Medal for Excellence for being the most distinguished executive of al Knight-Ridder companies, the 1990 Hispanic Alliance Heritage Award for Media, and the 1991 Leadership Award from ASPIRA.

Catalina Vásquez Villalpando (1940-)
Treasurer

Born on April 1, 1940, in San Marcos, Texas, Catalina Villalpando attended various universities, but really rose in her career through the ranks, beginning as a secretary and eventually becoming the director of the Community Services Administration, from 1969 to 1979. From there, she became a vice president of the Mid-South Oil Company in Dallas, and then a senior vice president of Communications International in Dallas. In 1983, she became a special assistant to President Ronald Reagan, and in 1988 she was appointed treasurer of the United States. She has been very active in Republican politics, serving as a vice president of the Republican National Assembly of Texas. Her honors include various special achievement awards from government agencies.

Reference

Unterberger, Amy L., ed. *Who's Who Among Hispanic Americans 1992-1993*. Detroit, Mich.: Gale Research, 1992.

Nicolás Kanellos

Illustrations

A Historical Overview: *p. 5:* Map of early European penetration of the United States (courtesy of the U.S. Department of the Interior and the National Park Service); *p. 13:* San José de Tumacacori Mission, Arizona (courtesy of the U.S. Department of the Interior and the National Park Service); *p. 14:* A *vaquero* in early California (courtesy of the Bancroft Library, University of California); *p. 15:* Rules issued by King of Spain regarding presidios on the frontier; *p. 18:* Soldier at the Monterey presidio in 1786 (courtesy of the Bancroft Library, University of California); *p. 19:* Wife of a presidio soldier in Monterey, 1786 (courtesy of the Bancroft Library, University of California); *p. 19:* A *patrón* in early California (courtesy of the Bancroft Library, University of California); *p. 20:* Presidio and pueblo of Santa Barbara in 1829 (from a lithograph by G. & W. Endicott. Courtesy of the Bancroft Library, University of California); *p. 21:* Ferdinand VII, King of Spain, 1814-1833 (from Manuel Rivera Cambas, Los gobernantes, 1872); *p. 23:* Pío Pico (1801-1894), last governor of California under Mexican rule (courtesy of the California Historical Society); *p. 24:* Confederate officers from Laredo, Texas: Refugio Benavides, Atanacio Vidaurri, Cristóbal Benavides and John Z. Leyendecker (courtesy of the Laredo Public Library); *p. 25:* Viceroy Francisco Fernández de la Cueva Enríquez, Duke of Albuquerque; *p. 25:* General Manuel Mier y Terán, Laredo, 1928; *p. 27:* Map of European claims in the United States to 1763 (courtesy of the U.S. Department of the Interior and the National Park Service);

p. 30: Albizu Campos at a press conference on December 16, 1947; *p. 30:* Luis Muñoz-Rivera; *p. 44:* Luis Muñoz Marín, architect of the present commonwealth status of Puerto Rico; *p. 47:* Fidel Castro; *p. 49:* The first flight of American citizens repatriated from Cuba on December 19, 1966 (courtesy of the *Texas Catholic Herald*); *p. 50:* Cubans arriving in Miami during the Mariel boat-lift (courtesy of the *Texas Catholic Herald*); *p. 51:* A legally immigrating Cuban woman is reunited with her granddaughter in Miami in 1980 (courtesy of the *Texas Catholic Herald*).

Spanish Explorers and Colonizers: *p. 60:* Queen Isabella la Católica; *p. 60:* Frontispiece from original 1493 edition of Cristóbal Colón's letter to the Catholic Kings describing his discoveries; *p. 66:* The title page of Cabeza de Vaca's *La relación* (*The Account of His Trip*), 1542; *p. 69:* A portrayal of Hernando de Soto by an unknown eighteenth-century artist (courtesy of the U.S. Department of the Interior and the National Park Service); *p. 71:* Pedro Menéndez de Avilés; *p. 71:* Drawing of free black militia (1795).

Historic Landmarks: *p. 138:* Royal Presidio Chapel, Monterey (courtesy of the U.S. Department of the Interior and the National Park Service); *p. 139:* San Francisco de Asís Mission (Mission Dolores) (Oriana Day Painting. Courtesy of the De Young Museum, San Francisco); *p. 140:* San Luis Rey de Francia Mission, Oceanside (photo by Henry F. Whitey, 1936. W.P.A.); *p. 140:* Santa Barbara Mission (photo by

Henry F. Whitey, 1936. W.P.A.); *p. 141:* General Vallejo House (photo by Roger Sturtevant, 1934); *p. 141:* Castillo de San Marcos, St. Augustine; *p. 142:* The Cabildo in New Orleans (courtesy of the U.S. Department of the Interior and the National Park Service); *p. 144:* The Convent of Porta Coeli in San Germán; *p. 144:* The Alamo, San Antonio (courtesy of the Department of the Interior and the National Park Service); *p. 145:* San Francisco de la Espada Mission, San Antonio; *p. 145:* La Bahía Mission (courtesy of the U.S. Department of the Interior and the National Park Service); *p. 146:* Monument honoring the fallen at the Alamo, San Antonio (courtesy of the U.S. Department of the Interior and the National Park Service); *p. 147:* A reconstruction of the San Francisco Mission in East Texas (courtesy of the *Texas Catholic Herald*); *p. 148:* San Miguel Mission, Santa Fe, New Mexico (courtesy of the U.S. Department of the Interior and the National Park Service); *p. 148:* San José y San Miguel Aguayo Mission (photo by Arthur W. Stewart, 1936. W.P.A.).

The Family: *p. 152:* The Lugo Family, circa 1888 (courtesy of Los Angeles County Museum of Natural History); *p. 153:* A child's birthday party in New York City (Justo A. Martí Collection, Center for Puerto Rican Studies Library, Hunter College, CUNY); *p. 154:* United Bronx Parents, Inc. (Records of the United Bronx Parents, Inc. Courtesy of the Center for Puerto Rican Studies Library, Hunter College, CUNY); *p. 154:* A Puerto Rican mine worker and his family, Bingham Canyon, Utah (Historical Archive, Departamento de Asuntos de la Comunidad Puertorriqueña. Courtesy of the Center for Puerto Rican Studies Library, Hunter College, CUNY); *p. 155:* Mexican Mother of the Year, 1969: Mrs. Dolores Venegas, Houston, Texas (courtesy of the *Texas Catholic Herald*); *p. 157:* A Hispanic family attends mass, Houston, Texas (photo by Curtis Dowell. Courtesy of the *Texas Catholic Herald*); *p. 158:* A *posada* rehearsal, Houston, Texas, 1988 (photo by Curtis Dowell. Courtesy of the *Texas Catholic Herald*).

Relations with Spain and Spanish America: *p. 177:* Rally in East Lower Harlem (El Barrio) in Manhattan in support of the independence of Puerto Rico (The Jesús Colón Papers. Courtesy of the Center for Puerto Rican Studies, Hunter College, CUNY; Benigno Giboyeaux for the Estate of Jesús Colón and the Communist Party of the United States of America); *p. 193:* Fidel Castro; *p. 194:* Archbishop Oscar Romero of El Salvador (courtesy of the *Texas Catholic Herald*); *p. 196:* Guerrillas of El Frente Farabundo Martí por la Liberación Nacional (FMLN) in El Salvador; *p. 198:* Demonstrators opposing U.S. mili-

tary aid to El Salvador in 1980 (courtesy of the *Texas Catholic Herald*).

Population Growth and Distribution: *p. 200:* Senior citizens at the Domino Park in Little Havana, Miami (courtesy of the *Texas Catholic Herald*); *p. 201:* Undocumented workers entering the United States at El Paso, Texas, 1990 (courtesy of the *Texas Catholic Herald*); *p. 201:* A group of Hispanics have just been issued their temporary residence cards, 1991 (photo by Les Fetchko. Courtesy of the *Texas Catholic Herald*); *p. 202:* The drive to legalize undocumented workers in Houston, Texas (photo by Curtis Dowell. Courtesy of the *Texas Catholic Herald*); *p. 203:* A poster for National Migration Week; *p. 204:* Mexican Independence Day Parade, Houston, Texas, 1982 (photo by Curtis Dowell. Courtesy of the *Texas Catholic Herald*); *p. 206:* A mass citizenship swearing in ceremony at Hoffheinz Pavilion of the University of Houston in 1987 (photo by Curtis Dowell. Courtesy of the *Texas Catholic Herald*).

Language: *p. 210:* The Teatro Puerto Rico in October, 1960 (Justo A. Martí Collection. Courtesy of the Center for Puerto Rican Studies Library, Hunter College, CUNY); *p. 214:* Downtown El Paso, Texas (courtesy of the *Texas Catholic Herald*); *p. 218:* A typical Hispanic grocery store in New York City (Justo A. Martí Collection. Courtesy of the Center for Puerto Rican Studies Library, Hunter College, CUNY); *p. 219:* Two scenes from the *Villa Alegre* television series; *p. 220:* A customer buying *La prensa* (Justo A. Martí Collection. Courtesy of the Center for Puerto Rican Studies Library, Hunter College, CUNY); *p. 222:* A voter registration drive in New York City (Justo A. Martí Collection. Courtesy of the Center for Puerto Rican Studies Library, Hunter College, CUNY); *p. 223:* Our Lady of Guadalupe Church in Queen Creek, Arizona (courtesy of the *Texas Catholic Herald*).

Law and Politics: *p. 240:* Four charts on law school enrollment (*Consultant's Digest*, May 1991); *p. 242:* Wilfredo Caraballo; *p. 243:* Antonia Hernández; *p. 244:* Mario G. Obledo; *p. 246:* Table 9.1, Hispanic Judges in State Courts (courtesy of the Hispanic National Bar Association Nationwide Summary of Hispanics in the State Judiciary, 1992); *p. 247:* Judge Reynaldo G. Garza; *p. 249:* Judge Raymond L. Acosta; *p. 249:* Justice John A. Argüelles; *p. 250:* Justice Joseph F. Baca; *p. 251:* Judge José A. Cabranes; *p. 253:* Judge George La Plata; *p. 254:* Judge Federico A. Moreno; *p. 255:* Chief Judge Manuel L. Real; *p. 256:* Justice Dorothy Comstock Riley; *p. 257:* Judge Joseph H. Rodríguez; *p. 257:* Chief Justice Luis D.

Rovirá; *p. 260:* Ben Blaz. Delegate to the U.S. Congress from Guam; *p. 261:* E. (Kika) de la Garza, U.S. Congressman (D-Texas); *p. 261:* Ron de Lugo. Delegate to the U.S. Congress from the U.S. Virgin Islands; *p. 262:* Matthew G. Martínez, U.S. Congressman (D-California); *p. 263:* Solomon *P. Ortiz, U.S. Congressman (D-Texas); p. 263:* Bill Richardson, U.S. Congressman (D-New Mexico); *p. 264:* Ileana Ros-Lehtinen, U.S. Congresswoman (R-Florida); *p. 264:* Edward R. Roybal, U.S. Congressman (D-California); *p. 265:* José E. Serrano, U.S. Congressman (D-New York); *p. 266:* Esteban E. Torres, U.S. Congressman (D-California); *p. 267:* Hispanic Members of the House of Representatives (courtesy of the Congressional Hispanic Caucus); *p. 268:* Herman Badillo, Former U.S. Congressman (D-New York); *p. 273:* Cari M. Domínguez, Director, Office of Federal Contract Compliance Programs; *p. 273:* Manuel Luján, Jr., Secretary of the Interior; *p. 274:* Robert Martínez, Director, Office of National Drug Control Policy, and Former Governor of Florida; *p. 275:* Antonia C. Novello, M.D., M.P.H., Surgeon General, United States Public Health Service; *p. 275:* Catalina Vásquez Villalpando, Treasurer of the United States; *p. 278:* Stephanie González, Secretary of State, New Mexico; *p. 279:* Ygnacio D. Garza, Mayor, Brownsville, Texas; *p. 280:* Gloria Molina, Los Angeles County Supervisor; *p. 281:* Federico Peña, Mayor, Denver (photo by Larry Lazlo); *p. 281:* Louis E. Saavedra, Mayor, Albuquerque; *p. 282:* Xavier L. Suárez, Mayor, Miami.

Education: p. 287: Children at recess, the Guadalupe Aztlán alternative school, Houston, 1981 (photo by Curtis Dowell. Courtesy of the *Texas Catholic Herald*); *p. 299:* Mexican fourth-graders at Drachman School (circa 1913) (courtesy of the Arizona Historical Society); *p. 300:* A poster encouraging Hispanics to register to vote; *p. 302:* Children at the Guadalupe Aztlán alternative school, Houston, 1981 (photo by Curtis Dowell. Courtesy of the *Texas Catholic Herald*); *p. 303:* A sixth-grade classroom in the Huelga School, an alternative school set up in St. Patrick's Chapel, Houston (photo by Curtis Dowell. Courtesy of the *Texas Catholic Herald*); *p. 304:* A poster encouraging affirmative action and equal opportunity in education in California; *p. 305:* Dr. Manuel Pacheco, President of the University of Arizona.

Business: p. 309: Table 11.1, Hispanic and Nonminority Businesses; *p. 309:* Poster for the 1985 United States Hispanic Chamber of Commerce convention; *p. 310:* Figure 11.1, Origin of U.S. Hispanic Business Owners; *p. 310:* Table 11.2, Number of Businesses, Sales Volume, Number of Employees, and Payroll by Hispanic Origin of Owners (source: United States Bureau of the Census, 1991); *p. 311:* Table 11.3, Hispanic Businesses by Major Industry Category (source: United States Bureau of the Census, 1991); *p. 311:* Table 11.4, Number and Sales Volume of Hispanic Businesses in the Ten Largest Metropolitan Statistical Areas versus Those in the Entire State (source: United States Bureau of the Census, 1991); *p. 312:* Table 11.5, Number of Employees in Hispanic Businesses (source: United States Bureau of the Census, 1992); *p. 312:* Table 11.6, Sales Volume of Hispanic Businesses (source: United States Bureau of the Census, 1987); *p. 313:* Table 11.7, The Thirty Largest Hispanic Businesses (courtesy of "The 500," 1991); *p. 314:* Table 11.8, Hispanic and Nonminority Business Owners by Age (source: United States Bureau of the Census, 1987); *p. 314:* Table 11.9, Hispanic and Nonminority Business Owners by Years of Education (source: United States Bureau of the Census, 1987); *p. 314:* Table 11.10, Hispanic and Nonminority Business Owners Across Four Characteristics (source: United States Bureau of the Census, 1987); *p. 315:* Table 11.11, Start-up Capital Required for Hispanic and Nonminority Business Owners; *p. 315:* Figure 11.2, Sources of Start-up Capital for Hispanic and Nonminority Business Owners; *p. 316:* Table 11.12, Profit and Loss for Hispanic and Nonminority Businesses (source: United States Bureau of the Census, 1987); *p. 316:* Table 11.13, Minority Employees in Hispanic and Nonminority Businesses (source: United States Bureau of the Census, 1987); *p. 318:* Gilbert Cuéllar, Jr; *p. 319:* Roberto C. Goizueta; *p. 319:* Frederick J. González; *p. 320:* Edgar J. Milán; *p. 322:* Lionel Sosa; *p. 323:* Clifford L. Whitehill.

Labor and Employment: p. 325: César Chávez exhorting people to start a new grape boycott in 1986 (courtesy of the *Texas Catholic Herald*); *p. 326:* Mexican women working at a commercial tortilla factory in the 1930s (courtesy of the Library of Congress); *p. 327:* A cotton picker in 1933 (photo by Dorothea Lange. Courtesy of the Library of Congress); *p. 328:* Mexican mine workers in the early 1900s (courtesy of the Arizona Historical Society); *p. 329:* Puerto Rican garment workers in New York City; *p. 329:* A Mexican worker being finger-printed for deportation (courtesy of the Library of Congress); *p. 330:* Southern Pacific railroad workers during World War II in Tucson, Arizona (courtesy of the Arizona Historical Society); *p. 332:* Unemployed workers at a relief office during the Depression (courtesy of the Library of Congress); *p. 332:* A fruit picker in California (courtesy of the *Texas Catholic Herald*); *p. 333:* A parade ending National Farm Workers Week, Union Square, New York, 1975 (courtesy of the *Texas Catholic Herald*); *p. 334:* A United Farm Workers picket line in Coachella,

California, 1973 (courtesy of the *Texas Catholic Herald*); *p. 336:* A scene from the Bracero Program (courtesy of the Library of Congress); *p. 337:* A field worker in the Bracero Program (courtesy of the Library of Congress); *p. 339:* A migrant work camp (courtesy of the Library of Congress); *p. 340:* The interior of a migrant labor shack (courtesy of the *Texas Catholic Herald*).

Women: *p. 354:* Poster advertising a Hispanic women's conference in Texas in 1987; *p. 354:* A beauty queen for the Fiestas Patrias celebration, Houston (photo by Curtis Dowell. Courtesy of the *Texas Catholic Herald*); *p. 357:* A workshop at the 1980 California Governor's Chicana Issues Conference; *p. 361:* Teresa Bernárdez, M.D; *p. 363:* Emyré Barrios Robinson; *p. 365:* Carmen Delgado Votaw, Director, Washington Office, Girls Scouts, USA.

Religion: *p. 368:* A Catholic charismatic prayer meeting (courtesy of the *Texas Catholic Herald*); *p. 369:* The Franciscan method of teaching the Indians by pictures (from an engraving based on Fray Diego Valdés, o.F.M., in his Rhetorica Christiana, Rome, 1579); *p. 369:* Bartolemé de las Casas (1474-1566); *p. 370:* San Juan Capistrano Mission, San Antonio, Texas (photo by Silvia Novo Pena. Courtesy of the *Texas Catholic Herald*); *p. 372:* The Image of Our Lady of Guadalupe (photo by Curtis Dowell. Courtesy of the *Texas Catholic Herald*); *p. 380:* Feast of the Crowning of Mary, Sacred Heart Cathedral, Houston, 1987 (photo by Curtis Dowell. Courtesy of the *Texas Catholic Herald*); *p. 382:* Annual mass on the feast day of Our Lady of Guadalupe, Houston, Texas (courtesy of the *Texas Catholic Herald*); *p. 383:* The celebration of the feast day of Our Lady of Caridad del Cobre, the patron of Cubans, Houston, 1986 (photo by Curtis Dowell. Courtesy of the *Texas Catholic Herald*); *p. 384:* A Christmas posada, Houston, 1988 (photo by Curtis Dowell. Courtesy of the *Texas Catholic Herald*); *p. 385:* Diversity in Hispanic evangelism (photo by Curtis Dowell. Courtesy of the *Texas Catholic Herald*).

Organizations: *p. 388:* A march from the Lower East Side of New York City over the Brooklyn Bridge to protest the poor conditions of public schools in the Puerto Rican community (Historic Archive of the Department of Puerto Rican Community Affairs in the United States. Courtesy of the Center for Puerto Rican Studies Library and Archives, Hunter College, CUNY); *p. 388:* A celebration of the Three Kings (Jesús Colón Papers. Courtesy of the Center for Puerto Rican Studies Library and Archives, Hunter College, CUNY); *p. 389:* A parade organized by the Tucson's Alianza Hispano-Americana (courtesy of the Arizona Historical Society); *p. 390:* President Ronald Reagan presents the Medal of Freedom to Dr. Héctor García; *p. 394:* Brooklyn Chapter of the Liga Puertorriqueña e Hispana (Puerto Rican and Hispanic League), circa 1927 (Jesús Colón Papers. Courtesy of the Center for Puerto Rican Studies Library and Archives, Hunter College, CUNY); *p. 396:* Poster for the Spanish-Speaking Coalition Conference of October, 1971.

Scholarship: *p. 400:* Albert Michael Camarillo; *p. 400:* Arthur León Campa; *p. 401:* Carlos E. Cortés; *p. 402:* Rodolfo J. Cortina; *p. 403:* Margarita Fernández Olmos; *p. 404:* Erlinda González-Berry; *p. 405:* Olga Jiménez-Wagenheim; *p. 406:* Luis Leal; *p. 407:* Raúl Moncarraz; *p. 408:* Sonia Nieto; *p. 408:* Julián Olivares; *p. 410:* Ricardo Romo; *p. 411:* Ramón Eduardo Ruiz.

Literature: *p. 414:* Miguel Antonio Otero (Miguel A. Otero Collection, Special Collections, General Library, University of New Mexico, Neg. No. 000-021-0004); *p. 415:* Eusebio Chacón (Miguel A. Otero Collection, Special Collections, General Library, University of New Mexico, Neg. No. 000-021-0168); *p. 415:* Title page of El hijo de la tempestad by Eusebio Chacón (Special Collections, General Library, University of New Mexico); *p. 416:* Cuban literary and patriotic figure, José Martí; *p. 418:* The cover of Daniel Venegas's satirical newspaper, *El Malcriado*; *p. 418:* Fray Angélico Chávez (Special Collections, General Library, University of New Mexico); *p. 419:* Cover of the first issue of *Gráfico* newspaper; *p. 421:* Lola Rodríguez de Tió (archives, Arte Público Press); *p. 423:* Abelardo Delgado, Ron Arias and Rolando Hinojosa at the Second National Latino Book Fair and Writers Festival, Houston, Texas, 1980 (archives, Arte Público Press); *p. 424:* The original manuscript of the Tomás Rivera poem, "When love to be?" (archives, Arte Público Press); *p. 425:* Evangelina Vigil-Piñón, reciting at the Third National Hispanic Book Fair, Houston, 1987 (photo: Julián Olivares. Archives, Arte Público Press); *p. 425:* The cover of Rudolfo Anaya's best-selling novel, *Bless Me, Ultima* (archives, Arte Público Press); *p. 426:* A vendor at the First National Latino Book Fair, Chicago, 1979 (archives, Arte Público Press); *p. 427:* Ana Castillo, 1979 (archives, Arte Público Press); *p. 427:* Helena María Viramontes, 1986 (photo by Georgia McInnis, Archives, Arte Público Press); *p. 428:* Luis Dávila at the First National Latino Book Fair, 1979 (archives, Arte Público Press); *p. 429:* The cover of Rudolfo Anaya's *Cuentos: Tales from the Hispanic Southwest* (archives, Arte Público Press); *p. 429:* Pat Mora, 1986 (archives, Arte Público Press); *p. 430:* The cover of Denise Chávez's *The Last of the Menu Girls* (archives, Arte Público Press); *p. 430:* The cover of *This Bridge Called My Back* (archives, Arte Público Press); *p. 431:* Gary Soto and Evangelina Vigil-Piñón, Third National Hispanic Book Fair and Writers Festival, Houston, Texas, 1987 (archives, Arte Público Press); *p. 432:* Ricardo Sánchez, Alejandro Morales, critic Salvador Rodríguez del Pino and Victor Villaseñor at a book fair in Mexico City, 1979; *p. 433:* Julia de Burgos; *p. 434:* José Luis González (archives, Arte Público Press); *p. 434:* Luis Rafael Sánchez (archives, Arte Público Press); *p. 435:* Pedro Juan Soto (archives, Arte Público Press); *p. 436:* Jesús Colón ca. 1950s (archives, Centro de Estudios Puertorriqueños, Hunter College); *p. 436:* Bernardo Vega in 1948 (archives, Centro de Estudios Puertorriqueños, Hunter College); *p. 437:* Sandra María Esteves, 1979 (archives, Arte Público Press); *p. 438:* Second National Latino Book Fair and Writers Festival, Houston Public Library Plaza, 1980 (archives, Arte Público Press); *p. 439:* Nicholasa Mohr, Nicolás Kanellos and Ed Vega at the Bookstop, Houston, Texas, 1985 (archives, Arte Público Press); *p. 440:* Virgil Suárez, 1991 (archives, Arte Público Press); *p. 441:* José Sánchez-Boudy; *p. 442:* Miguel Algarín reciting his poetry at the First National Latino Book Fair, Chicago, 1979 (archives, Arte Público Press); *p. 443:* Alurista, 1980 (archives, Arte Público Press); *p. 445:* Denise Chávez, 1989 (photo by Georgia McInnis. Archives, Arte Público Press); *p. 446:* Lorna Dee Cervantes, 1990 (photo by Georgia McInnis. Archives, Arte Público Press); *p. 446:* Judith Ortiz Cofer, 1989 (archives, Arte Público Press); *p. 447:* Victor Hernández Cruz, 1980 (archives, Arte Público Press); *p. 448:* Abelardo Delgado, 1979 (archives, Arte Público Press); *p. 449:* Roberto Fernández, 1989 (archives, Arte Público Press); *p. 450:* Lionel G. García, 1989 (archives, Arte Público Press); *p. 451:* Rolando Hinojosa, 1987 (archives, Arte Público Press); *p. 452:* Tato Laviera, 1990 (photo by Georgia McInnis. Archives, Arte Público Press); *p. 453:* Nicholasa Mohr, 1990 (archives, Arte Público Press); *p. 454:* Alejandro Morales, 1991 (archives, Arte Público Press); *p. 456:* Album cover of a live poetry recital by Pedro Pietri; *p. 457:* Ricardo Sánchez, 1987 (archives, Arte Público Press); *p. 457:* Gary Soto, 1991 (photo by M.L. Marinelli. Publicity Department, Chronicle Books); *p. 459:* Sabine Ulibarrí, 1989 (archives, Arte Público Press); *p. 460:* Ed Vega, 1991 (archives, Arte Público Press); *p. 461:* Victor Villaseñor, 1991 (photo by Tony Bullard. Archives, Arte Público Press).

Art: *p. 465:* Figure 18.1. Bell wall, San Juan Capistrano Mission, 1760-87. San Antonio, Texas (photograph by Jacinto Quirarte); *p. 466:* Figure 18.2. Facade, San José y San Miguel de Aguayo Mission, 1768-82. San Antonio, Texas (photograph by Kathy Vargas); *p. 467:* Figure 18.3. *Saint Joachim* portal sculpture (left side of the doorway), 1768-82, San José y San Miguel de Aguayo Mission. San Antonio, Texas (photograph by Kathy Vargas); *p. 467:* Figure 18.4. *Saint Anne* portal sculpture, 1768-82. San José y San Miguel de Aguayo Mission. San Antonio, Texas (photograph by Kathy Vargas); *p. 468:* Figure 18.5. Facade, 1783-97, San Xavier del Bac Mission. Tuscon, Arizona (photograph by Jacinto Quirarte); *p. 468:* Figure 18.6. *Saint Lucy*. Portal sculpture, 1783-97, San Xavier del Bac Mission. Tucson, Arizona (photograph by Jacinto Quirarte); *p. 469:* Figure 18.7. Main Portal, 1755, Nuestra Señora de la Purísma Concepción de Acúna Mission. San Antonio, Texas (photograph by Kathy Vargas); *p. 469:* Figure 18.8. Polychromy, 1768-82, San José y San Miguel de Aguayo Mission. San Antonio, Texas (photograph by Kathy Vargas); *p. 472:* Figure 18.9. José Benito Ortega. *Saint Isidore the Farmer*, 1880s-1907. Denver Art Museum; *p. 473:* Figure 18.10. José Dolores López. *Expulsion from the Garden of Eden;* *p. 476:* Figure 18.11. Theodora Sánchez. *Nicho* (Yard Shrine), dedicated to Saint Dymphna. 1957. Tucson, Arizona (photograph by Jacinto Quirarte); *p. 477:* Figure 18.12. Octavio Medellín. *Xtol* print (photograph courtesy of the artist); *p. 478:* Figure 18.13. Edward Chávez. *Indians of the Plains*. 1943. Egg Tempera on Plywood (photograph courtesy of the artist); *p. 482:* Figure 18.14. Rafael Ortiz. *Piano Destruction Concert, Duncan Terrace*. September 1966, London (photograph courtesy of the artist); *p. 486:* Figure 18.15. Judy Baca. Detail of *The Great Wall of Los Angeles*. 1980 (photograph by Jacinto Quirarte); *p. 487:* Figure 18.16. Carmen Lomas Garza. *Lotería—Table Llena,* 1974 (photograph courtesy of the artist); *p. 488:* Figure 18.17. Víctor Ochoa. Gerónimo, 1981, San Diego, CA (photograph by Jacinto Quirarte); *p. 489:* Figure 18.18. Víctor Ochoa. *Chicano Park*, 1981, San Diego, CA (photograph by Jacinto Quirarte); *p. 490:* Figure 18.19. Cesar Martinez. *La Pareja,* 1979 (photograph courtesy of the artist); *p. 491:* Figure 18.20. Jesse Treviño. *Panadería,* late 1970s (photograph courtesy of the artist); *p. 492:* Figure 18.21. José González. *Barrio Murals*. 1976. Cover design for *Revista Chicano-Riqueña* (photograph courtesy of the artist); *p. 493:* Figure 18.22. Marcos Raya. *Stop World War III* (photograph courtesy of the artist). Mural. Chicago, IL; *p. 497:* Figure 18.23. Willie Herrón and Gronk. *Black and White Mural,* 1973 and 1978. Estrada Courts, Los Angeles, CA (photograph by Jacinto Quirarte); *p. 497:* Figure 18.24. Willie Herrón and Gronk. *Black and White Mural,* 1973 and 1978.

Estrada Courts, Los Angeles, CA (diagram by Jacinto Quirarte); *p. 499:* Figure 18.25. Raymond Patlán and others. *History of the Mexican American Worker,* 1974-75. Blue Island, IL (photograph by Jose Gonzalcz); *p. 499:* Figure 18.26. Raymond Patlán and others. *History of the Mexican American Worker,* 1974-75. Blue Island, IL (diagram by Jacinto Quirarte); *p. 500:* Figure 18.27. Raúl Valdez and others. *La Raza Cósmica,* 1977. Austin, TX (photograph by Jacinto Quirarte); *p. 500:* Figure 18.28. Raúl Valdez and others. *La Raza Cósmica,* 1977. Austin, TX (diagram by Jacinto Quirarte); *p. 501:* Figure 18.29. Raúl Valdez and others. *La Raza Cósmica,* 1977. Austin, TX (diagram by Jacinto Quirarte); *p. 501:* Figure 18.30. Raúl Valdez and others. *La Raza Cósmica,* 1977. Austin, TX (diagram by Jacinto Quirarte); *p. 501:* Figure 18.31. Raúl Valdez and others. *La Raza Cósmica,* 1977. Austin, TX (diagram by Jacinto Quirarte); *p. 502:* Figure 18.32. Rogelio Cárdenas. *En la lucha ponte trucha,* 1978. Hayward, CA (photograph by Jacinto Quirarte); *p. 502:* Figure 18.33. Rogelio Cárdenas. *En la lucha ponte trucha,* 1978. Hayward, CA (diagram by Jacinto Quirarte); *p. 503:* Figure 18.34. Gilberto Garduño and others. *Multicultural Mural,* 1980. Santa Fe, NM (photograph by Jacinto Quirarte); *p. 503:* Figure 18.35. Gilberto Garduño and others. *Multicultural Mural,* 1980. Santa Fe, NM (diagram by Jacinto Quirarte).

Theater: *p. 507:* Don Antonio F. Coronel, ex-mayor of Los Angeles, and early theater owner and impresario (courtesy of Los Angeles County Museum of Natural History); *p. 507:* Los Angeles's California Theater; *p. 509:* The Mason Theater, Los Angeles; *p. 510:* Actress Rosalinda Meléndez; *p. 512:* The García girls chorus line from the Carpa García Tent show; *p. 513:* Don Fito, the Carpa García *peladito* from the Carpa García tent show; *p. 517:* The cover of a program for the performance of an operetta at the Centro Español in 1919; *p. 518:* Centro Asturiano, with director Manuel Aparicio at the center front of the audience in 1937 (courtesy of the Dorothea Lynch Collection, Special Collections, George Mason University Library); *p. 519:* A scene from *El niño judío* at the Centro Asturiano (courtesy of the Dorothea Lynch Collection, Special Collections, George Mason University Library); *p. 520:* Manuel Aparicio directing a rehearsal of Sinclair Lewis's *It Can't Happen Here* in Spanish at the Centro Asturiano (courtesy of the Dorothea Lynch Collection, Special Collections, George Mason University); *p. 521:* Manuel Aparicio in Jacinto Benavente's *La Malquerida* (courtesy of the Dorothea Lynch Collection, Special Collections, George Mason University Library); *p. 522:* A scene from El Teatro Urbano's *Anti-Bicentennial Special* in

1976; *p. 524:* A scene from El Teatro de la Esperanza's production of Rodrigo Duarte Clark's *Brujerías*; *p. 524:* New York's Teatro Hispano in 1939; *p. 525:* Poster from La Farándula Panamericana theater group's 1954 production of *Los árboles mueren de pie,* starring Marita Reid; *p. 526:* Postcard photo of the Bronx's Pregones theater company in 1985; *p. 527:* The elaborate costuming of a Miami production of José Zorrilla's *Don Juan Tenorio*; *p. 529: Romeo and Juliet* in Spanish in Miami; *p. 537:* A scene from the Los Angeles production of Dolores Prida's *Beautiful Señoritas* (archives, Arte Público Press); *p. 539:* Playwright-director Luis Valdez; *p. 540:* Actress-director Carmen Zapata portrays Isabel la Católica in *Moments to Be Remembered.*

Film: *p. 548:* María Montez, an early Hispanic film star; *p. 551:* Henry Darrow as Zorro; *p. 560:* Carmen Miranda; *p. 561:* The late Freddie Prinze; *p. 561:* Erik Estrada, star of "CHiPs"; *p. 563:* The Sharks face off with the Jets in *West Side Story*; *p. 564:* A scene from *Boulevard Nights*; *p. 565:* Anthony Quinn in *The Children of Sánchez*; *p. 567:* Andy García in *The Godfather, Part III*; *p. 569:* The poster for *El norte*; *p. 570:* Raúl Juliá as Salvadoran Archbishop Oscar Romero in *Romero*; *p. 571:* Jimmy Smits; *p. 574:* Director Jesús Salvador Treviño in 1978; *p. 583:* The late Academy-Award-winning cinematographer, Nestor Almendros; *p. 585:* Producer-Director Moctezuma Esparza; *p. 588:* Ricardo Montalbán in the T.V. series, "Fantasy Island"; *p. 589:* Silvia Morales, director-cinematographer; *p. 590:* Rita Moreno receives her second Emmy in 1978; *p. 591:* Edward James Olmos.

Music: *p. 596:* Mexican musicians in the 1890s in California (courtesy of the Huntington Library, San Marino, California); *p. 596:* Xavier Cugat and his orchestra in the 1940s; *p. 597:* Augusto Coen and his Golden Orchestra, ca. 1930s-1940s; *p. 599:* Lidia Mendoza with Marcelo, comic Tin Tan and Juanita Mendoza in Chicago in the 1950s; *p. 600:* A working-class *orquesta,* circa 1930 (courtesy of Thomas Kreneck); *p. 606:* An *orquesta típica* in Houston (courtesy of Thomas Kreneck); *p. 609:* Beto Villa y su Orquesta, circa 1946 (courtesy of Chris Strachwitz); *p. 610:* Alonzo y su Orquesta, circa 1950 (courtesy of Thomas Kreneck); *p. 611:* Octavo García y sus GGs, circa 1952 (courtesy of Octavio García); *p. 612:* An outdoor *salsa* concert in Houston, Texas (courtesy of the Arte Público Press archives); *p. 613:* Celia Cruz at the Hollywood Palladium; *p. 614:* The Joe Cuba Sextet; *p. 615:* A Machito album cover; *p. 616:* A Tito Puente album cover; *p. 616:* Eddie Palmieri.

Media: p. 628: Wanda de Jesús as "Santa Andrade" in NBC's "Santa Barbara"; p. 629: A. Martínez as "Cruz Castillo" in NBC's "Santa Barbara"; p. 630: Henry Darrow as "Cruz Castillo's" father in NBC's "Santa Barbara"; p. 633: Ignacio E. Lozano, Jr., Editor-in-Chief of La Opinión; p. 634: Mónica Lozano-Centanino, Associate Publisher of *La Opinión;* p. 634: José I. Lozano, Publisher of *La Opinión;* p. 635: Marti Buscaglia, Director of Marketing, *La Opinión;* p. 635: Peter W. Davidson, President, *El Diario-La Prensa;* p. 636: Carlos D. Ramírez, Publisher, *El Diario-La Prensa;* p. 637: Phillip V. Sánchez, Publisher, *Noticias del Mundo* and *New York City Tribune;* p. 640: Cover of *Temas* magazine; p. 640: Cover of *Réplica* magazine; p. 641: Cover of *Más* magazine; p. 641: Cover of *La Familia de Hoy* magazine; p. 642: Cover of *Hispanic* magazine; p. 643: Cover of *Hispanic Business* magazine; p. 643: Charlie Erikson, founding editor of Hispanic Link News Service; p. 644: Cover of *Saludos Hispanos* magazine; p. 645: Pedro J. González; p. 646: Pedro J. González's singing group, "Los Madrugadores"; p. 646: Banner headlines in *La Opinión* newspaper announcing the guilty verdict in the Pedro J. González case; p. 648: Table 22.1, Radio Stations Owned and Controlled by Hispanics (sources: National Association of Broadcasters, Department of Minority and Special Services, Minority Telecommunications Development Program of the National Telecommunications and Information Administration, U.S. Department of Commerce); p. 649: McHenry Tichnor, founder of the Tichnor Media Systems; p. 650: Amancio V. Suárez of the Viva America Media Group; p. 656: Gustavo Godoy, Hispanic American Broadcasting Corporation, founder; p. 657: Henry R. Silverman, Telemundo founder; p. 658: Saul P. Steinberg, Telemundo founder; p. 660: Table 22.2, Stations Owned and Operated by the Univisión Spanish-Language Television Group (Late 1991); p. 658: Table 22.3, UHF Affiliates of the Univisión Spanish-Language Television Group (Late 1991); p. 661: Joaquín F. Blaya, president of Univisión; p. 661: Rosita Perú, senior vice president and director of programming, Univisión; p. 662: Univisión news studio; p. 663: Jorge Ramos and María Elena Salinas of "Noticiero Univisión"; p. 664: Table 22.4, Univisión Programming (Mid-1991); p. 665: Cristina Saralegui, host of Univisión's "El Show de Cristina"; p. 665: Don Francisco, host of Univisión's "Sábado Gigante" (Giant Saturday); p. 666: Luca Bentivoglio, host of Univisión's "Desde Hollywood," with Julio Iglesias; p. 666: Table 22.5, Stations Owned and Operated by the Telemundo Spanish-Language Television Group (Late 1991); p. 667: Table 22.6, Stations Affiliated with the Telemundo Spanish-Language Television Group (Late 1991); p. 668: Table 22.7, Telemundo Programming (Mid-1991); p. 669: Enrique Gratas, host of Telemundo's "Ocurrió Así"; p. 669: Andrés García and Rudy Rodríguez, of "El Magnate"; p. 670: Table 22.8, Affiliates of the Galavisión Spanish-Language Television Group (Late 1991); p. 671: Table 22.9, Galavisión Programming; p. 672: Laura Fabián, of Telemundo's "El Magnate"; p. 672: María Laria, host of Telemundo's "Cara a Cara"; p. 673: Milagros Mendoza, Host of "Esta Noche con Usted"

Science: p. 678: Dr. Angeles Alvariño de Leira; p. 679: Alberto V. Baez; p. 680: Graciela Candelas; p. 681: Manuel Cardona; p. 682: David Cardús; p. 683: Guillermo B. Cintrón; p. 684: Antonio E. Colás; p. 684: Francisco Dallmeier; p. 685: George Castro; p. 685: José Alberto Fernández-Pol; p. 686: Jorge Fischbarg; p. 687: Celso Ramón García; p. 688: José D. García; p. 690: Teresa Mercado; p. 691: Isabel Pérez-Farfante; p. 693: Pedro A. Sánchez; p. 694: James J. Valdés.

Sports: p. 697: Ramón Ahumada, known as "El Charro Plateado." (photo, circa 1890. Courtesy of the Arizona Historical Society); p. 699: A baseball team of Mexicans and Anglos, Los Angeles, 1870s (courtesy of the Huntington Library, San Marino, California); p. 703: Rod Carew; p. 704: Roberto Clemente; p. 704: Dave Concepción; p. 705: Roberto Durán; p. 706: Sixto Escobar; p. 707: Tom Flores; p. 707: Pancho González, U.S. Men's Singles Lawn Tennis Championship, 1948 (courtesy of the National Archives); p. 708: Keith Hernández; p. 709: Nancy López; p. 710: Amleto Monacelli; p. 711: Anthony Muñoz; p. 712: Jim Plunkett; p. 713: Juan "Chi Chi" Rodríguez; p. 713: Alberto Bauduy Salazar; p. 715: José "Chegüí" Torres (José A. Martí Collection. Courtesy of the Center for Puerto Rican Studies Library, Hunter College, CUNY); p. 715: Lee Treviño.

Prominent Hispanics: p. 717: Michael Jules Aguirre; p. 718: Tomás A. Arciniega; p. 718: Philip Arreola; p. 719: Tony Bonilla; p. 720: Harry Caicedo; p. 720: Vikki Carr; p. 721: Lynda Carter; p. 722: César Chávez; p. 723: José R. Coronado; p. 724: Jaime Escalante; p. 725: Joseph A. Fernández; p. 726: Archbishop Patrick F. Flores; p. 726: Ernesto Galarza; p. 727: Elsa Gómez; p. 728: Carolina Herrera; p. 729: Dolores Fernández Huerta; p. 730: Tania León; p. 731: Modesto A. Maidique; p. 732: Eduardo Mata; p. 733: Julián Nava; p. 734: Miguel A. Nevárez; p. 735: Katherine D. Ortega; p. 735: Manuel Pacheco (photo by Julieta González); p. 735: Guadalupe C. Quintanilla; p. 736: Mario E. Ramírez (photo by Gittings); p. 736: Paul Rodríguez; p. 737: Luis Santeiro; p. 738: Cristina Saralegui; p. 738: Alberto Serrano; p. 739: Roberto Suárez.

Glossary

A

acto – a one-act Chicano theater piece developed out of collective improvisation.

adelantado – the commander of an expedition who would receive, in advance, the title to any lands that he would discover.

agringado – literally "Gringo-ized" or Americanized.

audiencia – a tribunal that ruled over territories.

Aztlán – originally the mythological land of origin of the Mechica nations, to which the Toltecs and the Aztecs belong. Chicanos identify this land of origin as the geographic region of the American Southwest, figuratively their homeland.

B

babalao – a spiritual healer, witch, or advisor, especially in *santería*.

barrio – neighborhood.

batos locos – See *pachuco(s)*.

behareque – thatched huts used by Indians of the Caribbean.

bodega – a small general store.

bohíos – thatched-roofed huts used by the Caribbean Indians.

botánica – a shop that specializes in herbs and folk potions and medicines.

bracero – from *brazo*, arm, literally someone who works with their arms or performs manual labor; originally applied to temporary Mexican agricultural and railroad workers, it is also occasionally used to refer to any unskilled Mexican worker.

bulto – a wooden sculpture in the image of a Catholic saint.

C

cacique – the American Indian village chieftain.

caló – a Mexican-American dialect, often associated with *pachucos*.

canción – song.

capilla – chapel.

carpa – from the Quechua word meaning an "awning of branches;" in Spanish it has come to mean a tent. Circuses and tent theaters have come to be known as *carpas* by extension.

carreta – cart.

caudillo – chief, leader, originally of the rural poor, but today quite often used to refer to any grass-roots political leader.

charrerías – contests of the Mexican cowboys.

charro – a Mexican cowboy of the Jalisco region, maintaining the dress and customs often associated with *mariachis*.

Chicano – derivative of *Mechicano*, the same Nahuatl word that gave origin to the name of Mexico. The term originally meant Mexican immigrant worker in the early twentieth century, but became the name adopted by Mexican Americans, especially during the days of the civil rights and student movements.

chinampa – a man-made island or floating garden, developed by Meso-American Indians as an agricultural technique.

cimarrones – runaway slaves.

colonia – literally a "colony," it refers to the enclave of Hispanic population within a city, much as the term *barrio* is used today.

compadrazgo – godparenthood, usually through the baptism of a child. *Compadrazgo* is the extension of kinship to non-relatives and the strengthening of responsibilities among kin.

compadres – co-parents; godparents.

confianza – trust, the basis of the relationships between individuals in many spheres of social activity, but especially among kin.

conjunto – said of a Texas, northern-Mexico musical style as well as of the ensemble that plays it, usually made up of a guitar, a base guitar, a drum, and a button accordion.

corrido – a Mexican ballad.

criollo – a Creole, that is, someone of Spanish (European) origin born in the New World.

crónica – a local-color newspaper column often satirizing contemporary customs.

cronista – the writer of a *crónica*.

curandero – a folk healer who combines the practices of the Mexican Indians and Spanish folk-healing.

E

encomendero – the owner of the *encomienda*.

encomienda – the system by which a Spaniard held in high esteem by the King and Queen was given ownership of land in the New World and authorized to "protect" the Indians who had occupied the land in exchange for their free labor. This failed attempt at establishing feudal baronies was marked by the exploitation of the Indians.

ex-voto – a gift presented to a saint as a show of gratitude for a favor conceded.

F

familia, la – the greater family, which includes the immediate nuclear household and relatives that are traced on the female and male sides.

finca – farm, ranch.

G

gallego – in Cuban farce, the stock Galician Spaniard, known for his hard head and frugality.

H

hacendados – the owner of a *hacienda*.

hacienda – a large ranch derivative of the *latifundia* system.

hermandad – brotherhood.

I

indigenismo – an emphasis on American Indian and Pre-Colombian origins and identity.

ingenios – plantations, especially of sugar.

Isleños – descendants of the Canary Island settlers in southern Louisiana.

J

jíbaro – originally an American Indian word for "highlander," it is what Puerto Ricans call the rural mountain folk, but has also come to be symbolic of the national identity of Puerto Ricans.

K

kiva – a secret underground ceremonial chamber, especially as used in Pueblo culture for ceremonies and meetings.

L

latifundia – a large estate or ranch originating in ancient Roman civilization.

lectores – professional (hired) readers who would read books, magazines, and newspapers to cigar-rollers as they performed their laborious tasks.

M

macana – a wooden war club.

manda – a sacrificial offering to a saint in order to receive some favor.

maquiladora – a factory on the Mexican side of the border that performs part of the manual assembly of products at the comparatively lower wages offered by the Mexican economy. These products would then be shipped back to the United States for finishing and marketing by the partner company.

Marielito – a Cuban refugee who arrived in the United States as a result of the Mariel boatlift in the 1980s.

mestizo – an individual of mixed Spanish (or European) and American Indian heritage.

milagro – a charm made of tin, gold, or silver, and shaped in the form of an arm, a leg, a baby, or a house, representing the favor (usually of healing) that is desired from a saint.

morada – the meeting house of the *Penitente* lay brotherhood.

mulata – the stock female Mulatto character in Cuban farce.

música norteña – *conjunto* music from the northern region of Mexico (also includes Texas).

mutualista – mutual aid society, an organization that engaged in social activities and provided basic needs for immigrant workers and their families, including insurance and death benefits for members.

N

nacimiento – a nativity.

Nañiguismo – membership in the secret society of Abakúa, which combines elements of the Efik culture of the southern coast of Nigeria and Freemasonry.

negrito – in Cuban farce, the stock character in black face.

nitainos – principal advisors among the Arawak Indians, quite often in charge of the labor force.

nopal – the prickly pear cactus.

norteño – of northern Mexican origin.

Nuyorican – literally "New York-Rican," a term developed colloquially by Puerto Ricans born or raised in New York to distinguish themselves from those identifying solely with the island.

O

orishas – the African deities of *santería*.

orquesta – a Mexican-American musical ensemble that develops its style around the violin.

P

pachuco – the member of a Mexican-American urban youth subculture, which characteristically developed its own style of dress (zoot suit), its own dialect (*caló*), and its own bilingual-bicultural ideology during the 1940s and 1950s.

padrinos – godparents.

parentesco – kinship sentiment.

parientes – blood relatives.

pastorela – the shepherds play; a folk drama reenacted during the Christmas season.

patria – fatherland.

patria chica – the home region within the fatherland.

pelado – literally the "skinned one" or shirtless one, he was the stock underdog, sharp-witted picaresque character of Mexican vaudeville and tent shows.

Penitente – literally "penitent;" it is the name of a religious brotherhood in New Mexico.

piraguas – a narrow, high-prowed canoe used by the Caribbean Indians.

posada – a community Christmas pageant where carolers go door to door asking for shelter in reenactment of Joseph and Mary's search for lodging.

presidio – a fort, especially characteristic of frontier settlements.

promesa – literally a "promise," it is a sacrificial offering to a saint in order to receive some favor.

R

renegado/a – a renegade, someone who denies his or her Mexican identity.

repartimiento – a form of the *encomienda* which vested the rights over the Indians in the civil authorities.

reredo – altar screen.

retablos – paintings on panels behind the altar in a Catholic church.

revista – a vaudeville musical revue.

S

salsa – literally "sauce," it refers to Afro-Caribbean music.

santería – a synchretic religious sect growing out of the original African religion and the Catholicism of slaves.

santerismo – the same as santería.

santero – in the Southwest, a sculptor of wooden saints; in the Caribbean, a devotee of an *orisha* in *santería*.

santos – the sculpted figures representing saints of the Catholic church; used in worship and prayer.

T

Taino (also Nitaino) – a group of sedentary tribes native to the Caribbean.

V

vaquero – cowboy.

vegas – plantations, especially of coffee.

Y

yerberías – shops specializing in medicinal plants, herbs and potions.

yerberos – folk healers and spiritualists who use herbs in their practices.

yuca – manioc root.

Z

zarzuela – a type of Spanish operetta.

zemíes – gods of the Arawak Indians, also the small Taino religious figure made of clay that represented these gods.

General Bibliography

A

Acosta-Belén, Edna, ed. *The Puerto Rican Woman.* New York: Praeger, 1986.

Acuña, Rodolfo. *Occupied America: A History of Chicanos.* New York: Harper & Row, 1981.

Alvarez, Robert R. *Familia: Migration and Adaptation in Alta and Baja California 1850-1975.* Berkeley: University of California Press, 1987.

B

Barrera, Mario. *Race and Class in the Southwest: A Theory of Racial Inequality.* Notre Dame, Ind.: University of Notre Dame Press, 1979.

Bean, Frank D., and Marta Tienda. *The Hispanic Population of the United States.* New York: Russell Sage Foundation, 1988.

Beardsley, John, and Jane Livingston. *Hispanic Art in the United States: Thirty Painters and Sculptors.* New York: Abbeville Press, 1987.

Boswel, T.D., and J.R. Curtis. *The Cuban American Experience.* Totawa, N.J.: Rowan and Allenheld, 1984.

C

Camarillo, Albert. *Chicanos in a Changing Society.* Cambridge, Mass.: Harvard University Press, 1979.

Cotera, Marta P. *Latina Sourcebook: Bibliography of Mexican American, Cuban, Puerto Rican and Other Hispanic Women Materials in the USA.* Austin, Texas: Information Systems Development, 1982.

E

Elías Olivares, Lucia, ed. *Spanish in the U.S. Setting: Beyond the Southwest.* Rosalyn, Va.: National Clearinghouse for Bilingual Education, 1983.

F

Fitzpatrick, Joseph P. *Puerto Rican Americans: The Meaning of Migration to the Mainland.* Englewood Cliffs, N.J.: Prentice Hall, 1987.

Furtaw, Julia C., ed. *Hispanic American Information Directory 1992-1993.* Detroit, Mich.: Gale Research, 1992.

G

García, Mario T. *Mexican Americans.* New Haven, Conn.: Yale University Press, 1989.

H

Hendricks, G.L. *The Dominican Diaspora: From the Dominican Republic to New York City.* New York: Teacher's College Press of Columbia University, 1974.

History Task Force of the Centro de Estudios Puertorriqueños. *Labor Migration under Capitalism: The Puerto Rican Experience.* New York: Monthly Review Press, 1979.

K

Kanellos, Nicolás. *A History of Hispanic Theater in the United States: Origins to 1940.* Austin: University of Texas Press, 1990.

———, ed. *Biographical Dictionary of Hispanic Literature.* Westport, Conn.: Greenwood Press, 1985.

Knight, Franklin W. *The Caribbean.* New York: Oxford University Press, 1990.

L

Llanes, J. *Cuban Americans, Masters of Survival.* Cambridge, Mass.: Harvard University Press, 1982.

Lomeli, Francisco and Julio A. Martínez. *Chicano Literature: A Reference Guide.* Westport, Conn.: Greenwood Press, 1985.

M

McKenna, Teresa Flora and Ida Ortiz, eds. *The Broken Web: The Education Experience of Hispanic American Women.* Berkeley, Calif.: Floricanto Press and the Tomás Rivera Center, 1988.

Meier, Kenneth J. and Joseph Stewart. *The Politics of Hispanic Education.* New York: Russell Sage Foundation, 1987.

Meier, Matt S. and Feliciano Rivera. *Dictionary of Mexican American History.* Westport, Conn.: Greenwood Press, 1981.

Moore, Joan, and Harry Pachón. *Hispanics in the United States.* Englewood Cliffs, N.J.: Prentice Hall, 1985.

Morales, Julio. *Puerto Rican Poverty and Migration: We Just Had to Try Elsewhere.* New York: Praeger, 1986.

P

Pedraza-Bailey, S. *Political and Economic Migrants in America.* Austin: University of Texas Press, 1985.

Portes, Alejandro, and Robert L. Bach. *Latin Journey: Cuban and Mexican Immigrants in the United States.* Berkeley: University of California Press, 1985.

R

Rodríguez, Clara. *Born in the U.S.A.* Boston, Mass.: Unwin Hyman, 1989.

Ryan, Bryan. *Hispanic Writers.* Detroit, Mich.: Gale Research, 1991.

S

Sánchez-Korrol, Virginia. *From Colonia to Community.* Westport, Conn.: Greenwood Press, 1983.

Sandoval, Moisés. *On the Move: A History of the Hispanic Church in the United States.* Maryknoll, N.Y.: Orbis Books, 1990.

Schorr, Edward Allen. *Hispanic Resource Directory.* Juneau, Alaska: Denali Press, 1988.

Shirley, Carl F., ed. *Chicano Writers: First Series.* Detroit, Mich.: Gale Research, 1989.

Suchliki, Jaime. *Cuba: From Columbus to Castro.* Washington, D.C.: Pergammon Press, 1986.

U

United States Commission on Civil Rights. *Puerto Ricans in the Continental United States: An Uncertain Future.* Washington, D.C.: U.S. Commission on Civil Rights, 1976.

Unterburger, Amy L., ed. *Who's Who among Hispanic Americans, 1992-1993.* Detroit, Mich.: Gale Research, 1992.

V

Veciana-Suárez, Ana. *Hispanic Media: Impact and Influence.* Washington, D.C.: The Media Institute, 1990.

Vivó, Paquita, ed. *The Puerto Ricans: An Annotated Bibliography.* New York: R.R. Bowker, 1973.

W

Wagenheim, Kal. *A Survey of Puerto Ricans in the U.S. Mainland in the 1970s.* New York: Praeger, 1975.

Weber, David. *The Mexican Frontier, 1821-1846: The American Southwest under Mexico.* Albuquerque, University of New Mexico Press, 1982.

Index

R   C.1
973
K

Kanellos, Nicolas, ed

Reference library of Hispanic
  America, VOLUME III